Vital Record of Rhode Island.

1636-1850.

FIRST SERIES,

BIRTHS, MARRIAGES AND DEATHS.

A FAMILY REGISTER FOR THE PEOPLE.

By JAMES N. ARNOLD,

EDITOR OF THE NARRAGANSETT HISTORICAL REGISTER.

"Is My Name Written in the Book of Life?"

| Volume 1. | WARWICK. | Part 1. |

Published under the Auspices of the General Assembly.

PROVIDENCE, R. I.:
NARRAGANSETT HISTORICAL PUBLISHING COMPANY.
1891.

Notice

In many older books, foxing (or discoloration) occurs and, in some instances, print lightens with wear and age. Reprinted books, such as this, often duplicate these flaws, notwithstanding efforts to reduce or eliminate them. The pages of this reprint have been digitally enhanced and, where possible, the flaws eliminated in order to provide clarity of content and a pleasant reading experience.

Originally published
Providence, Rhode Island
1891

Reprinted by:

Janaway Publishing, Inc.
732 Kelsey Ct.
Santa Maria, CA 93454
(805) 925-1038
www.JanawayGenealogy.com

2000, 2007, 2011

ISBN: 978-1-59641-146-3

Made in the United States of America

WARWICK.

MARRIAGES.

A

2-12	Aborn James, and Hannah Westgate, of Robert; m. by John Rhodes, Justice, Nov. 16, 1755.
2-156	" Polly, and Sylvester Rhodes, Apr. 22, 1770.
2-159	" Mary, and Peleg Rhodes, Apr. 9, 1797.
2-19	" Desire Burrows, and Phillip Crapo, Mar. 1, 1801.
4-48	" Caroline C., and Simon H. Grèene, March 13, 1822.
3-338	" Mary Elizabeth, and Averill Barlow, Sept. 14, 1847.
2-5	Adams Capt. John, and Elizabeth Westgate, widow; m. by Eld. John Hammett, Nov. 14, 1757.
2-3	" John, and Prescilla Warner; m. by John Warner, Justice, Oct. 2, 1760.
2-118	" Susannah, and Thomas Hackstone, Sept. 24, 1792.
2-143	" Patty, and William Remington, Apr. 12, 1804.
3-326	Albro Caroline, and William W. Warner [also 3-355], July 7, 1833
3-14	" Irus, Jr., son of Irus, deceased, and Thankful H. Loveland, of Leonard, of Chatham, Mass.; m. by Eld. Moses Fifield, Feb. 22, 1835.
3-301	" Eliza, and Jason P. Stone, Oct. 8, 1839.
3-19	" Samuel W., of George W., deceased, of Coventry, and Sophia Lewis, of Randall, of said Coventry; m. by Elder Moses Fifield, Oct. 27, 1840.
3-36	" Gardiner G., of Warwick, son of Gardiner, dec., of South Kingstown, and Nancy Harrington, of West Greenwich; m. by Eld. Moses Fifield, Nov. 23, 1843.
3-35	" Samuel W., of George, and Mrs. Sophia Albro, daughter of Crandall Lewis; m. by Eld. Zalman Tobey, July 12, 1846.
3-35	" Mrs. Sophia, and Samuel W. Albro, July 12, 1846.
3-350	" Frances F., and Russell B. Whitman, Aug. 6, 1846.
3-235	" Pauline G., and Wm. B. Merrell, Nov. 15, 1847.

3-374 Aldrich Tamer, and Jeremiah H. Cranston, Oct. 26, 1846.
3-6   Alexander Reuben, and Fannie Whitman; m. by C. Brayton, Justice, Apr. 22, 1810.
1-37   Allen Mary, and John Greene, Feb. 16, 1709-0.
2-6   "   James, of Capt. James, of Newport, and Elizabeth, Greene, of Richard, of Warwick, m. by John Westcott, Asst., Aug. 31, 1726.
2-37   "   Rachel, and Benjamin Fry, Jan. 19, 1756.
2-53   "   Anne, and James Griffins, Jan. 1, 1758.
2-173 "   Mercy, and Charles Sherman, Apr. 26, 1761.
2-3   "   Ebenezer, and Margaret Remington; m. by John Warner, Justice, May 21, 1761.
2-71   "   Barnard, of Jonathan and Elizabeth Bailey, (so called); m. by Eld. Charles Holden, Sept. 7, 1777.
2-1   "   James, and Mary Shearman; m. by Charles Holden, Apr. 8, 1779.
2-240 "   Lemuel, of Pomfret, Conn., son of Caleb, dec., of Providence, and Welthian Holden, of Charles, Jr.; m. by Eld. John Gorton, Apr. 22, 1781.
2-116 "   Freelove, and Phillip Arnold, Mar. 31, 1785.
2-37   "   George, of Dr. John, of Warwick, and Lydia Ellis of Gideon, of W. Greenwich, Sept. 28, 1785.
2-195 "   Sabina, and Pompey Mumford (col.) Aug. 19, 1789.
2-104 "   John, and Susan Westcott, of Capt. Thomas; m. by Joseph Arnold, Justice, June 2, 1799.
2-159 "   Sarah Bowen, and Peleg Rhodes, Feb. 8, 1808.
3-353 "   Susan G., and Paul Wheelock, Nov. 12, 1826.
3-20   "   Amanda W., and Daniel G. Allen, Nov. 26, 1840.
3-20   "   Daniel G., of East Greenwich, son of Thomas G., of North Kingstown, and Amanda W. Allen, of Ray G., dec., of North Kingstown; m. by Eld. Moses Fifield, Nov. 26, 1840.
3-25   "   Daniel R., of Coventry, son of Henry, of North Kingstown, and Eliza G. Sweet, of Coventry, dau. of James; m. by Eld. Moses Fifield, Oct. 20, 1842.
3-165 "   Mary E., and Henry Hubbard, M. D., Jan. 27, 1845.
3-31   "   William H., of Warwick, son of Thomas, dec., and Martha A. Weeden, of North Kingstown; m. by Eld. Moses Fifield, Sept. 7, 1845.
3-108 "   Hannah A., and Moses Fifield, Jr., May 24, 1846.
3-37   "   Charles, of Cranston, R. I., son of Henry, and Mrs. Mary Waite, dau. of Christopher Nichols; m. by Eld. Zalman Tobey, Mar. 14, 1847.

3-421	Allen Susan, and Henry Whitman, Mar. 23, 1848.
1-88	Allerton Mary, and Nathaniel Spencer, Oct. 22, 1740.
1-49	Almy Mary, and John Greene, Dec. 8, 1739.
3-32	Amsden George, of Providence, and Fannie B. Emerson, of Warwick; m. by Rev. Stephen A. Thomas, Jan. 18, 1846.
1-7	Andrews William, and Hester Dexter, widow; m. by John Greene, Justice, Oct. 30, 1680.
1-18	" Mary, and Simon Smith, Jan. 5, 1698-9.
2-8	" Peleg, of East Greenwich, and Freelove Wightman, of Warwick; m. by Ebenezer Slocum, Justice, Dec. 12, 1762.
2-241	" Jonathan, of William, of Barrington, R. I., and Susannah Miller, of Nathan, of Warwick; m. by Eld. John Gorton, Oct. 31, 1784.
2-6	" Christopher, of Phillip, and Mrs. Freelove Rice, of Job; m. by Eld. John Gorton, Feb. 5, 1786.
2-249	" Silas, of Benoni, and Anna Gorton, of Eld. John; m. by James Jerauld, Justice, Aug. 2, 1787.
2-253	" Sarah, and Joseph Card, Apr. 30, 1789.
2-258	" Jesse, of Phillip, deceased, and Sally Arnold, of Joseph; m. by James Jerauld, Justice, Feb. 22, 1795.
2-102	" Eleanor, and James Jerauld, July 5, 1798.
3-41	" Penelope, and Joseph Bennett, Mar. 25, 1805.
3-233	" Perlonia G., and Warren R. Mitchell, Sept. 23, 1844.
3-397	" Mary C., and Jared A. Culver, Sept. 9, 1845.
3-32	" John, of Matteson, and Abby Sedgwick, of John; m. by Eld. Moses Fifield, Nov. 30, 1845.
3-13	" Charles E., and Ann M. Mason; m. by Eld. Richard Knight, Dec. 24, 1846.
3-38	" Wheaton, and Catherine Johnson, both of Coventry; m. by Eld. Stephen A. Thomas, Jan. 25, 1847.
3-39	" Dr. Thomas E., son of Ray and Anne, and Elizabeth A. Tiffany, dau. of John and Olive; m. by Rev. George W. Wooding, Nov. 9, 1847.
4-87	" John T., and Mrs. Roby A. Leech; m. by Rev. George Champlain, Mar. 29, 1854.
1-95	Angell William, of James, and Almy Harding, of Stephen; m. by William Greene, Justice, Sept 1, 1731.
1-94	" Almy, or Mary, and Benjamin Greene, Sept 2, 1731.
3-162	" Triphena H., and Gardiner B. Hammond, May 21, 1839.
3-318	" Mercy Ann, and William D. Torrey, Aug. 3

1-1	Anthony Elizabeth, and James Greene, Aug. 3, 1665.
3-1	" William, and Mary Greene; m. by Eld. Samuel Littlefield, Dec. 18, 1803.
4-88	" Thomas Ellwood, of East Greenwich, formerly of North Kingstown, and Nancy Holden Greene, of Warwick; m. by Rev. D. H. Bannister, Oct. 17, 1838.
1-70	Arnold Phebe, and Benjamin Smith, Dec. 25, 1691.
1-34	" Isreal, Jr., and Elizabeth Smith, of Benjamin, Feb. 28, 1698-9.
1-22	" Mary, and John Low, Oct. 8, 1702.
1-25	" Stephen, of Isreal, and Sarah Greene, of Capt. Peter, Nov. 28, 1706.
1-78	" Elisha, of Isreal, and Hannah Carpenter, of Timothy, Dec. 9, 1709.
1-28	" James, of Isreal, and Elizabeth Roads, of Peleg, Oct. 25, 1711.
1-32	" Phillip, of Stephen, of Providence, and Susannah Greene, of Capt. Benjamin, of Warwick, June 10, 1714.
1-74	" Elizabeth and Josiah Arnold, Dec. 27, 1716.
1-74	" Josiah, of Isreal, and Elizabeth Arnold, of Elisha, Dec. 27, 1716.
1-42	" Isreal, Jr., and Dorothy Roads, widow of Malacha, Dec. 24, 1719.
1-25	" Stephen, and Jane Blount; m. by Eld. Timothy Cutler, Dec. 28, 1727.
1-105	" Ephraim, of Elisha, of Warwick, and Phebe Edmunds, of William, of Providence, Apr. 26, 1729.
3-103	" Mary, and John Matteson, July 24, 1729.
1-42	" Isreal, Jr., of Warwick, and Elizabeth Case, widow of William, of Kings Towne, June 27, 1730.
1-107	" Stephen, Jr., of Stephen, of Warwick, and Hannah Case, of William, of Kings Towne, Jan. 16, 1732.
1-54	" John, of Capt. William, and Desire Joyce, Mar. 1, 1732-3.
1-106	" William, of Elisha, and Phebe Stafford, of Thomas; m. by Stephen Arnold, Justice, May 6, 1733.
1-59,63	" Hannah, and Jeremiah Corps, Nov. 22, 1736.
1-44	" Elizabeth, and Peter Wells, Feb. 1, 1736-7.
1-63	" Simon, of Isreal, and Lydia Greene, of Barlo; m. by James Arnold, Asst., Mar. 1, 1738-9.
1-23	" Rebecca, and Joseph Stafford, May 27, 1739.
1-105	" Ephraim, and Rachel Warner; m. by William Greene, Justice, Jan. 18, 1741.

4-1	Arnold Elizabeth, and James Arnold, Jr., Mar. 24, 1744.
4-1	" James, Jr., and Elizabeth Arnold, of Phillip; m. by William Rice, Asst., Mar. 24, 1744.
1-46	" William, and Prudence Colliss; m. by William Rice, Asst., at Providence, Nov. 3, 1744.
2-1	" Elisha, of Warwick, and Patience Hide, of Providence; m. by William Rice, Asst., Dec. 23, 1744.
2-2	" Capt. Josiah, and Maplet Wickes, widow of William; m. by Eld Manassah Martin, Dec. 15, 1745.
2-4	" Stephen, of Phillip, and Ann Haynes, of Capt. Josiah; m. by Eld. John Hammett, June 16, 1751.
2-3	" Owen, and Elizabeth Parker; m. by Eld. John Hammett, Oct. 21, 1751.
2-5	" Sion, of James, and Sarah Lockwood, of Capt. Amos; m. by Eld. John Hammett, Jan. 23, 1752.
2-25	" Bersheba, and Urian Davis, May 24, 1752.
2-6	" Rhodes, of James, and Almy Remington; m. by John Warner, Jr., Justice, Nov. 4, 1756.
2-3	" John, of Coventry, and Deborah Matteson, of John of Warwick; m. by Ebenezer Slocum, Justice, Nov. 4, 1758.
2-7	" Stephen, of Capt Edward, of Cranston, and Rhoda Rice, of Capt. Randall, of Warwick; m. by Ebenezer Slocum, Justice, Mar. 6, 1760.
2-146	" Hester, and Peter Rhodes, Mar. 22, 1761.
2-2	" Job, of William, and Mary Wightman, of George; m. by Ebenezer Slocum, Justice, Mar. 26, 1761.
2-7	" Thomas, and Frances Haynes; m. by Samuel Gorton, Justice, June 1, 1761.
2-74	" Elizabeth, and Reuben Hopkins, Dec. 6, 1761.
2-4	" Oliver, and Almy Greene, of Samuel; m. by Ebenezer Slocum, Justice, Mar. 11, 1762.
2-74	" Phebe, and Joshua Hunt, Apr. 11, 1762.
2-141	" Margaret, and John Rice, Oct. 30, 1763.
2-8	" William, of William, and Patience Wightman, of George; m. by Ebenezer Slocum, Justice, July 1, 1764.
2-75	" Phebe, and Samuel Hopkins, Feb. 3, 1765.
2-10	" William, of John, and Mrs. Alice Wilcox, of Stephen; m. by Eld. John Gardiner, May 2, 1765.
2-10	" David, of Josiah, dec., and Waite Lippitt, of Moses; m. by Eld. John Gorton, Aug. 29, 1765.
2-176	" Patience, and Stephen Smith, Jr., Dec. 26, 1765.

2-7 Arnold Gideon, of Phillip, dec., and Patience Brown, of Elisha; m. by Eld. Charles Holden, Nov. 22, 1767.
2-51 " Sarah, and Jonathan Gorton, Nov. 23, 1767.
2-35 " Phebe, and William Waterman, Mar. 10, 1768.
2-94 " Sarah, and Abraham Lippitt, Apr. 8, 1770.
2-228 " Hester, and Thomas Mathewson, Jan. 19, 1772.
2-12 " James, of Col. James, and Elizabeth Stafford, of Stukeley; m. by Thomas Rice, Justice, Jan. 30, 1772.
2-83 " Joseph, of William, of Warwick, and Anne Foster, of Thomas, of East Greenwich; m. by Ebenezer Slocum, Justice, July 12, 1772.
2-181 " Mary, and John Stafford, Feb. 11, 1773.
2-9 " George, of Col. James, and Ruth Utter, of Zebulon; m. by Eld. Charles Holden, Dec. 5, 1773.
2-192 " Sarah, and William Tibbetts, Jr., Feb. 1, 1778.
2-139 " Joseph, of Caleb, and Sarah Stafford, of Stukeley; m. by Eld. John Gorton, Sept. 6, 1778.
2-5 " Phillip, of Col. James, of Warwick, and Phebe Harris of William, of Cranston; m. by Eld. Samuel Winsor, Jan. 10, 1779.
2-234 " Freelove, and Nathan Arnold, Mar. 10, 1779.
2-234 " Nathan, of Elisha, dec., and Freelove Arnold, of James; m. by James Jerauld, Justice, Mar. 10, 1779.
2-116 " Phebe, and Edward Burke, Mar. 14, 1799.
2-238 " Phillip, of Benjamin, and Robe Gorton, of Jonathan; m. by Eld. John Gorton, Feb. 3, 1780.
2-138 " Andrew, of Phillip, of Warwick, and Phebe Reynolds, of Jabez, of North Kingstown; m. by Eld. James Wightman, Jan. 18, 1781.
2-1 " Moses, of Col. James, and Mrs. Sally Greene, of Stephen; m. by Eld. James Manning, Jan. 25, 1781.
2-211 " Mercy, and Thomas Westcott, Feb. 4, 1781.
2-183 " Millen, and Henry Reynolds, May 6, 1781.
2-24 " Lucy, and Joseph Chace, Dec. 16, 1781.
2-9 " Benedict, of Capt. Josiah, and Sarah Potter, of Joseph, dec.; m. by Eld. Charles Holden, Mar. 31, 1782.
2-182 " Phebe, and Olney Stone, Apr. 25, 1782.
2-30 " George, and Mercy Hopkins, Sept. 7, 1782.
2-239 " John R., of Cranston, son of Benjamin, and Mercy Rice, of Henry, of Warwick; m. by James Jerauld, Justice, Sept. 8, 1782.

WARWICK—MARRIAGES. 7

2-95   Arnold Capt. Joseph, son of Joseph and Dinah, of Warwick, and Ruth Godfrey, of Joshua and Mary, of East Greenwich, Feb. 22, 1784.
2-242 " Edmund, of Job, and Robe Arnold, of Phillip; m. by Eld. John Gorton, May 2, 1784.
2-242 " Robe, and Edmund Arnold May 2, 1784.
2-243 " Phillip, Jr., and Dinah Rice, of Olney, dec.; m. by Eld. John Gorton, Sept. 26, 1784.
2-242 " Rhoda, and Giles Greene, Jan. 6, 1785.
2-116 " Phillip, of Warwick, and Freelove Allen, of Christopher, of North Kingstown; m. by Eld. Nathan Hill, Mar. 31, 1785.
2-244 " Sarah, and Olney Baker, Apr. 3, 1785.
2-206 " Lydia, and Nathan Westcott, Jr., Oct. 20, 1785.
2-161 " Sarah, and Thomas Rice, Dec. 11, 1785.
2-247 " Dutee, of Benjamin, and Naomi Rice; m. by James Jerauld, Justice, Aug. 27, 1786.
2-236 " Mary, and Lowry Church, Mar. 2, 1788.
2-133 " John, of Joseph, and Henrietta Jerauld, of James; m. by Eld. John Gorton, Oct. 5, 1788.
2-228 " Richard, of Thomas, and Mrs. Honor Havens; m. by Eld. John Gorton, Mar. 19, 1789.
2-241 " Anne, and Caleb Brayton, June 25, 1789.
2-84   " Robe, and Caleb Jerauld, Jan. 19, 1790.
2-185 " Lydia, and Jeremiah Greene, Oct. 7, 1790.
2-138 " Phebe and Sion Arnold, July 10, 1791.
2-138 " Sion, of Oliver, dec., and Phebe Arnold, of Stephen; m. by Eld. John Gorton, July 10, 1791.
2-149 " Almy, and Samuel Remington, July 17, 1791.
2-258 " Sally, and Jesse Andrews, Feb. 22, 1795.
2-102 " Harris, Jr., and Freelove Holden; m. by Henry Arnold, Justice, Dec. 24, 1795.
2-7   " Thomas, of Benjamin, and Sarah Gorton, of Jonathan; m. by Eld. Samuel Littlefield, May 1, 1796.
2-20   " Elizabeth, and Dr. Nicholas Cooke, Mar. 12, 1797.
2-130 " Lucy, and Henry Jerauld, Sept. 11, 1798,
2-116 " Phebe, and Edward Burke, Mar. 14, 1799.
2-32   " Wanton, and Elizabeth Martindil; m. by Eld. Samuel Littlefield, Mar. 28, 1799.
2-120 " Susanna, and Olney Potter, Jan. 23, 1800.
2-169 " George W., of James, and Mary Price, of Nathan; m. by James Jerauld, Justice, June 1, 1800.

2-85   Arnold Barbara, and Thomas Eldridge, Aug. 7, 1800.
2-85   "   Russell, of Nicholas and Hannah, and Polly Rice, of Henry, Jr., dec.; m. by Joseph Arnold, Justice, Nov. 2, 1800.
2-144   "   Mercy, and John Briggs, Nov. 9, 1800.
2-165   "   Frederick, of Warwick, son of Thomas and Dorcas Matteson, of Coventry, dau. of Daniel; m. by Joseph Manchester, Justice, Apr. 26, 1801.
2-198   "   Bowen, and Elizabeth Briggs, widow of Charles, Jr., m. by James Jerauld Justice, June 14, 1801.
2-221   "   Daniel, and Welthian Holden; m. by Eld. Samuel Littlefield, Sept. 12, 1801.
2-30   "   Lydia, and Reuben Arnold, Nov. 8, 1801.
2-30   "   Reuben, of William, and Lydia Arnold, of Nathaniel, Jr.; m. by James Jerauld, Justice, Nov. 8, 1801.
2-180   "   George, of Thomas, and Hannah Randall; m. by Eld. Samuel Littlefield, Apr. 4, 1802.
3-1   "   Nathaniel, of Joseph, and Almy Greene, of David; m. by Caleb Jerauld, Justice, May 5, 1805.
3-309   "   Henritta, and Benjamin Tibbetts, Jan. 5, 1806.
3-1   "   Elisha, of James, dec., and Sarah Gorton, of William; m. by Caleb Jerauld, Justice, Mar. 6, 1806.
3-1   "   Daniel, of Oliver, and Sarah Rice; m. by Eld. Samuel Littlefield, Oct. 2, 1806.
3-115   "   Mary L., and Robert W. Greene, Feb. 22, 1807.
3-2   "   David, Jr., and Rebecca Stafford; m. by Eld. Samuel Littlefield, Nov. 1, 1807.
3-44   "   Phebe, and Caleb Baker, Mar. 12, 1809.
3-13   "   Olney R., and Lydia Remington; m. by Eld. Samuel Littlefield, Nov. 19, 1809.
3-170   "   Elizabeth, and Stephen Jerauld, July 17, 1810.
3-8   "   Elisha, of Nathan, and Hannah Gorton, of Dea. Benjamin; m. by Eld. Thomas Manchester, Apr. 26, 1810.
3-9   "   Benedict, and Mary Greene; m. by Eld. Samuel Littlefield, Dec. 6, 1810.
3-11   "   Oliver, of Warwick, and Sally Williams, of Cranston; m. by Eld. Bela Jacobs, Oct. 11, 1812.
3-10   "   Joseph, of Caleb, of Warwick, and Betsey Carpenter, of Cranston; m. by Eld. Bela Jacobs, Dec. 30, 1813.
3-77   "   Mary Ann, and Benjamin M. Cole, Oct. 20, 1822.
3-123   "   Abbie Ann, and Richard Gorton, Dec. 29, 1825.
3-225   "   Lydia W., and Charles Morse, Jr., Dec. 28, 1826.

3-21	Arnold Russell, and Susan Reynolds, of North Kingstown; m. by Rev. Michael Burdick, Jan. 11, 1830.
4-83	" Mary, and Peleg R. Bennett, Mar. 27, 1830.
3-15	" Joseph W., of Nathaniel, and Mary T. Spencer, of Ephraim; m. by Eld. Moses Fifield, July 29, 1838.
3-16	" Whipple A., and Avis Carr; m. by Rev. Thomas Dowling, Apr. 8, 1839.
3-17	" Nathaniel, and Mary Smith, m. by Rev. Thomas Dowling, Aug. 8, 1839.
3-18	" Mary Ann, and Peleg Arnold, Dec. 9, 1839.
3-18	" Peleg, of Coventry, son of Peleg, dec., and Mary Ann Arnold, of Benjamin; m. by Eld. Moses Fifield, Dec. 9 1839.
3-51	" Mary A., and Jabez Ballou, Aug. 17, 1840.
3-22	" Lyman, of Benjamin, of Scituate, and Waity Ann Remington, of William; m. by Eld. Moses Fifield, Feb. 14, 1841.
3-5	" Henry, and Ruth Daniel; m. by Levin Smith, Justice, Apr. 19, 1841.
3-334	" Experience, and Samuel Whitman, July 11, 1841.
3-23	" Capt. John William, son of John and Betsey, and Phebe Holdredge Wightman, of Samuel W., and Hannah; m. by Eld. Job Manchester, Mar. 7, 1842.
3-154	' Hannah G., and Thomas Hathaway, May 16, 1842.
3-325	" William W., of Benjamin, of Warwick, and Mahala Tiffany, of Daniel, of Coventry; m. by Eld. Pardon Tillinghast, June 13, 1842.
3-26	" Alban, of Christopher, of Warwick, and Mary Davis Benjamin, of Wickford; m. by Eld. Nathaniel W. Warner, Jan. 10, 1843.
3-33	" Israel, of John, and Cordelia W. Knowlton, of James; m. by Rev. Gardner Dean, June 8, 1844.
3-28	" John M., of Coventry, son of Samuel W., and Sarah M. Parker, of Arnold, of Warwick, m. by Rev. Jonathan Brayton, July 10, 1844.
3-29	" Edwin W., of Christopher, and Mary L. S. Reynolds, of Thomas; m. by Eld. Nathaniel W. Warner, Dec. 16, 1844.
3-30	" Nelson H., and Harriet A. Wells; m. by Rev. Edward K. Fuller, Nov. 11, ——recorded Aug. —, 1845.
3-318	" Elizabeth G., and Lewis H. Thurber, Oct. 8, 1845.

3-34	Arnold Joseph R., and Hannah Wells; m. by Rev. Edward K. Fuller, Mar. 22, 1846.	
3-3	"	Horace, and Phebe A. Arnold; m. by Rev. S. A. Thomas, Jan. 17, 1848.
3-3	"	Phebe A., and Horace Arnold, Jan. 17, 1848.
4-76	"	Reuben, of William, dec., and Lydia Vaughn, of North Kingstown, dau. of Charles; m. by Rev. Thomas Hardman, Feb. 15, 1848.
3-4	"	Uriah, of Christopher O., of Warwick, and Esther Ann Collins, of Rowland, of Scituate; m. by Eld. Daniel Slocum, April 11, 1849.
4-11	"	Almarah J., and Allen B. Burt, May 20, 1849.
4-23	"	Mercy W. and William H. Hudson, Jan. 1, 1850.
4-70	"	Thomas, of Warwick, and Freelove R. Colvin, of Cranston; m. by Rev. S. A. Thomas, June 24, 1852.
4-82	"	Ann E., and James Kettell, Jan. 23, 1853.
3-305	Ashton Abbie, and Peleg Sisson, Dec. 12, 1847.	
4-17	"	Abbie B., and Olney Luther, Oct. 7, 1849.
2-23	Atwood Elizabeth, and Daniel Brayton, Jan. 30, 1772.	
2-240	"	Caleb, of Charles, dec., and Marian Walton, of John; m. by Thomas Rice, Jr., Justice, July 29, 1781.
2-248	"	Nehemiah, and Joanna Snell, of Daniel; m. by James Jerauld, Justice, Dec. 31, 1786.
3-4	"	Francis B., of Warwick, and Freelove Baker, of Jeremiah, of Scituate; m. by Peleg Fiske, Justice, Sept. 23, 1802.
2-392	"	Robey, and Amos Hopkins, Mar. 27, 1803.
3-345	"	Ruth, and Rufus Wakefield, Oct. 9, 1811.
3-368	"	Almy B., and Dr. Otis Cooper, Oct. 30, 1843.
3-250	"	Charlotte, and Nicholas G. Potter, Apr. 22, 1844.
3-386	"	Charlotte B., and Stukeley B. Briggs, June 20, 1847.
4-38	"	Harriet T., and Lucius Briggs, Apr. 21, 1851.
2-250	Austin Jonathan, of Scituate, son of Pasque, of Exeter, dec., and Mehitable Casey, widow, daughter of John Baker, of Gloucester; m. by Eld. John Gorton, July 22, 1787.	
3-194	"	Celia, A., and Benoni Knight, Jan. 12, 1842.
3-24	"	Clarke, and Mary Wilbur, of Hazard; m, by Rev. William Stovyer, Mar. 23, 1842.
3-189	"	Eleanor B., and Caleb Kenyon, July 3, 1843.
3-27	"	Allen, of Stephen and Olive, aged 20 years, and Elizabeth Randall Card, of William and Sarah, aged 18 years; m. by Rev. M. J. Stone, Sept. 17, 1844.

4-78 Austin Harriet, and Potter P. Straight, Aug. 2, 1857,
2-9   Aylsworth Anthony, and Mary Marks; m. by Ebenezer Slocum, Justice, Nov. 26, 1762.
2-211 " Ruth, and Isaac Gardner, Jr., Oct. 11, 1767.

B

2-232 Babcock Thomas, of Westerly, son of Thomas, and Sarah Waterman, of Capt. John, dec., of Coventry; m. by Eld. Charles Holden, Nov. 3, 1774.
3-55 " Daniel, of William, dec., of South Kingstown, and Lucinda Kenyon, of Jonathan, of Cranston; m. by Eld. Moses Fifield, Aug. 9, 1841.
3-239 " Abby, and Charles C. Noyes, Feb. 29, 1844.
3-381 " John, of Gideon, and Almira Jackson, of William; m. by Rev. Jonathan Brayton, Oct. 18, 1846.
3-215 " Susan C., and Henry Love, Nov. 13, 1848.
4-23 " Margaret, and Barber Hoxsie, Mar. 19, 1850.
3-393 Babson Ann Elizabeth, and George W. Bailey, Sept. 3, 1845.
4-29 " Sarah S., and Halesey H. Richardson, July 4, 1850.
1-48 Backer William, and Mary Remington; m. by Anthony Low, Justice, July 28, 1724.
2-71 Bailey Elizabeth, and Barnard Allen, Sept. 7, 1777.
2-241 " Elizabeth, and Daniel Clap, June 15, 1783.
2-230 " Gideon, of East Greenwich, son of William, and Margaret Gardner, of Capt. Oliver; m. by James Jerauld, Justice, Oct. 2, 1796.
3-382 " Henry A., of Warwick, son of Wheaton, and Mercy A. Pearce, of Warwick, formerly of North Kingstown, daughter of Merchant; m. by Rev. Jonathan Brayton, Dec. 16, 1844.
3-393 " George W., of Jeremiah and Ann Elizabeth Babson, of Isaac N.; m. by Rev. Jonathan Brayton, Sept. 3, 1845.
3-299 " Clarissa A., and Jared H. Smith, Dec. 26, 1847.
4-5   " Margaret, and Robert G. Card, Oct. 31, 1849.
4-81 " Jeremiah, and Ann Whitman, both of Coventry; m. by Rev. David Curtis, Oct. 30, 1863.
3-49 Bagley Edmund, and Esther N. Hazard; m. by Rev. Daniel Curtis, Aug. 15, 1815.
4-91 Bajnotti Paul, and Carrie Matilda Brown; m. by Rev. Henry Waterman, June 17, 1876.

1-8	Baker Mary, and Mark Roberts, Jan. 1, 1682.
1-8	" Sarah, and Peter Roberts, Apr. 27, 1685.
2-78	" Patience, and Benjamin Howard, Dec. 10, 1772.
2-228	" Abraham, of Warwick, and Sarah Westcott, of Benjamin of Cranston; m. by James Harris, Justice, May 2, 1773.
2-230	" Isaac, and Marvel Inman, (mulattoes); m. by Thomas Rice, Jr., Justice, Jan. 4, 1774.
2-229	" George, of Elisha, and Hannah Baker, of Capt. Phillip; m. by Thomas Rice, Jr., Justice, Jan 6, 1774.
2-229	" Hannah, and George Baker, Jan. 6, 1774.
2-116	" Mary, and David Knight, Dec. 25, 1777.
2-181	" Temperance, and Thomas Sailes, Jan. 22, 1778.
2-233	" Elisha, of Philip dec., and Mary Stone, of Thomas; m. by James Jerauld, Justice, May 3, 1778.
2-206	" Robey, and Stukeley Westcott, May 24, 1778.
2-126	" Elizabeth, and Christopher Potter, Dec. 14, 1783.
2-244	" Olney, and Sarah Arnold, of Gideon; m. by Eld. John Gorton, Apr. 3, 1785.
3-7	" Silas, of Moses, and Patience Brown, of Joseph; m. by Eld. John Gorton, Mar. 31, 1785.
2-160	" Anna, and Henry Reynolds, June 16, 1785.
2-114	" William, of Elisha, and Truth LeValley, of Peter, Dec. 24, 1789.
2-140	" Joseph, of Joseph, and Sarah Wightman, of Capt. Reuben, dec.; m. by Eld. John Gorton, Feb. 28, 1790.
2-173	" Samuel, of Warwick, and Sarah Williams, dau. of Elisha, of Cranston; m. by Wm. Warner, Justice, Dec. 3, 1795.
2-170	" Moses, and Sarah Baker; m. by Eld. Samuel Littlefield, Mar. 5, 1797.
2-170	" Sarah, and Moses Baker, Mar. 5, 1797.
2-113	" Eleanor, and William Tillinghast, Mar. 12, 1797.
2-229	" Burton, of George, of Warwick, and Ruth Bennett, of Samuel, of Cranston, June 4, 1798.
2-36	" Elisha, of Joseph, and Charlotte Chace, of Abraham, dec.; m. by Joseph Arnold, Justice, Nov. 30, 1800.
2-27	" Earl, of Joseph, of Warwick, and Freelove Baker, of Thomas, of Cranston; m. by Nicholas Congdon, Justice, Feb. 14, 1802.
2-27	" Freelove, and Earl Baker, Feb. 14, 1802.
2-32	" Josiah, of Joseph, and Sallie Carder, of James; m. by Caleb Westcott, Justice, Sept. 2, 1802.

3-4	Baker	Freelove, and Frances B. Atwood, Sept. 23, 1802.
2-1	"	Elizabeth, and William Anthony Holden, June 5, 1803.
3-151	"	Mary, and William Harrison, Apr. 11, 1805.
3-44	"	Caleb, of Cranston, and Phebe Arnold, of Coventry, dau. of Phillip, m. by C. Brayton, Justice, Mar. 12, 1809.
4-346	"	Robey, and Reuben Wickes, Apr. 8, 1810.
3-156	"	Phebe, and John Howard, Dec. 1, 1816.
3-51	"	Joseph, of Silas, and Susan Tiffany, of James; m. by Rev. Levi Walker, July 1, 1819.
3-48	"	Charles W., of Charles, dec., and Phebe R. A. Brown, of Elisha; m. by Rev. Moses Fifield, Jan. 1, 1840.
3-191	"	Susan, and James Kingsley, June 3, 1840.
3-54	"	William H., of Burton, and Mary Ann Potter, of Henry; m. by Eld. William Stovyer, June 27, 1841.
3-59	"	Albert, of Elisha, dec., and Roby Tiffany, of Daniel, m. by Rev. Moses Fifield, Oct. 11, 1841.
3-322	"	Phebe A., and Charles F. Thurston, Apr. 4, 1842.
3-61	"	Almira, and Henry A. Bowen, Sept. 15, 1842.
3-389	"	William, of Cranston, and Eliza Mathewson, of Providence; m. by Joseph S. Gladding, Dec. 8, 1845.
3-236	"	Latilda K., and John W. Martin, Dec. 22, 1845.
3-384	"	Johiel, of Orin, and Elizabeth Keech, of George, both of Cranston; m. by Eld. Zalmon Tobey, July 25, 1847.
4-28	"	Charles H., of Warwick, aged 19 years, son of Richard and Alice, and Mrs. Ann Francis Gorton, of Warwick, aged 25 years, dau. of Isaac and Lucy; m. by Rev. Benjamin Phelan, July 28, 1850.
4-44	"	Mary E., and John G. Bissell, Sept. 10, 1851.
4-43	"	Windwell M., and Thomas W. Gorton, Sept. 11, 1851.
4-81	"	Paulina R., and Ambrose Lawton, June 28, 1852.
3-363	"	Susan, J., and William D. Brayton, July 12, 1866.
3-51	Ballou Jabez, of Warwick, son of Simeon dec., of Burrillville, and Mary A. Arnold, of Oliver C. W., of Warwick; m. by Rev. Moses Fifield, Aug. 17, 1840.	
3-306	Bamford Sarah, and Daniel Sharples, Dec. 3, 1842.	
	Barber Susan, and William W. Warner, Nov. 7, 1844.	
3-236	" Alzada G., and William B. Niles, Dec. 14, 1846.	
4-72	" Sarah, and William A. Rice, Sept. 17, 1848.	
3-52	Barbour William, of Warwick, son of John, of Johnston, Scotland, and Mary Temple, of Warwick, dau. of James, of Johnston, Scotland; m. by Rev. Moses Fifield, Oct. 30, 1840.	

3-388   Barlow   Averill, of Woodstock, Conn., son of Darius, and Mary Elizabeth Aborn, of Joseph R., dec.; m. by Rev. Zalman Tobey, Sept. 14, 1847.
4-73   Barnes   Ezra N., of Warwick, son of Peleg, of Scituate, and Amey Leach, of Warwick, dau. of Isaac; m. by Rev. Moses Fifield, Mar. 17, 1836.
3-384   Barney Nathaniel, of Seekonk, Mass., son of Enock, of Rehoboth, Mass., and Olive M. Jones, of Providence, dau. of Thomas; m. by Rev. Jonathan E. Farbush, Apr. 14, 1844.
4-92   "   Dorcas P., and William M. Spink, Oct. 24, 1853.
1-88   Barne Elizabeth, and William Clark, July 13, 1732.
3-138   Bartlett Lucy A., and Benjamin H. Gifford, July 18, 1843.
2-139   Barthalake Thomas, and Merebe Utter; m. by Silas Clapp, Justice, Sept. 20, 1761.
3-47   Bartholick John, of Stewart, and Hannah Eldredge, of Samuel; m. by Joseph Arnold, Justice, Dec. 15, 1811.
1-5   Barton Benjamin, and Susan Gorton, of Samuel, Sr.; m. by John Greene, Justice, June 18, 1672.
1-40   "   Mary, and Jabez Greene, Mar. 17, 1697-8.
1-73   "   Benjamin, of Andrew, and Mary Hail, of Richard, ——— 28, 1727.
2-14   "   John Jr., of Providence, and Mary Johnson, of Elkanah, of Warwick; m. by Phillip Arnold, Asst., July 21, 1734.
1-101   "   Samuel, of Andrew, and Lilas Tanner, of William, Mar. 23, 1737-8.
2-222   "   Mary, and Joseph Gorton, Jan. 1, 1763.
2-13   "   Andrew, of Rufus, and Penelope Palmer, of Simeon; m. Eld. Charles Holden, Oct. 2, 1763.
2-201   "   Phebe, and Jeremiah Westcott, Apr. 26, 1764.
2-226   "   Benjamin, of Rowland, dec., of Warwick, and Sarah Hall, of Abial, of East Greenwich; m. by Allen Johnson, Justice, Feb. 25, 1776.
2-223   "   Sarah, and Moses Burlingame, Nov. 24, 1776.
2-98   "   Sarah, and Thomas Lockwood, Dec. 14, 1800.
2-198   Bateman Thomas, son of Hector, late of Coventry, and Elizabeth Marill, of Spencer; m. by Eld. Thomas Manchester, Jan. 1, 1795.
3-54   "   Capt. Benjamin, of East Greenwich, and Sarah Hart, of Warwick; m. by Rev. Benjamin Hazelton, Sept. 24, 1826.

2-264	Bates Lydia, and Joseph Coggeshall, Nov. 21, 1762.
3-63	" James H., of William, dec., and Hannah Reaves, of Olney; m. by Rev. Moses Fifield, Apr. 30, 1843.
	[NOTE—Was this man's name Baxter. See below.]
3-353	" Mrs. Robey W., and John Wilcox, Feb. 2, 1846.
3-359	" Elizabeth F., and Josiah Welch, June 21, 1845.
3-394	" George W., Jr., of George, and Malissa M. Rice, of Lorey, dec.; m. by Rev. Moses Fifield, Feb. 14, 1847.
3-287	" Dorcas, and Charles E. Remington, Aug. 14, 1848.
1-17	Battey John, of Samson, and Margaret Carr, of Nicholas, both of Jamestown, Sept. 18, 1707.
2-24	" Dinah, and Fones Greene, Mar. 15, 1710-1.
1-67	" Nicholas, of John, and Hannah Davis, of Robert; m. by Stukeley Stafford, Justice, Nov. 26, 1735.
1-59	" William, of John, and Hopestill Peirce, of Aziekim, Oct. 9, 1740.
3-52	" Rebeckah, and Thomas Corp, Aug. 2, 1741.
2-219	" John, of John, of Scituate, and Ruth Lockwood, of Capt. Amos; m. by Eld Charles Holden, Mar. 10, 1765.
2-86	" Mary, and Amos Kimball, June 29, 1769.
3-386	" Mrs. Margaret M. and Nathan H. Ralph, June 26, 1843.
3-63	Baxter James H., of William, dec., and Hannah Reaves, of Olney, m. by Rev. Moses Fifield, April 30, 1843.
	[NOTE.—Was this man's name Bates? See above.]
2-15	Bebe James, and Mary Cahoon, of Samuel; m. by James Greene, Justice, Oct. 27, 1757.
3-64	Beybee Thomas, of Warwick, son of John, of Scotland, and Jenette Temple, of Warwick, dau. of James, of Scotland; m. by Rev. Moses Fifield, Dec. 29, 1843.
3-26	Benjamin Mary Davis, and Alban Arnold, Jan. 10, 1843.
1-31	Bennett Priscilla, and Stukeley Westcott, Dec. 21, 1693.
1-66	" Samuel Jr., and Mary Stafford, of Amos, July 15, 1716.
1-40	" Penelope, and Charles Holden, Jr., Dec. 13, 1716.
1-38	" Sarah, and Ezekiel Warner, May 30, 1717.
1-33	" Hannah, and Samuel Stafford, June 20, 1717.
1-102	" William, and Hannah Capwell, of Samuel; m. by Thomas Stafford, Justice, Oct. 2, 1731.
2-121	" Ann, and William Proud, Feb. 17, 1750.
2-14	" Samuel, of John, of Warwick, and Margeret Potter, of Abel, of Coventry; m. by Eld. John Hammett, Mar. 25, 1750.

2-219	Bennett Jonathan, of William, of East Greenwich, and Alice Greene, of Nathaniel, of Coventry; m. by Eld. John Gorton, May 12, 1765.
2-227	" David, of John, and Mary Wight, of George; m. by Thomas Rice, Jr., Justice, July 26, 1772.
2-226	" Abel, of Samuel, and Rosanna Remington, of Peleg; m. by Eld. Charles Holden, Nov. 12, 1772.
2-231	" Joseph, of John, and Mary Remington, of Thomas; m. by Eld. Charles Holden, Dec. 9, 1773.
2-229	" Ruth, and Burton Baker, June 4, 1798.
2-131	" Samuel, of Warwick, and Elizabeth Morris, of East Greenwich; m. by James Jerauld, Justice, Aug. 30, 1798.
2-88	" Caleb, of David, and Lydia Doud, of Noah; m. by James Jerauld, Justice, Nov. 12, 1799.
2-99	" Stephen, of David, and Phebe Straight, of Joseph; m. by James Jerauld, Justice, Oct. 12, 1800.
2-138	" Nancy Dyre, and James Price, Nov. 5, 1801.
2-116	" John, of Joseph, and Robey Burlingame, of Samuel; m. by Alexander Havens, Justice, May 20, 1802.
2-190	" Elizabeth, and John W. Bennett, Feb. 3, 1803.
2-190	" John W., of Abel, and Elizabeth Bennett, of David; m, by Caleb Jerauld, Justice, Feb. 3, 1803.
2-105	" Abel, of Abel, and Nabby Straight, of Joseph; m. by Alexander Havens, Justice, May 22, 1803.
3-41	" Joseph, of Warwick, son of Joseph, and Penelope Andrews, of Scituate, dau. of James, dec.; m. by Eld. John Westcott, Mar. 25, 1805.
3-309	" Rest, and Thomas Hackstone, Dec. 8, 1805.
3-42	" Margaret, and Peleg R. Bennett, May 19, 1808.
3-42	" Peleg Remington, of Abel, and Margeret Bennett, of David; m. by C. Brayton, Justice, May 19, 1808.
4-83	" Peleg R., and Mary Arnold; m. by Rev. Henry Tatem, Mar. 27, 1830.
4-66	" Elizabeth, and William Burden, May 1, 1836.
3-238	" Eliza R., and David Nickerson, Nov. 24, 1836.
3-133	" Rhoda, and William D. Greene, Oct. 5, 1840.
3-383	" John R., and Margeret Rowen; m. by Rev. Jonathan Brayton, Apr. 29, 1844.
3-386	" Samuel, and Martha Carr; m. by Rev. Edward K. Fuller, May 21, 1845.
3-389	" Jeremiah, of Charles, dec., and Mary Williams, of Caleb; m. by Rev. Moses Fifield, Feb. 23, 1846.

3-402	Bennett Almond G., and Lucy C. Briggs; m. by Rev. Edward K. Fuller, —— 14, 1846.
4-4	" Lucinda, and Samuel L. Hunt, Nov. 23, 1848.
3-326	" Mary L., and William W. Tarbox, Feb. 11, 1849.
4-6	" Asahel A., of Coventry, son of Samuel, and Hannah Kingsley, of Warwick, dau. of James; m. by Rev. Jonathan Brayton, Mar. 11, 1849.
4-77	" Allen H., and Jane A. Corey, m. by Rev. Moses Fifield, Dec. 9, 1855.
1-52	Benson Hannah, and Abner Corp, Nov. 25, 1734.
3-41	" Martin, and Amey Smith; m. by Rev. Mr. Ellis, Feb. 22, 1809.
3-42	" Nelson H., of Squire, of Heath Mass., and Matilda Davis, of Benjamin, of Warwick; m. by Eld. Moses Fifield, Nov. 26, 1835.
1-66	Bentley Elizabeth, and Isreal Tripp, Sept. 2, 1744.
2-18	" Caleb, of East Greenwich, and Martha Foster, of Thomas, of Warwick; m. by Eld. John Gorton, June 14, 1761.
2-16	" Benjamin, and Barbara Pearce, both of East Greenwich; m. at Warwick, by Eld. John Gorton, Nov. 21, 1762.
2-177	" Thomas, of Caleb, of Warwick, and Catherine Boyd, of Andrew, of East Greenwich; m. by James Jerauld, Justice, Sept. 20, 1797.
3-69	" Patience, and Wilbour Carpenter, Jr., Oct. 7, 1810.
3-105	" Betsey Ann, and Samuel I. France, May 14, 1848.
3-62	Bicknell William Henry, and Nancy Eliza Johnson; m. by Rev. Edward K. Fuller, July 4, 1844.
3-88	Bigby Hugh, and Margaret Manuel; m. by Rev. Edward K. Fuller, July 4, 1845.
4-44	Bissell John G., of Depere, Wisconsin, aged 26 years, son of Samuel, and Mary E. Baker, of Warwick, aged 23 years, dau. of Joseph B., and Mary E.; m. by Rev. Benjamin Phelan, Sept. 10, 1851.
4-75	Bitgood Joseph A., and Hannah Tanner; m. by Rev. Eleazer Bellows, Jan. 20, 1860.
3-45	Blair David, of William, dec., of East Greenwich, and Alice Stafford, of Warwick; m. by C. Brayton, Justice, Sept. 3, 1809.
1-399	Blanchard Benjamin, and Ann Reaves; m. by William Rice, Justice, Jan. 8, 1739, or 40.

1-100   Blanchard Moses, of Scituate, R. I., son of William, and Ann Whaley, of Samuel; m. by Rev. Francis Bates, Jan. 1, 1734-5.

1-100   " Theophilis, of William, of Scituate, and Patience Jefford, of Joshua, of Warwick; m. by Eld. Francis Bates, Jan. 1, 1734-5.

1-89   " John, and Sarah Wood, of William; m. by William Rice, Justice, Oct. 14, 1739.

2-152   " Rosannah, and Thomas Rice, Apr. 17, 1777.

3-80   " Huldah, and Benjamin Cornell, Jr., Aug. 15, 1839.

3-132   " Betsey T., and Esbon Greene, July 26, 1840.

4-15   " Ada, and Benjamin C. Tillinghast, Aug. 26, 1849.

4-20   " Mary, and John M. Williams, Dec. 25, 1849.

3-32   Blesborough Agnes, and John Tourgee, Oct. 8, 1848.

1-25   Blount Jane, and Stephen Arnold, Dec. 28, 1727.

3-5, 45   Bonn John Henry, of John H., and Celia Church, of Lowry; m. by C. Brayton, Justice, Oct. 5, 1808.

3-105   Boss Almira, and Samuel Fenner, Aug. 15, 1841.

4-20   " Charles L., of Providence, and Sylvia M. Sarle, of Warwick; m. by Rev. Reuben Allen, Jan. 1, 1849.

2-113   Bosworth Almy and Benjamin Nichols, May 15, 1757.

4-30   " Joseph H., of Warwick, son of Smith, and Mary E. Rousemaniere, of Warwick, dau. of Lewis; m. by Rev. Jonathan Brayton, Sept. 2, 1850.

1-27   Bowen Hannah, and Edward Casey, Sept. 12, 1742.

2-109   " Barbara, and Nathaniel Millard, July 1, 1758.

2-38   " Barbara, and Daniel Fish, Apr. 8, 1760.

2-17   " Isreal, of Coventry, and Sarah Gorton, of Warwick; m. by Eld. Peter Werden, Apr. 5, 1761.

2-168   " Nathan, of Capt. Isreal, of Coventry, and Betsey Gardner, of Capt. Oliver; m. by James Jerauld, Justice, June 10, 1798.

2-228   " Aaron, of Coventry, son of Phillip, and Hannah Merrell, of Spencer, of Warwick; m. by Nathan Arnold, Justice, Aug. 9, 1801.

3-57   " Russell, of James, of Shaftesbury, Vt., and Mary Ann Cornell, of Richard, of Warwick; m. by Rev. Moses Fifield, June 3, 1830.

3-60   " Cyrel C., of Foster, son of Asaph, and Hannah W. Johnson, of Warwick, dau. of Obadiah, of Coventry; m. by Rev. Moses Fifield, May 20, 1839.

3-338   " Caroline A., and Jonathan R. Weaver, Oct. 3, 1839.

3-239	Bowen Sarah Ann, and Charles E. Kinne, Feb. 11, 1840.
3-61	" Henry Augustus, of Warwick, son of Thomas, of Coventry, and Almira Baker, of Earl, of Warwick, m. by Rev. Moses Fifield, Sept. Sept. 15, 1842.
3-387	" James, and Elizabeth Gould; m. by Rev. Edward K. Fuller, July 1, 1845.
3-50	" Samuel G., of Warwick, and Mary Gardiner, of East Greenwich; m. by Rev. Daniel Waldo, Apr. 4, 1818.
3-382	" Susan, and Gideon C. Briggs, Dec. 7, 1846.
3-363	Bowman William, of Warwick, and Laura Hunt, of North Providence; m. by Rev. S. A. Thomas, Jan. 23, 1848.
4-31	" George, aged 19 years, son of William, dec., and Mary Caroline Sunderland, aged 19 years, dau. of Daniel, of North Kingstown; m. by Rev. Moses Fifield, Oct. 7, 1850.
4-35	" William H., aged 21 years, son of William, and Susan F. Nichols, aged 18 years, dau. of Lowry; m. by Rev. Moses Fifield, Jan. 26, 1851.
2-133	Bowtwell Capt. John, a resident of West Greenwich, and Polly Olin, of Peter, of Warwick; m. by James Jerauld, Justice, Aug. 23, 1798.
2-177	Boyd Catherine, and Thomas Bentley, Sept. 20, 1797.
2-122	" Hannah, and Darius Havens, Oct. 15, 1798.
4-75	" Catherine J., and Benjamin G. Holden, Mar. 29, 1855.
3-59	Bradford Daniel W., of Plympton, Mass., and Harriet N. Rice, of Warwick; m. by Rev. Charles S. Weaver, Apr. 12, 1832.
3-42	Brayman John G., and Sarah K. Pollock; m. by Elder John Gorton, Aug. 20, 1837.
2-17	Brayton William, of Thomas, of Coventry, and Mary Webb, of Jeremiah, of Warwick; m. by Ebenezer Slocum, Justice, Aug. 24, 1760.
2-223	" Daniel, of Coventry, son of Francis, and Elizabeth Atwood, of Charles; m. by Thomas Rice, Justice, Jan. 30, 1772.
2-241	" Caleb, of Francis, of Coventry, and Anne Arnold, of Stephen; m. by Eld. John Gorton, June 25, 1789.
2-188	" Charles, of Daniel, and Rebecca Havens, of William; m. by Eld. Thomas Manchester, Apr. 26, 1795.
2-231	" Mary, and Thomas Havens, Feb. 6, 1803.
2-119	" Susannah, and Caleb Pearce, June 23, 1803.
3-220	" Sophia, and Russell Miller, Nov. 11, 1813.

3-362	Brayton	William D., son of Hon. Charles, dec., and Anna W. Clarke, of Warwick, dau. of Ray, of East Greenwich; m. by Rev. Martin Cheney, Sept. 19, 1839.
4-57	"	Nehemiah, aged 32 years, son of Lodowick, of Cranston, and Lydia Sarle, aged 30 years, dau. of Joseph, of Cranston; m. by Rev. B. F. Hedden, Sept. 26, 1852.
3-36	"	William D., of Charles, dec., and Susan J. Baker, of Josiah; m. by Rev. Jonathan Brayton, July 12, 1866.
3-87	Brennan	Margaret, and Owen Drury, Sept. 21, 1845.
1-11	Briggs	James, of Kingstown, and Sarah Wickes, of John, of Warwick, Feb. —, 1734-5.
1-30	"	Susannah, and William Warner, Jan. 27, 1739-0.
2-16	"	George, and Hannah Wightman, widow of John, Jr.; m. by Eld. Peter Warden, Mar. 8, 1756.
2-15	"	Benjamin, and Rachel Warner, of Samuel; m. by Eld. John Hammett, May 18, 1757.
2-15	"	Joseph, of Job, and Lydia Miller, of Nathaniel, dec.; m. by Eld. Charles Holden, Nov. 26, 1767.
2-229	"	Isaac, of Job, and Sarah Gorton, of William, Jr.; m. by Eld. Charles Holden, Nov. 28, 1773.
2-238	"	Stephen, of George, and Huldah Gorton, of Nathan; m. by Eld. John Gorton, Aug. 27, 1780.
2-182	"	Amey, and Simmons Spencer, June 7, 1789.
2-158	"	Charles, Jr., son of Charles, of East Greenwich, and Elizabeth Rice, of William, of Warwick; m. by James Jeruald, Justice, Aug, 21, 1796.
2-134	"	James, of Joseph, and Cynthia Jenckes, of John, both of Smithfield; m. by Benoni Paine, Justice, June 4, 1797.
2-183	"	Samuel, and Nancy Rhodes; m. by Eld. Samuel Littlefield, May 3, 1798.
2-219	"	William, and Isabel W. Greene; m. by Eld. Samuel Littlefield, Nov. 21, 1799.
2-144	"	John, of Warwick, and Mercy Arnold, of Coventry; m. by Eld. Samuel Littlefield, Nov. 9, 1800.
2-198	"	Elizabeth, and Bowen Arnold, June 14, 1801.
2-87	"	Lydia, and Clarke Gorton, Oct. 25, 1801.
3-252	"	Betsey, and Pardon Potter, Jr., Aug. 6, 1809.
3-55	"	Susan R., and Rhodes Burke, Oct. 14, 1821.
3-53	"	Wanton R., of Samuel, and Celia Greene, of Capt. Benjamin, dec.; m. by Eld. Thomas Manchester, Sept. 5,1822.
3-275	"	Betsey R., and Daniel Remington, Dec. 6, 1820.
3-260	"	Mercy Ann, and Gen. Thomas A. Potter, June 17, 1832.

3-58	Briggs	George A., of John, of Warwick, and Mary Brown, of Joshua, of Exeter; m. by Eld. Thomas Tillinghast, Aug. 28, 1834.
3-58	"	George A., of John, and Julia Ann Tibbetts, of Charles; m. by Eld. Pardon Tillinghast, June 5, 1836.
3-98	"	Renery, and Thomas Eldredge, Aug. 31, 1840.
3-303	"	Sybel, and David Spencer, Jan. 3, 1841.
3-56	"	Samuel A., of Samuel, and Annah Fifield, of Rev. Moses; m. by Rev. John C. Goodrich, July 1, 1841.
3-57	"	Benjamin R., of Warwick, son of James, of Coventry, and Eliza A. Thurston, of Waterman, of Exeter; m. by Rev. Moses Fifield, Aug. 23, 1841.
3-60	"	Andrew, of Cranston, son of Alfred, and Mary L. Capwell, of Warwick, dau. of John; m. by Rev. Junia S. Mowry, Apr. 3, 1842.
3-304	"	Lucy, and John W. Sherman, Apr. 7, 1842.
3-381	"	Stephen A., of Benjamin, dec., and Maria E. Mitchell, of Samuel; m. by Rev. Moses Fifield, Feb. 19, 1844.
3-83	"	Nelson T., of Palmer T. and Amey, and Hannah Francis Place, of Sarah; m. by Rev. M. J. Steere, Aug. 14, 1844.
3-314	"	Huldah G., and Thomas T. Taylor, Apr. 28, 1845.
3-235	"	Nancy, and Augustus S. Mitchell, Oct. 27, 1845.
3-396	"	Ruth Ann, and John Campbell, Jan. 19, 1846.
3-390	"	Nicholas C., of Nicholas, and Lucy M. Tillinghast, of Horace, both of Providence; m. by Rev. Joseph Macreading, Mar. 29, 1846.
3-382	"	Gideon C., of Paul, and Susan Bowen, dau. of Hazard Boss; m. by Rev. Jonathan Brayton, Dec. 7, 1846.
3-402	"	Lucy C., and Almond G. Bennett, 14, 1846.
3-392	"	Jonathan F., of Warwick, and Susan D. Searle, of Cranston; m. by Rev. Stephen A. Thomas, Jan. 1, 1847.
3-386	"	Stukeley B., and Charlotte B. Atwood; m. by Rev. Stephen A. Thomas, June 20, 1847.
3-385	"	Benjamin N., of Coventry, son of David and Hannah Spencer, of Warwick, dau. of Pardon; m. by Rev. George A. Willard, Aug. 22, 1847.
4-38	"	Lucius, of Warwick, and Harriet T. Atwood, of Coventry; m. by Rev. Thomas F. Waterman, Apr. 21, 1851.
3-364	Brooks	Henry, of Warwick, and Hannah Carruthors, of East Greenwich; m. by Rev. George Uhleer, Feb. 18, 1849.

3-44	Brownell John G., and Mary Brown; m. by Rev. Thomas Tew, Sept. 30, 1839.
3-158	Browning Charlotte M., and Benjamin Hill, June 24, 1822.
3-56	" John G., and Mary Wood; m. by Rev. Henry Tatem, Nov. 2, 1827.
1-16	Brown Mary, and Joseph Carpenter, Mar. 18, 1702-3.
1-37	" Dorothy, and Nathaniel Medbury, Mar. 27, 1718.
1-42	" John, of North Brittain, and Mary Fox, of Ipswich, Mass.; m. by John Wickes, Asst., Dec. 19, 1723.
1-67	" Deborah, and Samuel Cross, Nov. 28, 1728.
1-61	" Abigail, and John Warner, Jr., June 26, 1729.
1-68	" Keziah, and Samuel Warner, Feb. 19, 1729-0.
1-107	" Elisha, and Patience Edmunds, of Joseph; m. by Phillip Arnold, Asst., Jan. 14, 1734-5.
1-1	" Phebe, and William Utter, Jr., Jan. 20, 1740.
1-52	" Major James, and Catherine Greene; m. by Eld. Manassah Martin, Apr. 27, 1740.
2-89	" Lucy, and Joseph Lippitt, Feb. 19, 1746.
2-216	" Ruth, and Thomas Wickes, Jan. 16, 1752.
2-47	" Mary, and Caleb Gorton, Sept. 20, 1753.
2-190	" Waite, and John Tibbetts, Jan. 7, 1760.
2-13	" Elisha, and Mary Tibbetts; m. by Samuel Gorton, Justice, May 21, 1761.
2-7	" Patience, and Gideon Arnold, Nov. 22, 1767.
3-7	" Patience, and Silas Baker, Mar. 31, 1785.
2-250	" Samuel, of Daniel, dec., of East Greenwich, and Mary Greene, of Richard, dec.; m. by Eld. John Gorton, Oct. 22, 1787.
2-185	" Elisha, of Joseph, and Sally Rice, of Henry; m. by James Jerauld, Justice, Feb. 24, 1796.
3-48	" James, Jr., of James, and Anna, of Smithfield, and Tabitha Lippitt, of Moses, and Tabitha, of Warwick; m. by Rev. Edward Hyde, Oct. 26, 1815.
3-52	" John H., of Nathan, late of North Kingstown, and Emeline Freeman, of Peter, of Warwick; m. by Eld. Thomas Manchester, Nov. —, 1819.
4-1	" Anne Carter, and John Brown Francis, June 18, 1822.
4-36	" Naomi, and George Burton, Jr., Apr. 3, 1825.
3-58	" Mary, and George A. Briggs, Aug. 28, 1834.
3-422	" Lydia, and Alvin Wickes, June 9, 1836.
3-314	" Beriah S., of John, and Mehitable Wilbur, of Hazard; m. by Rev. Moses Fifield, June 13, 1839.

3-61	Brown Beriah L., of Jessie, and Mehitable Wilbour, of Hazard; m. by Rev. Moses Fifield, June 13, 1839.
3-44	" Mary, and John G. Brownell, Sept. 30, 1839.
3-63	" Harris O., of Warwick, son of Jerimoth, dec., of Scituate, and Mary Ann Seabury, of Warwick, dau. of George B.; m. by Rev. Moses Fifield, Oct.'7, 1839.
3-45	" Willett G., and Mary Potter; m. by Rev. Thomas Dowling, Oct. 27, 1839.
3-48	" Phebe R. A., and Charles W. Baker, Jan. 1, 1840.
3-49	" Nicholas, of Jesse, and Phebe Ann Wilcox, of Ishmael, dec.; m. by Rev. Moses Fifield, Feb. 24, 1840.
3-315	" Dorcas, and John W. Tew, Mar. 15, 1840.
3-50	" Daniel A., of Warwick, son of Jaumoth, dec., of Scituate, and Lucy Spink, of Silas, of Cranston; m. by Rev. Moses Fifield, Aug. 3, 1840.
3-329	" Ann M., and Benjamin D. Vickery, Dec. 28, 1840.
3-421	" William M., of Jesse, and Susan A. Clapp, of widow Hannah; m. by Rev. George A. Williams, Jan.13,1848.
3-365	" Joseph P., of Charlestown, R. I., son of Henry, of Waterford, Conn., and Artemissia Thurston, of Warwick, dau. of George, dec., of Charlestown; m. by Rev. John H. Baker, May 30, 1848.
4-74	" Samuel G., and Sarah G. Kettle; m. Rev. Thomas Hardman, Mar. 5, 1849.
4-21	" Joseph O., of Abial, and Margaret Whitford, of Rodman; m. by Rev. Jonathan Brayton, Nov. 4, 1849.
4-51	" Lucy A., and Daniel B. Burke, Mar. 22, 1852.
4-91	" Carrie M., and Paul Bajanotti, June 17, 1876.
2-17	Brussel John, and Dorcas Fry (so called); m. by Eld. John Gorton, Sept. 29, 1783.
1-57	Bucklin Joseph, and Mary Worden; m. by Thomas Stafford, Justice, Oct. 23, 1737.
1-3	Budlong Francis, and Rebecca Hazard, widow of Joseph; m. by John Greene, Asst., Mar. 19, 1668-9.
1-61	" Rebecca, and Samuel Peirce, Nov. 26, 1721.
1-46	" John, of Warwick, and Tabitha Perce, dau. of Azriekim, of Rehoboth, Mass.; m. by John Warner, Justice, Jan. 8, 1729-0.
1-24	" Mary, and Benjamin Pearce, Jan. 8, 1729-0.
1-62	" Moses, of John, and Hannah Staples, of Samuel, July 4, 1734.
2-62	" Isabel, and Elisha Greene, Jr., Dec, 4, 1748.

24   VITAL RECORD OF RHODE ISLAND.

2-15	Budlong	Samuel, of Moses, and Katherine Rhodes, of Capt. John, Jr.; m. by Eld. Charles Holden, Sept. 28, 1758.
2-149	"	Rosanna, and John Rhodes, Aug. 25, 1763.
2-26	"	Susannah, and James Carder, Jr., Apr. 27, 1766.
2-14	"	Pearce, of John, dec., and Prudence Remington, of Thomas, m. by Eld. Charles Holden, Aug. 27, 1769.
2-234	"	Almy, and Benjamin Budlong, Aug. 28, 1778.
2-234	"	Benjamin, of John, dec., and Almy Budlong, of Samuel; m. by Eld. Charles Holden, Aug. 28, 1778.
2-238	"	Capt. Moses, and Mary Nichols, otherwise, Davis, dau. of Eleanor Briggs, wife of Job; m. by James Jerauld, Justice, Oct. 19, 1780.
2-140	"	Stephen, of Warwick, and Huldah Burlingame, of Phillip, of Cranston, Apr. 17, 1784.
2-255	"	Samuel, Jr., son of Samuel, of Warwick, and Waitey Salsbury, of Nathan, of Cranston; m. by Eld. John Gorton, Apr. 3, 1791.
2-226	"	Pearce, of Nathan, and Mary Littlefield, of Samuel; m. by Eld. David Corpe, Nov. 18, 1792.
2-181	"	Job, of Samuel, and Rebecca Budlong; m. by Eld. David Corpe, Jan. 7, 1793.
2-181	"	Rebecca, and Job Budlong, Jan. 7, 1793.
2-100	"	Mary, and Jeremiah Webb, Dec. 13, 1797.
2-106	"	Joseph, of Moses, and Robey Kimball, of Amos; m. by Joseph Arnold, Justice, June 10, 1798.
2-18	"	John, Jr., and Dorcas Pearce, of Azrikim; m. by Eld. Charles Holden, July 31, ———.
2-161	"	Amos, and Betsey Lippitt, of Ceaser, (both col.,) m. by James Jerauld, Justice, Apr. 6, 1800.
2-80	"	Nathan, Jr., of Nathan, and Lucy Carder, of James; m. by James Jerauld, Justice, Jan. 13, 1802.
3-269	"	Susanna, and Charles Remington, Feb. 16, 1805.
3-43	"	Stephen, and Isbie Lippitt; m. by Alexander Havens, Justice, July 28, 1805.
4-76	"	Oliver C., of Warwick, and Sarah B. Wood, of Coventry; m. by Rev. Jonathan Wilson, Apr. 27, 1826.
4-66	"	Almy, and Eld. John Joslin, May 18, 1830.
3-313	"	Lydia W., and James B. Tillinghast, Mar. 25, 1845.
3-392	"	Ann M., and Alfred Stone, Nov. 20, 1848.
4-58	"	Sarah L., and William G. Sherman, July 13, 1852.
2-76	Bugbee	Elizabeth, and John Hudson, Aug. 6, 1778.
3-75	Bunn	Mary A., and James Cole, Mar. 19, 1835.

4-19	Bunn James H., of Providence, and Bethiah P. Sarle, of Warwick; m. by Rev. Reuben Allen, Nov. 18, 1849.
3-395	Burch William C., of Groton, Conn., and Mary E. Taber, of Coventry; m. by Rev. Stephen A. Thomas, Jan. 10, 1847.
3-385	Burdick Wilbour J., and Almira Herd; m. by Rev. Edward K. Fuller, Sept. 15, 1845.
3-387	" S. Maria, and George W. Burrows, Nov. 7, 1847.
4-66	Burden William, of Warwick, son of Henry, dec., of Bristol, and Elizabeth Bennett, of Warwick, dau. of Thomas, dec., of East Greenwich; m. by Rev. Moses Fifield, May 1, 1836.
3-72	Burguess Lydia, and Thankful Collins, Dec. 3, 1733.
3-128	" Sophia, and Phillip Greene, Mar. 4, 1832.
4-43	" Olive W., and William R. Wilson, July 14, 1851.
3-78	Burke Mary, and Benjamin Carpenter, Aug. 29, 1790.
2-128	" Richard, of William, and Mary Greene, of Caleb; m. by Eld. John Gorton, July 17, 1791.
2-188	" Seth, of William, and Lucy Tiffany, of Thomas; m. by Eld. Thomas Manchester, Mar. 26, 1795.
2-105	" Edmund, of William, and Betsey Taylor, of Ambrose; m. by Joseph Arnold, Justice, Apr. 5, 1798.
2-116	" Edward, of William, and Phebe Arnold, of Dea. John; m. by Joseph Arnold, Justice, Mar. 14, 1799.
2-13	" Christopher, of William, and Elizabeth Millard, of Samuel; m. by Caleb Jerauld, Justice, Aug. 14, 1803.
3-55	" Rhodes, of Coventry, son of Capt: Seth, of Warwick, and Susan R. Briggs, of Capt. Samuel, of Warwick; m. by Rev. Thomas Manchester, Oct. 14, 1821.
3-352	" Sarah, and Austin Wilson, May 4, 1826.
3-354	" Fannie T., and William G. Wood, July 4, 1831.
4-51	" Daniel B., of Providence, aged 26 years, son of Rhodes, and Susan, of Coventry, and Lucy A. Brown, of Warwick, aged 25 years, dau. of Daniel and Lucy; m. by Rev. Benjamin Phelan, Mar. 22, 1852.
1-12	Burlingame Mary, and Amos Stafford, Dec. 19, 1689.
1-49	" Margaret, and Joseph Remington, Sept. 29, 1717.
1-36	" Mary, and John Warner, Jr., Oct. 23, 1719.
2-223	" Moses, Jr., of Coventry, son of Moses, and Sarah Barton, of Andrew, of Warwick; m. by Thomas Rice, Jr., Justice, Nov. 24, 1776.
2-140	" Huldah, and Stephen Budlong, Apr. 17, 1784.

2-75	Burlingame Sarah, and Edward Holden, Jan. 16, 1785.
2-153	" Mercy, and Benjamin Rhodes, July 17, 1785.
2-153	" Phebe, and Benjamin Rhodes, Dec. 4, 1791.
2-116	" Robey, and John Bennett, May 20, 1802.
2-99	" Nancy, and Caleb Ladd, Feb. 10, 1803.
2-154	" Elizabeth, and Jeffrey Amhurst Rice, Dec. 8, 1803.
3-97	" Sarah, and Andrew Essex, Sept. 30, 1832.
3-189	" Mrs. Mary, and Nathan Knight, Aug. 29, 1839.
3-43	" Robert, of Warwick, son of Stephen, of Cranston, and Prescilla C. Sarle, of Warwick; m. by Rev. Moses Fifield, Nov. 17, 1839.
3-53	" Gorton, son of Stephen, of Cranston, and Sally A. Sarle, of Warwick, dau. of Benjamin; m. by Rev. Moses Fifield, Mar. 4, 1841.
3-117	" Frances, and John Gardner, Dec. 31, 1843.
3-169	" Adeline M., and Daniel T. Hart, Feb. 18, 1846.
3-391	" Pardon, of Warwick, son of George, and Susan H. Wilbour, of Cranston, dau. of Jeremiah; m. by Rev. Jonathan Brayton, Apr. 26, 1846.
3-364	" George, and Hannah Collins; m. by Rev. S. A. Thomas, Sept. 16, 1847.
3-64	Burrell Isaiah, Jr., of Lynn, Mass., and Mary Woodmansee, of John, of Warwick, formerly of Richmond; m. by Rev. Moses Fifield, Oct. 20, 1839.
3-160	" Mercy, and William Hare, Nov. 6, 1842.
4-68	Burr Molly, and Hollis K. Jenckes, Apr., 1813.
3-387	Burrows George W., of Warwick, son of Benjamin, of Groton, Conn., and S. Maria Burdick, of Voluntown, Conn.; m. by Rev. Moses Fifield, Nov. 7, 1847.
1-6	Burton Elizabeth, and Thomas Hedjer, Oct. 30, 1674.
1-7	" Susannah, and Samuel Gorton, Dec. 11, 1684.
2-14	" Rufus, of John, of Cranston, and Abigail Snell, of Daniel, of Warwick; m. by James Jerauld, Justice, Dec. 14, 1777.
2-115	" John, of Benjamin, and Polly Card, of Joseph; m. by Henry Remington, Justice, Apr. 16, 1801.
2-122	" Sally, and Caleb Holden, Apr. 9, 1802.
4-36	" George, Jr., of Warwick, son of George, of Cranston, and Naomi Brown, of Elisha, Apr. 3, 1825.
4-32	" William, of Cranston, aged 28 years, formerly of Stockport, Eng., son of William and Mary, and Margaret Jane Palmer, of Cranston, aged 17 years, dau. of John and Jane; m. by Rev. Zalman Tobey, Oct. 27, 1850.

3-276 Burt Sarah L., and Joseph B. Rice, Sept. 14, 1832.
4-11 " Allen B., of Taunton, Mass., son of Allen and Almarah J. Arnold, of Warwick, dau. of George; m. by Rev. Jonathan Brayton, May 20, 1849.
3-390 Burvee Almoran, of Warwick, son of Henry, of Salesbury, N. Y., and Margaret Davis, of Warwick, dau. of Benjamin, of East Greenwich; m. by Rev. Moses Fifield, Oct. 13, 1834.
1-4 Busecott Mary, and Peter Spicer, Dec. 15, 1670.
3-383 Bushee James, of Warwick, and Abbie B. Gardiner, of East Greenwich; m. by Eld. Thomas Tillinghast, Aug. 2, 1847.
3-166 Bushnell Amanda, and Bernard M. Hall, Sept. 16, 1840.
2-163 Button Anne, and Peirce Reynolds, Oct. 15, 1788.
3-72 Butts Susannah, and John Cooke; Aug. 5, 1813.
2-16 Byles Samuel, and Ruth Dexter; m. by James Arnold, Asst., Jan. 28, 1749-0.
2-17 " Capt. Samuel, of Cranston, and Sarah Carpenter, of Warwick; m. by Eld. John Warner, Jr., Apr. 2, 1757.

C

3-73 Cady Joseph, of Joel, and Mary Himes, of Lydia; m. by Rev. Moses Fifield, Mar. 28, 1842.
3-367 " Alferese, of Joel, and Mary Northup, of Smith; m. by Rev. Moses Fifield, May 29, 1843.
1-13 Cahoone Nathaniel, and Jane Jones, of Thomas, Feb. 25, 1702.
1-39 " Joseph, and Elizabeth Scranton, of Thomas,———1713.
1-65 " Rebecca, and James Greene, Dec. 18, 1717.
1-64 " Samuel, of Joseph, of Warwick, and Susannah Nichols, of John, of East Greenwich, Feb. 9, 1720-1.
2-20 " Samuel, and Margaret Nichols, of James; m. by James Greene, Justice, Jan 13, 1750.
2-15 " Mary, and James Bebe, Oct. 27, 1757.
2-109 " Patience, and Moses Mathewson, Jan. 26, 1758.
3-94 Calvert Ann, and William Eaton, Sept. 19, 1846.
2-215 Cammet Freelove, and Caleb Weaver, Apr. 7, 1787.
3-396 Campbell John, and Ruth Ann Briggs; m. by Rev. Edward K. Fuller, Jan. 19, 1846.
1-86 Capron Edward, and Marian Greene, widow; m. by William Greene, Justice, Feb. 26, 1729-0.

2-148	Capron Marian, and Benjamin Rouse, July 16, 1761.
3-74	" Caleb B., of Greene, of East Greenwich, and Betsey Essex, of Corpe; m. by Rev. Thomas Manchester, Dec. 1, 1811.
3-228	" Betsey Ann, and George G. Mathewson, Mar. 2, 1840.
3-205	" Sarah, and Charles A. Lake, Nov. 5, 1840.
3-378	" Charles B., of Warwick, son of Pliney, and Almira Fisher, of Smithfield, dau. of Obed, dec.; m. by Rev. Zalman Tobey, Sept. 28, 1847.
4-41	" Sarah A., and Lon Jessup, Apr. 26, 1851.
1-102	Capwell Hannah, and William Bennett, Oct 2, 1731.
4-87	" James, of North Providence, son of John, and Mary B. Wickes, of Reuben; m. by Rev. Benjamin Phelan, Apr. 7, 1836.
3-60	" Mary L., and Andrew Briggs, Apr. 3, 1842.
4-21	" George W., of Jabez W., and Mariah White, of Benjamin; m. by Rev. Jonathan Brayton, Dec. 20, 1849.
1-5	Carder John, of Richard, and Mary Holden, of Capt. Randall, and Frances; m. by John Greene, Justice, Dec. 1, 1671.
1-6	" Sarah, and Benjamin Gorton, Dec. 5, 1672.
1-7	" Mary, and Malacha Roades, May 27, 1675.
1-31	" Capt. James, and Mary Whipple, of Providence, dau. of John, Jan. 6, 1686-7.
1-54	" Mary, and Richard Greene, ——— 1700.
1-30	" John, and Elizabeth Paine, of William, of Boston, Dec. 25, 1701.
1-47	" Elizabeth, and William Collins, Aug. 20, 1723.
1-92	" Joseph, of John, and Ann Low, of Anthony, July 25, 1724.
1-92	" Ann, and Josiah Haynes, Jan. 1, 1729.
1-106	" John, Jr., of Warwick, and Mary Westcott, of Robert; m. by John Wickes, Asst., Nov. 30, 1732.
1-106	" John, Jr., and Mary Westgate, of Robert, Nov. 30, 1732.
1-45	" Susanna, and Edward Case, Jan. 24. 1733-4.
1-59	" James, of John, and Sarah Davis, of Urian; m. by Eld. Manassah Martin, Feb. 6, 1736.
2-70	" Sarah, and Benjamin Hudson, Aug. 14, 1760.
2-168	" Elizabeth, and Thomas Stone, Jr., Mar. 5, 1761.
2-175	" Mary, and Thomas Slocum, June 21, 1761.
2-26	" James, Jr., son of Capt. James, and Susannah Budlong, of Capt. Moses; m. by Eld. Charles Holden, Apr. 27, 1766.

2-27	Carder Capt.	James, and Anne Hammett, widow of John, Jr.; m. by Eld. Charles Holden, Dec. 28, 1766.
2-78	"	Hannah, and William Holden, June 20, 1773.
2-243	"	Joseph, of John, dec., of Warwick, and Esther Sheldon, of Eld. Benjamin, of Cranston; m. by Eld. John Gorton, Mar 27, 1785.
2-131	"	Randall, and Dianna Rice; m. by Eld. Samuel Littlefield, Dec. 28, 1794.
2-173	"	Catherine, and Webb Straight, May 31, 1795.
2-194	"	George, and Anne Carpenter, of Wilbour; m. by James Jerauld, Justice, June 14, 1801.
2-80	"	Lucy and Nathan Budlong, Jr., Jan. 13, 1802.
2-32	"	Sally, and Josiah Baker, Sept. 20, 1802.
3-226	"	Harriet, and E——— Qurman, Apr. 5, 1845.
3-315	"	Nancy M., and Daniel B. Thurston, Sept. 22, 1845.
4-44	"	James N., aged 21 years, son of James, dec., and Elizabeth, and Phebe Gorton, aged 16 years, dau. of John, dec., and Hannah; m. by Rev. Benjamin Phelan, Aug. 4, 1851.
4-62	"	Alma D., and Isreal R. Sheldon, Nov. 4, 1852.
2-253	Card	Joseph, of Richard, and Sarah Andrew, of Benoni, both of East Greenwich; m. by Eld. John Gorton, Apr. 30, 1789.
2-115	"	Polly, and John Burton, Apr. 16, 1801.
3-279	"	Olive C., and Thomas C. Rice, May 27, 1839.
3-297	"	Sarah B., and Greene A. Sweet, Sept. 2, 1839.
3-71	"	Joseph, of Richard, of East Greenwich, and Henrietta Leach, of Coventry, widow of Owen, dau. of Eleazer Fiske, dec., m. by Rev. Moses Fifield, May 18, 1841.
3-27	"	Elizabeth R., and Allen Austin, Sept. 17, 1844.
3-398	"	William H. N., and Harriet Dawley; m. by Rev. Edward K. Fuller, Oct. 2, 1845.
3-399	"	William H., and Hannah M. Tyler: m. by Rev. Stephen A. Thomas, June 29, 1846.
3-377	"	Stephen E., and Esther E. Parker; m. by Eld. Thomas Tillinghast, June 9, 1847,
3-408	"	Nathan, and Rhoda A. Sunderland; m. by Rev. Stephen A. Thomas, Jan. 27, 1848.
4-5	"	Robert G., of Robert, and Margaret Bailey, of Jeremiah; m. by Rev. Jonathan Brayton, Oct. 31, 1849.

4-88	Card William Amos, and Georgiana A. Williams, both of Warwick; m. at North Kingstown, by Rev. Joseph C. Butler, Dec. 7, 1870.
2-237	Carey Ichabod, of Dighton, and Elizabeth Millard, of Nathaniel; m. by James Jerauld, Justice, Aug. 27, 1779.
1-16	Carpenter Joseph, of Abiah, of Warwick, and Mary Brown, of Beriah, of Kings Towne, Mar. 18, 1702-3.
1-78	" Hannah, and Elisha Arnold, Dec. 9, 1709.
1-86	" Martha, and John Lee, Jr., Mar. 13, 1740.
2-19	" Oliver, of Providence, and Martha Greene, of Barlo, of Warwick; m. by Eld. Manassah Martin, Apr. 7, 1743.
2-17	" Sarah, and Samuel Byles, Apr. 2, 1757.
2-219	" Job, and Barbara Miller; m. by Eld. Charles Holden, Dec. 27, 1764.
2-220	" John, of Providence, and Sarah Utter, of William, Jr., dec., of Warwick; m. by Eld. Charles Holden, Oct. 27, 1765.
2-164	" Lucy, and William Rice, Dec. 15, 1772.
2-236	" Job, Jr., of Job, dec., and Elisha York, of James, dec.; m. by Thomas Rice, Jr., Justice, July, 14, 1776.
2-215	" Lydia, and Daniel Wightman, Oct. 6, 1782.
2-168	" Mary, and Peter Sprague, Feb. 19, 1789.
3-78	" Benjamin, of Wilbour, and Mary Burke, of William; m. by Eld. John Gorton, Aug 29, 1790.
2-127	" Sarah, and Benjamin Pearce, June 26, 1791.
2-194	" Anne, and George Carder, June 14, 1801.
2-28	" Mercy, and William Price, Aug. 9, 1801.
2-172	" Wilbour, and Millesent Lockwood; m. by Eld. Samuel Littlefield, June 28, 1802.
3-328	" Millesent, and Benjamin Vaughn, Oct. 5, 1809.
3-69	" Wilbour, Jr., of Wilbour dec., and Patience Bentley, of Caleb; m. by Caleb Gerald, Justice, Oct. 7. 1810.
3-10	" Betsey, aud Joseph Arnold, Dec. 20, 1813.
4-401	" Welthia, and William B. Spencer, Apr., 20, 1834.
3-78	" George B., of Joshua, and Rhoda Covel, of Thomas; m. by Rev. Moses Fifield, Sept. 11 1842.
3-364	Carruthors Hannah, and Henry Brooks, Feb. 18, 1849.
1-17	Carr Margaret, and John Battey, Sept. 18, 1707.
1-32	" Deborah, and John Greene, Dec. 6, 1711.
1-35	" Avis, and Hezekiah Gorton, Aug. 20, 1719.
1-48	" Patience, and Robert Westgate, July 9, 1723.
2-98	" Sarah, and Resolved Waterman, Oct. 12, 1732.

2-253 Carr Sails, of Warwick, and Mary Hatch, of East Greenwich; m. by Eld. David Corpe, Nov. 5, 1789.
3-16 " Avis, and Whipple A. Arnold, Apr. 8, 1839.
3-34 " Sally Russell, and George G. Watson, Oct. 12, 1840.
3-369 " John C., of Exeter, now of Warwick, son of William, and Alice S. Rathbun, of North Kingstown, now of Providence, dau. of Baldwin; m. by Rev. Jonathan Brayton, May 19, 1844.
3-386 " Martha, and Samuel Bennett, May 21, 1845.
3-86 " Frances, and Alvin G. Dodge, Aug. 3, 1845.
4-59 " Sarah Ann, and Abraham Lockwood, Apr. 21, 1850.
4-83, 84 " Nathaniel S., of West Greenwich, and Harriet N. Watson, of South Kingstown; m. by Rev. A. Sherwin, Jan. 16, 1857.
4-78 " Susan B., and Willard Wilcox, Jan. 29, 1860.
4-78 Carter James A., and Marcella A. Remington, Jan. 6, 1853.
4-99 " Mary A., and Thomas P. Remington, Jan 6, 1853.
1-27 Casey Edward, of Lieut. Adam, and Hannah Bowen; m. by John Greene, Justice, Sept. 12, 1742.
2-215 " Mary and Benjamin Wood, Mar. 17, 1765.
2-250 " Mehitable, and Jonathan Austin, July 22, 1787.
2-101 " William, of Easton, Washington Co., N. Y., and Betsey Peirce, of Giles; m. by Joseph Arnold, Justice, Jan. 7, 1798.
1-42 Case Elizabeth, and Isreal Arnold, Jr., June 27, 1730.
1-107 " Hannah, and Stephen Arnold, Jr., Jan. 16, 1732.
1-45 " Edward, of William, of South Kingstown, and Susannah Carder, of John, of Warwick, Jan. 24, 1733-4.
2-171 " Frances, and James Sherman, Nov. 8. 1759.
4-27 Caswell Luther L., of James, and Abbie Eliza Hazard, of Peleg; m. by Rev. Moses Fifield, May 14, 1850.
3-409 Caucrofte William, and Elizabeth Pelgington; m. by Rev. Stephen A. Thomas, Mar. 12, 1848.
2-243 Ceazer William, of Providence, and Bathsheba Rice, of Warwick, (col.); m. by Eld. John Gorton, Feb. 3, 1788.
2-195 " Joseph, of North Kingstown, and Freelove King, of East Greenwich, (col.); m. by Benjamin Barton, Justice, Aug. 3, 1789.
2-263 Chace Mercy, and John Weeden, Jan. 7, 1776.
2-237 " Lorey, of Abraham, and Mary Wightman, of Elisha; m. by James Jerauld, Justice, Apr. 2, 1780.

2-24 Chace Joseph, of Abraham, of Warwick, and Lucy Arnold, of Oliver, of East Greenwich; m. by Eld. John Gorton, Dec. 16, 1781.
2-65 " Sarah, and Stephen Greene, May 5, 1782.
2-92 " Cynthia, and Thomas Snell, Oct. 5, 1798.
2-36 " Charlotte, and Elisha Baker, Nov. 30, 1800.
3-367 " William W., of Warwick, son of William, of Providence, and Martha Lockwood, of Warwick, dau. of Joseph, dec., of Manchester, Eng.; m. by Eld. Moses Fifield, May 8, 1844.
3-373 " Carlton, of Providence, and Sarah A. Fones, of Warwick, m. by Rev. Edward K. Fuller, Nov. 11, 1844.
1-102 Chadsey Mary, and Thomas Spicer, June 1, 1744.
4-57 Champlain George, aged 21 years, of Kingstown, son of Eld. George, and Sarah E. Proffet, (col.); m. by Eld. William P. Place, Sept. 23, 1852.
4-64 Chapin Dianna M., and Richard Waterman, Feb. 15, 1831.
2-25 Chapman Nathaniel, and Phebe Greene, widow of Giles; m. by Eld. Charles Holden, Mar. 2, 1767.
2-111 " Dorcas, and Daniel Matteson, Mar. 1, 1770.
4-97 " Capt. William Rhodes, son of Benjamin and Zilpha, and Mercy Burlingame Rhodes, of Capt. Benjamin and Phebe, Nov. 12, 1820.
3-398 Chappell Edward, and Mary Singer; m. by Rev. John C. Brown, Aug. 16, 1846.
3-376 " John H., of Hopkinton, son of John H., and Mary A. Gardiner, of Warwick, dau. of Ezekiel; m. by Rev. Jonathan Brayton, Oct. 18, 1846.
4-52 " Belinda, and William J. Johnson, Mar. 2, 1852.
4-26 Chase William L., of Burrillville, son of Buffum, and Annette Tyler, of Warwick, dau. of William; m. by Rev. Zalman Tobey, June 2, 1850.
4-79 Cheese Thomas S., of Cranston, and Eliza Sweet, of Warwick; m. by Rev. James E. Phillips, May 15, 1838.
3-372 " Henry F., of Sarah, and Julia Proffet, of Joseph, (col.); m. by Rev. Martin J. Steere, Apr. 3, 1845.
3-370 Cheves James M., and Betsey Ann Sypwood, of James; by Rev. Jonathan E. Forbush, June 27, 1844.
4-34 Chipman Harriet F., and Albert G. Scholfield, Jan. 1, 1851.
2-236 Church Lowry, of William, and Mary Arnold, of William; m. by Eld. John Gorton, Mar. 2, 1788.
3-5, 45 " Celia, and John Henry Bonn, Oct. 5, 1808.

3-256 Church Sally Ann, and George W. Price, Dec. 20, 1813.
3-378 Chute Josiah, of Curtis, of Cumberland, Me., and Abbie Reynolds, of Charles, of Warwick; m. by Eld. Thomas Hardman, Nov. 8, 1847.
1-29,52 Cindrick Anne, and Joseph Hicks, Nov. 18, 1738.
2-22 Clapp Silas, of Rye, N. Y., and Mary Greene, of John, of Warwick; m. by Eld. John Hammett, Apr. 19, 1752.
2-42 " John, of Silas, and Anna, Waterman, of John, dec.; m. by Charles Holden, Aug. 31, 1775.
2-241 " Daniel, of Warwick, and Elizabeth Bailey, of Robert, of East Greenwich; m. by Eld. James Wightman, June 15, 1783.
3-70 " John G., of John, of Warwick, and Catherine Godfrey, of Joshua, late of East Greenwich; m. by Rev. Thomas Manchester, Aug. 12, 1810.
3-79 " Gardner, of Nathaniel, of Dorchester, Mass., and Lucy Anne Greene, of John, of Warwick; m. by Rev. Moses Fifield, June 3, 1839.
3-76 " James H., of Thomas, dec., and Ruth A. Coggeshall, of Robert; m. by Rev. Moses Fifield, June 16, 1842.
3-421 " Susan A., and William M. Brown, Jan. 13, 1848.
4-45 " Ann A, W., and Stephen Tiffany, Oct. 20, 1850.
1-50 Clark Joseph, and Elizabeth Nichols, of Thomas, Nov. 6, 1718.
1-88 " William, and Elizabeth Borne, of Samuel, July 13, 1732.
2-72 " Phebe, and Bartholomew Hunt, Dec. 30, 1759.
2-20 " Joseph, and Susanna Latham; m. by Thomas Rice, Justice, Sept. 22, 1768.
2-227 " Mary, and John Gorton, Jr., Feb. 28, 1773.
3-68 " Weeden, and Hannah Spink; m. by Eld. David Curtis, Feb. 11, 1810.
3-62 " Anna W., and William D. Brayton, Sept. 19, 1839.
3-67 " Ethan Ray, of Warwick, son of Ray, of Brookfield, N. Y., formerly of East Greenwich, and Mary E. Millard, of Augustus; m. by Rev. Moses Fifield, Oct. 29, 1840.
3-77 " Ann, and Hyrum Clark, Aug. 22, 1842.
3-77 " Hyrum, of Elias, and Ann Clark, of Benjamin; m. by Thomas Wickes, Aug. 22, 1842.
3-348 " Betsey M., and Stowell White, Sept. 18, 1842.
4-32 " Susan C., and Nathan K. Gleason, Dec. 1, 1861.
2-21 Clemons Hannah, and John Cranston, June 10, 1804.
4-16 Cleveland Sally Maria, and Thomas Jackson, Oct. 7, 1849.
3-66 Cobb Almy, and Joseph Congdon, Sept. 21, 1840.

1-4 Codner Richard, of Swansea, and Phebe Lorton, of Warwick; m. by John Greene, Justice, May 23, 1671.
1-20 Coggeshall Elizabeth, and John Warner Jr., Nov. 27, 1694.
1-42 " Daniel, and Rebecca Heath, wife of Josiah, Nov. 12, 1738.
2-23 " Benjamin, of Stratford, Conn., and Comfort Mathewson, of Warwick; m. at Middletown, R. I., by Joshua Coggshall, Justice, June 1, 1758.
2-264 " Joseph, and Lydia Bates; m. by Eld. Charles Holden, Nov. 21, 1762.
2-79 " Violette, and Martin Johnson, Dec. 15, 1769.
3-66 " Joseph, of Almy, and Elizabeth Godfrey, otherwise Graft, dau. of Waite Godfrey; m. by C. Brayton, Justice, June 18, 1809.
3-69 " Robert H., of Warwick, son of Christopher, dec., of East Greenwich, and Sally Sholes, widow of Lyman, of Valley Falls, and dau. of Lemuel Bennett; m. by Rev. Moses Fifield, Mar. 31, 1841.
3-76 " Ruth A., and James H. Clapp, June 16, 1842.
1-68 Cogshall Sarah, and Samuel Greene, Mar. 11, 1724-5.
3-110 Colburn Lucy A., and Henry A. Franklin, Sept. 27, 1847.
2-254 Colebee Sarah, and Richard Sephton, Dec. 29, 1791.
1-2-56 Cole Nathaniel, now of Long Island, and Martha Jackson, of Hamstead, N. Y.; m. by John Greene, Asst., Aug. 30, 1667.
1-90 " Ann, and Thomas Wickes, Feb. 10 or 20, 1701-2.
1-56 " Nathaniel, and Deborah Lockwood, of Abraham; m. by Randall Holden, Asst., Nov. 29, 1725.
2-195 " Sarah, and David Vaughn, Dec. 5, 1745.
2-21 " Nathaniel, and Sarah Lockwood; m. by John Warner, Jr., Justice, Apr. 28, 1757.
2-178 " Joseph, of Benjamin, of North Kingstown, and Almy Moon, of Robert, of Exeter; m. by Eld. Charles Holden, Dec. 17, 1773.
2-236 " John, of Nathaniel, and Phebe Remington, of Thomas; m. by Eld. Charles Holden, Feb. 4, 1779.
2-22 " John, Jr., and Catherine Low; m. by Eld. Samuel Littlefield, Aug. 14, 1804.
3-67 " Lockwood, and Deborah Gorton; m. by C. Brayton, Justice, Nov. 13, 1808.
3-119 " Deborah, and James Greene, Aug. 2, 1818.
3-77 " Benjamin M., and Mary Ann Arnold; m. by Rev. Jonathan Smith, Oct. 20, 1822.

3-75	Cole James, and Mary A. Bunn; m. by Rev. Henry Tatem, Mar. 19, 1835.
4-30	" Mary L., and Thomas W. Whitford, Aug. 4, 1850.
1-8	Collins Sarah, and John Potter, Jan. 7, 1684.
1-25	" Thomas, and Abigail House, Feb. 17, 1692.
1-14	" Elizabeth, and Samuel Gorton, May 9, 1695.
1-64	" Sarah, and John Ruttenberge, Apr. 14, 1719.
1-47	" William, of Thomas, and Elizabeth Carder, of John, Aug. 20, 1723.
1-103	" Ann, and William Wood, July 2, 1727.
1-72	" Thankful, of Thomas, and Sarah Gorton, of Samuel, May 19, 1728.
1-72	" Thankful, and Lydia Burguess, Dec. 3, 1733.
2-23	" Thomas, of Mr. Thankful, of Warwick, and Ann Sweet, of Richard, of West Greenwich; m. by John Warner, Jr., Justice, May 29, 1755.
3-208	" Maria B , and Daniel G. Littlefield, Nov. 28, 1842.
3-364	" Hannah, and George Burlingame, Sept. 16, 1847.
3-4	" Esther Ann, and Uriah Arnold, Apr. 11, 1849.
4-84, 86	" Moses W., and Cynthia A. Walker; m. by Rev. Stephen A. Thomas, Nov. 9, 1855.
1-46	Collis Prudence, and William Arnold, Nov. 3, 1744.
2-107	Colvin Temperance, and Michael Martin, Oct. 1, 1785.
3-71	" George, and Huldah Davis; m. by C. Brayton, Justice, Sept. 27, 1812.
3-79	" Phillip A., of John, and Mary Rowand; m. by Rev. Moses Fifield, Oct. 31, 1843.
3-285	" Sally C., and James H. Reynolds, Jan 1, 1844.
4-70	" Freelove R., and Thomas Arnold, June 24, 1852.
2-239	Comstock Jabez, of Chatham, Conn., and Almy Greene, of James, of Warwick; m. by James Jerauld, Justice, Jan. 1, 1784.
3-73	Congdon Peleg, of Exeter, and Mary Remington, of Warwick; m. by Eld. Samuel Littlefield, Jan. 7, 1816.
3-66	" Joseph, of John, dec., and Almy Cobb, dau. of Anthony A. Rice, dec.; m. by Eld. Moses Fifield, Sept. 21, 1840.
3-72	" Francis H., of William, and Hannah B. Rice, of Low ; m. by Rev. Jonathan Brayton, Mar. 20, 1842.
3-371	" George T., of James, and Julia E. Weaver, of John; m. by Rev. Jonathan E. Forbush, Oct. 20, 1842.
3-449	" Maria, and James Vaughn, Nov. 3, 1845.

4-24	Congdon John, of William, and Jane Love, of Leonard; m. by Rev. Jonathan Brayton, May 2, 1847.
4-50	" John, of Cranston, age 65 years, son of James and Mary, and Sarah Ann Hollis, of Warwick, age 25 years, dau. of Ira and Lucy; m. by George Greene, Justice, Dec. 16, 1851.
1-2	Cooke Elizabeth, and John Harrude, Dec. 24, 1666.
2-110	" Abigail, and Nicholas Mathewson, May 20, 1773.
2-20	" Dr. Nicholas, and Elizabeth Arnold, of David, Mar. 12, 1797.
3-72	" John, and Susannah Butts; m. by C. Brayton, Justice, Aug. 5, 1813.
3-74	" George H., of George, and Mary W. Remington, of William; m. by Rev. Junia S. Mowry, Mar. 28, 1842.
1-50	Cook Samuel, and Enfield Greene, of John; m. by James Greene, Asst., Mar. 25, 1719.
2-45	" Patience, and Capt. Samuel Greene, Apr. 28, 1757.
2-85	" Thomas, of Portsmouth, and Sarah Moot, of Warwick; m. by Ebenezer Slocum, Justice, Dec. 12, 1763.
2-47	" Polly, and Cuffe Greene, Jan. 18, 1779.
2-145	" Sarah, and Thomas Remington, May 7, 1786.
2-88	" Martha, and Anthony Rice, Jan. 3, 1790.
3-399	" George, of Warwick, son of Thomas, of Tiverton, and Jane Franklin, of James R., dec., of Perth, Scotland; m. by Rev. Moses Fifield, Apr. 16, 1846.
3-368	Cooper Dr. Otis, and Almy B. Atwood, of John; m. by Rev. Jonathan Brayton, Oct. 30, 1843.
3-70	Corey Charles E., of Warwick, son of Peleg, of North Kingstown, and Mary H. Dawley, of James, of Warwick; m. by Eld. Moses Fifield, May 20, 1841.
3-89	" Betsey, and Benjamin Dawley, Jr., June 16, 1842.
3-575	" Abraham R., or Anthony, and Mary Anna Stokes, of Samuel, both of Cranston; m. by Rev. Zalman Tobey, Jan. 20, 1847.
3-272	" Mary, and George W. Rathbun, Oct., 11, 1847.
4-77	" Jane A., and Allen H. Bennett, Dec. 9, 1855.
3-57	Cornell Mary Ann, and Russell Bowen, June 3, 1830.
3-80	" Benjamin, Jr., of Coventry, son of Benjamin, and Huldah Blanchard, of Coventry, dau. of Samuel, of Warwick; m. by Rev. Moses Fifield, Aug. 15, 1839.

4-52 Cornell Harvey, of East Greenwich, aged 23 years, son of Clarke and Mary, of Abington, Penn., and Sarah H. Remington, of Warwick, aged 20 years, dau. of Henry and Lucy Ann; m. by Rev. Benjamin Phelan, Mar. 31, 1852.
4-78 " Marthin, of Providence, and Clarrissa L. Greene, of Warwick; m. by Eld. Henry B. Lock, May 1, 1859.
1-52 Corpe Abner, of John, and Hannah Ransom, of Joshua, Nov. 25, 1734.
1-59-63 " Jeremiah, of Providence, and Hannah Arnold, of Warwick, widow of Stephen; m. by Eld. Manassah Martin, Nov. 22, 1736.
1-52 " Thomas, of John, and Rebecca Battey, of John; m. by James Rhodes, Justice, Aug. 2, 1741.
2-31 " Rebecca, and Hugh Essex, Mar. 25, 1747.
2-23 " Benajah, of Warwick, and Margaret Gesling, of North Kingstown; m. by Eld. Samuel Albro, May 1, 1758.
2-265 " David, and Susanna Essex; m. by Eld. John Gorton, Feb. 6, 1773.
2-36 " Anna, and Stephen Le Valley, Apr. 8, 1798.
2-239 Cottrell Hannah P., and James H. Nicholas, July 6, 1846.
3-153 Covill Sally H., and Paul Himes, Apr. 5, 1842.
3-78 " Rhoda, and George B. Carpenter, Sept. 11, 1842.
1-27 Cowell Elizabeth, and John Warner, Sept. 24, 1730.
4-81 Coyle James Henry, and Anna Levina Faulkner; m. by Rev. James P. Gibson, Mar. 12, 1864.
1-5 Crandall John, Jr., of Newport, and Elizabeth Gorton, of Samuel, Sr,. of Warwick; m. by John Greene, Justice, June 18, 1672.
3-87 " Betsy, and Nehemiah Dexter, Dec. 13, 1841.
3-88 " Sibine, and Elisha Dickerson, Feb. 28, 1842.
3-80 " Asa, Jr., of Asa, and Rhoda Crandall, of Rowland; m. by Rev. Moses Fifield, Apr. 24, 1843.
3-80 " Rhoda, and Asa Crandall, Jr., Apr. 24, 1843.
3-243 " Abbie H., and Daniel E. Newman, Feb. 18, 1844.
3-400 " William, of Coventry, and Mrs. Eliza Pike; m. by Rev. Stephen A. Thomas, Apr. 21, 1846.
4-19 " Pardon, of Asa, dec., and Catherine Tefft, of Benjamin, dec.; m. by Rev. Moses Fifield, Jan. 1, 1850.
2-21 Cranston John, of Samuel, of Foster, R. I., and Hannah Clemmons, of John, dec.; m. by John Barton, Justice, June 10, 1804.

4-95	Cranston Sarah, and William Nichols, Oct. 5, 1837.
3-68	" William H., of Warwick, son of Thomas, dec., of North Kingstown, and Safety Reed, of Warwick, widow of John, of Hopkinton; m. by Rev. Moses Fifield, Jan. 7, 1841.
3-423	" Hannah E., and A. W. Jillson, Aug. 3, 1845.
3-374	" Jeremiah H., of Willian S., and Tamer Aldrich, of Lyman, dec.; m. by Rev. Zalman Tobey, Oct. 26, 1846.
4-60	" Mary Ann, and Albert R. Johnson, Feb. 6, 1853.
2-19	Crapo Phillip, of Providence, and Desire Burrows Aborn, of Warwick; m. by Eld. Enos Hitchcock, Mar. 1, 1801.
1-67	Cross Samuel, and Deborah Brown, of Juda, Nov. 28, 1728.
2-223	Cruff Mary, and Asa Wightman, July 30, 1771.
2-19	Culverson John, of Newport, and Almy Greene, of William, of Warwick; m. by Eld. John Hammett, July 2, 1749.
3-397	Culver Jared A., of Warwick, son of Benjamin, of Waklingford, Conn., and Mary C. Andrews, of Warwick, dau. of Ray G.; m. by Rev. Moses Fifield, Sept. 9, 1845.
3-141	Curian Mary E., and Oliver P. Griffen, June 17, 1847.
3-75	Curtis Rev. David, of Warwick, and Phebe Keech, of Providence; m. by Rev. Stephen Gano, June 21, 1810.

D

2-212	Dailey Margery, and Benoni West, Aug. 25, 1782.
3-81	" Joseph, of Warwick, and Philena Mitchell, of Norwich, Conn.; m. by Ephriam Arnold, Justice, Apr. 27, 1820.
3-92	" Ceaser L., and Marceny Proffet, (col.); m. by Rev. George Champlain, Mar. 8, 1846.
4-87	" Sarah, and Andrew Wallen, Aug. — 1858.
2-97	Daly Sarah, and Ceaser Lippitt, Aug, 26, 1779.
3-125	Dana Martha B., and George Sears Greene, Feb. 21, 1837.
3-86	" John W., of Providence, son of Jaykel, dec., and Sarah M. Hammond, of William; m. by Rev. Moses Fifield, June 9, 1840.
3-5	Daniel Ruth, and Henry Arnold, Apr. 19, 1841.
1-65	Davice Ann, and Thomas Ruttenberge, July 4, 1726.
1-26	Davis Kezia, and Peter Greene, June 29, 1710.
1-53	" Jerusha, and Sylvanus Westgate, Dec. 13, 1711.
1-26	" John, and Rebecca Peck, Oct. 7, 1735.
1-67	" Hannah, and Nicholas Battey. Nov. 26, 1735.

1-59	Davis Sarah, and James Carder, Feb. 6, 1736.
2-25	" Urian, and Bersheba Arnold; m. by Eld. John Hammett, May 24, 1752.
2-27	" Thomas, of Samuel, of East Greenwich, and Almy Rhodes, of John, of Warwick; m. by Eld. Charles Holden, Dec. 5, 1771.
2-28	" Samuel, of Samuel, of East Greenwich, and Alice Whipple, of Eleazer, of Warwick; m. by Eld. Charles Holden, Nov. 26, 1772.
2-65	" Sarah, and Peter Greene, Aug. 3, 1777.
3-71	" Huldah, and George Colvin, Sept. 27, 1812.
3-390	" Margaret, and Almoran Burvee, Oct. 13, 1834.
3-42	" Matilda, and Nelson H. Benson, Nov. 26, 1835.
3-264	" Sybel D., and Smith W. Pierce, Nov. 4, 1838.
3-83	Dawley John G., and Sally Tanner; m. by Rev. Jonathan Wilson, Nov. 30, 1826.
3-70	" Mary H., and Charles E. Corey, May 20, 1841.
3-89	" Benjamin, Jr., of Coventry, son of Benjamin, and Betsey Corey, of Scituate, dau. of Jesse; m. by Rev. Moses Fifield, June 16, 1842.
3-90	" William, of Phillip, and Mary P. Rice, of Benjamin; m. by Rev. Moses Fifield, Dec. 6, 1842.
3-398	" Harriet, and William H. N. Card, Oct. 2, 1845
3-88	" Alfred, of Warwick, son of Jesse, and Susan Ann Wilbour, of Coventry, dau. of Hazard; m. by Rev. Jonathan Brayton, Nov. 2, 1846.
2-26	Deway Elias, and Almy Vaughn, of Christopher, both of East Greenwich; m. by Ebenezer Slocum, Justice, Sept. 25, 1761.
1-7	Dexter Hester, and William Andrews, Oct. 30, 1680.
1-67	" John, of Thomas, of Provencetown, Mass., and Ruth Utter, of William, of Warwick; m. by Jonathan Arnold, Asst., Mar. 3, 1735-6.
2-25	" Benjamin, of John, of East Greenwich, and Sarah Wightman, of John, of Warwick; m. by Eld. John Hammett, Jan. 16, 1745-6.
2-16	" Ruth, and Samuel Byles, Jan. 28, 1749-0.
2-25	" Jonathan, of John, and Alice Low, of Col. Stephen; m. by Eld. Charles Holden, Dec. 31, 1761.
2-184	" Robey, and John Tibbitts, Dec. 13, 1772.
2-38	" Phebe, and William Le Valley, Sept. 25, 1788.
3-281	" Olive H., and George W. Remington, Sept. 12, 1839.

3-87   Dexter Nehemiah, of Jeremiah, and Betsey Crandall, of Asa ; m.. by Rev. Jonathan Brayton, Dec. 13, 1841.
3-137   "   Emeline, and Henry W. Greene, July 18 or 28, 1842.
3-88   Dickenson Elisha, of Samuel, dec., of Saybrook, Conn., and Sibine Crandall, of Rowland, of Warwick ; m. by Rev. Moses Fifield, Feb. 28, 1842.
1-5   Dodge Jane, and Thomas Stafford, Jr., Dec. 20, 1671.
3-88   "   Alvin G., and Frances Carr, of Caleb ; m. by Rev. M. J. Steere, Aug. 3, 1845.
2-29   Doud Ezekiel, of Warwick, and Ruth Johnson, of Elijah, of East Greenwich ; m. by James Jerauld, Justice, July 12, 1780.
2-88   "   Lydia, and Caleb Bennett, Nov. 12, 1799.
3-255   Douglass Martha, and Ezekiel Potter, Sept. 13, 1812.
3-91   "   Henry Gardner, of Warwick, son of James, of South Kingstown, and Mary Ann Reaves, of Warwick, dau. of Ira B., of Long Island; m. by Rev. Moses Fifield, July 15, 1844.
1-2   Downe Mary, and John Worrell, alias Johnson, Dec. 7, 1668.
1-46   Draper Sarah, and John Garnadi, Nov. 3, 1720.
3-87   Drury Owen, and Margaret Brennan, of Providence ; m. by Rev. Edward Putnum, Sept. 21, 1845.
4-74   Duffy John, and Mary Heenan ; m. by Rev. M. A. Wallace, Feb. 21, 1860.
3-84   Durfee Albert C., of Warwick, son of Benjamin, of Newport, dec., and Betsey C. Gardner, of Warwick, dau. of Joseph, of Cranston ; m. by Rev. Moses Fifield, Dec. 22, 1844.
4-7   "   Morris, and Ariadne Tillinghast, both of Providence ; m. by Rev. B. T. Hedden, May 27, 1849.
3-89   Dutemple William, of North Kingstown, and Hannah Fry, of West Greenwich ; m. by Rev. Stephen A. Thomas, Aug. 4, 1845.
3-82   Dyer John C., of Warwick, son of Samuel, and Hannah, of North Kingstown, and Ann L. Manchester, of James, and Mary, of Warwick ; m. by Rev. Benjamin Hazelton, May 21, 1826.
3-84   "   Daniel, and Sally C. Merrill ; m. by Rev. Moses Fifield, Dec. 27, 1829.
3-85   "   Carey C. of Warwick, son of Samuel D., of North Kingstown, and Mary Manchester, of James, dec. ; m. by Rev. Moses Fifield, Apr. 29, 1832.

3-282	Dyer Amey Ann, and John Roward, Jr., Oct. 25, 1841.
3-82	" Edward T., of Warwick, son of William T., and Phebe Peckham, of Samuel; m. by Rev. Moses Fifield, Oct. 2, 1844.
4-8	" Patience T., and Samuel Tillinghast, June 28, 1849.

E

3-102	Eager Calvin, of Sutton, Mass., son of Jasper, and Dorotha Titus, of Warwick, dau. of Isaac; m. by Rev. Jonathan Brayton, Mar. 18, 1847.
1-93	Earl Benjamin, and Reckah Westgate, May 28, 1726.
1-67	" Elizabeth, and George Westgate, Oct. 5, 1727.
2-53	" Sarah, and Benjamin Gorton, Sept. 6, 1757.
3-197	East Patience, and William Lippitt, (col.); about 1786.
3-94	Eaton William, of William, and Ann Calvert, of Robert; m. by Rev. Edward Putnam, Sept. 19, 1846.
3-95	Eddy Uriah, Jr., of Cranston, and Mary Gallup, dau. of Samuel, of West Greenwich; m. by Eld. Thomas Manchester, Nov. 24, 1822.
4-84	" Samuel R., of Warwick, and Anna D. Wye, of Cranston; m. by Rev. Jonathan Brayton, Dec. 21, 1859.
1-105	Edmunds Phebe, and Ephriam Arnold, Apr. 26, 1729.
1-107	" Patience, and Elisha Brown, Jan. 14, 1734-5.
1-60	" Joseph, Jr., and Mary Potter, of John; m. by Phillip Arnold, Asst., Dec. 19, 1739.
2-33	" Hannah, and Richard Estes, Mar. 10, 1760.
2-84	" Mary, and John Jencks, May 15, 1796.
3-94	" Esek, of Anthony, dec., and Eleanor Eldred, of Samuel; m. by C. Brayton, Justice, Mar. 3, 1811.
3-99	Edwards Dexter A., of Providence, son of Martin, dec., of Cranston, and Rebecca A. Tillinghast, of Warwick, dau. of Horace; m. by Rev. Moses Fifield, Jan. 9, 1842.
3-93	Eldredge Thomas, of Warwick, and Anne Greene, of Coventry, m. by Stephen Potter, Justice, July 15, 1784.
3-93	" Thomas, of Richard, and Barbara Arnold, of Stephen; m. by Thomas Holden, Justice, Aug. 7, 1800.
3-47	" Hannah, and John Bartholick, Dec. 15, 1811.
3-357	" Eliza, and Benjamin C. Wood, Jan. 6, 1836.
3-98	" Thomas, of Cranston, son of Wilbur, and Renery Briggs, of Aaron; m. by Eld. Job Manchester, Aug. 31, 1840.

2-142	Eldred Abigail, and Thomas Remington, Dec. 14, 1744.	
3-94	" Eleanor, and Esek Edmunds, Mar. 3, 1811.	
2-37	Ellis Lydia, and George Allen, Sept. 28, 1785.	
2-119	" Mary, and William Potter, May 1, 1786.	
3-284	" Amey Ann, and George B. Richardson, Aug. 14, 1842.	
3-32	Emerson Fannie B., and George Amsden, Jan. 18, 1846.	
1-1	England Ellen, and Jeremy Westcott, July 27, 1665.	
4-22	" George King, of Warwick, son of Isaac, of Wiltshire, Eng., and Mrs. Elizabeth H. Hitch, of Warwick, dau. of John Vaughn, of Newport, R. I.; m. by Rev. Benjamin Phelan, Jan. 13, 1850.	
2-31	Essex Hugh, and Rebecca Corpe; m. by Eld. Daniel Fish, Mar. 25, 1747.	
2-265	" Susannah, and David Corpe, Feb. 6, 1773.	
2-116	" John, of Warwick, and Amey Hambleton, of North Kingstown; m. by Eld. James Wightman, Dec. 25, 1781.	
2-34	" David, of Warwick, and Mary Hampleton, of East Greenwich; m. by Eld. Nathan Hill, Sept. 17, 1782.	
2-137	" Corps, late of North Kingstown, and Mary Matteson, of North Kingstown, dau. of Richard, of Coventry; m. by Eld. Nathan Hill, July 27, 1783.	
2-136	" Benajah, of Warwick, and Penelope Jones, of North Kingstown; m. by Eld. Nathan Hill, Aug. 24, 1786.	
3-289	" Elizabeth, and Elisha Sprague, Apr. 4, 1805.	
3-74	" Betsey, and Caleb B. Capron, Dec. 1, 1811.	
3-96	" James, and Susan Smith, m. by Eld. Samuel Littlefield, Jan. 17, 1823.	
3-97	" Andrew, and Sarah Burlingame; m. by Rev. Richard Knight, Sept. 30, 1832.	
3-100	" Joseph P., and Emeline Wood; m. by Rev. Edward K. Fuller, Jan. 1, 1846.	
3-101	" Benjamin, of Reuben, formerly of Hopkinton, and Sally Maria Tillinghast, of Warwick, dau. of John R. Congdon; m. by Rev. Moses Fifield, Feb. 9, 1847.	
3-102	" Stephen, and Mary A. Whitford; m. by Rev. Stephen A. Thomas; Oct. 11, 1847.	
2-33	Estes Richard, and Hannah Edmunds; m. by Samuel Gorton, Justice, Mar. 10, 1760.	

F

2-133 Fairbanks, Ruth, and Samuel Holmes, Jan. 10, 1779.
2-111 " Elizabeth, and Spicer Miller, Jan. 30, 1783.
3-421 Farmer Margaret, and Albert Gorton, Apr. 1, 1848.
3-106 Farnum Albert, of Providence, son of Zabodee, dec., and Ann Tennant, of Havens, of Warwick; m. by Rev. Moses Fifield, Apr. 27, 1843.
3-104 Farris William H., of Joseph, and Everline A. Pollard, of Franklin; m. by Rev. Moses Fifield, Nov. 22, 1847.
4-81 Faulkner Anne L. and James H. Coyle, Mar. 12, 1864.
3-101 Fenner Lillie, and Samuel Barton, Mar. 23, 1737-8.
2-39 " Daniel, of Cranston, and Sarah Haynes, of Warwick, dau. of William; m. by Eld. Charles Holden, Oct. 3, 1762.
2-41 " Jeremiah, of Jeremiah, of Coventry, and Elizabeth Greene, of Col. Christopher, dec., of Warwick; m. by Eld. Thomas Manchester, Sept. 25, 1789.
3-104 " Charles, of Bowen, and Martha B. West, of Amos; m. by Rev. Moses Fifield, Feb. 8, 1841.
3-105 " Samuel, of Lorey, and Almira Boss, of Charles; m. by Eld. William Stovyer, Aug. 15, 1841.
3-179 " Susan A., and Joseph N. W. Johnson, May 3, 1847.
4-48 " Ellen, and Edmund Potter, Nov. 16, 1851.
3-56 Fifield Annah, and Samuel A. Briggs, July 1, 1841.
3-108 " Moses, Jr., of Moses, and Hannah A. Allen, of Christopher; m. by Rev. Moses Fifield, May 24, 1846.
1-52,58 Finney Samuel, and Elizabeth Tibbitts, widow of Thomas; m. by John Greene, Justice, Mar. 12 or 17, 1726-7.
1-11 Fisher Ruth, and John Potter, June 2, 1664.
4-63, 65 " James, of Cranston, late of Waltham, Mass., and Amanda Potter, of Warwick, of Job; m. by Eld. David Curtis, June 16, 1821.
3-298 " Harriet, and Erastus G. Spaulding, Nov. 11, 1839.
3-378 " Almira, and Charles B. Capron, Sept. 28, 1847.
2-38 Fish Daniel, of Dighton, Mass., and Barbara Bowen, of Warwick; m. by Samuel Gorton, Justice, Apr. 8, 1760.
2-61 Flagg Jane, and Elisha Greene, Dec. 5, 1776.
2-187 " Mary Magdalene, and Ray Greene, July 23, 1794.
3-73 Fleming Catherine, and Thomas Hennessey, Apr. 15, 1854.
2-41 Fletcher William, of Thomas, and Sarah Young, of James; m. by Eld. Thomas Manchester, Nov. 17, 1796.

1-9	Fones Mary, and "Ensign" James Greene, Jr., Jan. 29, 1688-9.
3-373	" Sarah A., and Carlton Chace, Nov. 11, 1844.
4-9	Foss Benjamin L., of Providence, son of Wallace D., and Eliza Smith, of Providence, dau. of Robert Dearborne; m. by Eld. Zalman Tobey, Apr. 23, 1849.
1-76	Foster Thomas, of Warwick, and Martha Hazelton, of Charles, of East Greenwich, Mar. 3, 1732.
3-51	" Elizabeth, and John Greene, June 12, 1737.
2-18	" Martha, and Caleb Bentley, June 14, 1761.
2-83	" Anne, and Joseph Arnold, July 12, 1772.
2-37	" Thomas, of Thomas, dec., of East Greenwich, and Alse Greene, widow of Amos, of Warwick; m. by Eld. John Gorton, Mar. 18, 1781.
3-251	" Amey, and John Price, Dec. 11, 1808.
3-107	" William, of Warwick, son of Henry, dec., of Aerintos, Eng., and Mary Walker, of Warwick, widow of John, of Preston, Eng.; m. by Rev. Moses Fifield, Oct. 8, 1843.
1-42	Fox Mary, and John Brown, Dec. 19, 1723.
3-105	France Samuel I., and Betsey Ann Bentley, both of Waterford, Mass.; m. by Rev. Alfred Colburn, May 14, 1848.
1-8, 2-5	Francis Abraham, of Abraham, and Anne Lippitt, of Moses; m. by Eld. Arthur Brown, June 18, 1736.
2-39	" William, and Hester Knapp; m. by John Warner, Jr., Justice, Sept. 6, 1761.
4-1	" John B., son of John and Abby, and Anne Carter Brown, of Nicholas, June 18, 1822.
4-2	" Elizabeth, and John Brown Francis, May 23, 1832.
4-2	" John Brown, and Elizabeth Francis, dau. of Willing, of Philadelphia, Penn., May 23, 1832.
4-1, 3	" Anne B., and Marshall Wood, July 12, 1848.
3-340	Franklin Ann, and Hazard B. Woodmansee, Oct. 11, 1840.
3-399	" Jane, and George Cook, Apr. 16, 1846.
3-110	" Henry A., of Jeremiah, and Lucy A. Colburn, of Jonathan; m. by Rev. Jonathan Brayton, Sept. 27, 1847.
4-14	Frazer Liza, and James White, June 21, 1849.
4-22	" Martha, and Robert White, Nov. 29, 1849.
1-49	Freeborn Thomas, of Gideon, of Portsmouth, and Elizabeth Thomas, of George, of Kings Towne, Jan. 30, 1735-6.
2-195	" Elizabeth, and Christopher Vaughn, May 10, 1747.
2-38	" Noel, of Portsmouth, and Phillipa Low, of Warwick; m. by Jeremiah Lippitt, Asst., Apr. 22, 1756.

2-41	Freeman Peter, late of France, and Mary Gammett, of Isaac; m. by James Jerauld, Justice, Oct. 15, 1785.
3-52	" Emeline, and John H. Brown, Nov. —, 1819.
3-234	" Mary Jane, and George B. Money, Aug. 10, 1846.
3-308	" Susan E., and Henry Shippee, Aug. 10, 1846.
2-39	Frothingham Nathaniel, of Providence, and Barbara Wells, widow of Arnold, of Warwick; m. by Eld. Charles Holden, May 13, 1767.
1-42	Fry Thomas, of East Greenwich, and Mary Greene, of Capt. Samuel; m. by Anthony Low, Justice, Dec. 31, 1719.
1-69	" Hannah, and John Holden, Jan. 6, 1731-2.
1-15	" Thomas, and Eleanor Greene, of Richard, dec., Nov. 16, 1740.
2-44	" Sarah, and Richard Greene, Sept. 28, 1746.
2-37	" Benjamin, of East Greenwich, and Rachel Allen, of Capt. James, of Newport; m. by Jeremiah Lippitt, Asst., Jan. 19, 1756.
2-41	" Capt. Samuel, of East Greenwich, and Deborah Greene, of John, of Potowomut; m. by Joseph Lippitt, Asst., Aug. 23, 1764.
2-17	" Dorcas, and John Brushel, Sept. 29, 1783.
3-89	" Hannah, and William Dutemple, Aug. 4, 1845.
3-379	Fullerton John, and Isabella Kenyon; m. by Rev. Stephen A. Thomas, Feb. 2, 1848.
2-197	Fuller Liscomb, and Elizabeth Weaver, of Abigail; m. by James Jerauld, Justice, June 23, 1793.

G

3-95	Gallup Mary, and Uriah Eddy, Jr., Nov. 24, 1822.
2-41	Gammett Mary, and Peter Freeman, Oct. 15, 1785.
1-104	Gardiner Mary, and Barnard Hill, Jan. 13, 1731-2.
3-50	" Mary, and Samuel G. Bowen, Apr. 4, 1818.
3-343	" Phebe Ann, and Lewis Weaver, Dec. 30, 1841.
3-167	" Sarah, and John Hanop, Feb. 24, 1846.
3-376	" Mary A., and John H. Chappell, Jr., Oct. 18, 1846.
3-383	" Abbie B., and James Bnshee, Aug. 2, 1847.
4-27	" Harriet N., and Benjamin Waterhouse, June 2, 1850.
4-86	" Francis W., and Harriet E. Seamons; m. by Rev. Stephen A. Thomas, Aug. 26, 1851.

4-34   Gardiner Francis C., of Providence, (aged 39,) son of Samuel E., of North Kingstown, dec., and Cynthia Phillips, of Warwick, (aged 21,) dau. of Job; m. by Rev. Moses Fifield, June 6, 1851.
4-48   "   Benjamin W., of North Kingstown, aged 22 years, son of Jeffrey H., and Hannah C. Shippee, of Coventry, aged 22 years; m. by Rev. Benjamin Phelan, Nov. 9, 1851.
4-85   "   William, of Providence, and Mrs. Lucy A. Smith, of South Kingstown; m. by Rev. O. P. Fuller, May 27, 1867.
2-58   Gardner Daniel, of Coventry, and Mary Greene, widow of Stephen, of Warwick; m. by Eld. Charles Holden, Oct. 4, 1761.
2-64   "   Oliver, of Isaac, of East Greenwich, and Mrs. Mercy Gorton, of William, of Warwick; m. by Eld. John Gorton, Sept. 25, 1766.
2-211 "   Isaac, Jr., of East Greenwich, and Ruth Aylesworth, of East Greenwich, dau. of Anthony, m. by Thomas Casey, Justice, Oct. 11, 1767.
2-66   "   Thustian, of Pawtucket, and Avis Waterman, of Capt. Resolved, of Warwick; m. by Eld. Charles Holden, Dec. 22, 1768.
2-151 "   Mercy, and Wanton Rice, Oct. 2, 1791.
2-140 "   Benjamin, of Caleb, of East Greenwich, and Sarah Gardner, of Capt. Oliver, of Warwick; m. by James Jerauld, Justice, Oct. 10, 1791.
2-140 "   Sarah, and Benjamin Gardner, Oct. 10, 1791.
2-257 "   Isaac, of Isaac, dec., of East Greenwich, and Alce Wickes, of Stuteley, of Warwick; m. by Eld. Phillip Jenkins, July 2, 1794.
2-230 "   Margaret, and Gideon Bailey, Oct. 2, 1796.
2-168 "   Betsey, and Nathan Bowen, June 10, 1798.
2-29   "   Wickes, and Waitey Rhodes; m. by Eld. Samuel Littlefield, Dec. 19, 1802.
3-136 "   John A., of Cranston, son of Oliver, and Orrilla Hopkins, of Coventry, dau. of Reuben; m. by Rev. Jonathan Baxter, Apr. 10, 1842.
3-135 "   James A., of North Kingstown, son of Beriah, and Martha E. Hamilton, of Henry; m. by Rev. Thomas Wilkes, Aug. 9, 1841.
3-117 "   John, of South Kingstown, son of William, and Francis Burlingame, of Thomas; m. by Rev. Jonathan Brayton, Dec. 31, 1843.

3-128	Gardner Benjamin, of Wickes, and Caroline Greene, of Richard W.; m. by Rev. Jonathan E. Forbush, Sept. 26, 1844.
3-84	" Betsey C., and Albert C. Durfee, Dec. 22, 1844.
3-413	" Joseph W., of Warwick, son of Joseph, and Harriet Hill, of Providence, dau. of Robert; m. by Rev. Jonathan Brayton, July 27, 1846.
3-271	" Susan C., and Caleb A. Rice, Jan. 31, 1847.
3-192	" Maria R., and Ambrose E. Kenyon, Sept. 13, 1847.
3-416	" Frances, and Robert Hampson, Nov. 2, 1847.
3-420	" James, of Samuel, and Martha, and Emeline Wright, of Nathan and Betsey; m. by Rev. Charles E. Bennett, Oct. 2, 1848.
1-46	Garnardi John, and Sarah Draper; m. by Daniel Pierce, Justice, Nov. 3, 1720.
1-4	Garner George, and Tabitha Teffe, both of Pettesquamscott; m. by Henry Gardiner, Feb. 13, 1670.
3-140	Gavitt Arnold, of Warwick, and Barbara Shaw, of Johnston; m. by Rev. Edward K. Fuller, Nov. 10, 1844.
1-6	Gerreard Mary, and Jeremiah Smith, Jan. 2, 1672.
2-23	Gesling Margaret, and Benajah Corpe, May 1, 1758.
3-138	Gifford Benjamin H., of Bristol, and Lucy A. Bartlett, of Warwick; m. by Rev. Martin S. Steere, July 18, 1843.
1-5	Gisborne Francis, of Portsmouth, and Mary Wickes, of John, of Warwick; m. by John Greene, Justice, Jan. 8, 1671.
4-82	Gleason Nathan K., and Susan C. Clarke; m. by Rev. Jonathan Brayton, Dec. 1, 1861.
1-72	Godfrey Elizabeth, and Richard Greene, June 9, 1727.
2-95	" Ruth, and Capt. Joseph Arnold, Feb. 22, 1784.
2-57	" John, of Joshua, of East Greenwich, and Welthian Wickes, of Stukeley, of Warwick; m. by James Jerauld, Justice, Feb. 24, 1802.
3-66	" Elizabeth, otherwise Graft, and Joseph Coggeshall, June 18, 1809.
3-70	" Catherine, and John G. Clapp, Aug. 12, 1810.
3-229	" Dorcas, and Benjamin G. Mawney, Dec. 3, 1840.
1-3	Gorton John, and Margaret Weston; m. by John Greene, Asst., Jan. 25, 1665.
1-4	" Anna, and John Warner, Aug. 7, 1670.
1-5	" Elizabeth, and John Crandall, Jr., June 18, 1672.
1-5	" Susan, and Benjamin Barton, June 18, 1672.
1-5	" Benjamin, and Sarah Carder, of Richard; m. by John Greene, Justice, Dec. 5, 1672.

1-7	Gorton	Samuel, and Susannah Burton, of William and Hannah; m. by John Greene, Justice, Dec. 11, 1684.
1-11	"	Mary, and Samuel Greene, Jan. 24, 1694-5.
1-14	"	Samuel, of John, and Elizabeth Collins, of Eliza, May 9, 1695.
1-21	"	Sarah, and John Wickes, Dec. 15, 1698.
1-55	"	John Jr., of John, of Warwick, and Patience Hopkins of Thomas, of Providence, Feb. 2, 1699-0.
1-27	"	Samuel, of Capt. Benjamin, dec., and Elizabeth Greene, of Thomas, dec., July 25. 1706.
1-28	"	Maplet, and Thomas Remington, Dec. 28, 1710.
1-45	"	Samuel, Jr., and Freelove Masson, of Joseph, June 1, 1715.
1-35	"	Hezekiah, of Warwick, and Avis Carr, of Jamestown; m. Nicholas Carr, Warden, Aug. 20, 1719.
1-69	"	Ann, and Daniel Remington, Feb. 16, 1722-3.
1-54	"	Margaret, and Samuel Whitman, Nov. 11, 1724.
2-21		Pub. and m. same day.
1-57	"	Alice, and Stephen Low, Feb. 18, 1725.
1-57	"	Cloe, and Stephen Low, Feb. 18, 1725-6.
1-72	"	Sarah, and Thankful Collins, May 19, 1728.
1-84	"	Samuel Jr., and Mary Rice, of Capt. John; m. by William Greene, Justice, Jan. 21, 1730-1.
1-96	"	William, and Mercy Matteson; m. by William Greene, Justice, Jan. 7, 1731.
1-1	"	Elizabeth, and Benjamin Tallman, Jan. — 1735.
1-45	"	Othniel, of Othniel, and Theodosia Hopkins, June 3, 1736.
2-166	"	Sarah, and Stukeley Stafford, May 26, 1748.
2-47	"	Caleb, of Edward, and Mary Brown, of Elisha; m. by John Greene, Justice, Sept. 20, 1753.
2-49	"	Edward, Jr., and Mary Greene; m. by Joseph Edmunds, Justice, Nov. 27, 1755.
2-53	"	Benjamin, of Samuel, 2d, and Sarah Earle, of Benjamin; m. by Eld. Charles Holden, Sept. 6, 1757.
2-54	"	Nathan, of William, and Mary Pearce, of Eld. Benjamin; m. by Eld. Charles Holden, June 29, 1758.
2-51	"	Jonathan, and Sarah Arnold; m. by Samuel Gorton, Justice, Nov. 23, 1759.
2-148	"	Anne, and Job Rice, Nov. 27, 1760.
2-17	"	Sarah, and Isreal Bowen, Apr. 5, 1761.
2-214	"	Mary, and Phillip Wightman, May 27, 1762.

2-63	Gorton Benjamin, of Samuel, of Warwick, and Avis Hulet, of Capt. John, of Scituate; m. by Eld. Reuben Hopkins, July 18, 1762.
2-222	" Joseph, of Samuel, of Warwick, and Mrs. Mary Barton of Warren; m. by Rev. Solomon Townsend, Jan. 1, 1763.
2-61	" Thomas, of Benjamin, of West Greenwich, and Susanna Pearce, of Capt. John, of East Greenwich; m. by Eld. John Gorton, May 27, 1764.
2-216	" Mary, and Thomas Wilbur, Dec. 2, 1764.
2-64	" Mercy, and Oliver Gardiner, Sept. 25, 1766.
2-65	" Samuel, and Frances Graves, widow of Ebenezer; m. by Eld. Charles Holden, May 5, 1768.
2-117	" Phebe, and Peleg Olin, Feb. 5, 1769.
2-221	" John, of Eld. John, and Deborah Spink; m. by Samuel Soule, Justice, Aug. 26, 1770.
2-227	" John, Jr., of Eld. John, and Mary Clarke, of William; m. by Thomas Rice, Jr., Justice, Feb. 28, 1773.
2-122	" Mary, and Jeremiah Pearce, Jr., May 2, 1773.
2-229	" Sarah, and Isaac Briggs, Nov. 28, 1773.
2-263	" Elizabeth, and William Wood, July 2, 1775.
2-60	" Slade, of Dr. Samuel, and Mary Whitford, of George; m. by Eld. John Gorton, Dec. 11, 1777.
2-126	" Mary, and William Potter, Mar. 26, 1778.
2-238	" Robe, and Phillip Arnold, Feb. 3, 1780.
2-66	" Benjamin, of Dr. Samuel, and Thankful Whitford, of George, m. by Eld. John Gorton, May 30, 1780.
2-238	" Huldah, and Stephen Briggs, Aug. 27, 1780.
2-109	" Mary, and Earle Morey, Sept. 1, 1782.
2-208	" Freelove, and Daniel Wickes, Nov. 24, 1785.
2-244	" William, of Dr. Samuel, and Sarah Whitford, of George; m. by Eld. John Gorton, Nov. 24, 1785.
2-248	" William, of Benjamin, and Hannah Wightman, of Phillip; m. by Eld. John Gorton, Oct. 1, 1786.
2-249	" Anna, and Silas Andrews, Aug. 2, 1787.
2-252	" David, of Joseph, and Alice Whitford, of George; m. by Eld. John Gorton, Mar. 19, 1789.
2-255	" Nathan, and Anne Warner; m. by Eld. Abraham Lippitt, Dec. 2, 1792.
2-255	" Deborah, and John Warner, Dec. 6, 1792.
2-195	" Hannah, and William Waterman, June 9, 1793.
2-7	" Sarah, and Thomas Arnold, May 1, 1796.

3-11 Gorton Anthony, and Phebe Gorton; m. by Rev. Samuel Littlefield, Sept. 10, 1797.
3-11 " Phebe, and Anthony Gorton, Sept. 10, 1797.
2-87 " Clarke, of John, and Lydia Briggs, of Joseph; m. by James Jerauld, Justice, Oct. 25, 1801.
3-1 " Sarah, and Elisha Arnold, Mar. 6, 1806.
3-67 " Deborah, and Lockwood Cole, Nov. 13, 1808.
3-269 " Sarah and Holden Rhodes, Dec. 4, 1808.
3-8 " Hannah, and Elisha Arnold, Apr. 26, 1810.
3-120 " Barton W., of Dea. Benjamin, and Mercy R. Stafford, of John, dec.; m. by Eld. Thomas Manchester, Dec. 3, 1818.
3-122 " Samuel of Dea. Benjamin, and Elizabeth H. Whitmarsh, of Walker, of Dighton, Mass.; m. by Eld. Thomas Manchester, June 3, 1821.
3-350 " Barbara H., and Freeman Wing, Feb. 2, 1823.
3-123 " Richard, of Dea. Benjamin, and Abbie Ann Arnold, of Cyrus; m. by Eld. Jonathan Wilson, Dec. 29, 1825.
2-273 " Phebe, and Thomas Rhodes, Mar. 2, 1828.
3-358 " Elizabeth, and Henry J. Wilbur, June 14, 1837.
3-131 " Job P., of Warwick, son of Benjamin, of West Greenwich, and Deborah D. Sweet, of Warwick, dau. of Lindsey; m. by Rev. Moses Fifield, Oct. 7, 1839.
3-134 " Hale, of Hale, dec., and Ann Frances Phillips, of Lucy; m. by Henry S. Tillinghast, Justice, Mar. 20, 1841.
3-127 " Charles, of Hannah, of West Greenwich, and Theodosia Spencer, of Rufus, dec., of Warwich; m. by Rev. Moses Fifield, May 29, 1843.
3-421 " Albert, of William, G., and Margaret Farmer, of Thomas; m. by Rev. George A Williams, Apr. 1, 1848.
4-28 " Mrs. Ann F., and Charles H. Baker, July 28, 1850.
4-44 " Phebe, and James N. Carder, Aug. 4, 1851.
4-43 " Thomas W., aged 20 years, son of Thomas and Betsey, and Windwell M. Baker, aged 23 years, dau. of Burton, and Ruth; m. by Rev. Benjamin Phelan, Sept. 11, 1851.
3-401, 4-57 " Harriet C., and William B. Spencer, Oct. 6, 1852.
1-24 Gould Anne, and Nathaniel Greene, Feb. 27, 1703.
1-57 " Elizabeth, and James Greene, Feb. 17, 1726-7.
3-387 " Elizabeth, and James Bowen, July 1, 1845.

2-46	Graves Ebenezer, and Francis Rice, of Thomas; m. by Eld. John Hammett, May 19, 1751.
2-71	" Sarah, and Thomas Hathaway, Sept. 28, 1759.
2-65	" Frances, and Samuel Gorton, May 5, 1768.
1-5	Greene Elizabeth, and Thomas Greene, last of June, 1659.
1-5	" Thomas, and Elizabeth Greene, m. last of June, 1659.
1-1	" James, of Warwick, and Elizabeth Anthony, of Portsmouth, Aug. 3, 1665.
1-6	" William, of Capt. John, of Warwick, and Mary Sayles, of John, of Providence, Dec. 17, 1674.
1-7	" Mary, and John Holmes, Oct. 12, 1680.
1-15	" Job, of Major John, and Phebe Sayles, of John, Jan. 22, 1684-5.
1-8	" Mary, and James Renals, Feb. 19, 1684-5.
1-5	" Ann, and Thomas Greene, Jr., May 27, 1686.
1-5	" Thomas, Jr., and Ann Greene, May 27, 1686.
1-9	" "Ensign" James Jr., and Mary Fones, of Capt. John, Jan. 29, 1688-9.
1-62	" Benjamin, of Thomas, and Susannah Holden, of Randall, Jan. 21, 1689-0.
1-10	" Richard, of Major John, of Warwick, and Ellen Sayles, of John, of Providence, Feb. 16, 1692-3.
1-11	" Samuel, of Major John, and Mary Gorton, of Capt. Benjamin, Jan. 24, 1694-5.
1-14	" Peter, of James, of Warwick, and Elizabeth Slocum, of Ebenezer, of Jamestown, Feb. 12, 1695-6.
1-40	" Jabez, of James, and Mary Barton, of Benjamin and Susannah, Mar. 17, 1697-8.
1-54	" Richard, and Mary Carder, of John ——— 1700.
1-24	" Nathaniel, of Thomas, and Anne Gould, of Thomas, and Frances, of Boston, Mass., Feb. 27, 1703.
1-27	" Elizabeth, and Samuel Gorton, July 25, 1706.
1-25	" Sarah, and Stephen Arnold, Nov. 28, 1706.
1-35	" Anne, and Thomas Stafford, Dec. 25, 1707.
1-37	" John, of James, Jr., and Mary Allen, of Increase, of Dartmouth, Feb. 16, 1709-0.
1-26	" Peter, of Capt. Peter, and Kezia Davis, June 29, 1710.
1-24	" Fones, of Capt. James, and Dinah Battey; m. at Jamestown, by Edward Townsend, Warden, Mar. 15, 1710-1.
1-32	" John, of Thomas, dec., and Deborah Carr, of Caleb, of Jamestown, Dec. 6, 1711.
1-24	" Fones, and Rebecca Tibbits, of Henry, Feb. 5, 1712-3.

1-29	Greene	William, of Capt. Peter, and Sarah Medbury, Feb. 14, 1712-3.
1-32	"	Susanna, and Phillip Arnold, June 10, 1714.
1-40	"	Jabez, and Grace Whitman, of Valentine, of Providence, May 23, 1716.
1-60	"	Barlo, of Capt. Peter, and Lydia Hardin, of Isreal, Oct. 21, 1717.
1-65	"	James, of John, and Rebeckah Cahoone, of Nathaniel, Dec. 18, 1717.
1-50	"	Enfield, and Samuel Cook, Mar. 25, 1719.
1-36	"	Audrey, and Thomas Stafford, July 16, 1719.
1-43	"	John, of Capt. Peter, and Mary Greene, of Major Job; m. by Anthony Low, Justice, Oct. 25, 1719.
1-43	"	Mary, and John Greene, Oct. 25, 1719.
1-41	"	Katherine, and William Greene, Dec. 30, 1719.
1-41	"	William, of Capt. Samuel, and Katherine Greene, of Capt. Benjamin; m. by Anthony Low, Justice, Dec. 30, 1719.
1-42	"	Mary, and Thomas Fry, Dec. 31, 1719.
1-51	"	Ebenezer, of Peter, dec., and Marian Remington, widow of John, Aug. 1, 1724.
1-68	"	Samuel, of Capt. Samuel, and Sarah Cogshall, of Joshua, Mar. 11, 1724-5.
2-6	"	Elizabeth, and James Allen, Aug. 31, 1726.
1-57	"	James, of Jabez, of Warwick, and Elizabeth Gould, of Jeremiah, of North Kingstown, Feb. 17, 1726-7.
1-60	"	Ueal, of John, of Warwick, and Susanna Hill, of Henry, of East Greenwich, Jan. — 1727.
1-72	"	Richard, of Warwick, and Elizabeth Godfrey, of Newport, m. by Rev. James Honeyman, June 9, 1727.
1-79	"	Margaret, and Pardon Tillinghast, Jan. 8, 1729.
1-86	"	Marian, and Edward Capron, Feb. 26, 1729-0.
1-34	"	Almy, and John Greene, Jan. 28, 1730-1.
1-34	"	John, of Thomas, dec., and Almy Greene, of Richard, Jan. 28, 1730-1.
1-85	"	Phillip, of Job, and Elizabeth Wickes, of John, Aug. 12, 1731.
1-94	"	Benjamin, of Samuel, dec., and Almy or Mary Angell, of James; m. by William Greene, Justice, Sept. 2, 1731.
1-97	"	Daniel, and Temperance Harris; m. by Isaac Ray, Justice, Nov. 11, 1731.
1-73	"	Ann, and John Nichols, Jr., Mar. 22, 1733.

1-58	Greene	Nathaniel, of Jabez, and Phebe Greene, of Benjamin, Sept. 13, 1733.
1-58	"	Phebe, and Nathaniel Greene, Sept. 13, 1733.
1-57	"	James, of Jabez, of Warwick, and Hannah Tucker, of Abraham, of Dartmoath, June 22, 1734.
1-1	"	Thomas, of John, and Elnathan Rice, of John; m. by William Greene, Justice, Jan. 18, 1735.
1-99	"	Ann, and Nathan Westcott, Mar. 6, 1735.
1-63	"	Capt. Benjamin, and Mary Hudson, widow; m. by Stukeley Stafford, Justice, July 3, 1735.
1-93	"	Benjamin, of Jabez, of Warwick, and Ann Hoksey, of South Kingstown; m. by Jeremiah Lippitt, Justice, Nov. 27, 1735.
1-38	"	Dinah, and Randall Rice, Mar. 16, 1736.
1-57	"	Welthian, and Jeremiah Lippitt, Sept. 12, 1736.
1-51	"	John, of Peter, of Warwick, and Elizabeth Foster, of George, of East Greenwich, June 12, 1737.
1-66	"	Elizabeth, and Benjamin Jefferson, Aug. 9, 1737.
1-49	"	John, of Richard, and Mary Taft; m. by Rev. James Searing, Dec. 8, 1737.
1-52	"	Deborah, and Charles Rhodes, Jan. 31, 1738-9.
1-63	"	Lydia, and Simon Arnold, Mar. 1, 1738-9.
1-58	"	Nathaniel, of James, and Alce Lee, of John, Mar. 8, 1738-9.
1-66	"	Sarah, and John Roades, Jr., Apr. 25, 1738.
1-58	"	Nathaniel, of Jabez, and Mary Mott, Apr. 18, 1739.
1-4	"	Caleb, of John, and Ann Rodman, of Thomas, of South Kingstown, Nov. 22, 1739.
1-52	"	James, of Fones, and Patience Waterman, of Capt. John; m. by Eld. Manassah Martin, Apr. 10, 1740.
1-52	"	Catherine, and Major James Brown, Apr. 27, 1740.
1-69	"	Jonathan, and Mary Stafford, of Samuel; m. by William Rice, Justice, July 27, 1740.
1-15	"	Ellena, and Thomas Fry, Nov. 16, 1740.
1-104	"	Rachel, and Henry Matteson, Dec. 13, 1740.
1-2	"	Mary, and Joseph Wickes, July 30, 1741.
1-39	"	Richard, of Major Peter, and Mary Rice, of Capt. Thomas; m. by Jeremiah Lippitt, Justice, June —, 1742.
2-19	"	Martha, and Oliver Carpenter, Apr. 7, 1743.
1-93	"	Ann, and John Greene, Feb. 10, 1744.
1-93	"	John, of Jabez, dec., and Ann Greene, widow of Benjamin; m. by Jeremiah Lippitt, Justice, Feb. 10 or 16, 1744.

2-165	Greene Elizabeth, and John Stafford, Jr., Oct. 22, 1744.
2-43	" Job, of Fones, and Mercy Greene, of William; m. by Eld. John Hammett, May 30, 1745.
2-43	" Mercy, and Job Greene, May 30, 1745.
2-44	" Richard, of John, of Warwick, and Sarah Fry, of Thomas, of East Greenwich; m. by Peter Mawney, Justice, Sept. 28, 1746.
2-62	" Elisha, Jr., of Capt. Elisha, and Isabel Budlong, of John, Dec. 4, 1748.
2-46	" Phebe, and Thomas Greene, Apr. 6, 1749.
2-46	" Thomas, of Fones, and Phebe Greene, of John; m. by Eld. John Hammett, Apr. 6, 1749.
2-204	" Phebe, and Capt. Thomas Warner, June 22, 1749.
2-19	" Almy, and John Culverson, July 2, 1749.
2-203	" Mary, and John Walton, Jr., Jan. 6, 1750.
2-47	" John, of Thomas, and Patience Greene, grand dau. of John; m. by James Greene, Justice, Oct. 27, 1751.
2-47	" Patience, and John Greene, Oct. 27, 1751.
2-22	" Mary, and Silas Clapp, Apr. 19, 1752.
2-48	" Stephen, of William, and Mary Hammett, of John; m. by James Greene, Justice, Feb. 8, 1753.
2-90	" Phebe, and Anthony Low, Jan. 1, 1754.
2-58	" Stephen, of Thomas [also 2-143], and Mary Rhodes, of Malachi; m. by Eld. John Gorton, Oct. 24, 1754.
2-49	" Mary, and Edward Gorton, Nov. 27, 1755.
2-51	" Catherine, and John Greene, Mar. 11, 1756.
2-51	" John, of Boston, Mass., son of Thomas, and Catherine Greene, dau. of Gov. William; m. by Jeremiah Lippitt, Asst., Mar. 11, 1756.
2-59	" Freelove, and Godfrey Greene, July 23, 1756.
2-59	" Godfrey, of Richard, and Freelove Greene, of William; m. by Jeremiah, Lippitt, Asst., July 23, 1756.
2-60	" Christopher, and Ann Lippitt; m. by Eld. J. Graves, Jan. 6, 1757.
2-45	" Capt. Samuel, of Gov. William, of Warwick, and Patience Cook, of Ebenezer, of East Greenwich; m. by Eld. John Hammett, Apr. 28, 1757.
2-54	" Mary, and Thomas Greene, Feb. 5, 1758.
2-54	" Thomas, of Fones, and Mary Greene, widow, of Capt. Fones; m. by Eld. Charles Holden, Feb. 5, 1758.

2-56	Greene	William, Jr., son of Hon. William, dec., of Warwick, and Catherine Ray, of Capt. Simon, of New Shoreham; m. by Edward Sands, Warden, Apr. 30, 1758.
2-211	"	Susanna, and Silas Weaver, June 8, 1758.
2-65	"	Oliver, of Barlo, and Penelope Wells, of John; m. by Eld. Charles Holden, Mar. 20, 1760.
2-57	"	Jacob, of Nathaniel, and Margaret Greene, of Jabez; m. by Ebenezer Slocum, Justice, Mar. 26, 1761.
2-57	"	Margaret, and Jacob Greene, Mar. 26, 1761.
2-173	"	Margaret, and Capt. Rufus Spencer, July 12, 1761.
2-57	"	Stephen, of John, and Mercy Lockwood, of Capt. Amos; m. by Eld. Charles Holden, Sept. 20, 1761.
2-58	"	Mary, and Daniel Gardner, Oct. 4, 1761.
2-59	"	Comfort, and William Greene, Feb. 18, 1762.
2-59	"	William, of Richard, and Comfort Greene, of John: m. by Eld. Charles Holden, Feb. 18, 1762.
2-4	"	Almy, and Oliver Arnold, Mar. 11, 1762.
2-43	"	William, and Phebe Johnson, widow; m. by Eld. Charles Holden, Oct. 16, 1763.
2-61	"	Hannah, and Nathan Greene, June 14, 1764.
2-61	"	Nathan, and Hannah Greene, of James; m. by Ebenezer Slocum, Justice, June 14, 1764.
2-41	"	Deborah, and Capt. Samuel Fry, Aug. 23, 1764.
2-44	"	Giles, of James, and Phebe Rhodes, of John, Jr.; m. by Eld. Charles Holden, Sept. 13, 1764.
2-63	"	Benjamin, of Richard, and Anne Low, of Col. Stephen; m. by Eld. Charles Holden, Sept. 30, 1764.
2-176	"	Ruth, and Mial Salisbury, Dec. 9, 1764.
2-219	"	Alice, and Jonathan Bennett, May 12, 1765.
2-214	"	Elizabeth, and Stuteley Wickes, Dec. 26, 1765.
2-54	"	Thomas, of Fones, dec., and Hannah Hill, widow of Nathaniel; m. by Eld. Charles Holden, Nov. 13, 1766.
2-25	"	Phebe, and Nathaniel Chapman, Mar. 2, 1767.
2-66	"	Caleb, of Richard, and Mary Lippitt, of Moses, dec.; m. by Eld. Charles Holden, Jan. 21, 1768.
2-65	"	Peter, of John, and Elizabeth Johnson, of Esek; m. by Eld. Charles Holden, Aug. 7, 1768.
2-23, 93	"	Tabitha, and Moses Lippitt, Dec. 25, 1768.
2-221	"	John, of Richard, of Potowomut, and Barbara Holden, of Col. Randall, dec.; m. by Eld. Charles Holden, Sept. 30, 1770.

2-246   Greene John, of Richard, and Mary Greene, of Phillip; m. by Eld. Charles Holden, Sept. 22, 1771.
2-246   "   Mary, and John Greene, Sept. 22, 1771.
2-224   "   William, of John, and Wait Lockwood, of Capt. Amos; m. by Eld. Charles Holden, Mar. 8, 1772.
2-231   "   David, Jr., of David, and Isabel Warner, of John; m. by Thomas Rice, Jr., Justice, Apr. 16, 1772.
2-62   "   Christopher, of Nathaniel, of Warwick, and Catherine Ward, of Westerly; m. by Eld. Joshua Clarke, Dec. 23, 1773.
2-230   "   William, and Welthian Lippitt; m. by Eld. J. Graves, Jan. 13, 1774.
2-179   "   Phebe, and John Stone, Jr., Mar. 17, 1774.
2-232   "   Nathaniel, of Nathaniel, of Warwick, and Catherine Littlefield, of John, of New Shoreham; m. by Eld. John Gorton, July 20, 1774.
2-233   "   Patience, and Capt. Abraham Lockwood, Dec. 24, 1775.
2-61   "   Elisha, of Nathaniel, of Warwick, and Jane Flagg, of William, of Boston, Mass; m. by Eld. Charles Holden, Dec. 5, 1776.
2-65   "   Peter, of Warwick, and Sarah Davis, of North Kingstown; m. by Eld. James Wightman, Aug. 3, 1777.
2-216   "   Phebe, and Major Samuel Ward, Mar. 8, 1778.
2-53   "   Charles, of Rufus, of East Greenwich, and Phebe Sheffield, of Benjamin, dec. of Jamestown; m. by Eld. John Gorton, Dec. 6, 1778.
2-47   "   Cuffe, servant of James, now a soldier in the Continental Army, and Polly Cook, servant of Sally, (col.); m. by Adam Comstock, Justice, Jan. 18, 1779.
2-209   "   Susanna, and Caleb Westcott, Sept. 10, 1780.
2-1   "   Mrs. Sally, and Moses Arnold, Jan. 25, 1781.
2-97   "   Bethiah, and John LeValley, Mar. 15, 1781.
2-37   "   Alse, and Thomas Foster, Mar. 18, 1781.
2-49   "   James, of James, of Nesocut, Warwick, and Phebe Warner, of Thomas, son of Eld. John Gorton, Jan. 6, 1782.
2-218   "   Welthian, and John Waterman, Jr., Feb. 3, 1782.
2-54   "   Welthian, and Capt. Thomas Hughes, Feb. 27, 1782.
2-65   "   Stephen, of Coventry, son of Job, and Sarah Chace, of Abraham, of Warwick; m. by James Jerauld, Justice, May 5, 1782.

2-242	Greene James, 4th,	and Rebecca Pitman, of Providence, dau. of Saunders; m. by Rev. Joseph Snow, Nov. 17, 1782.
2-62	"	Col. Christopher, Jr., of Nathaniel, of Warwick, and Deborah Ward, of Hon. Samuel, of Newport; m. by Eld. William Bliss, May 12, 1783.
2-239	"	Almy, and Jabez Comstock, Jan. 1, 1784.
2-252	"	Sarah, and Caleb Hill, Jan. 4, 1784.
3-93	"	Anne, and Thomas Eldredge, July 15, 1784.
2-242	"	Giles, of Giles, and Rhoda Arnold, of William, Jr.; m. by Eld. John Gorton, Jan. 6, 1785.
2-55	"	Job, of Warwick, and Abigail Rhodes, of Stonington; m. by Eld. Gardiner Thurston, Nov. 29, 1785.
2-245	"	Elizabeth, and Sylvester G. Hazard, Mar. 5, 1786.
2-49	"	Celia, and William Greene, Nov. 7, 1786.
2-49	"	William, of Capt. Benjamin, and Celia Greene, of Gov. William; m. by Eld. John Gorton, Nov. 7, 1786.
2-247	"	Rachel, and Thomas Whitaker, Dec. 28, 1786.
2-98	"	Mary, and Benjamin LeValley, Mar. 18, 1787.
2-250	"	Mary, and Samuel Brown, Oct. 22, 1787.
2-251	"	George, and Sally Waterman; m. by Eld. Abraham Lippitt, Dec. 16, 1787.
2-41	"	Elizabeth, and Jeremiah Fenner, Sept. 25, 1789.
2-251	"	Thomas, Jr., and Barbara Low, of Col. John; m. by Eld. Abraham Lippitt, Aug. 22, 1790.
2-185	"	Jeremiah, of Col. Christopher, dec., of Warwick, and Lydia Arnold, of Col. William, of East Greenwich; m. at East Greenwich by Eld. John Gorton, Oct. 7, 1790.
2-128	"	Benjamin, of Caleb, and Penelope Westcott; m. by Eld. Abraham Lippitt, Nov. 12, 1790.
2-128	"	Mary, and Richard Burke, July 17, 1791.
2-195	"	Stephen, of Warwick, and Mercy Jencks, of Smithfield, dau. of Joseph; m. by Eld. John Winsor, Dec. 1, 1791.
2-255	"	Sarah, and William Rice, Oct. 28, 1792.
2-255	"	Dorcas, and Isaac Hall, Jan. 6, 1793.
2-197	"	Betsey, and Nathaniel Millard, June 2, 1793.
2-187	"	Ray, and Mary Magdalene Flagg; m. at Charlestown, Mass., by Rev. Robert Smith, Pastor of St. Phillip's Church, July 23, 1794.
2-66	"	Caleb, and Sarah Robinson Greene; m. by Eld. Samuel Littlefield, Mar. 8, 1795.
2-66	"	Sarah Robinson, and Caleb Greene, Mar. 8, 1795.

2-186		Greene Howland, of East Greenwich, son of Gideon, and Nancy Pearce, otherwise Brown, dau. of Hannah Pearce; m. by James Jerauld, Justice, May 29, 1796.
2-132	"	Samuel, of Caleb, and Elizabeth Stafford, of John; m. by James Jerauld, Justice, Mar. 19, 1797.
2-99	"	Catherine, and Caleb Ladd, July 30, 1797.
2-97	"	Deborah, and William Morris, July 5, 1798.
2-118	"	Catherine, and Christopher Greene, Jan. 7, 1799.
2-118	"	Christopher, and Catherine Greene; m. by Eld. Samuel Littlefield, Jan. 7, 1799.
2-219	"	Isabel W., and William Briggs, Nov. 21, 1799.
2-101	"	Nicholas, of Greenfield, N. Y., and Hannah Hammett, of Warwick; m. by Eld. Samuel Littlefield, Aug. 10, 1800.
2-257	"	Almy, and William Hammett, Nov. 9, 1800.
2-34	"	Christopher, and Ann Low; m. by Eld. Samuel Littlefield, Apr. 24, 1803.
2-27	"	Thomas L., and Anne Greene Holden; m. by Eld. Samuel Littlefield, May 1, 1803.
3-1	"	Mary, and William Anthony, Dec. 18, 1803.
3-1	"	Almy, and Nathaniel Arnold, May 5, 1805.
3-342	"	Mary, and James Warner, Dec. 15, 1805.
3-113	"	Emily, and Franklin Greene, June 29, 1806.
3-113	"	Franklin, and Emily Greene; m. by Eld. Samuel Littlefield, June 29, 1806.
3-115	"	Robert W., and Mary L. Arnold; m. by Eld. Samuel Littlefield, Feb. 22, 1807.
3-247	"	Elizabeth, and Olney Potter, Nov. 20, 1808.
3-114	"	Jeremiah, and Phebe Hughes; m. by Eld. Samuel Littlefield, Feb. 19, 1809.
3-9	"	Mary, and Benedict Arnold, Dec. 6, 1810.
3-117	"	James, and Mercy Waterman; m. by Rev. Samuel Littlefield, Oct. 29, 1812.
3-114	"	Jeremiah, and Sarah Littlefield; m. by Eld. Samuel Littlefield, June 8, 1817.
3-119	"	James, and Deborah Cole; m. by Rev. Samuel Littlefield, Aug. 2, 1818.
4-80	"	Simon H., of Warwick, a resident of Providence, and Cornelia Caroline Aborn; m. by Rev. James Wilson, Mar. 13, 1822.
3-53	"	Celia, and Wanton R. Briggs, Sept. 5, 1822.
3-121	"	William M., and Sarah Warner; m. by Eld. Samuel Littlefield, Dec. 11, 1823.

WARWICK—MARRIAGES.

3-124　　Greene Lieut. George Sears, U. S. A., son of Caleb, and Elizabeth Vinton, of David; m. by Rev. C. B. Kellogg, July 14, 1828.
3-126　　" Thomas H., and Mary Ann, Lockwood; m. by Eld. Job Manchester, Jan. 10, 1830.
3-128　　" Phillip, and Sophia Burguess; m. by Eld. Job Manchester, Mar. 4, 1832.
3-127　　" Catherine Celia, and Stephen G. Warner, Feb. 2, 1833.
3-336　　" Elizabeth, and William Warner, Mar. 5, 1835.
3-125　　" George Sears, of Caleb, of Warwick, and Martha Barrett Dana, dau. of Hon. Samuel, dec., of Groton, Mass.; m. by Rev. James Walker, Feb. 21, 1837.
4-88　　" Nancy H., and Thomas E. Anthony, Oct. 17, 1838.
3-79　　" Lucy Anne, and Gardner Clapp, June 3, 1839.
3-130　　" Benjamin, of John, of Nantucket, and Prescilla S. Tourjee, of Thomas, of North Kingstown; m. by Rev. Moses Fifield, June 10, 1839.
3-163　　" Anstress C. A., and John J. Harvey, Sept. 23, 1839.
3-132　　" Esbon, of Warwick, son of Sally, of Coventry, and Betsey T. Blanchard, of Warwick, dau. of Martha, of Coventry; m. by Rev. Moses Fifield, July 26, 1840.
3-133　　" William D., of Spicer, and Rhoda Bennett; m. by Rev. Moses Fifield, Oct. 5, 1840.
3-342　　" Sarah L., and Henry Waterman, June 14, 1841.
3-241　　" Elizabeth W., and William K. Nichols, Sept. 30, 1841.
3-126　　" Rufus, of Thomas, dec., and Sally Ann Low, of John, dec.; m. by Rev. Junia S. Mowry, Dec. 23, 1841.
3-137　　" Henry W., of Warner I., and Emeline Dexter, of Jeremiah, of Exeter, dec.; m. by Rev. Moses Fifield, July 18, or 28, 1842.
3-332　　" Susan S., and Richard Valpey, Oct. 31, 1842.
3-161　　" Sarah S., and William S. Holden, Mar. 9, 1843.
3-210　　" Lucy A., and Thomas Lynch, Apr. 4, 1843.
3-162　　" Betsey T., and Edward H. Holden, Nov. 19, 1843.
3-139　　" Charles J., of Thomas, of Warwick, and Susan Ann Head, of Warwick, son of Asa, of Portsmouth; m. by Rev. Moses Fifield, July 14, 1844.
3-234　　" Abby, and Jenckes Mowry, Sept. 26, 1844.
3-128　　" Caroline, and Benjamin Gardner, Sept. 26, 1844.
3-352　　" Octavia, and John Webster, June 7, 1845.
3-263　　" Mary Eliza, and Paxhall A. Parker, Jan. 19, 1846.
　　　　" Sarah Maria, and Charles Morrison, Apr. 19, 1847.

3-142 Greene Stephen A., of Stephen, and Susan C. Tanner, of John; m. by Rev. Jonathan Brayton, Oct. 24, 1847.
3-195 " Celia, and Truman Knowles, Dec. 14, 1847.
3-143 " Stephen, of East Greenwich, son of Valentine, and Almira B. Sherman, of East Greenwich; m. by Rev. Daniel Slocum, Nov. 3, 1848.
4-28 " Sarah P., and C. C. Shute, July 2, 1850.
4-49 " Jane, and William H. Pratt, Nov. 17, 1851.
4-49 " Catherine C., and Caleb Westcott, Dec. 15, 1851.
4-63 " Mary H., and Austin W. Otis, Mar. 6, 1853.
4-78 " Clarissa L., and Martin Cornell, May 1, 1859.
3-129 Grennell John, of Portsmouth, and Hannah Whitman, of Exeter; m. by Rev. Thomas Tillinghast, Nov. 5, 1837.
3-125 Griffin Stephen C., son of Joseph and Mary, and Mary Ann Whaley, of Martha; m. by Eld. Gersham Palmer, Jan. 1, 1826.
3-291 " Sarah B., and Thomas C. Sweet, May 17, 1847.
3-141 " Oliver P., and Mary E. Curian; m. by Rev. Stephen A. Thomas, June 17, 1847.
2-53 Griffis James, and Anne Allen, widow; m. by Eld. Charles Holden, Jan. 1, 1758.
4-93 Grimshaw Mary Jane, and Albert Rice, Aug. 17, 1873.
1-1 Grove Ann, and John Lippitt, Jr., Feb. 9, 1664.
2-156 Grummuch Elizabeth, and Cuff Roberts (col.), Feb. 27, 1788.

H

2-68 Hackstone Nathaniel, and Ruth Seabin; m. by Eld. John Hammett, Feb. 9, 1752.
2-124 " Elizabeth, and Matthew Price, Dec. 14, 1777.
2-118 " Thomas, of Warwick, and Susanna Adams, of Coventry; m. by Job Randall, Justice, Sept. 24, 1792.
3-309 " Thomas, of Warwick, and Rest Bennett, of Ezekiel, of Coventry; m. by Samuel Rice, Justice, Dec. 8, 1805.
1-73 Hail Mary, and Benjamin Barton, —— 28, 1727.
1-28 Hall George, of John, and Jane Voighn, of George, Mar. 11, 1737.
1-65 " William, and Mary Slocum; m. by William Rice, Asst., June 7, 1744.
2-226 " Sarah, and Benjamin Barton, Feb. 25, 1776.

2-255	Hall	Isaac, of North Kingstown, son of William, and Dorcas Greene, of Caleb, of Warwick; m. by James Jerauld, Justice, Jan. 6, 1793.
2-126	"	Mary, and Capt. Oliver Holden, Feb. 21, 1798.
3-153	"	William, of Sutton, Mass., and Almy Hammett, of Warwick; m. by Eld. Samuel Littlefield, Mar. 27, 1808.
3-173	"	Ruth Ann, and George W. Jordan, Nov. 28, 1839.
3-166	"	Bernard M., of William, of Coventry, and Amanda Bushnell, of Warwick, dau. of Stephen, late of Coventry, deceased; m. by Rev. Moses Fifield, Sept. 16, 1840.
3-158	"	David, and Silvia Sweet, both of Coventry; m. by Rev. Henry Tatem, Dec. 10, 1840.
3-166	"	Dudley D., of Isaac, and Waitey A. Spink, of Clarke; m. by Rev. Martin J. Steere, Apr. 14, 1845.
3-167	"	Mary, and Alba Hopkins, July 3, 1845.
4-24	"	Henry T., of Daniel, and Angenette Walker; m. by Rev. Jonathan Brayton, Nov. 4, 1849.
4-37	Halsted	William M., aged 25 years, son of David W., and Harriet, and Mary R. Thompson, aged 19 years; m. by Rev. Benjamin Phelan, Oct. 16, 1850.
2-34	Hambleton	Amie, and John Essex, Dec. 25, 1781.
3-135	Hamilton	Martha E., and James A. Gardner, Aug. 9, 1841·
1-59	Hammett	John, of John and Dorothy Roades, of Malachi; m. by Eld. George Pigott, Dec. 13, 1726.
2-48	"	Mary, and Stephen Greene, Feb. 8, 1753.
2-72	"	Malachi, of Eld. John, of Warwick, and Maplet Hawkins, of James, of Providence; m. by Eld., Charles Sheldon, Mar. 8, 1761.
2-77	"	Malachi, and Hannah Wickes, widow of William; by Eld. Charles Holden, Jan. 10, 1765.
2-27	"	Anne, and Capt. James Carder, Dec. 28, 1776.
2-77	"	Caleb, of Eld. John, of Warwick, and Keziah Potter, of William, of Cranston; m. by Eld. Charles Holden, Nov. 15, 1772.
2-218	"	Susanna, and Benjamin Weaver, Dec. 20, 1772.
2-101	"	Hannah, and Nicholas Greene, Aug. 10, 1800.
2-257	"	William, of Malachi, and Amey Greene, of Christopher, dec.; m. by Joseph Arnold, Justice, Nov. 9, 1800.
2-247	"	Clarke, of Warwick, and Mary Standish, of Middleborough, Mass.; m. by Eld. Samuel Littlefield, Sept. 8, 1801.
3-153	"	Almy, and William Hall, Mar. 27, 1808.

3-162 Hammond Gardiner B., of Warwick, son of Benjamin, dec., of North Kingstown, and Triphena H. Angell, of Warwick, dau. of Jeremiah, dec., of Scituate; m. by Rev. Moses Fifield, May 21, 1839.
3-86 " Sarah M., and John W. Dana, June 9, 1840.
2-116 Hampleton Mary, and David Essex Sept. 17, 1782.
3-168 Hampson William, and Frances Tew; m. by Rev. Edward K. Fuller, Oct. 13, 1843.
3-416 " Robert, and Frances Gardner; m. by Rev. Stephen A. Dexter, Nov. 2, 1847.
3-167 Hanop John, of George, and Sarah Gardiner, of Samuel; m. by Rev. James Mulchahy, Feb. 24, 1846.
1-60 Hardin Lydia, and Barlo Greene, Oct. 21, 1717.
1-95 " Almy, and William Angell, Sept. 1, 1731.
3-160 Hare William, and Mercy Burrell; m. by Eld. Jonathan Brayton, Nov. 6, 1842.
4-77 Harper Isabel, and Alonzo Tourjee, Aug. 16, 1855.
4-79 Harrup Mary, and Nathan Hunter, June, 18, 1864.
3-26 Harrington Nancy, and Gardiner G. Albro, Nov. 23, 1843.
3-403 " Randall R. H., son of Augustus, of Warwick, and Mary R. Matteson, of Coventry, dau. of William, dec.; m. by Rev. Moses Fifield, Sept. 12, 1847.
2-86 Harrison Sarah, and Andrew Kinnecom, Dec. 27, 1795.
3-151 " William, and Mary Baker; m. by Eld. Samuel Littlefield, April 11, 1805.
3-151 " John, and Mary Randall; m. by Eld. Samuel Littlefield, May 5, 1805.
3-155 " Capt. William, aud Catherine T. Warner; m. by Rev. David Curtis, Jan. 1, 1816.
3-196 " Ann E., and John H. Kenyon, Jr., Jan. 21, 1842.
1-23 Harris Patience, and William Smith, Mar. 17, 1708-9.
1-97 " Temperance, and Daniel Greene, Nov. 11, 1731.
2-78 " Nicholas, of Jedediah, of Cranston, and Phebe Tibbetts, of Warwick, dau. of Henry; m. by Eld. Charles Holden, Feb. 25, 1773.
2-5 " Phebe, and Phillip Arnold, Jan. 10, 1779.
3-154 " Andrew, of Andrew, late of Johnston, dec., and Sarah Remington: m. by C. Brayton, Justice. Apr. 2, 1809.
3-274 " Sarah, and William Rice, Oct. 13, 1829.
3-164 " Henry, of William, dec., and Mercy A. Ney, of William; m. by Rev. Moses Fifield, Feb. 6, 1840.

3-167	Harris Stephen, Jr., of Warwick, son of Stephen, and Eliza Morse, of Benjamin, of Coventry; m. by Eld. Job Manchester, Oct. 29, 1840.
3-167	" Ezra, of Dedham, Mass., son of Daniel, of Moreton, Vt., and Hannah L. Wright, of Dedham, dau. of Josiah, of Plympton, Mass.; m. by Rev. Moses Fifield, Nov. 27, 1840.
1-2	Harrude John, and Elizabeth Cooke; m. by John Greene, Asst., Dec. 24, 1666.
3-302	Harry Mary, and Pardon Sweet, Jan. 11, 1847.
3-54	Hart Sarah, and Capt. Benjamin Bateman, Sept. 24, 1826.
3-169	" Daniel T., of Warwick, and Adeline M. Burlingame, of Cranston; m. by Rev. Stephen A. Thomas, Feb. 18, 1846.
3-163	Harvey John J., and Anstress Clarke Allen Greene; m. by Rev. Thomas Dowling, Sept. 23, 1839.
2-253	Hatch Mary, and Sails Carr, Nov. 5, 1789.
2-135	" Abigail, and Rice Millard, Sept. 30, 1798.
1-91	Hathaway Jeremiah, and Ruth Ruttenberge, of John, Mar. 10, 1725-6.
2-26	" Mary, and Pardon Relph, alias Dailey, Mar. 2, 1758.
2-71	" Thomas, and Sarah Graves; m. by Ebenezer Slocum, Justice, Sept. 28, 1759.
2-108	" Catherine, and Joseph Mathewson, Feb. 5, 1761.
2-67	" William, of Caleb, and Jane Stafford, dau. of John Ripley; m. by Eld. Charles Holden, June 4, 1775.
2-68	" Nathan, of Caleb, and Mercy LeValley, of Michael; m. by James Jerauld, Justice, Feb. 27, 1783.
3-154	" Thomas, of Scituate, son of Thomas, and Hannah G. Arnold, of Warwick, dau. of Dea. Benjamin; m. by Rev. Jonathan Brayton, May 16, 1842.
4-29	" Alanson F., of Warwick, aged 20 years, son of Silas, and Sarah A. Woodmansee, of Warwick, aged 22 years, dau. of Betsey, of Richmond; m. by Rev. Moses Fifield, July 28, 1850.
1-75	Havens Phebe, and John Whitman, June 14, 1722.
1-61	" Ruth, and Edward Pigot, Oct. 9, 1733.
2-212	" Desire, and Joseph Whitford, Oct. 9, 1761.
2-150	" Susanna, and Fones Rice, Feb. 16, 1764.
2-70	" William, of Alexander, dec., and Deliverance Stafford, of Joseph, Jr.; m. by Eld. John Gorton, Sept. 9, 1764.
2-152	" Mary, and Jonathan Remington, June 15, 1769.

2-228	Havens Honor, and Richard Arnold, Mar. 19, 1789.
2-164	" Alexander, of William, and Anne Ladd, of Capt. John, dec.; m. by Eld. John Gorton, Jan. 31, 1790.
2-188	" Rebecca, and Charles Brayton, Apr. 26, 1795.
2-135	" William, of William, and Elizabeth Jerauld, of James; m. by Joseph Arnold, Justice, Oct. 18, 1795.
2-122	" Darius, a resident of Warwick, and Hannah, Boyd, of Andrew, of East Greenwich; m. by James Jerauld, Justice, Oct. 15, 1798.
2-231	" Thomas, of William, and Mary Brayton, of Daniel; m. by Caleb Jerauld, Justice, Feb. 6, 1803.
2-205	Hawkins Mary, and Robert Westgate, Nov. 19, 1753.
2-72	" Maplet, and Malachi Hammett, Mar. 8, 1761.
1-164	" Thomas, of Warwick, son of Elijah, of Gloucester, and Lydia A. Newman, of Warwick, dau. of Noah; m. by Rev. Moses Fifield, Nov. 14, 1844.
1-92	Haynes Josiah, of Charles, and Ann Carder, widow of Joseph, Jan. 1, 1729.
1-19	" Ann, and Capt. Thomas Rice, June 19, 1740.
2-4	" Ann, and Stephen Arnold, June 16, 1751.
2-89	" Mary, and Peter LeValley, May 11, 1755.
2-7	" Frances, and Thomas Arnold, June 1, 1761.
2-39	" Sarah, and Daniel Fenner, Oct. 3, 1762.
1-3	Hazard Joseph, and Rebecca Lippitt; m. by Walter Todd, Asst., Feb. 2, 1664.
2-3	" Rebecca, and Francis Budlong, Mar. 19, 1668-9.
2-245	" Sylvester G., of Dr. Robert, dec., of South Kingstown, and Elizabeth Greene, of Richard, dec., of Potowomut; m. by Eld. John Gorton, Mar. 5, 1786.
3-49	" Esther N., and Edmund Bayley, Aug. 15, 1815.
3-168	" Benjamin M., of North Kingstown, son of Robinson, and Jane G. Knox, of Thomas P. R. A., of Warwick, m. by Rev. Moses Fifield, Sept. 16, 1841.
4-12	" Sarah F., and William E. Remington, July 25, 1849.
4-27	" Abbie E., and Luther L. Caswell, May 14, 1850.
1-7	Hazelton James, and Rathvun Westcott, widow of Robert, Aug. 10, 1678.
1-76	" Martha, and Thomas Foster, Mar. 3, 1732.
3-139	Head Susan Ann, and Charles J. Greene, July 14, 1844.
2-70	Healey John, of Providence, and Ellis Lockwood, of Warwick; m. by Eld. John Gorton, July 25, 1756.

3-165	Healey Rowland G., of Peter D., and Susan M. Morey, of Benjamin; m. by Rev. Moses Fifield, Sept. 3, 1840.
4-10	Heap John, Jr., of Cranston, son of John, and Mary Palmer, of Cranston, dau. of John; m. by Rev. Zalman Tobey, June 10, 1849.
1-42	Heath Rebecca, and Daniel Coggeshall, Nov. 12, 1738.
4-67	Hebbard Lucy A, and William Matteson, Nov. 18, 1846.
1-6	Hedjer Thomas, and Elizabeth Burton, of William and Hannah; m. by Arthur Fenner, Asst., Oct. 30, 1674.
4-74	Heenan Mary, and John Duffy, Feb. 21, 1860.
3-169	Henderson Andrew, of George, and Ann Young, of James; m. by Thomas Wilkes, Justice, Sept. 6, 1841.
4-73	Hennessey Thomas, and Catherine Fleming; m. by Rev. James P. Gibson, Apr. 15, 1854.
4-72	Henry John, of Cumberland, aged 32 years, son of Zimri, of Foster, and Phebe Sheldon, of Scituate, aged 36 years; m. by Eld. Richard Knight, Nov. 13, 1853.
3-385	Herd Almira, and Wilbour J. Burdick, Sept. 15, 1845.
1-29,52	Hicks Joseph, and Ann Cindrick; m. by Eld. Manassah Martin, Nov. 18, 1738.
2-1	Hide Patience, and Elisha Arnold, Dec. 23, 1744.
1-60	Hill Susanna, and Usal Greene, Jan. — 1727.
1-58	" Mary, and William Nichols, June 23, 1728.
1-104	" Barnard, of Jonathan, and Mary Gardiner, of Samuel, all of Swansey, Jan. 13, 1731-2.
1-55	" Thomas, of Jonathan, dec.,and Abigail Perce, of Preserved; m. at North Kingstown, Nov. 4, 1736.
2-68	" Caleb, of North Kingstown, and Mercy Stafford, of Stuteley, dec., of Warwick; m. by Eld. John Gorton, Mar. 23, 1755.
2-67	" Nathaniel, of Dea. Thomas, dec., of North Kingstown, and Hannah Waterman, of Capt. John, of Coventry; m. by Eld. Charles Holden, Mar. 29, 1761.
2-54	" Hannah, and Thomas Greene. Nov. 13, 1766.
2-224	" Mary, and Thomas Warner, Nov. 24, 1782.
2-252	" Caleb, and Caleb, of North Kingstown, and Sarah Greene, of Thomas, of Naussocut, Warwick; m. by Eld. John Gorton, Jan. 4, 1784.
3-158	" Benjamin, of Christopher, and Charlotte Matilda Browning, of John; m. by Elder Thomas Manchester, June 24, 1822.

3-159	Hill	James F., of James, and Penelope Thurston, dau. of Sebbens Northup; m. by Rev. Jonathan Brayton, Sept. 19, 1842.
3-413	"	Harriet, and Joseph W. Gardiner, July 27, 1846.
3-73	Himes	Mary, and Joseph Cady, Mar. 28, 1842.
3-153	"	Paul, of William, and Sally H. Covell, of Thomas; m. by Rev. Junia S. Mowry, Apr. 5, 1842.
3-312	"	Robey, and Alanson Tefft, Nov. 19, 1843.
4-85	"	Samuel, and Mary C. Parker; m. by Rev. Jonathan Brayton, May 25, 1851.
3-159	"	Stephen P., and Abbie B. Reynolds; m. by Eld. Jonathan Wilson, Oct. 16, 1823.
4-12	Hiscox	Emily, and Jerman Y. Potter, Sept. 3, 1849.
4-22	Hitch	Elizabeth H., and George K. England, Jan. 13, 1850.
1-43	Hitt	James, Jr., and Renewed Sweet, of James; m. by Wm. Greene, Justice, July 5, 1727.
2-108	Hix	Bathsheba, and John Morimer, Dec. 4, 1757.
2-73	"	Joseph, and Deliverance Whipple, widow of Eleazer; m. by Eld. Charles Holden, Feb. 8, 1767.
1-93	Hoksey	Ann, and Benjamin Greene, Nov. 27, 1735.
1-5	Holden	Frances and John Holmes, Dec. 1, 1671.
1-5	"	Mary, and John Carder, Dec. 1, 1671.
1-6	"	Elizabeth, and John Rice, July 16, 1674.
1-62	"	Susannah, and Benjamin Greene, Jan. 21, 1689-0.
1-30	"	Catherine, and John Rhodes, Jan. 29, 1714.
1-40	"	Charles Jr., of Warwick, and Penelope Bennett, of John, of Newport, Dec. 13, 1716.
1-41	"	Wait, and William Holden, Apr. 30, 1721.
1-41	"	William, of Charles, and Wait Holden, of Randall, Apr. 30, 1721.
1-51	"	"Ensign" Randall, son of Major Randall, and Rose Wickes, of John, July 3, 1724.
1.69	"	John, of Charles, and Hannah Fry, of Thomas, Jan. 6, 1731-2.
1-20	"	Barbara, and Richard Wickes, Mar. 20, 1735.
1-88	"	Catherine, and Christopher Lippitt, Jan. 2, 1736.
2-67	"	John, of Capt, Charles, and Dorothy Rice, of Capt. Thomas; m. by Eld. Manassah Martin, Aug. 5, 1744.
2-108	"	Hannah, and James Mason, Jan. 11, 1750.
2-68	"	Charles, and Hannah Martin; m. by Eld. John Gorton, Jan. 23, 1757.
2-151	"	Mary, and William Rhodes, Aug. 18, 1765.

2-69	Holden	Anthony, of William, and Elizabeth Rice, of William, dec., m. by Thomas Rice, Jr., Justice, May 25, 1769.
2-221	"	Barbara, and John Greene, Sept. 30, 1770.
2-218	"	Sarah, and John Wells, Dec. 23, 1770.
2-76	"	Charles, 3d, of John, dec., and Sarah Remington, of Thomas; m. by Thomas Rice, Justice, Nov. 3, 1771.
2-78	"	William, of William, and Hannah Carder, of James; m. by Eld. Charles Holden, June 20, 1773.
2-95	"	Anstress, and Moses Lippitt, Jan. 8, 1775.
2-75	"	Anthony, of Randall, and Sarah Warner, of Thomas, dec; m. by Eld. Charles Holden, Jan. 27, 1780.
2-240	"	Welthian, and Lemuel Allen, Apr. 22, 1781.
2-75	"	Edward, of Thomas, and Sarah Burlingame, of Samuel; m. by James Jerauld, Justice, Jan. 16, 1785.
2-206	"	Ishmael, servant of Thomas, and Sarah West, of Ishmael (col.); m. by James Jerauld, Justice, Apr. 29, 1787.
2-71	"	Thomas, and Mercy Wightman, widow of Phillip; m. by James Jerauld, Justice, June 9, 1793.
2-102	"	Freelove, and Harris Arnold, Jr., Dec. 24, 1795.
2-104	"	Elizabeth, and Capt. Samuel Low, Apr. 2, 1797.
2-126	"	Capt. Oliver, and Mary Hall, of widow Mary; m. by Joseph Arnold, Justice, Feb. 21, 1798.
2-221	"	Welthian, and Daniel Arnold, Sept. 12, 1801.
2-122	"	Caleb, of Thomas, Jr., of Warwick, and Sally Burton, dau. of Freelove, dec., of Cranston; m. by Nicholas Congdon, Justice, Apr. 9, 1802.
2-27	"	Anne Greene, and Thomas L. Greene, May 1, 1803.
2-1	"	William Anthony, of William, and Elizabeth Baker, of Thomas; m. by Caleb Westcott, Justice, June 5, 1803.
3-160	"	William A., and Celinda Williams; m. by Eld. Samuel Littlefield, June 8, 1817.
3-156	"	Cyrus, of John, and Amanda Westcott; m. by Rev. Jonathan Brayton, June 30, 1842.
3-161	"	William S., of William, dec., and Sarah S. Greene, of Christopher; m. by Rev. Moses Fifield, Mar. 9, 1843.
3-162	"	Edward H., of George, and Betsey T. Greene, dau. of George Taft; m. by Rev. E. L. Ervins, Nov. 19, 1843.
4-75	"	Benjamin G., and Catherine J. Boyd; m. by Rev. Benjamin Phelan, Mar. 29, 1855.
4-50	Hollis	Sarah Ann, and John Congdon, Dec. 16, 1851.
1-5	Holmes	John, of Newport, and Frances Houldon, of Randall, of Warwick; m. by John Greene, Justice, Dec. 1, 1671.

1-7   Holmes John, and Mary Greene, widow of William; m. by John Greene, Justice, Oct. 12, 1680.
2-133   "   Samuel, late of New York, and Ruth Fairbanks, of Nathaniel, of Warwick; m. by Adam Comstock, Justice, Jan. 10, 1779.
1-55   Hopkins Patience, and John Gorton, Jr., Feb. 2, 1699-0.
1-45   "   Theodosia, and Othniel Gorton, June 3, 1736.
2-73   "   William, and Mary Westgate; m. by John Warner, Jr., Justice, Dec. 5, 1760.
2-74   "   Reuben, of Scituate, and Elizabeth Arnold, of Warwick, widow of Owen; m. by Eld. Charles Holden, Dec. 6, 1761.
2-75   "   Jeremiah, of Scituate, and Ann Sweet, of Phillip, Jr., of Warwick; m. by Ebenezer Slocum, Justice, Sept. 30, 1762.
2-75   "   Samuel, of Scituate, and Phebe Arnold, of William, of Warwick; m. by Ebenezer Slocum, Justice, Feb. 3, 1765.
2-30   "   Mercy, and George Arnold, Sept. 7, 1782.
2-194   "   Frances, and Sylvester Tiffany, July 28, 1784.
2-39   "   Amos, of Samuel, of West Greenwich, and Robey Atwood, of Charles, dec., of Warwick; m. by Eld. Thomas Manchester, Mar. 27, 1803.
3-155   "   Charles F., of Elisha, and Harriet N. Sweet, of Samuel; m. by Thomas Wilkes, Justice, Apr. 4, 1842.
3-136   "   Orrilla, and John A. Gardner, Apr. 10, 1842.
3-167   "   Alba, of Duty, and Mary Hall, of Isaac; m. by Rev. Moses Fifield, July 3, 1845.
3-415   "   George G., of Providence, and Cordelia W. Place, of East Greenwich; m. by Rev. S. A. Thomas, Oct. 17, 1847.
3-415   "   Stanton, and Harriet Johnson; m. by Rev. Stephen A. Thomas, Oct. 17, 1847.
1-25   House Abigail, and Thomas Collins, Feb. 17, 1692.
3-403   Houson William O., and Anstress Ann Shippee; m. by Rev. Edward K. Fuller, Dec. 16, 1845.
2-76   Howard Benjamin, of Benjamin, dec., and Ann Sisco; m. by Eld. Charles Holden, July 14, 1771.
2-78   "   Benjamin, of Soloman, and Patience Baker, of Jonathan; m. by Eld. Charles Holden, Dec. 10, 1772.
2-160   "   Ann, and Jerauld Remington, May 12, 1782.

3-156	Howard John, and Phebe Baker, widow; m. by Stephen Budlong, Justice, Dec. 1, 1816.
3-161	" Nathan, of Ebenezer, of Mendon, Mass., and Sarah J. Reynolds, of Nicholas, dec., formerly of North Kingstown; m. by Rev. Moses Fifield, May 4, 1834.
3-262	" Eleanor, and Samuel Palmer, June 15, 1834.
3-212	" Mary P., and William M. King, Sept. 5, 1843.
3-207	" Sarah Ann, and James W. Locke, Oct. 3, 1842.
4-53	" John B., aged 20 years, son of John and Hannah, and Margaret J. Wheeler, aged 18 years, dau. of Henry G·, and Sarah P,; m. by Rev. Benjamin Phelan, May 6, 1852.
4-60	" Elisha P., of Warwick, aged 23 years, son of John, and Hannah Wheeler, aged 16 years, dau. of Henry; m. by Rev. Benjamin Phelan, Feb. 4, 1853.
1-1	How Abigail, and Daniel Kee, July 15, 17—.
4-23	Hoxsie Barber, of Rouse of Richmond, R. I., and Margaret Babcock, of Warwick, dau. of William, dec., of South Kingstown; m. by Rev. Moses Fifield, Mar. 19, 1850.
3-163	Hoyt Edwin, of Newport, and Susan Sprague, of Hon. William; m. by Rev. Moses Fifield, Nov. 29, 1843.
3-165	Hubbard Henry, M. D., son of J. Calvin, of Killingly, Conn., and Mary E. Allen, of Christopher; m. by Rev. Moses Fifield, Jan. 27, 1845.
4-67	" Lucy A., and William Matteson, Nov. 18, 1846.
3-304	" Lydia M., and Raymond G. Spencer, May 2, 1847.
1-63	Hudson Mary, and Benjamin Greene, July 3, 1735.
2-67	" Daniel, and Eleanor Rice; m. by William Rice, Asst., Jan. 19, 1745.
2-70	" Benjamin, and Sarah Carder; m. by John Warner Jr., Justice, Aug. 14, 1760,
2-76	" John, of Thomas, of Cranston, and Elizabeth Bugbee, widow, of Warwick; m. by Adam Comstock, Justice, Aug. 6, 1778.
4-23	" William H., of Providence, son of William, dec., and Mercy Waterman Arnold, dau. of George B.; m. by Rev. Zalman Tobey, Jan. 1, 1850.
2-54	Hughes Capt. Thomas, of Capt. Joseph, dec., of Newport, and Welthian Greene, of Christopher, of Warwick; m. by Eld. John Gorton, Feb. 27, 1782.
3-114	" Phebe, and Jeremiah Greene, Feb. 19, 1809.
2-63	Hulet Avis, aud Benjamin Gorton, July 18, 1762.

3-178   Hull Louisa, and Norris Jackson, Dec. 31, 1846.
4-79   Hunter Nathan, and Mary Harrup; m. by Rev. Silas M. Rogers, June 18, 1864.
2-72   Hunt Bartholomew, of North Kingstown, and Phebe Clark, of Warwick; m. by Eld. John Gorton, Dec. 30, 1759.
2-73   " Zebadee, and Catherine Potter; m. by John Warner, Jr., Justice, Aug. 23, 1760.
2-74   " Joshua, and Phebe Arnold, of Simon; m. by Eld. Charles Holden, Apr. 11, 1762.
3-295   " Hannah, and Sion R. Sweet, Aug. 14, 1843.
3-445   " Avis, and Joseph B. Richardson, May 7, 1846.
3-363   " Laura, and William Bowman, Jan. 23, 1848.
4-46   " Samuel L., of Silas, and Lucinda Bennett, of Ephriam; m. by Rev. Jonathan Brayton, Nov. 23, 1848.
4-18   " Mary E., and George S. Wilcox, Jan. 1, 1850.
3-105   Hutchins Susan A., and Henry Walker, Oct. 28, 1845.
4-50   " Thankful G., and Seth Sweetzer, Nov. 26, 1851.

I

3-171   Ingalls Eliza Ann, and John B. Jacoy, Nov. 19, 1826.
2-230   Inman Marvel, and Isaac Baker, (mul.), Jan. 4, 1774.
1-26   Irish Sarah, and William Schreech, Dec. 4, 1712.

J

1-2,56 Jackson Martha, and Nathaniel Cole, Aug. 30, 1667.
3-381   " Almira, and John Babcock, Oct. 18, 1846.
3-178   " Norris, of East Greenwich, son, of Richard, and Louisa Hull, of Warwick, dau. of Abraham; m. by Rev. Jonathan Brayton, Dec. 31, 1846.
4-16   " Thomas, of Robert, of Warwick, and Sally Maria Cleveland, of Albro, of East Greenwich; m. by Rev. Daniel Slocum, Oct. 7, 1849.
3-171   Jacoy John B., of North Kingstown, son of Elisha, and Mary, and Eliza Ann Ingalls, of Caleb, and Anne; m. by Rev. Benjamin Hazelton, Nov. 19, 1826.

2-100	Jeffard Patience, and Theophilus Blanchard, Jan. 1 or 5, 1734-5.
1-66	Jefferson Benjamin, and Elizabeth Greene, of William, Aug. 9, 1737.
2-110	Jenckes Mary, and Nathaniel Manchester, Aug. 21, 1763.
2-195	" Mercy, and Stephen Greene, Dec. 1, 1791.
2-84	" John, and Mary Edmond; m. by Eld. Samuel Littlefield, May 15, 1796.
2-134	" Cynthia, and James Briggs, June 4, 1797.
4-68	" Hollis King, of Cumberland, and Molly Burr, of Rehoboth, Mass.; m. by Samuel Macomber, Justice Apr. — 1813.
3-176	" John Davis, of Providence, son of Capt. William C. dec., and Mary Rhodes Manchester, of Warwick, dau. of Job m. by Eld. Job Manchester, Sept. 14, 1843.
2-81	Jerauld James, of Dutee, and Mary Rice, of Henry; m. by Ephriam Westcott, Justice, Jan. 1, 1769.
2-154	" Freelove, and Caleb Rice, Jan. 9, 1772.
2-82	" Gorton, of Dr. Dutee, and Elizabeth Stafford, of Capt. John; m. by John Rice, Justice, Dec. 18, 1774.
2-111	" Sarah, and Samuel Millard, Jan. 29, 1776.
2-124	" Hannah, and Samuel Peirce, Jr., Dec. 22, 1776.
2-82	" Gorton, of Dr. Dutee, and Phebe Rice, of Henry; m. by Eld. John Gorton, Feb. 22, 1778.
2-125	" Martha, and Thomas Pearce, Oct. 10, 1779.
2-157	" Susannah, and Henry Rice, Sept. 22, 1782.
2-133	" Henrietta, and John Arnold, Oct. 5, 1788.
2-84	" Caleb, of Dr. Dutee, and Robe Arnold, of Caleb; m. by Eld. John Gorton, Jan. 19, 1790.
2-135	" Elizabeth, and William Havens, Oct. 18, 1795.
2-102	" James, of Warwick, and Eleanor Andrews, of Benoni, of East Greenwich; m. by Henry Remington, Justice, July 5, 1798.
2-130	" Henry, and Lucy Arnold, of Gideon, dec.; m. by Joseph Arnold, Justice, Sept. 11, 1798.
2-135	" John, of Dr. Gorton, and Nancy Westcott, of Caleb; m. by Joseph Arnold, Justice, Nov. 23, 1800.
2-214	" Freelove, and Stuteley Wood, Jan. 13, 1803.
3-170	" Stephen, and Elizabeth Arnold; m. by Eld. Samuel Littlefield, July 17, 1810.
4-41	Jessep Low, of Benjamin, aged 22 years, and Sarah A. Capron, adopted dau. of Russell Corey, aged 17 years; m. by Eld. William H. Richards, Apr. 26, 1851.

3-423 Jillson A. W., of Willimantic, Conn., son of Asa, and Hannah E. Cranston, of Warwick, dau. of Thomas; m. by Rev. Jonathan Brayton, Aug. 3, 1845.
1-2 John, alias Johnson, and Mary Anna, both of Pawtuxet; m. by Benjamin Smith, Asst., Dec. 15, 1665.
1-3 Johnson Hannah, and Richard Suske Smith, Sept. 3, 1669.
1-45 " John, of Elkanah, and Sarah Phillips, of John, of Jamestown; m. by John Rice, Justice, Oct. 13, 1721.
2-14 " Mary, and John Barton, Jr., July 21, 1734.
1-56 " John, and Elizabeth Moon, of Ebenezer, of N. Kingstown —— 1738.
2-43 " Phebe, and William Greene, Oct. 16, 1763.
2-65 " Elizabeth, and Peter Greene, Aug. 7, 1768.
2-79 " Martin, of John, and Violette Coggeshall, of Rebecca; m. by Eld. Charles Holden, Dec. 15, 1769.
2-80 " Elijah, Jr., of East Greenwich, son of Elijah, and Isabel Wightman, grand dau. of Margaret; m. by James Greene, Justice, May 7, 1775.
2,29 " Ruth, and Ezekiel Doud, July 12, 1780.
2-83 " Isaac, and Elizabeth Remington; m. by Eld. Abraham Lippitt, Oct. 28, 1784.
2-100 " Simeon, and Bethany Needham; m. by James Jerauld, Justice, Dec. 13, 1797.
4-99 " Palmer T., and Susan J. Remington, Mar. 7, 1838.
3-60 " Hannah W., and Cyrel C. Bowen, May 20, 1839.
3-172 " James M., of Warwick, son of Jonathan, and Fidelia Putney, of Cranston, dau. of Moses; m. by Eld. Job Manchester, June 10, 1839.
3-174 " Barrish, of James, and Roby Knight, of Charles; m. by Rev. Thomas Dowling, Feb. 10, 1840.
3-302 " Eliza, and Jeremiah Stafford, Mar. 25, 1841.
3-320 " Maria F., and Samuel H. Tefft, Nov. 22, 1841.
3-323 " Abbie R., and Stephen W. Thurston, May 2, 1842.
3-175 " Lawton, of Coventry, son of Joseph dec., and Freelove Manchester, of Gideon, dec., of Warwick; m. by Rev. Moses Fifield, Dec. 24, 1843.
3-62 " Nancy E., and William H. Bicknell, July 4, 1844.
3-177 " James C., of East Greenwich, and Dianna Ralph, of Coventry; m. by Rev. Stephen A. Thomas, Oct. 12, 1846.

3-355   Johnson Amelia, and Ira West, Nov. 1, 1846.
3-38   "   Catherine, and Wheaton Andrews, Jan. 25, 1847.
3-179   "   Joseph N. W., of Warwick, son of Isreal, of Coventry, and Susan A. Fenner, of Bowen, of Warwick; m. by Rev. Moses Fifield, May 3, 1847.
3-415   "   Harriet, and Stanton Hopkins, Oct. 17, 1847.
4-52   "   William J., of Cranston, aged 27 years, son of Benedict, and Belinda Chappell, of Warwick, aged 23 years, dau. of John, dec.; m. by Rev. William H. Richards, Mar. 2, 1852.
4-60   "   Albert R., of Warwick, aged 19 years, son of James, and Mary Ann Cranston, of William S., m. by Rev. Benjamin Phelan, Feb. 6, 1853.
1-13   Jones Jane, and Nathaniel Cahoone, Feb. 25, 1702.
2-136   "   Penelope, and Benajah Essex, Aug. 24, 1786.
3-168   "   Lislet, and Thomas, P. R. A. Knox, Jan 21, 1810.
3-384   "   Olive M., and Nathaniel Barney, Apr. 14, 1844.
3-173   Jordan George W., of Warwick, son of John, of Coventry, and Ruth Ann Hall, of Isaac, formerly of Westerly; m. by Rev. Moses Fifield, Nov. 28, 1839.
4-66   Joslin Eld. John, and Almy Budlong; m. by Eld. Job Manchester, May 18, 1830.
1-54   Joyce Desire, and John Arnold, Mar. 1, 1732-3.
2-83   "   John, of John, dec., and Elizabeth Remington, of Thomas; m. by Eld. John Gorton, May 29, 1785.
3-213   Justin Eliza, and Edward M. Luther, Aug. 8, 1847.

K

2-189   Keas Alice, and Jonathan Tarbox, Dec. 19, 1756.
2-85   "   Nathan, of William, dec., and Barbara Low, of Capt. John, dec.; m. by Eld. Charles Holden, Aug. 20, 1769.
3-75   Keech Rhoda, and Rev. David Curtis, June 21, 1810.
3-192   "   William R., and Rebecca P. Randall, of Abraham, dec., m. by Rev. Moses Fifield, June 7, 1840.
3-384   "   Elizabeth, and Johiel Baker, July 25, 1847.
1-101   Kee Sarah, and Richard Rice, Sept. 21, 1732.
1-1   "   Daniel, of Ebenezer and Abigail Howe, of Samuel; m. by Eld. Francis Bates, July 15, ———.
3-55   Kenyon Lucinda, and Daniel Babcock, Aug. 9, 1841.

3-196   Kenyon John H. Jr., and Ann Elizabeth Harrison; m. by Rev. Merrett Bates, Jan. 21, 1842.
3-189   " Caleb, of Charlestown, son of Caleb, dec., and Eleanor B. Austin, of Warwick, dau., of Nicholas, dec., of North Kingstown; m. by Rev. Moses Fifield, July 3, 1843.
3-191   " James, of Cranston, son of Samuel, and Mary Malcolm, of Samuel, of said town; m. by Rev. Zalman Tobey, July 27, 1847.
3-192   " Ambrose E., of Eunice E., and Maria R. Gardner, of Joseph; m. by Rev. Moses Fifield, Sept. 13, 1847.
3-379   " Isabella, and John Fullerton, Feb. 2, 1848.
4-82   Kettell James, of Coventry, son of Seneca, of Exeter, and Ann Elizabeth Arnold, of Warwick, dau. of Oliver; m. by Rev. Jonathan Brayton, Jan. 23, 1853.
1-48   Kettle Giffe, and Nathaniel Sweet, Sept. 7, 1721.
4-74   " Sarah G., and Samuel G. Brown, Mar. 5, 1849.
2-86   Kimball Amos, son of Dean, of Johnston, and Mary Battey, dau. of William, of Warwick; m. by Eld. Charles Holden, June 29, 1769.
2-106   " Robey, and Joseph Budlong, June 10, 1798.
3-217   " Polly, and Cyrus Manchester, Feb. 3, 1805.
1-59   Kindrick Rosannah, and Oliver Roades, Dec. 2, 1736.
3-313   Kingsley Elizabeth, and James M. Tourjee, June 10, 1839.
3-191   " James, of James, and Susan Baker, of Thomas; m. by Sidney S. Tillinghast, Justice, June 3, 1840.
3-193   " Noah, of James, of Warwick, and Sarah A. Worden, of Warwick, dau. of Isaac, dec., of Charlestown; m. by Rev. Moses Fifield, Oct. 6, 1840.
3-194   " Dyer, of James, dec., and Alice A. Sweet, of Warwick, dau. of William, dec., of West Greenwich; m. by Rev. Moses Fifield, Jan. 3, 1848.
4-6   " Hannah, and Asahel Bennett, Mar. 11, 1849.
2-119   King Joanna, and Thomas Price, Jan. 22, 1744-5.
2-195   " Freelove, and Joseph Ceaser, (col.), Aug. 3, 1789.
3-272   " Caroline, and William Rice, Aug. 28, 1825.
3-195   " William M., of Sweet, and Mary P. Howard, of John; m. by Rev. Moses Fifield, Sept. 5, 1842.
3-301   " Mrs. Harriet A., and Isaac W. Slack, Sept. 13, 1846.
3-212   " William M., of Sweet, and Waity S. Lawton, of Benjamin, dec.; m. by Rev. Moses Fifield, Dec. 7, 1846.
2-86   Kinnecome Andrew, and Sarah Harrison; m. by Rev. Samuel Littlefield, Dec. 27, 1795.

4-67	Kinnecome John, and Betsey Potter, of Cranston; m. by Rev. Henry Tatem, Dec. 13, 1833.
3-190	" William, of Andrew, and Louisa V. Westcott, of Jahleel; m. by Rev. Thomas Dowling, Mar. 1, 1840.
3-239	Kinne Charles E., of Warwick, son of Nathan, dec., of Kinsman, Ohio, and Sarah Ann Bowen, of Warwick, widow of William, of Pittsfield, Mass., and dau. of John Nye, of Exeter; m. by Rev. Moses Fifield, Feb. 11, 1840.
1-22	Kippey John, and Mereby Lee, of John; m. by Phillip Arnold, Asst., Sept. 26, 1739.
2-39	Knapp Hester, and William Francis, Sept. 6, 1761.
2-92	Knight Mary, and Amos Lockwood, Jr., Mar. 14, 1756.
2-116	" David, of Jonathan, of Scituate, and Mary Baker, of Elisha, of Warwick; m. by James Jerauld, Justice, Dec. 25, 1777.
3-220	" Mary, and Russell Miller, Oct. 9, 1825.
6-189	" Nathan, and Mrs. Mary Burlingame, of Coventry; m. by Rev. Thos. Dowling, Aug. 29, 1839.
3-174	" Roby, and Barrish Johnson, Feb. 10, 1840.
3-194	" Benoni, of Johnston, son of Earl, and Celia A. Austin, of Abel, of Warwick; m. by Rev. Junia S. Mowry, Jan. 12, 1842.
2-292	" Ann Maria, and Joseph Ney, Apr. 2, 1848.
4-25	" Albert H., of Scituate, son of William W., and Jane W. Taft, of Warwick, dau. of George; m. by Rev. Jonathan Brayton, Feb. 21, 1850.
4-25	" Zilpha S., and Josiah Taylor, Mar. 1, 1850.
1-2	Knowles Mary, and Moses Lippitt, Nov. 19, 1668.
3-324	" Mary, and William Townsend, May 24, 1842.
3-195	" Truman, and Celia Greene; m. by Rev. Thomas Hardman, Dec. 14, 1847.
3-33	Knowlton Cordelia W., and Israel Arnold, June 8, 1844.
3-168	Knox Thomas P. R. A., and Lislet Jones, Jan. 21, 1810.
3-168	" Elizabeth Mariah, of Thomas P. R. A. and Lislet; m. ——— Apr. 23, 1840.
3-168	" Jane G., and Benjamin M. Hazard, Sept. 16, 1841.

L

1-52	Ladd Sarah, and George Whitman, Aug. 13, 1738.
2-164	" Anne, and Alexander Havens, Jan. 31, 1790.

2-99 Ladd Caleb, of John, dec., and Catherine Greene, of Christopher; m. by James Jerauld, Justice, July 30, 1797.
2-99 " Caleb, of Capt. John, dec., and Nancy Burlingame, of Samuel, formerly of Cranston; m. by Alexander Havens, Justice, Feb. 10, 1803.
3-205 Lake Charles A., of Providence, son of Charles, dec., and Sarah Capron, of William, of Warwick; m. by Rev. Moses Fifield, Nov. 5, 1840.
3-360 " Levinia B., and Fenner B. Williams, Feb. 4, 1844.
3-447 Lane William R., of Cranston, son of Rowland, and Pauline Potter, of Scituate, dau. of Moses; m. by Rev. Jonathan Brayton, Feb. 10, 1846.
3-316 Langford Ruth, and John Tennant, Sept. 7, 1846.
2-201 Lanphere Elisha, of Warwick, son of Elisha, late of Westerly, and Lydia LeValley, of Robert; m. by Elder Job Manchester, Nov. 25, 1839.
2-20 Latham Susanna, and Joseph Clarke, Sept. 22, 1768.
3-214 Lothrop Richard S., of Griswold, Conn., son of Septimus, dec., and Jane F. Thompson, of Warwick, dau. of Festes L., [also 3-325]; m. by Rev. John P. Cleaveland, Sept. 26, 1848.
2-91 Lawrence John, of Providence, and Elizabeth Little, widow of Major Otis, of Warwick; m. by Elder Charles Holden, Dec. 22, 1761.
1-80 Lawton Margaret, and Samuel Sparks, Dec. 4, 1736.
3-211 " Isaac D., and Mary P. Reynolds; m. by Rev. Edward K. Fuller, June 16, 1845.
3-429 " James B., of Seth J. and Mary Ann LeValley, of Peter; m. by Rev. Jonathan Brayton, Feb. 9, 1846.
3-212 " Waitey S., and William M. King, Dec. 7, 1846.
4-81 " Ambrose, and Paulina R. Baker; m. by Rev. Jonathan Brayton, June 28, 1852.
4-73 Leach Amey, and Ezra N. Barnes, Mar. 17, 1836.
3-71 " Henrietta, and Joseph Card, May 18, 1841.
4-87 " Mrs. Robey A., and John T. Andrew, Mar. 29, 1854.
1-58 Lee Alce and Nathaniel Greene, Mar. 8, 1738-9.
1-22 " Mereby, and John Kippey, Sept. 26, 1739.
1-86 " John, Jr., of John, and Martha Carpenter, of Joseph; m. by William Greene, Justice, Mar. 13, 1740.
2-89 LeValley Peter, and Mary Haynes; m. by Elder John Gorton, May 11, 1755.
2-178 " Mary, and Joseph Straight, Jr., Dec. 16, 1773.

2-97	LeValley John, of John, and Bethia Greene, of Richard; m. by Eld. John Pendleton, Mar. 15, 1781.
2-98	" Peter, of Michael, of Warwick, and Katherine Parker, of Peter, of Coventry; m. by Isaac Johnson, Justice, July 11, 1782.
2-68	" Mercy, and Nathan Hathaway, Feb. 27, 1783.
2-143	" Margaret, and Henry Remington, Sept. 18, 1785.
2-98	" Benjamin, of Michael, dec., and Mary Greene, of Rebecca; m. by James Jerauld, Justice, Mar. 18, 1787.
2-38	" William, of Peter, and Phebe Dexter, of Benjamin; m. by Elder John Gorton, Sept. 25, 1788.
2-114	" Truth, and William Baker, Dec. 24, 1789.
2-36	" Stephen, and Anne Corpe; m. by James Jerauld, Justice, Apr. 8, 1798.
3-254	" Sarah, and Henry Parish, Aug. 31, 1810.
3-201	" Lydia, and Elisha Lanphere, Nov. 25, 1839.
4-231	" Mary A., and William B. Morrell, Nov, 2, 1840.
3-429	" Mary Ann, and James B. Lawton, Feb. 9, 1846.
2-19	Lewis Sophia, and Samuel W. Albro, Oct. 27, 1840.
1-3	Lippitt Rebecca, and Joseph Hazard, Feb. 2, 1664.
1-1	" John, Jr., and Ann Grove; m. by Randall Rice, Asst., Feb. 9, 1664.
1-2	" Moses, and Mary Knowles; m. by Benjamin Smith, Asst., Nov. 19, 1668.
1-4	" Ann, and Edward Searle, Jr., Feb. 13, 1670.
1-33	" Moses, and Anne Phillis Whipple, of Joseph and Alice, of Providence, Nov. 20, 1707.
1-83	" Moses, Jr., and Wait Rhodes, of John, Apr. 26, 1732.
1-88	" Christopher, of Moses, and Catherine Holden, of Anthony; m. by William Greene, Justice, Jan. 2, 1736.
1-8, 2-5	" Anne, and Abraham Francis, June 18, 1736.
1-57	" Jeremiah, of Moses, and Wealthian Greene, of Richard, dec., Sept. 12, 1736.
2-89	" Joseph, of Warwick, and Lucy Brown, of Capt. Thomas, of Rehoboth, Mass.; m. by Rev. William Greenwood, Feb. 19, 1746.
2-60	" Ann, and Christopher Greene, Jan. 6, 1757.
2-10	" Wait, and David Arnold, Aug. 29, 1765.
2-66	" Mary, and Caleb Greene, Jan. 21, 1768.
2-93	" Moses, of Moses, dec., of Warwick, and Tabitha Greene, of Elisha, of East Greenwich [also 2-23]; m. by Eld. Charles Holden, Dec. 25, 1768.

2-94	Lippitt Abraham, of Moses, dec., and Sarah Arnold, of Capt. Josiah; m. by Eld. Charles Holden, Apr. 8, 1770.
2-230	" Wealthian, and William Greene, Jan. 13, 1774.
2-95	" Moses, of Christopher, late of Cranston, dec., and Anstress Holden, of Charles, Jr., of Warwick; m. by Eld. Charles Holden, Jan. 8, 1775.
2-96	" John, and Amey Warner; m. by J. Graves, Justice, May 19, 1776.
2-97	" Ceaser (nig.), and Sarah Daly (Ind.); m. by Eld. Charles Holden, Aug. 26, 1779.
2-96	" Charles, of Christopher, of Cranston, and Penelope Low, of Col. John; m. by Eld. John Gorton, Jan. 12, 1783.
2-92	" Betsey, and Moses Lippitt, Nov. 7, 1785.
2-92	" Moses, of Jeremiah, and Betsey Lippitt, of Joseph; Nov. 7, 1785.
3-197	" William, and Patience East (col.); m. by Eld. Abraham Lippitt, about ———, 1786.
2-161	" Betsey, and Amos Budlong (col.), Apr. 6, 1800.
3-289	" Ann, and James Spywood, Aug. 30, 1804.
3-43	" Isbie, and Stephen Budlong, July 28, 1805.
3-340	" Sarah, and William Weekes, Sept. 3, 1809.
3-48	" Tabitha, and James Brown, Jr., Oct. 26, 1815.
3-280	" Anstress G., and Esau Rhodes, July 11, 1839.
2-232	Littlefield Catherine, and Nathaniel Greene, July 20, 1774.
2-226	" Mary, and Pearce Budlong, Nov. 18, 1792.
3-114	" Sarah, and Jeremiah Greene, June 8, 1817.
3-205	" Lorenzo D., of John, and Harriet B. Reaves, of Olney, dec.; m. by Rev. Moses Fifield, Mar. 7, 1842.
3-208	" Daniel G., of John, and Maria B. Collins, of Alpheus; m. by Rev. Moses Fifield, Nov. 28, 1842.
2-91	Little Elizabeth, and John Lawrence, Dec. 22, 1761.
3-204	Locke Thomas W., of Warwick, son of Edward, dec., of South Kingstown, and Hannah Wood, of Warwick, dau. of Peleg, of Coventry; m. by Rev. Moses Fifield, July 18, 1841.
3-207	" James W., of Warwick, son of Charles, of Richmond, and Sarah Ann Howard, of John, of Warwick; m. by Rev. Moses Fifield, Oct. 3, 1842.
1-56	Lockwood Deborah, and Nathaniel Cole, Nov. 29, 1725.
1-53	" Amos, and Sarah Utter; m. by John Warner, Justice, Dec. 23, 1725.
3-58	" Sarah, and Abel Potter, June 16, 1728,

1-43	Lockwood	Adam, of Abraham, of Warwick, and Sarah Straight, of Henry, of East Greenwich, Dec. 24, 1734.
2-5	"	Sarah, and Sion Arnold, Jan. 23, 1752.
2-92	"	Amos, Jr., and Mary Knight; m. by John Warner, Jr., Justice, Mar. 14, 1756.
2-70	"	Ellis, and John Healey, July 25, 1756.
2-21	"	Sarah, and Nathaniel Cole, Apr. 28, 1757.
2-57	"	Mercy, and Stephen Greene, Sept. 20, 1761.
2-189	"	Phebe, and George Thomas, Sept. 25, 1763.
2-219	"	Ruth, and John Battey, Mar. 10, 1765.
2-224	"	Wait, and William Greene, Mar. 8, 1772.
2-94	"	Benjamin, of Cranston, son of Capt. Amos, dec., and Phebe Waterman, of Capt. Resolved, dec.; m. by Eld. Charles Holden, April 5, 1772.
2-233	"	Capt. Abraham, of Capt. Amos, dec., and Patience Greene, of Capt. James; m. by Eld. Charles Holden, Dec. 24, 1775.
2-93	"	Nathaniel, and Lydia Webb; m. by Eld. Samuel Littlefield, July 7, 1799.
2-98	"	Thomas, and Sarah Barton; m. by Eld. Samuel Littlefield, Dec. 14, 1800.
2-93	"	Abraham, of Adam, and Elizabeth Webb, of William, [also 2-186]; m. by James Jerauld, Justice, Feb. 14, 1802.
2-172	"	Millesent, and Wilbur Carpenter, June 28, 1802.
3-351	"	Hannah, and William Webb, Sept. 20, 1812.
4-96	"	Lucy, and Thomas Lockwood, July 29, 1821.
4-96	"	Thomas, and Lucy Lockwood; m. by Eld. Samuel Littlefield, July 29, 1821.
3-199	"	Robinson, and Amey Young; m. by Eld. Job Manchester, Sept. 7, 1829.
3-126	"	Mary Ann, and Thomas H. Greene, Jan. 10, 1830.
3-202	"	Nathan W., of Amos, dec., and Amey Perkins, of Jacob; m. by Eld. Job Manchester, Sept. 1, 1840.
4-38	"	Abbie, and Albert Lockwood, Sept. 22, 1842.
4-38	"	Albert, and Abbie Lockwood; m. by Rev. Jonathan E. Forbush, Sept. 22, 1842.
4-38	"	Albert, and Eliza Lockwood; m. by Rev. Jonathan E. Forbush, Sept. 22, 1842.
4-38	"	Eliza, and Albert Lockwood, Sept. 22, 1842.
4-75	"	Mary M., and Albert Phillips, Aug. 16, 1843.
3-367	"	Martha, and William W. Chace, May 8, 1844.

3-358 Lockwood Sarah B., and William G. Weaver, Dec. 27, 1847.
4-59 " Abraham, of Warwick, and Sarah Ann Carr, of Mass.; m. by Eld. William Stovyer, Apr. 21, 1850.
1-4 Lorton Phebe, and Richard Codner, May 23, 1671.
3-206 Lovell Rowland G., of Cranston, son of Nathan, of Scituate, and Lucinda Whipple, of Stephen B., of Warwick; m. by Rev. Moses Fifield, June 2, 1842.
3-14 Loveland Thankful H., and Irus Albro, Jr., Feb. 22, 1835.
3-200 Love Henry A., of Coventry, son of William, and Catherine E. Newell, of Cumberland, dau. of Ziba, resident of Providence; m. by Rev. Nicholas G. Potter, Sept. 22, 1839.
4-24 " Jane, and John Congdon, May 2, 1847.
3-109 " Ann C., and Albert B. Waterman, June 13, 1847.
3-215 " Henry, of Coventry, son of Leonard, and Susan C. Babcock, of William, dec.; m. by Rev. Moses Fifield, Nov. 13, 1848.
1-6 Low John, of Anthony and Frances, and Mary Roades, of Zachary; m. by Job Almy, Justice, Mar. 3, 1674-5.
1-22 " John, of Anthony, and Mary Arnold, of Israel, Oct. 8, 1702.
1-92 " Ann, and Joseph Carder, July 25, 1724.
1-57 " Stephen, of Anthony, and Cloe Gorton, of Samuel; m. by John Wickes, Asst., Feb. 18, 1725-6.
1-21,57 " Stephen, of Anthony, and Alce Gorton, of Samuel, (published) Feb. 18, 1725, m. same day.
2-120 " Elizabeth, and John Parker, Nov. 6, 1744.
2-120 " Mary, and Joseph Potter, Jan. 1, 1747.
2-90 " Anthony, of Capt. John, and Phebe Greene, of Phillip; m. by Eld. John Gorton, Jan. 1, 1754.
2-90 " John, and Sarah Wickes; m. by Eld. John Gorton, Oct. 26, 1755.
2-38 " Phillippa, and Noel Freeborn, Apr. 22, 1756.
2-208 " Rebecca, and James Warner, Jan. 6, 1757.
2-169 " Sarah, and Benjamin Spencer, Jan. 20, 1757.
2-213 " Hannah, and William Wickes, Aug. 7, 1760.
2-25 " Alice, and Jonathan Dexter, Dec. 31, 1761.
2-63 " Anne, and Benjamin Greene, Sept. 30, 1764.
2-85 " Barbara, and Nathan Rice, Aug. 20, 1769.
2-200 " John, of John, Jr., dec., and Barbara Wells, of Col. John; m. by Eld. Charles Holden, Sept. 7, 1775.
2-96 " Penelope, and Charles Lippitt, Jan. 12, 1783.
2-251 " Barbara, and Thomas Greene, Jr., Aug. 12, 1790.

2-233 Low Rosannah, and Charles Wells, Mar. 22, 1795.
2-104 " Capt. Samuel, of Anthony, and Elizabeth Holden, of Capt. Randall, Apr. 2, 1797.
2-34 " Anne, and Christopher Greene, Apr. 24, 1803.
2-22 " Catherine, and John Cole, Jr., Aug. 14, 1804.
3-126 " Sally Ann, and Rufus Greene, Dec. 23, 1841.
3-213 Luther Edward M., of Warwick, son of Mason, and Eliza Justin, of Joseph, of Cranston; m. by Rev. Zalman Tobey, Aug. 8, 1847.
4-17 " Olney, of Sheldon and Mary, and Abbie B. Ashton, of Samuel B. and Freelove; m. by Rev. Benjamin Phelan, Oct. 7, 1849.
3-210 Lynch Thomas, of Cambridge, Mass., son of Patrick, and Lucy A. Greene, of Jeremiah, of Warwick; m. by Rev. Jonathan Brayton, Apr. 4, 1843.

M

3-323 Maguire Sarah Jane, and Francis S. Turner, June 1, 1848.
3-222 Mahoney Timothy, and Alice Rice, of Matthew; m. by Albro Anthony, Justice, Nov. 18, 1821.
3-219 " Timothy, of Warwick, son of Timothy, and Ruth Roberts, dau. of James Lindsley; m. by Rev. Junia S. Mowry, Nov. 4, 1841.
3-191 Malcolm Mary, and James Kenyon, July 27, 1847.
2-251 Malone Michael, of Ireland, and Elizabeth Rice, of Henry; m. by James Jerauld, Justice, Nov. 11, 1787.
2-110 Manchester Nathaniel, of Scituate, and Mary Jenckes, of Warwick; m. by Ebenezer Slocum, Justice, Aug. 21, 1763.
2-159 " Phebe, and Benjamin Remington, Apr. 18, 1779.
3-217 " Cyrus, of Gideon, and Polly Kimball, of Amos; m. by Caleb Westcott, Justice, Feb. 3, 1805.
3-230 " Catherine L., and William B. Merrill, Oct. 9, 1825.
4-82 " Ann L. and John L. Dyer, May 21, 1826.
3-261 " Lydia S., and Samuel D. Peirce, Feb. 6, 1831.
3-85 " Mary, and Cary C. Dyer, Apr. 29, 1832.
3-218 " Nancy, and Junia S. Mowry, Dec. 2, 1841.
3-176 " Mary R., and John D. Jenckes, Sept. 14, 1843.
3-175 " Freelove, and Lawton Johnson, Dec. 24, 1843.
3-231 Marble Thomas, of William, dec., and Ruth B. Tibbetts; m. by Rev. Moses Fifield, Aug. 11, 1842.

2-108   Mariner John, of Newport, and Bathsheba Hix, of Joseph, of Warwick; m. by Eld. Charles Holden, Dec. 4, 1757.
2-9   Marks Mary, and Anthony Aylesworth, Nov. 26, 1762.
2-32   Martindil Elizabeth, and Wanton Arnold, Mar. 28, 1799.
2-68   Martin Hannah, and Charles Holden, Jan. 23, 1757.
2-107   " Michael, of Warwick, and Temperance Colvin, of Coventry; m. by James Jerauld, Justice, Oct. 1, 1785.
3-236   " John W., of Otis, and Latilda K. Baker, of Burton; m. by Rev. Moses Fifield, Dec. 22, 1845.
3-322   " Esther, and Samuel W. Thurston, Nov. 26, 1846.
1-3   Mary Anna, and John, alias Johnson, Dec. 15, 1665.
1-45   Masson Freelove, and Samuel Gorton, Jr., June 1, 1715.
2-108   Mason James, of Warren, Esq., and Hannah Holden, widow; m. by Eld. John Hammett, Jan. 11, 1750.
2-110   " Pelatiah, of Cumberland, and Judah Tibbetts, widow of William, of Warwick; m. by Eld. Charles Holden, Sept. 4, 1766.
3-13   " Ann M., and Charles E. Andrews, Dec. 24, 1846.
1-96   Mathewson Mercy, and William Gorton, Jan. 7, 1731.
2-107   " Henry, of Francis, of Warwick, and Comfort Pearce, of George, dec., of Bristol; m. by Samuel Greene, Justice, Nov. 21, 1745.
2-109   " Moses, and Patience Cahoon; m. by Ebenezer Slocum, Justice, Jan. 26, 1758.
3-23   " Comfort, and Benjamin Coggeshall, June 1, 1758.
2-108   " Joseph, of John, dec., of Warwick, and Catherine Hathaway, of Coventry; m. by Ebenezer Slocum, Justice, Feb. 5, 1761.
2-195   " Hannah, and David Vaughn, Jr., Jan. 24, 1762.
2-228   " Thomas, of John, and Hester Arnold, of Elisha; m. by Thomas Rice, Justice, Jan. 19, 1772.
2-110   " Nicholas, of Henry, dec., and Abigail Cooke, of Capt. Silas; m. by Eld. Charles Holden, May 20, 1773.
3-228   " George G., of Providence, son of Russell, of Coventry, and Betsey Ann Capron, of Warwick, dau. of William, formerly of East Greenwich; m. by Rev. Moses Fifield, Mar. 2, 1840.
3-389   " Eliza, and William Baker, Dec. 8, 1845.
1-103   Matteson John, and Mary Arnold; m. by Stutely Stafford, Justice, July 24, 1729.
2-96   " Mercy, and William Gorton, Jan. 7, 1731.

1-69	Matteson Francis, of Francis, and Dinah Tibbetts, of Rebeckah; m. by Phillip Arnold, Justice, July 10, 1740.
1-104	" Henry, and Rachel Greene, of John, (of James), Dec. 13, 1740.
2-3	" Deborah and John Arnold, Nov. 4, 1758.
2-111	" Daniel, of John, dec., and Dorcas Chapman, of Stephen; by Eld. Charles Holden, Mar 1, 1770.
2-108	" Edmund, of Ebenezer, dec., of West Greenwich, and Susanna Matteson, of Warwick; m. by Adam Comstock, Justice, Apr. 30, 1775.
2-108	" Susanna, and Edmund Matteson, Apr. 30, 1775.
2-137	" Mary, and Corps Essex, July 27, 1783.
2-257	" George, of Thomas, of Coventry, and Susannah Snell, of Daniel, of Warwick; m. by Eld. Thomas Manchester, Sept. 11, 1794.
2-165	" Dorcas, and Frederic Arnold, Apr. 26, 1801.
3-283	" Margeret, and Sheffield Reynolds, Jan. 6, 1842.
3-225	" Jacob, of Phillip, of West Greenwich, and Betsey Webb, of Jeremiah, of Warwick; m. by Eld. Thomas Tillinghast, Dec. 4, 1843.
3-224	" Stukely, of Phillip, of West Greenwich, and Phebe Ann Webb, of Jeremiah; m. by Rev. Thomas Tillinghast, Dec. 4, 1843.
4-67	" William, and Lucy A. Hubbard, both of Cumberland; m. by Rev. R. Arvine, Nov. 18, 1846.
3-403	" Mary R., and Randall R. H. Harrington, Sept. 12, 1847.
3-229	Mawney Benjamin G., son of John G., of Warwick, and Dorcas Godfrey, of Warwick, dau. of Jonathan, dec., of East Greenwich; m. by Rev. Moses Fifield, Dec. 3, 1840.
2-112	Maxwell Adam, and Ann Proud, of John, of Newport; m. by Eld. Charles Holden, Mar 28, 1771.
1-91	McGregor Alexander, and Susannah Stafford of Major Joseph; m. by John Rice, Justice, Jan. 4, 1738-9.
4-18	McKensie Hector, of Providence, son of Alexander, and Mary E. Taylor, of John, dec.; m. by Rev. Benjamin Phelan, Nov. 4, 1849.
4-95	McMahon Peter, and Mary Monaghan; m. by Rev. J. A. Couch, Oct. 16, 1865.
1-29	Medberry Sarah, and William Greene, Feb. 14, 1712-3.
1-37	Medbury Nathaniel, and Dorothy Brown, both of Barrington; m. by Richard Waterman, Justice, Mar. 27, 1718.
2-157	Menden Rebecca, and Randall Rice, Oct. 6, 1773.

2-228	Merrill Hannah, and Aaron Bowen, Aug. 9, 1801.
3-230	" William B., and Catherine L. Manchester; m. by Rev. Jonathan Wilson, Oct. 9, 1825.
3-84	" Sally C., and Daniel Dyer, Dec. 27, 1829.
3-226	" Sylvester K., of William, and Almy R. Tillinghast, dau. of widow Sally, formerly of East Greenwich; m. by Rev. Moses Fifield, July 4, 1830.
3-284	" Desire G., and John R. Rice, Nov, 14, 1842.
3-235	" William B., son of William G., and Paulina G. Albro, of John, dec.; m. by Rev. Moses Fifield, Nov. 15, 1847. [See also Morrell.]
2-109	Millard Nathaniel, and Barbara Bowen, widow; m. by Eld. Charles Holden, July 1, 1758.
2-112	" Esquire, of Nathaniel, dec., of Warwick, and Patience Pearce, of Jonathan, of Providence; m. by Eld. Charles Holden, Oct. 20, 1771.
2-179	" Nathan, of Nathan, and Ann Rice, of Major Henry; m. by Eld. Charles Holden, June 23, 1774.
2-111	" Samuel, of Nathaniel, dec., and Sarah Jerauld, of Dr. Dutee; m. by Eld. John Gorton, Jan. 29, 1776.
2-237	" Elizabeth, and Ichabod Carey, Aug. 27, 1779.
2-249	" John, Jr., of Nathaniel, of Warwick, and Eunice Pearce, of Jonathan, of Portsmouth; m. by William Anthony, Jr., Justice, Dec. 23, 1785.
2-197	" Nathaniel, of Esquire, and Betsey Greene, of Christopher; m. by Eld. David Corpe, June 2, 1793.
2-106	" Martin, of Samuel, and Rebecca Olin, of Peleg; m. by James Jerauld, Justice, Jan. 25, 1798.
2-135	" Rice, of Nathan, Jr., and Abigail Hatch, of Eleazer, dec.; m. by James Jerauld, Justice, Sept. 30, 1798.
2-134	" Samuel, and Susannah Rice; m. by Eld. Thomas Manchester, Nov. 25, 1798.
2-116	" Ruth, and ——Simmons, Jan. 25, 1801.
2-13	" Elizabeth, and Christopher Burke, Aug. 14, 1803.
3-223	" Gulielmus B., of Samuel, and Eliza A. Tillinghast, of Eld. Thomas, of East Greenwich; m. by Eld. Thomas Manchester, Aug. 23, 1818.
3-67	" Mary E., and Ethan Ray Clarke, Oct. 29, 1840.
3-344	" Isabella A., and Peleg W. Westcott, Sept. 7, 1841.
4-17,102	" Sarah A., and William Phillips, Dec. 13, 1849.
2-219	Miller Barbara, and Job Carpenter, Dec. 27, 1764.
2-15	" Lydia, and Joseph Briggs, Nov. 26, 1767.

2-111	Miller Spicer, of Nathaniel, and Elizabeth Fairbanks, of Jonathan; m. by Eld. John Gorton, Jan. 30, 1783.	
2-241	" Susannah, and Jonathan Andrews, Oct. 31, 1784.	
3-219	" John, and Phebe Stone, Nov. 28, 1806.	
3-220	" Russell, of Samuel, and Sophia Brayton, of Daniel, dec.; m. by Eld. Thomas Manchester, Nov. 11, 1813.	
3-220	" Russell, of Warwick, and Mary Knight, of Coventry; m. by Rev. Jonathan Wilson, Oct. 9, 1825.	
3-226	" William, and Eliza Shreives, both of Providence; m. by Rev. David Pickering, June 7, 1829.	
3-226	" Rice A., of Warwick, son of Rice, and Sarah L. Randall, of Cranston, dau. of Benjamin; m. by Rev. Zalman Tobey, Sept. 6, 1846.	
4-36	" Mrs. Eliza, and Henry Potter, Jan. 30, 1851.	
2-110	Mitchell James Reynolds, of James, of North Kingstown, and Sibbel Wightman, of John, of Cranston; m. by Caleb Jerauld, Justice, Mar. 9, 1804.	
3-218	" John, and Robe Tibbetts; m. by C. Brayton, Justice, Mar. 12, 1809.	
3-270	" Sarah, and John S. Reynolds, Apr. 22, 1812.	
3-81	Mitchell Philena, and Dr. Joseph Dailey, Apr. 27, 1820.	
3-381	" Maria E., and Stephen A. Briggs, Feb. 19, 1844.	
3-233	" Warren R., of Samuel, and Perlonia G. Andrews, of Whipple; m. by Rev. Jonathan Brayton, Sept. 23, 1844.	
3-235	" Augustus S., of Samuel, and Nancy Briggs, of Robert; m. by Rev. Moses Fifield, Oct. 27, 1845.	
4-58	" Mary L., and Holden B. Remington, Oct. 18, 1852.	
4-95	Monaghan Mary, and Peter McMahon, Oct. 16, 1865.	
3-222	Money John W. of Allen, and Hannah H. Seager, of David; m. by Rev. Jonathan Brayton, Nov. 7, 1842.	
3-234	" George B., of Warwick, son of Allen, of Providence, and Mary Jane Freeman, of Warwick, dau. of Henry, of East Greeewich; m. by Rev. Moses Fifield, Aug. 10, 1846.	
1-56	Moon Elizabeth, and John Johnson, ———, 1738.	
2-178	" Almy, and Joseph Cole, Dec. 17, 1773.	
2-85	Moot Sarah, and Thomas Cook, Dec. 12, 1763.	
2-109	Morey Earle, of Exeter, son of John, of North Kingstown, and Mary Gorton, of William, Jr., of Warwick; m. by Eld. John Gorton, Sept. 1, 1782.	
2-70	" Susan M., and Rowland G. Healey, Sept. 3, 1840.	

2-198 Morrell Elizabeth, and Thomas Bateman, Jan. 1, 1795.
4-231 " William B., of William G., of Warwick, and Mary A. LeValley, of Mary; m. by Rev. C. S. Macreading, Nov. 2, 1840.
[See also Merrill.]
2-97 Morris William, of East Greenwich, and Deborah Greene, of Amos, of Warwick; m. by James Jerauld, Justice, July 5, 1798.
2-131 Elizabeth, and Samuel Bennett, Aug. 30, 1798.
3-225 Morse Charles, Jr., of Charles, of Coventry, and Lydia W. Arnold, of Thomas, dec., of Warwick; m. by Eld. Thomas Manchester, Dec. 28, 1826.
3-167 " Eliza, and Stephen Harris, Jr., Oct. 29, 1840.
1-58 Mott Mary, and Nathaniel Greene, Apr. 18, 1739.
4-47 " Oliver A., aged 23 years, son of Oliver C., and Ann Pilkington, aged 19 years, dau. of John; m. by Rev. Benjamin Phelan, Oct. 21, 1851.
3-388 Manuel Margaret, and Hugh Bigby, Sept. 26, 1845.
3-294 Mowry Levinia B., and Thomas M. Southwick, Feb 11, 1839.
3-218 " Junia S., son of Reuben, of Smithfield, and Nancy Manchester, of John, dec., of Tiverton; m. by Rev. Martin Cheney, Dec. 2, 1841.
3-122 " George, of Ira, and Eliza Ann Spencer, of Thomas; m. by Rev. Junia S. Mowry, Mar. 6, 1842.
3-234 " Jenckes, of Warwick, son of Joseph, of Smithfield, and Abby Greene, of Richard; m. by Rev. Jonathan E. Forbush, Sept. 26, 1844.
1-3 Mudge Moses, and Elizabeth Weeden; m. by Benjamin Smith, Asst., Dec. 17, 1665.
2-195 Mumford Pompey, and Sabina Allen, (col.), both of East Greenwich; m. by Eld. John Gorton, Aug. 19, 1789.
3-232 Myric Joseph, Jr., son of Joseph, and Sally Walker, of Stephen; m. by Rev. Jonathan Brayton, Dec. 12, 1843.

N

2-242 Nason Joseph, Jr., of Newport, son of Joseph, and Mary Wilcox, of Warwick, dau. of Ishmael, dec.; m. by Rev. Moses Fifield, Mar. 3, 1842.
3-354 " Mary A., and Edwin S. Walker, Nov. 26, 1846.
2-100 Needham Bethany, and Simon Johnson, Dec. 13, 1797.

3-200 Newell Catherine E., and Henry A. Love, Sept. 22, 1839.
2-148 Newfield Clintha, and Ishmael Rhodes, Nov. 20, 1791.
3-243 Newman Daniel E., of Noah, and Abbie H. Crandall, of Rowland; m. by Rev. Moses Fifield, Feb. 18, 1844.
1-164 " Lydia A., and Thomas Hawkins, Nov. 14, 1844.
3-297 " Eliza B., and Andrew D. Shreaves, Mar. 13, 1845.
3-164 Ney Mercy, and Henry Harris, Feb. 6, 1840.
2-242 " Joseph, of Isaac, and Ann Maria Knight, of Sanford, both of Cranston; m. by Rev. Moses Fifield, Apr. 2, 1848.
3-230 Nickerson David, of Warwick, son of Valentine, dec., of Yarmouth, Mass., and Eliza R. Bennett, of Warwick, dau. of John, dec.; m. by Rev. Moses Fifield, Nov. 24, 1836.
2-238 Nicholas Mary, and Capt. Moses Budlong, October 19, 1780.
3-237 " Christopher, of Cranston, and Phebe Ann Rice, of Warwick, dau. of Josephus; m. by C. Brayton, Justice, Oct. 25, 1812.
3-239 " James H., of Cranston, and Hannah P. Cottrell, of South Kingstown; m. by Elder Thomas Tillinghast, July 6, 1846.
1-50 Nichols Elizabeth, and Joseph Clark, Nov. 6, 1718.
1-64 " Susannah, and Samuel Cahoon, Feb. 9, 1720-1.
1-58 " William, of John, of Warwick, and Mary Hill, of Henry, of West Greenwich; m. by William Greene, Justice, June 23, 1728.
1-81 " Benjamin, of John, and Hannah Tibbetts; m. by William Greene, Justice, Feb. 4, 1730-1.
1-73 " John, Jr., and Ann Greene, of John; m. by John Spencer, Justice, Mar. 22, 1733.
2-20 " Margaret, and Samuel Cahoon, Jan. 13, 1750.
2-113 " Benjamin, and Almy Bosworth; m. by Joseph Edmonds, Asst., May 15, 1757.
2-113 " Caleb, of James, of East Greenwich, and Ann Reed, of Warwick; m. by Ebenezer Slocum, Justice, May 29, 1758.
2-116 " Jonathan, of Benjamin, and Mary Wight, of Phillip; m. by Eld. John Gorton, June 27, 1790.
4-95 " William, of Benjamin, and Sarah Cranston, of Thomas; m. by Rev. Nathaniel W. Warner, Oct. 5, 1837.
" Mary, and John Raymond, Nov. 16, 1837.

3-241 Nichols William K., of Warwick, son of William, of Cranston, and Elizabeth W. Greene, of Thomas F., of Warwick; m. by Rev. Moses Fifield, Sept. 30, 1841.
3-244 " William, of Warwick, son of John P., of North Kingstown, and Susan Tripp, of Warwick, dau. of David; m. by Rev. Moses Fifield. July 1, 1844.
3-240 " Charles Morrison, of Providence, of Jonathan Bassett, and Sarah Maria Greene, of Warwick, dau. of Thomas R.; m. by Rev. Zalman Tobey, Apr. 19. 1847.
4-35 " Susan F., and William H. Bowman, Jan. 26, 1851.
4-59 " Sally G., and David A. Spencer, Nov. 25, 1852.
2-115 Niles Jonathan, of Samuel, of West Greenwich, and Avice Rice, of Henry, of Warwick; m. by Eld. John Gorton, Feb. 23, 1764.
2-177 " Martha, and Lawton Spencer, Aug. 7, 1791.
3-245 " Charles H., of James, and Ruth A. Northup, of John; m. by Rev. Jonathan Brayton, Nov. 28, 1844.
3-238 " William B., of West Greenwich, and Alsada G. Barber, of Coventry; m. by Rev. Stephen A. Thomas, Dec. 14, 1846
3-240 Northup Stephen S., son of Lebbens, of North Kingstown, and Experience A. Reynolds, dau. of Ezekiel, of Exeter; m. by Rev. Moses Fifield, Sept. 20, 1841.
3-367 " Mary, and Alferene Cady, May 29, 1843.
3-245 " Ruth A., and Charles H. Niles, Nov. 28, 1844.
3-241 " Charles T., of William, and Theresa H. A. Wood, of John J.; m. by Rev. George A. Willard, Nov. 8, 1847.
4-16 " Stephen H. of Stephen N. dec., and Sally Vickery, of George C., dec.; m. by Rev. Moses Fifield, Nov. 15, 1849.
3-239 Noyes Charles C., of Warwick, son of John, and Abby Babcock, of Warwick, dau. of William, dec., of South Kingstown; m. by Rev. Moses Fifield, Feb. 29, 1844.

O

4-15 Odell Abigail R., and George J. Taft, Aug. 8, 1849.
2-190 Olin Mary, and Benjamin Tiffany, Nov. 6, 1768.
2-117 " Peleg, of Warwick, son of Henry, of West Greenwich, and Phebe Gorton, of Eld. John, of Warwick; m. by Thomas Casey, Justice, Feb. 5, 1769.

2-118 Olin David, and Hannah Riley; m. by James Jerauld, Justice, Oct. 28, 1793.
2-106 " Rebecca, and Martin Millard, Jan. 25, 1798.
2-133 " Polly, and Capt. John Boutwell, Aug. 23, 1798.
4-63 Otis Austin W., of New York, aged 46 years, and Mary H. Greene, of Warwick, aged 24 years, dau. of Thomas and Emeline; m. by George Peirce, Justice, Mar. 6, 1853.

P

3-262 Padelford Abraham H., and Ann Maria Pulsifer, of Providence; m. by Rev. Edward K. Fuller, July 3, 1845.
1-30 Paine Elizabeth, and John Carder, Dec. 25, 1701.
2-13 Palmer Penelope, and Andrew Barton, Oct. 2, 1763.
3-262 " Samuel, of Bristol, son of Hezekiah, of Woodstock, Conn., and Eleanor Howard, of William, of Smithfield; m. by Rev. Moses Fifield, June 15, 1834.
3-330 " Martha, and John B. Whitaker, Mar. 8, 1841.
3-307 " Betsey Ann, and Stephen P. Salsbury, July 30, 1843.
4-10 " Mary, and John Heap, June 10, 1849.
4-32 " Margaret Jane, and William Burton, Oct. 27, 1850.
2-123 Parce Mial, of Johnston, and Elizabeth Potter, of Samuel, of Cranston; m. by Andrew Harris, Justice, Nov. 2, 1788.
3-254 Parish Henry, of Richmond, and Sarah LeValley, of Warwick; m. by Rev. Samuel Littlefield, Aug. 31, 1810.
2-120 Parker John, and Elizabeth Low, of Lieut. Stephen; m. by Eld. Manassah Martin, Nov. 6, 1744.
2-3 " Elizabeth, and Owen Arnold, Oct. 21, 1751.
2-98 " Katherine, and Peter LeValley, July 11, 1782.
4-99 " Isabella, and James Remington, Mar. 15, 1811.
3-266 " William S., of Warwick, son of John, dec., and Hannah Pilkinton, of Warwick, dau. of George, of Pawtucket, Mass.; m. by Rev. Moses Fifield Dec. 3, 1842.
3-28 " Sarah M., and John M. Arnold, July 10, 1844.
3-263 " Paxhall A. Jr., U. S. N., son of Com. Paxhall, and Mary Eliza Greene, of John; m. by Rev. Moses Fifield, Jan. 19, 1846.
3-377 " Esther E., and Stephen E. Card, June 9, 1847.
4-85 " Mary C., and Samuel Himes, May 25, 1851.

1-24 Pearce Benjamin, and Mary Budlong, of John; m. by John Warner, Justice, Jan. 8, 1729-0.
2-107 " Comfort, and Henry Mathewson, Nov. 21, 1745.
2-54 " Mary, and Nathan Gorton, June 29, 1758.
2-146 " Freelove, and William Ross, June 30, 1760.
2-16 " Barbara, and Benjamin Bentley, Nov. 21, 1762.
2-122 " Azrikam, of Eld. Benjamin, dec., and Louis Warner, of William; m. by Eld. Charles Holden, Feb. 13, 1763.
2-61 " Susanna, and Thomas Gorton, May 27, 1764.
2-112 " Patience, and Esquire Millard, Oct. 20, 1771.
2-122 " Jeremiah, Jr., of East Greenwich, and Mary Gorton, of Eld. John, of Warwick; m. by Thomas Rice, Jr., Justice, May 2, 1773.
2-125 " Thomas, of Samuel, of Tolland, Conn., and Martha Jerauld, of Dr. Dutee, of Warwick; m. by Eld. John Gorton, Oct. 10. 1779.
2-249 " Eunice, and John Millard, Jr., Dec. 23, 1785.
2-127 " Benjamin, of Coventry, son of Azrikam, and Sarah Carpenter, of Elisha, of Warwick; m. by Peter Greene, Justice, June 26, 1791.
2-186 " Nancy, and Howland Greene, May 29, 1796.
2-254 " Susannah, and Powers Wickes, Oct. 1, 1797.
2-119 " Caleb, of Thomas, dec., and Susannah Brayton, of Daniel; m. by Alexander Havens, Justice, June 23, 1803.
3-382 " Mercy A., and Henry A. Bailey, Dec. 16, 1844.
3-321 " Meranda, and James H. Titus, July 19, 1846.
4-32 " Jeremiah G., of Cranston, aged 26 years, son of Nathan and Caroline, and Mary Steere, of Cranston, aged 23 years, dau. of Hardin and Mary, of Johnston; m. by Rev. Zalman Tobey, Oct. 6, 1850.
2-18 " Dorcas, and John Budlong, July 31, ——.
3-82 Peckham Phebe, and Edward T. Dyer, Oct. 2, 1844.
1-26 Peck Rebecca, and John Davis, Oct. 7, 1735.
2-165 " Martha, and Simeon Smith, Dec. 12, 1773.
1-27 Peirce Susannah, and John Warner, Aug. 6, 1713.
1-61 " Samuel, of Aziekam, of Rehoboth, and Rebeckah Budlong, of John, of Warwick; m. by Anthony Low, Justice, Nov. 26, 1721.
1-95 " Nathaniel, of Preserved, of East Greenwich, and Sarah Wilkes, of Thomas, of Warwick; m. by William Greene, Justice, May 22, 1735.
1-59 " Hopestill, and William Battey, Oct. 9, 1740.

2-119	Peirce Thomas, of John, dec., of East Greenwich, and Rebecca Scranton, of Stephen, of Warwick; m. by Jabez Greene, Justice, Oct. 14, 1744.
2-123	" Mrs. Elizabeth, and Giles Peirce, Oct. 13, 1775.
2-123	" Giles, of Thomas, of East Greenwich, and Mrs. Elizabeth Peirce, of Caleb, dec., of Warwick; m. by Eld. John Gorton, Oct. 13, 1775.
2-124	" Samuel, Jr., and Hannah Jerauld, of Dr. Dutee; m. by Eld. John Gorton, Dec. 22, 1776.
2-101	" Betsey, and William Casey, Jan. 7, 1798.
3-271	" Fannie, and William Roberts, Jr., Oct. 18, 1812.
3-261	" Samuel D., of Warwick, son of Marchant, dec., of No. Kingstown, and Lydia S. Manchester, of James; m. by Rev. Moses Fifield, Feb. 6, 1831.
3-265	" Willard T., of Warwick, son of Marchant, dec., of North Kingstown, and Sarah Stafford, of Thomas R., of Warwick; m. by Rev. Moses Fifield, Sept. 17, 1838.
3-264	" Smith W., of Warwick, son of Marchant, dec., of North Kingstown, and Sybel D. Davis, of Ezra D., dec., of North Kingstown; m. by Eld. Joseph W. Allen, Nov. 4, 1838.
3-339	" Susan, and Jahleel Westcott, May 1, 1840.
3-287	" Susan S., and John H. Rice, Nov. 25, 1844.
4-13	Pepperell Robert, of Warwick, son of Robert, of London, Eng., and Sophrona A. Tibbetts, of William, of Warwick; m. by Rev. Moses Fifield, Sept. 23, 1849.
1-46	Perce Tabitha, and John Budlong, Jan. 8, 1729-0.
1-16	" Judah, and William Tibbetts Apr. 26, 1736.
1-55	" Abigail, and Thomas Hill, Nov. 4, 1736.
3-202	Perkins Amey, and Nathan W. Lockwood, Sept. 1, 1840.
3-296	" Susan M., and William H. Snell, June 3, 1844.
3-254	" Nancy, and Henry A. Potter, May 15, 1845.
3-267	" Horace E., of Sterling, Conn., and Mary W. Remington, of Warwick; m. by Eld. Thomas Tillinghast, Nov. 9, 1845.
4-35	Perry William G., and Nancy A. Shaw; m. by Eld. James L. Phillips, Dec. 12, 1837.
3-261	" John R., of Smithfield, son of George C., of Coventry, and Cornelia B. Vinton, of Smithfield, dau. of Leonard, of Warwick; m. by Rev. Moses Fifield, May 3, 1847.
1-45	Phillips Sarah, and John Johnson, Oct. 13, 1721.
-89	" Patience, and Alfred Smith, Jan. 15, 1832.

3-134　Phillips Ann Frances, and Hale Gorton, Mar. 20, 1841.
3-267　"　Amey and George G. Potter, Oct. 13, 1842.
4-75　"　Albert, and Mary M. Lockwood; m. by Rev. D. Dorchester, Aug. 16, 1843.
3-238　"　Arnold F., of Nathan, and Mary A. Searl, of Lyndia, both of Smithfield; m. by Rev. Martin J. Steere, July 6, 1845.
3-357　"　Patience, and Augustus L. White, July 30, 1846.
4-17,102　"　William, of James, and Sarah A. Millard, of Charles; m. by Rev. Benjamin Phelan, Dec. 13, 1849.
4-34　"　Cynthia, and Francis C. Gardiner, June 6, 1851.
1-61　Pigot Edward, and Ruth Havens, of Robert, Oct. 9, 1733.
3-400　Pike Mrs. Eliza, and William Crandall, Apr. 21, 1846.
4-13　"　Susan, and James A. Whitman, Sept. 18, 1849.
3-409　Pilgington Elizabeth, and William Caucrofte, Mar. 12, 1848.
3-266　Pilkinton Hannah, and William S. Parker, Dec. 3, 1842.
4-47　"　Ann, and Oliver A. Mott, Oct. 21, 1851.
3-259　Pirse Hannah J., and Earl P. Pollard, Nov. 3, 1827.
2-242　Pitman Rebecca, and James Greene, 4th, Nov. 17, 1782.
3-83　Place Hannah F., and Nelson T. Briggs, Aug. 14, 1844.
3-415　"　Cordelia N., and George G. Hopkins, Oct. 17, 1847.
4-77　Platt Janette A., and Louis B. Wilson, Jan. 25, 1860.
3-259　Pollard Earl P., of Rachel, and Hannah J. Pirse, of Caleb; m. by Rev. Francis Dana, Nov. 3, 1827.
3-438　"　Benjamin, of Providence, son of James, and Maria Quackinbush, of Warwick, dau. of John; m. by Rev. Jonathan Brayton, Nov. 2, 1845.
3-320　"　Abbie A., and Daniel Tanner, May 7, 1846.
3-104　"　Everline A., and William H. Farris, Nov. 22, 1847.
3-42　Pollock Sarah K., and John G. Brayman, Aug. 20, 1837.
1-11　Potter John, and Ruth Fisher; m. by William Burleston, Asst., June 2, 1664.
1-3　"　Abell, and Rachel Warner; m. by John Greene, Asst., Nov. 16, 1669.
1-8　"　John, and Sarah Collins, widow; m. by John Greene, Justice, Jan. 7, 1684-5.
1-23　"　Content, and Sarah Wright, of Providence, June 1, 1703.
1-58　"　Abel, and Sarah Lockwood, of Abraham; m. by John Wickes, Asst., June 16, 1728.
1-60　"　Mary, and Joseph Edmonds, Jr., Dec. 19, 1738.

2-120	Potter William, of Capt. William, of Providence, and Barbara Stafford, of Capt. Samuel, of Warwick; m. by Eld. John Hammett, Feb. 2, 1745.
2-120	" Joseph, of Providence, and Mary Low, of Capt. John, of Warwick; m. by Jeremiah Lippitt, Justice, Jan. 1, 1747.
2-14	" Margaret, and Samuel Bennett, Mar. 25, 1750.
2-207	" Sarah, and John Waterman, June 13, 1754.
2-168	" Mercy, and Samuel Sweet, Sept. 23, 1754.
2-73	" Catherine, and Zebadee Hunt, Aug. 23, 1760.
2-77	" Keziah, and Caleb Hammett, Nov. 15, 1772.
2-126	" William, of Caleb, of Cranston, and Mary Gorton, of Benjamin, of Warwick; m. by Elder Charles Holden, Mar. 26, 1778.
2-125	" Pardon, of Capt. William, and Mary Snell, of Daniel; m. by James Jerauld, Justice, Oct. 17, 1779.
2-9	" Sarah, and Benedict Arnold, Mar. 31, 1782.
2-126	" Christopher, of John, and Elizabeth Baker, of Oliver; m. by Eld. John Gorton, Dec. 14, 1783.
2-119	" William, of William, and Mary Ellis, of Benjamin, dec.; m. by Thomas Rice, Jr., Justice, May 1, 1786.
2-123	" Elizabeth, and Mial Parce, Nov. 2, 1788.
2-120	" Olney, of Coventry, and Susannah Arnold, of Warwick; m. by Eld. Samuel Littlefield, Jan. 23, 1800.
3-247	" Olney, and Elizabeth Greene; m. by Rev. Samuel Littlefield, Nov. 20, 1808.
3-252	" Pardon, Jr., and Betsey Briggs, of Joseph; m. by C. Brayton, Justice, Aug. 6, 1809.
3-255	" Ezekiel, of Arnold, and Martha Douglass, of James; m. by C. Brayton, Justice, Sept. 13, 1812.
4-63,65	" Amanda, and James Fisher, Jan. 16, 1821.
3-258	" Simon, and Marian Slocum; m. by Randall Carder, Justice, May 11, 1822.
3-263	" Otis W., of Benjamin, of Cranston, and Lydia A. Tillinghast of Eld. Thomas, dec., of East Greenwich; m. by Eld. Pardon Tillinghast, July 25, 1831.
3-260	" Gen. Thomas A., and Mercy Ann Briggs; m. by Eld. Thomas Tillinghast, June 17, 1832.
4-67	" Betsey, and John Kinnecome, Dec. 13, 1833.
3-45	" Mary, and Willett G. Brown, Oct. 27, 1839.
3-54	" Mary Ann, and William H. Baker, June 27, 1841.
3-345	" Joanna, and John J. Wood, Oct. 4, 1841.

3-267 Potter George G., of West Greenwich, and Amey Phillips, of Warwick (both Or.); m. by Rev. Jonathan E. Forbush, Oct. 13, 1842.
3-250 " Nicholas G., of Coventry, son of Andrew, and Charlotte Atwood, of Caleb; m. by Rev. Jonathan Brayton. Apr. 22, 1844.
3-253 " James R., of Cranston, son of Jabez J., and Marcella A. Remington, of James [also 4-99]; m. by Rev. Jonathan Brayton, Aug. 14, 1844.
3-254 " Henry A., and Nancy Perkins, both of Coventry; m. by Rev. Stephen A. Thomas, May 15, 1845.
3-437 " Willis, of Knight, and Elizabeth P. Searl, of Benjamin; m. by Rev. Jonathan Brayton, Aug. 3, 1845.
3-447 " Paulina, and William R. Lane, Feb. 10, 1846.
4-12 " Jerman Y., of Thomas, and Emily Hiscox, dau. of Potter Kivan; m. by Rev. Benjamin Phelan, Sept. 3, 1849.
4-36 " Henry, aged 69 years, son of Pardon, and Mrs. Eliza Miller, aged 39 years, dau. of John Shreive; m. by Rev. Benjamin Phelan, Jan. 30, 1851.
4-48 " Edmund, of Coventry, aged 21 years, son of Lowry, and Ellen Fenner, of Warwick, aged 27 years, dau. of Bowen; m. by Rev. Benjamin Phelan, Nov. 16, 1851.
4-49 Pratt William H., of Providence, aged 20 years, son of Chester, and Jane Greene, of Warwick, aged 20 years, dau. of Alphonso; m. by Rev. Benjamin Phelan, Nov. 17, 1851.
2-215 Preston Margaret, and Benjamin Wood, Mar. 13, 1763.
3-268 " Joseph, of Plaisfield, Conn., son of Aaron, and Lydia Stafford, of Allen, of Warwick; m. by Rev. Moses Fifield, Sept. 4, 1843.
2-119 Price Thomas, of Warwick, and Joanna King, of Providence; m. by William Rice, Asst., Jan. 22, 1744-5.
2-209 " Bridget, and Joseph Wickes, June 22, 1758.
2-124 " Matthew, of Benoni, and Elizabeth Hackstone. of John; m. by James Jerauld, Justice, Dec. 14, 1777.
2-169 " Mary, and George W. Arnold, June 1, 1800.
2-28 " William, of Matthew, and Mercy Carpenter, of Elisha; m. by James Jerauld, Justice, Aug. 9, 1801.
2-138 " James, of Samuel, and Nancy Dyre Bennett, of Abel; m. by James Jerauld, Justice, Nov. 5, 1801.
3-251 " John, resident, of Coventry, and Amey Foster of Warwick, dau. of William; m. by C. Brayton, Justice, Dec. 11, 1808.

3-256	Price George W., and Sally Ann Church; m. by Rev. David Curtis, Dec. 20, 1813.
3-222	" Alice, and Timothy Mahoney, Nov. 18, 1821.
3-349	" Elizabeth, and Benoni West (col.), Jan. 4, 1822.
3-310	" Betsey, and John Kerr Trumball, Jan. 27, 1828.
3-251	Prophet James, of Warwick, son of Thomas, and Susannah Prophet, of Watt, of Cranston (col.); m. by Thomas Potter, Justice, Mar. 31, 1774.
3-251	" Susannah, and James Prophet, Mar. 31, 1774.
3-372	" Julia, and Henry F. Chase (col.), Apr. 3, 1845.
3-92	" Marceny, and Ceaser L. Dailey (col.), Mar. 8, 1846.
4-57	" Sarah E., and George Champlin, Jr. (col.), Sept. 23, 1852.
2-121	Proud William, of Providence, and Ann Bennett, of Capt. Samuel, dec., of Warwick; m. by Eld. John Hammett, Feb. 17, 1750.
2-112	" Ann, and Adam Maxwell, Mar. 28, 1771.
3-262	Pulsifer Ann Maria, and Abraham H. Padelford, July 3, 1845.
3-172	Putney Fidelia, and James M. Johnson, June 10, 1839.

Q

3-438	Quackinbush Maria, and Benjamin Pollard, Nov. 2, 1845.
3-266	Quiman E———, and Harriet Carder; m. by Rev. Edward K. Fuller, Apr. 5, 1845.

R

3-386	Ralph Nathan H., of Coventry, und Mrs. Margaret M. Battey, of West Greenwich; m. by Rev. Jonathan Brayton, June 26, 1843.
3-177	" Dianna, and James C. Johnson, Oct. 12, 1846.
2-180	Randall Hannah, and George Arnold, Apr. 4, 1802.
3-151	" Mary, and John Harrison, May 5, 1805.
3-192	" Rebecca P., and William R. Keech, June 7, 1840.
3-226	" Sarah L. and Rice A. Miller, Sept. 6, 1846.
4-74	" Phebe, and Edwin Stone, Mar. 25, 1860.
1-52	Ransom Hannah, and Abner Corps, Nov. 25, 1734.
3-272	Rathburn George W., and Mary Corey; m. by Rev. S. A. Thomas, Oct. 11, 1847.
3-369	" Alice S., and John C. Carr, May 19, 1848.

2-56 Ray Catherine, and William Greene, Jr., Apr. 30, 1758.
1-39 Reaves Ann, and Benjamin Blanchard, Jan. 8, 1739-40
3-205 " Harriet B., and Lorenzo D. Littlefield, Mar. 7, 1842.
3-63 " Hannah, and James H. Bates, Apr. 30, 1843.
[NOTE.—Was this man's name Baxter? See page 15].
3-91 " Mary Ann, and Henry G. Douglass, July 15, 1844.
2-113 Reed Ann, and Caleb Nichols, May 29, 1758.
3-68 " Safety, and William H. Cranston, Jan. 7, 1841.
2-26 Relph Pardon, alias Daly, and Mary Hathaway; m. by Eld. John Gorton, Mar. 2, 1758.
1-28 Remington Thomas, of Thomas, dec., and Maplet Gorton, of Capt. Benjamin, dec., Dec. 28, 1710.
1-49 " Joseph, of Thomas, and Margaret Burlingame, of Thomas, Sept. 29, 1717.
1-69 " Daniel, and Ann Gorton, of Samuel, Feb. 16, 1722-3.
1-48 " Mary, and William Backer, July 28, 1724.
1-51 " Marian, and Ebenezer Greene, Aug. 1, 1724.
2-142 " Thomas, and Abigail Eldred, Dec. 14, 1744.
2-143 " Anna, and Peleg Rice, May 19, 1754.
2-6 " Almy, and Rhodes Arnold, Nov. 4, 1756.
2-3 " Margaret, and Ebenezer Allen, May 21, 1761.
2-191 " Hannah, and Henry Tibbetts, Dec. 15, 1763.
2-154 " Maplet, and William Rice, Jan. 29, 1769.
2-152 " Jonathan, of Warwick, and Mary Havens, of Nathaniel, of North Kingstown; m. by Eld. Charles Holden, June 15, 1769.
2-14 " Prudence, and Pearce Budlong, Aug. 27, 1769.
2-76 " Sarah, and Charles Holden, Nov. 3, 1771.
2-226 " Rosanna, and Abel Bennett, Nov. 12, 1772.
2-156 " Thomas, of Capt. Thomas, and Mary Rice, of Capt. Holden; m. by Thomas Rice, Jr., Justice, Dec. 20, 1772.
2-231 " Mary, and Joseph Bennett, Dec. 9, 1773.
2-142 " Mary, and Josephus Rice, May 18, 1777.
2-162 " Thomas, Jr., of Thomas, and Mary Wood, of William; m. by Eld. Charles Holden, June 7, 1778.
2-236 " Phebe, and John Cole, Feb. 4, 1779.
2-159 " Benjamin, of Warwick, and Phebe Manchester, of North Kingston; m. by Eld. James Wightman, Apr. 18, 1779.
2-159 " John, of Thomas, and Mary Tillinghast, of Samuel; m. by Eld. John Gorton, Dec. 17, 1780.

2-160	Remington Jerauld, of Thomas, and Anne Howard, of Soloman; m. by James Jerauld, Justice, May 12, 1782.
2-83	" Elizabeth, and Isaac Johnson, Oct. 28, 1784.
2-83	" Elizabeth, aud John Joyce, May 29, 1785.
2-143	" Henry, of Thomas, and Margaret LeValley, of Peter; m. by Eld. John Gorton, Sept. 18, 1785.
2-145	" Thomas, of Thomas dec., and Sarah Cook, widow of Silas, dau. of Joseph Crofford, dec.; m. by Eld. John Gorton, May 7, 1786.
2-220	" Rosanna, and Olney Wood, Mar. 8, 1787.
2-149	" Samuel, of Ruel, and Almy Arnold, of Thomas; m. by Eld. John Gorton, July 17, 1791.
2-143	" William, of Thomas, and Pattey Adams, of Andrew; m. by Alexander Havens, Justice, Apr. 12, 1804.
3-269	" Charles, and Susanna Budlong; m. by Eld. Thomas Spooner, Feb. 16, 1805.
3-309	" Maplet, and Charles Tibbetts, June 1, 1806.
3-154	" Sarah, and Andrew Harris, Apr. 2, 1809.
3-13	" Lydia, and Olney R. Arnold, Nov. 19, 1809.
4-99	" James, and Isabella Parker, of Thomas and Lusanna, of Scituate, Mar. 15, 1811.
3-73	" Mary and Peleg Congdon, Jan. 7, 1816.
3-275	" Daniel, and Betsey R. Briggs; m. by Eld. Job Manchester, Dec. 6, 1829.
3-295	" Caroline, and Thomas J. Spencer, Apr. 27, 1834.
3-356	" Lydia E. and Reuben Whitman, Apr. 12, 1835.
4-99	" Susan J., and Palmer T. Johnson, Mar. 7, 1838.
3-281	" George W., of William, of Warwick, and Olive H. Dexter, of Warwick, dau. of Benjamin, dec., of Chatham, Mass.; m. by Eld. Moses Fifield, Sept. 12, 1839.
3-22	" Waitey Ann, and Lyman Arnold, Feb. 14, 1841.
4-74	" Mary W., and George H. Cooke, Mar. 28, 1842.
3-285	" John H., and Mrs. Martha A. Thomas; m. by Eld. Jonathan Brayton, May 8, 1843.
3-253	" Marcelia A., and James R. Potter, [also 4-99,] Aug. 14, 1844.
3-267	" Mary W., and Horace E. Perkins, Nov. 9, 1845.
3-288	" Thomas M., of Thomas, of Warwick, and Scynthia Tillinghast, of Samuel, of Foster; m. by Rev. Martin J. Steere, Jan. 1, 1846.
4-54	" Henry A., of William, and Sally W. Reynolds, of Thomas A. and Charity; m. by Rev. Zalman Tobey, May 7, 1848.

3-287 Remington Charles E., of James E., dec., and Sarah R., and Dorcas Bates, of Samuel, dec., and Roby B.; m. by Rev. George A. Willard, Aug. 14, 1848.
4-54 " Elizabeth, and William O. Vaughn, Apr. 1, 1849.
4-12 " William E., of Peleg, dec., and Sarah F. Hazard, of Peleg; m. by Rev. Moses Fifield, July 25, 1849.
4-52 " Sarah H., and Harvey Cornell, Mar. 31, 1851.
4-58 " Holden B., aged 20 years, of Warwick, son of Arastus and Susan, and Mary L. Mitchell, aged 17 years, of Portsmouth, dau. of Jonathan and Martha; m. by Rev. Benjamin Phelan, Oct. 18, 1852.
4-78 " Marcelia A., and James A. Carter, Jan. 6, 1853.
4-99 " Thomas P., and Mary A. Carter, Jan. 6, 1853.
1-8 Renals James, of Kings Towne, and Mary Greene, of Warwick; m. by John Greene, Justice, Feb. 19, 1684-5.
2-155 Reynolds Henry, Jr., son of Henry, of West Greenwich, and Jemima Wightman, of George, Jr.; m. by Eld. John Gorton, Sept. 27, 1772.
2-138 " Phebe, and Andrew Arnold, Jan. 18, 1781.
2-163 " Henry, of Thomas, of East Greenwich, and Millen Arnold, of Mrs. Mary; m. by Eld. John Gorton, May 6, 1781.
2-160 " Henry, of North Kingstown, son of Jabez, and Anna Baker, of Warwick; m. by James Jerauld, Justice, June 16, 1785.
2-163 " Peirce, of Shibnah, and Anne Burton, of Rufus, of Hopkinton, now both of East Greenwich; m. by Eld. John Gorton, Oct. 15, 1788.
2-121 " Mary, and William Tayler, Dec. 30, 1797.
3-270 " John S., of Henry, and Sarah Mitchell, of Samuel; m. by C. Brayton, Justice, Apr. 22, 1812.
3-159 " Abbie B., and Stephen P. Himes, Oct. 16, 1823.
3-21 " Susan, and Russell Arnold, Jan. 11, 1830.
3-161 " Sarah J., and Nathan Howard, May 4, 1834.
3-240 " Experience A., and Stephen S. Northup, Sept. 20, 1841.
3-283 " Sheffield, of Warwick, son of William, and Margaret Matteson, of Asel, dec., of Coventry; m. by Rev. Moses Fifield, Jan. 6, 1842.
3-347 " Lucy Ann, and Gardner G. Wood, Dec. 25, 1842.
3-285 " James H., of Warwick, aud Sally C. Colvin, of Coventry; m. by Rev. Albert Colvin, Jan. 1, 1844.
3-29 " Mary L. S., and Edwin W. Arnold, Dec. 16, 1844.

3-211	Reynolds	Mary P., and Isaac D. Lawton, June 16, 1845.
3-307	"	Edeth B., and William D. Shearman, Feb. 22, 1846.
3-378	"	Abbie, and Josiah Chute, Nov. 8, 1847.
4-54	"	Sally W., and Henry A. Remington, May 7, 1848.
1-29	Rhodes	Malachi, and Dorothy Whipple, of John, of Providence, May 8, 1699-0.
1-83	"	Wait, and Moses Lippitt, Apr. 26, 1732.
1-52	"	Charles, and Deborah Greene; m. by Eld. Manassah Martin, Jan. 31, 1738-9.
2-199	"	Deliverance, and Eleizer Whipple, June 24, 1744.
2-141	"	Joseph, of Major John, and Anne Weaver, of Clement, dec.; m. by John Walton, Justice, Feb. 4, 1747.
2-58, 143	"	Mary, and Stephen Greene, Oct. 24, 1754.
1-25	"	Katherine, and Samuel Budlong, Sept. 28, 1758.
2-146	"	Peter, of Charles, of Cranston, and Hester Arnold, of Simon, of Warwick; m. by Eld. Charles Holden, Mar. 22, 1761.
2-149	"	Robert, of James, and Phebe Smith, of Christopher; m. by Eld. Charles Holden, Apr. 7, 1763.
2-149	"	John, of John, Jr., and Rosanna Budlong, of Eld. Daniel; m. by Eld. Charles Holden, Aug. 25, 1763.
2-43	"	Phebe, and Giles Greene, Sept. 13, 1764.
2-151	"	William, of Anthony, and Mary Holden, of John; m. by Eld. Charles Holden, Aug. 18, 1765.
2-42	"	Holden, and Susannah Wall, of John, Mar. 12, 1769.
2-151	"	William, of Anthony, and Ann Westcott, of Nathan; m. by Eld. Charles Holden, July 21, 1769.
2-156	"	Sylvester, of James, of Warwick, and Polly Aborn, of Capt. Joseph, late of Cranston; m. by Eld. Elisha Greene, Apr. 22, 1770.
2-27	"	Almy, and Thomas Davis, Dec. 5, 1771.
2-153	"	Benjamin, of Peter, and Mercy Burlingame, of Samuel; m. by James Jerauld, Justice, July 17, 1785.
2-55	"	Abigail, and Job Greene, Nov. 29, 1785.
2-162	"	Polly, and Thomas Stafford, Jr., Jan. 1, 1789.
2-148	"	Ishmael, of Warwick, and Clintha Newfield, of Cranston; m. by Eld. John Gorton, Nov. 20, 1791.
2-153	"	Benjamin, and Phebe Burlingame, of Samuel, Dec. 4, 1791.
2-159	"	Peleg, of Malachi, of Warwick, and Mary Aborn, of Daniel, of Cranston, Apr. 9, 1797.
2-183	"	Nancy, and Samuel Briggs, May 3, 1798.
2-29	"	Watey, and Wickes Gardiner, Dec. 19, 1802.

2-159	Rhodes	Peleg, of Malachi, of Warwick, and Sarah Bowen Allen, Feb. 8, 1808.
3-269	"	Holden, and Sarah Gorton; m. by C. Brayton, Justice, Dec. 4, 1808.
4-97	"	Mercy B., and Capt. William R. Chapman, Nov. 12, 1820.
3-273	"	Thomas, and Phebe Gorton; m. by Rev. Jonathan Wilson, Mar. 2, 1828.
3-280	"	Esau, of Nehemiah, and Anstress G. Lippitt, widow, of George (col.); m. by Eld. Job Manchester, July 11, 1839.

[NOTE.—See also Roades].

1-6	Rice	John, and Elizabeth Holden; m. by Benjamin Barton, Justice, July 16, 1674.
1-38	"	John, Jr., and Elnathan Whipple, of John, July 25, 1695.
1-79	"	William, of Warwick, and Phebe Tripp, of South Kingstown; m. by Rouse Helme, Asst., Dec. 10, 1730.
1-84	"	Mary, and Samuel Gorton, Jr., Jan. 21, 1730-1.
1-101	"	Richard, of Randall, and Sarah Kee, of Ebenezer, Sept. 21, 1732.
1-101	"	Richard, of Randall, of Warwick, and Sarah Rice, of Killingly, Conn., dau. of Ebenezer; m. by William Greene, Justice, Sept. 21, 1732.
1-101	"	Sarah, and Richard Rice, Sept. 21, 1732.
1-1	"	Elnathan, and Thomas Greene, Jan. 18, 1735.
1-38	"	Randall, of John, and Dinah Greene, of Thomas, Mar. 16, 1736.
2-167	"	Lydia, and Phillip Sweet, Jr., Jan. 25, 1740.
1-81	"	Isaac, of Randall, and Deborah Sweet, of James; m. by William Rice, Justice, June 8, 1770.
1-80	"	Freelove, and Jeremiah Webb, June 19, 1740.
1-19	"	Capt. Thomas, and Ann Haynes; m. by Eld. Manassah Martin, June 19, 1740.
1-39	"	Mary, and Richard Greene, June —, 1742.
2-67	"	Dorothy, and John Holden, Aug. 5, 1744.
2-67	"	Eleanor, and Daniel Hudson, Jan. 19, 1745.
2-46	"	Francis, and Ebenezer Graves, May 19, 1751.
2-142	"	Holden, of Thomas, and Elizabeth Warner, of John; m. by Eld. John Hammett, June 2, 1751.
2-143	"	Peleg, of Nathan, and Anna Remington; m. by Eld. John Gorton, May 19, 1754.
2-192	"	Hannah, and Job. Tripp, May 16, 1757.
2-7	"	Rhoda, and Stephen Arnold, Mar. 6, 1760.

2-148	Rice	Job and Anne Gorton; m. by John Warner, Jr., Justice, Nov. 27, 1760.
2-141	"	John, of William, dec., and Margaret Arnold, of Capt. Josiah, dec.; m. by Eld. Charles Holden, Oct. 30, 1763.
2-150	"	Fones, of Randall, and Susanna Havens, of Alexander; m. by Eld. John Gorton, Feb. 16, 1764.
2-115	"	Avice, and Jonathan Niles, Feb. 23, 1764.
2-189	"	Mary, and James Thurber, Dec. 8, 1765.
2-81	"	Mary, and James Jerauld, Jan. 1, 1769.
2-154	"	William, of Thomas, and Maplet Remington of Thomas; m. by Eld. John Gorton, Jan. 29, 1769.
2-155	"	Freelove, and Thomas Rice, Apr. 6, 1769.
2-155	"	Thomas, of Capt. Randall, and Freelove Rice, widow of Olney; m. by Eld. Charles Holden, Apr. 6, 1769.
2-69	"	Elizabeth and Anthony Holden, May 25, 1769.
2-154	"	Caleb, of Major Henry, and Freelove Jerauld, of Dr. Dutee; m. by Thomas Rice, Jr., Justice, Jan. 9, 1772.
2-164	"	William, of Nathan, and Lucy Carpenter, of Wilbour; m. by Thomas Rice, Justice, Dec. 15, 1772.
2-156	"	Mary, and Thomas Remington, Dec. 20, 1772.
2-157	"	Randall, of Nathan, and Rebecca Mendon; m. by Eld. John Gorton, Oct. 6, 1773.
2-179	"	Ann, and Nathan Millard, June 23, 1774.
2-152	"	Thomas, of Thomas, and Rosanna Blanchard, of John, dec.; m. by Eld. John Gorton, Apr. 17, 1777.
2-142	"	Josephus, of Capt. Thomas, and Mary Remington, of Capt. Thomas; m. by Thomas Rice, Justice, May 18, 1777.
2-82	"	Phebe, and Gorton Jerauld, Feb. 22, 1778.
2-160	"	Reuben (colored servant of Thomas Rice), and Bersheba Roberts (col.), of Abigail; m. by Adam Comstock, Justice, Feb. 4, 1779.
2-172	"	Tamar, and Ceaser Sweet (col.), Mar. 21, 1779.
2-239	"	Mercy, and John R. Arnold, Sept. 8, 1782.
2-157	"	Henry, of Henry, and Susannah Jerauld, of Dr. Dutee; m. by Eld. John Gorton, Sept. 22, 1782.
2-243	"	Dinah, and Phillip Arnold, Jr., Sept, 26, 1784.
2-161	"	John, and Sarah Utter; m. by Eld. Abraham Lippitt, Apr. 7, 1785.
2-161	"	Thomas, of Henry, and Sarah Arnold, of Phillip; m. by Eld. John Gardiner, Dec. 11, 1785.
2-6	"	Mrs. Freelove, and Christopher Andrews, Feb. 5, 1786.

2-247	Rice	Naomi, and Dutee Arnold, Aug. 27, 1786.
2-251	"	Elizabeth, and Michael Malone, Nov. 11, 1787.
2-243	"	Barsheba, and William Ceaser, Feb. 3, 1788,
2-88	"	Anthony, of Holden, dec., and Martha Cook, of Capt. Silas; m. by Eld. John Gorton, Jan. 3, 1790.
2-151	"	Wanton, of Henry, and Mercy Gardner, of Capt. Oliver; m. by Eld. John Gorton, Oct. 2, 1791.
2-255	"	William, of Henry, and Sarah Greene, of Caleb; m. by James Jerauld, Justice, Oct. 28, 1792.
2-131	"	Dianna, and Randall Carder, Dec. 28, 1794.
2-185	"	Sally, and Elisha Brown, Feb. 24, 1796.
2-158	"	Elizabeth, and Charles Briggs, Jr., Aug. 21, 1796.
2-134	"	Susannah, and Samuel Millard, Nov. 25, 1798.
2-85	"	Polly, and Russell Arnold, Nov. 2, 1800.
2-154	"	Jeffrey Amhurst, of William, and Elizabeth Burlingame, of Joseph; m. by Caleb Jerauld, Justice, Dec. 8, 1803.
3-1	"	Sarah, and Daniel Arnold, Oct. 2, 1806.
3-277	"	Joseph W., and Elizabeth Wilbour; m. by Eld. Samuel Littlefield, June 13, 1811.
3-237	"	Phebe Ann, and Christopher Nichols, Oct. 25, 1812.
3-291	"	Deborah V., and Stephen Sweet, July 2, 1818.
3-272	"	William, of Jeffrey A., dec., and Caroline King, of Benjamin; m. by Eld. Pardon Tillinghast, Aug. 28, 1825.
3-274	"	William, and Sarah Harris; m. by Rev. Moses, Fifield, Oct. 13, 1829.
3-59	"	Harriet N., and David W. Bradford, Apr. 12, 1832.
3-276	"	Joseph B., of Warwick, and Sarah L. Burt, of Bristol; m. by Eld. Thomas Tillinghast, Sept. 14, 1832.
3-279	"	Thomas C., of Plainfield, Conn., and Olive C. Card, of Warwick; m. by Rev. Thomas Dowling, May 27, 1839.
3-296	"	Nancy, and William K. Sprague, Sept. 19, 1839.
3-72	"	Hannah B., and Francis H. Congdon, Mar. 20, 1842.
3-284	"	John R., of Richard, and Desire G. Merrill, of Josiah; m. by Rev. Moses Fifield, Nov. 14, 1842.
3-90	"	Mary P., and William Dawley, Dec. 6, 1842.
3-287	"	John H., of Low, dec., and Susan S. Peirce, of Warwick, dau. of Marchant, of North Kingstown, dec.; m. by Rev. Moses Fifield, Nov. 25, 1844.
3-270	"	Jason W., of Richard, and Esther Ann Tefft, of Nathan, of Thompson, Conn.; m. by Rev. Moses Fifield, Nov. 16, 1846.

3-271	Rice	Caleb A., of Richard, and Susan C. Gardner, of Jeffrey H.; m. by Rev. Moses Fifield, Jan. 31, 1847.
3-394	"	Malissa M., and George W. Bates, Jr., Feb. 14, 1847.
4-72	"	William A., and Sarah Barber; m. by Eld. William P. Place, Sept. 17, 1848.
4-78	"	John C., and Susan Wilcox; m. by Rev. Jonathan Brayton, Sept. 10, 1862.
4-93	"	Albert, of Albert and Ann, and Mary Jane Grimshaw, of Thomas and Jane; m. by Rev. Jonathan Brayton, Aug. 17, 1873.
3-284	Richardson	George B., of Cranston, son of George, and Amy Ann Ellis, of Warwick, dau. of Jeremiah, of Providence, dec.; m. by Rev. Moses Fifield, Aug. 14, 1842.
3-445	"	Joseph B., of Abijah, and Avis Hunt, of William; m. by Rev. Jonathan Brayton, May 7, 1846.
3-286	"	Franklin, of Warwick, son of John, of Vt., and Lovice C. Taylor, of Warwick, dau. of David; m. by Rev. Alfred Colburn, Nov. 26, 1846.
4-29	"	Halsey H., of Coventry, son of Joseph B., and Sarah S. Babson, of Warwick, dau. of Isaac N.; m. by Rev. Jonathan Brayton, July 4, 1850.
2-144	Richmond	Jeremiah, of Providence, and Elizabeth Warner, of Samuel, of Warwick; m. by Eld. Charles Holden, Feb. 23, 1766.
2-118	Riley	Hannah, and David Olin, Oct. 28, 1793.
2-201	Risby	Isabella, and Capt. John Warner, Jr., Apr. 16, 1747.
1-6	Roades	Mary, and John Low, Mar. 3, 1674-5.
1-7	"	Malachy, of Zachary and Joanna, and Mary Carder, of Richard and Mary; m. by Benjamin Smith, Jr., Justice, May 27, 1675.
1-19	"	John, of Zachariah, and Wait Waterman, of Resolved, Feb. 12, 1684-5.
1-28	"	Elizabeth, and James Arnold, Oct. 25, 1711.
1-30	"	John, of John, dec., and Catherine Holden, of Lieut. Charles, Jan. 29, 1714.
1-42	"	Dorothy, and Isreal Arnold, Jr., Dec. 24, 1719.
1-59	"	Dorothy, and John Hammett, Dec. 13, 1726.
1-87	"	Malachy, Jr., and Deborah Whitman, of George; m. by William Greene, Justice, May 27, 1731.
1-83	"	Wait, and Moses Lippitt, Jr., Apr. 26, 1732.
1-64	"	James, of Malacha, dec., and Sarah Westgate, of Silvanus, dec., Feb. 22, 1732-3.

1-59	Roades Oliver, and Roseannah Kindrick; m. by Manassah Martin, Dec. 2, 1736.
66	" John, Jr., and Sarah Greene, of William, Apr. 25, 1738.
1-8	Roberts Mark, and Mary Baker; m. by Samuel Gorton, Justice, Jan. 1, 1682.
1-8	" Peter, and Sarah Baker; m. by John Greene, Justice, Apr. 27, 1685.
2-160	" Bersheba, and Reuben Rice (col.), Feb. 4, 1779.
2-156	" Cuff, of Coventry, and Elizabeth Grummuck, of Warwick (col.); m. by James Jerauld, Justice, Feb. 27, 1788.
3-289	" Anne, and Daniel Snell, Dec. 27, 1804.
3-271	" William, Jr., of Scituate, and Fanny Peirce, of East Greenwich; m. by Rev. David Curtis, Oct. 18, 1812.
3-278	" William A., of Scituate, son of William, Jr., of Killingly, Conn., and Mary Vaughn, of Amos, of East Greenwich; m. by Eld. Moses Fifield, Jan. 15, 1835.
3-219	" Ruth, and Timothy Mahoney, Nov. 4, 1841.
1-4	Rodman Ann, and Caleb Greene, Nov. 22, 1739.
2-157	Roomes Pero, of North Kingstown, and Bettey Slocum, of Warwick (col.); m. by Eld. Thomas Tillinghast, Aug. 18, 1804.
2-146	Ross William, of Newport, and Freelove Pearce, of Samuel, of Warwick; m. by Eld. Charles Holden, June 30, 1760.
4-30	Rousemaniere Mary E., and Joseph H. Bosworth, Sept. 2, 1850.
2-148	Rouse Benjamin, and Marian Capron, of Edward; m. by Ebenezer Slocum, Justice, July 16, 1761.
2-150	" Sandee, and Hannah Sweet, of John; m. by Eld. John Gorton, Apr. 8, 1764.
3-79	Rowand Mary, and Phillip A. Colvin, Oct. 31, 1843.
3-282	" John, Jr., of John, and Amey Ann Dyer, of John, dec.; m. by Rev. Moses Fifield, Oct. 25, 1841.
3-383	Rowan Margaret, and John R. Bennett, Apr. 29, 1844.
1-64	Ruttenberge John, of John, and Sarah Collins, of Thomas, Apr. 14, 1719.
1-91	" Ruth, and Jeremiah Hathaway, Mar. 10, 1725-6.
1-65	" Thomas, and Ann Davice, of Robert, July 4, 1726.
2-200	" Mary, and Nathan Westcott, June 16, 1745.

S

2-204 Salsberry Sybel, and Elisha Wightman, Feb. 27, 1752.
2-171 Salisbury Peleg, of Cranston, and Mercy Sweet, of Warwick; m. by Eld. John Gorton, Dec. 14, 1758.
2-176 " Mial, of Martin, of Cranston, and Ruth Greene, of Dea. Thomas, of Warwick; m. by Eld. John Gorton, Dec. 9, 1764.
2-255 " Waity, and Samuel Budlong, Jr., Apr. 3, 1791.
3-307 " Stephen P., of Warwick, son of Cromwell D., of East Greenwich, and Betsey Ann Palmer, of Warwick, dau. of Oliver G.; m. by Rev. Moses Fifield, July 30, 1843.
2-181 Sailes Thomas, of Edward, of Cranston, and Temperance Baker, of Silas, m. by Eld. Charles Holden, Jan. 22, 1778.
3-43 Sarle Precilla C., and Robert Burlingame, Nov. 17, 1839.
3-53 " Sally A., and Gorton Burlingame, Mar. 4, 1841.
4-20 " Silvia M., and Charles L. Boss, Jan. 1, 1849.
4-19 " Bethiah P., and James H. Bunn, Nov. 18, 1849.
4-57 " Lydia, and Nehemiah Brayton, Sept. 26, 1852.
1-6 Sayles Mary, and William Greene, Dec. 17, 1674.
1-15 " Phebe, and Job Greene, Jan, 22, 1684-5.
1-10 " Ellen, and Richard Greene, Feb. 16, 1692-3.
4-34 Scholfield Albert G., aged 43 years, son of John and Betsey, of Jewett City, Conn., aud Harriet F. Chipman, aged 38 years, of Warwick, dau. of Francis and Sally; m. by Rev. Zalmon Tobey, Jan. 1, 1851.
1-26 Schreech William, of Warwick, and Sarah Irish, of Little Compton, Dec. 4, 1712.
3-305 Scott James M., of Scituate, son of Thomas, and Susan Tennant, of Warwick, dau. of Daniel; m. by Rev. Jonathan Brayton, May 23, 1842.
1-1 Scranton Margaret, and David Shippee, Aug. 15, 1664.
1-39 " Elizabeth, and Joseph Cahoon, ——— 1713.
2-119 " Rebecca, and Thomas Peirce, Oct. 14, 1744.
2-166 " Mary, and Eber Sweet, Mar. 3, 1747.
2-172 " Stukeley, and Hannah Sisco; m. by John Warner, Jr., Justice, Jan. 25, 1759.
2-68 Seabin Ruth, and Nathaniel Hackstone, Feb. 9, 1752.
3-63 Seabury Mary A., and Harris O. Brown, Oct. 7, 1839.
3-222 Seager Hannah H., and John W. Morey, Nov. 7, 1842.
4-864 Seamans Harriet E., and Francis W. Gardiner, Aug. 26, 1851.

(8W)

1-4	Searle Edward, Jr., of Meshanticut, and Ann Lippitt, widow; m. by James Greene, Justice, Feb. 13, 1670.
3-311	" Julia A., and Samuel R. Tillinghast, Feb. 26, 1843.
3-298	" Isaac, of Silas, and Ruth Tennant, of James; m. by Rev. Martin J. Steere, Apr. 7, 1845.
3-258	" Mary A., and Arnold F. Phillips, July 6, 1845.
3-437	" Elizabeth P., and Willis Potter, Aug. 3, 1845.
3-392	" Susan D., and Jonathan F. Briggs, Jan. 1, 1847.
3-32	Sedgwick Abby, and John Andrew, Nov. 30, 1845.
2-254	Sephton Richard, formerly of Great Brittain, and Sarah Colbee, widow of Abraham, dec.; m. by James Jerauld, Justice, Dec. 29, 1791.
3-306	Sharples Daniel, of Warwick, son of Thomas, dec., of Lowell, Mass., and Sarah Bumford, of Warwick, dau. of Simson, of Pawtucket, Mass.; m. by Rev. Moses Fifield, Dec. 3, 1842.
1-35	Shaw Elizabeth, and Peter Stone, June 25, 1696.
4-35	" Nancy A., and William G. Perry, Dec. 12, 1837.
3-140	" Barbara, and Arnold Gavitt, Nov. 10, 1844.
2-53	Sheffield Phebe, and Charles Greene, Dec. 6, 1778.
2-243	Sheldon Esther, and Joseph Carder, Mar. 27, 1785.
4-62	" Isreal R., of Cranston, aged 25 years, son of Pardon, and Rebecca, m. Mrs. Alma D. Carder, aged 20 years of Warwick, dau. of William; m. by Rev. George Pearce, Nov. 4, 1852.
4-72	" Phebe, and John Henry, Nov. 13, 1853.
2-171	Sherman James, of Eleazer, and Francis Case, of Edward; m. by John Warner, Jr., Justice, Nov. 8, 1759.
2-173	" Charles, and Mercy Allen; m. by John Warner, Jr., Justice, Apr. 26, 1761.
2-1	" Mary, and James Allen, Apr. 8, 1779.
3-361	" Mary, and Willett Young, Aug. 9, 1826.
3-304	" John W., of Portsmouth, son of Caleb, dec., and Lucy Briggs, of Warwick, dau. of Palmer; m. by Rev. Junia S. Mowry, Apr. 7, 1842.
3-307	" William D., of Isbon, and Edith B. Reynolds, dau. of Thomas A. Remington; m. by Rev. Martin J. Steere, Feb. 22, 1846
3-292	" Lorenzo D., of Johnston, and Lucy Ann Sweet, of Warwick (also 4-70); m. by Rev. Stephen A. Thomas, Sept. 7, 1846.
3-143	" Almira B., and Stephen Greene, Nov. 3, 1848.

4-47	Sherman Henry C., aged 21 years, son of Roswell, and Harriet K. Stone, aged 21 years, dau. of Walton; m. by Rev. Benjamin Phelan, Oct. 30, 1851.	
4-58	" William G., aged 27 years, of North Attleboro, son of David, dec., and Sarah L. Budlong, aged 17 years, dau. of Edmund D.; m. by Rev. Benjamin Phelan, July 13, 1852.	
4-77	" Elisha O., and Isabella Tourjee; m. by Rev. C. H. Titus, Dec. 7, 1864.	
1-1	Shippee David, of Maidfield, and Margaret Scranton; m. by Walter Todd, Asst., Aug. 15, 1664.	
3-308	" Barbara, and Colonel Shippee, Dec. 18, 1843.	
3-308	" Colonel, of Spencer, and Barbara Shippee, of Rufus, dec.; m. by Rev. Moses Fifield, Dec. 18, 1843.	
3-403	" Anstress Ann, and William O. Houson, Dec. 16, 1845.	
3-308	" Henry, of Thomas, of Warwick, and Susan E. Freeman, of Warwick, dau. of Henry, of East Greenwich; m. by Rev. Moses Fifield, Aug. 10, 1846.	
4-48	" Hannah C., and Benjamin W. Gardner, Nov. 9, 1851.	
4-65	" Olive C., and Edwin Westcott, May 22, 1853.	
3-69	Sholes Sally, and Robert H. Coggeshall, Mar. 31, 1841.	
3-226	Shreives Eliza, and William Miller, June 7, 1829.	
3-297	" Andrew D., of Nicholas W. and Elissa B. Newman, of Noah; m. by Rev. Moses Fifield, Mar. 13, 1845.	
4-28	Shute C. C., of Providence, son of Isaac and Lucy, and Sarah P. Greene, of Warwick, dau. of Robert and Sarah; m. by Rev. Benjamin Phelan, July 2, 1850.	
3-306	Sidebottom Ebenezer, and Mary Ann Tunguad, m. by Rev. Edward K. Fuller, Apr. 19, 1845.	
2-116	Simmons ———— and Ruth Millard, of Capt. Nathan; m. by Rev. Abraham Lippitt, Nov. 11, 1792.	
4-79	" Hattie, and Alonzo B. Sweet, Nov. 29, 1862.	
3-398	Singer Mary, and Edward Chappell, Aug. 16, 1846.	
2-170	Sisco Eleazer, of Richard, and Phebe Sparron; m. by John Warner, Jr., Justice, Oct. 24, 1756.	
2-172	" Hannah, and Stuteley Scranton, Jan. 25, 1759.	
2-76	" Ann, and Benjamin Howard, July 14, 1771.	
3-300	Sisson Sarah R., and John B. Smith, Nov. 2, 1845.	
3-305	" Peleg, of Scituate, son of Elisha and Catherine, and Abbie Ashton, of Samuel B. F. of Scituate; m. by Rev. George W. Brewster, Dec. 12, 1847.	

3-301	Slack Isaac W., of North Kingstown, son of Benjamin, and Mrs. Harriet A. King, of Cranston, dau. of William L. Martin; m. by Rev. Zalman Tobey, Sept. 13, 1846.
1-14	Slocum Eliazbeth, and Peter Greene, Feb. 12, 1695-6.
1-44	" Ruth, and Peter, Wells, Nov. 23, 1740.
1-65	" Mary, and William Hall, June 7, 1744.
2-167	" Mercy, and Capt. John Spencer, Feb. 9, 1752.
2-172	" Jonathan, and Ruth Tripp, both of Portsmouth; m. by Ebenezer Slocum, Justice, Feb. 23, 1759.
2-175	" Thomas, and Mary Carder; m. by Ebenezer Slocum, Justice, June 21, 1761.
2-157	" Bettey, and Pero Roomes (col.), Aug. 18, 1804.
3-258	" Marian, and Simon Potter, May. 11, 1822.
1-3	Smith Richard Suske, and Hannah Johns, late of Salem; m. by John Greene, Asst., Sept. 3, 1669.
1-6	" Jeremiah, of John, and Mary Girreard, of John; m. by John Greene, Justice, Jan. 2, 1672.
1-6	" Mrs. Anna, widow; married Nov. 2, 1678.
1-70	" Benjamin, of Benjamin, and Phebe Arnold, of Stephen, Dec. 25, 1691.
1-18	" Simon, of Benjamin, and Mary Andrews, of William, Jan. 5, 1698-9.
1-34	" Elizabeth, and Isreal Arnold, Jr., Feb. 28, 1698-9.
1-23	" William, of Warwick, and Patience Harris, of Providence; m. by Thomas Fry, Justice, Mar. 17, 1708-9.
2-149	" Phebe, and Robert Rhodes, Apr. 7, 1763.
2-176	" William, of Dartmouth, Mass., and Sarah Waterman, of Resolved, dec., of Warwick; m. by Eld. Charles Holden, Nov. 17, 1765.
2-176	" Stephen, Jr., of Stephen, and Patience Arnold, of Simeon; m. by Eld. Charles Holden, Dec. 26, 1765.
2-164	" Simeon, of Warwick, and Martha Peck, of Cranston, R. I.; m. by Eld. Charles Holden, Dec. 12, 1773.
3-41	" Amey, and Martin Benson, Feb. 22, 1809.
3-96	" Susan, and James Essex, Jan. 17, 1823.
4-89	" Alfred, of Pawtuxet, and Patience Phillips, of Warren; m. by Rev. George W. Anthony, Jan. 15, 1832.
3-17	" Mary, and Nathaniel Arnold, Aug. 8, 1839.
3-303	" George, and Elizabeth W. Stone; m. by Rev. Edward K. Fuller, Sept. 1, 1845.

3-300	Smith	John B., of Providence, son of George W. dec., and Sarah R. Sisson, of Samuel; m. by Rev. Moses Fifield, Nov. 2, 1845.
3-299	"	Jared H., of William, and Clarrissa A. Bailey, of Jeremiah; m. by Rev. John H. Barker, Dec. 26, 1847.
3-407	"	John L., and Susan E. Wellman; m. by Rev. George Uhler, Jan. 7, 1849.
4-9	"	Eliza, and Benjamin L. Foss, Apr. 23, 1849.
4-37	"	Lucy L., and Seth H. Steere, Feb. 23, 1851.
4-85	"	Mrs. Lucy A., and William Gardiner, May 27, 1867.
1-5	Smyte	Mrs. Anna, widow, and —— ——, Nov. 2, 1678.
2-14	Snell	Abigail, and Rufus Burton, Dec. 14, 1777.
2-125	"	Mary, and Pardon Potter, Oct. 17, 1779.
2-248	"	Joanna, and Nehemiah Atwood, Dec. 31, 1786.
2-257	"	Susannah, and George Matteson, Sept. 11, 1794.
2-92	"	Thomas, of Daniel, and Cynthia Chace, of Lowry; m. by James Jerauld, Justice Oct. 5, 1798.
3-289	"	Daniel, of Warwick, and Anne Roberts, of William, of Scituate; m. by Caleb Westcott, Justice, Dec. 27, 1804.
3-296	"	William H., of Henry, and Susan M. Perkins, of Elisha; m. by Rev. Jonathan Brayton, June 3, 1844.
3-294	Southwick	Thomas M., of Uxbridge, Mass., son of Enoch, and Levinia B. Mowry, of Warwick, dau. of Osborne; m. by Eld. Moses Fifield, Feb. 11, 1839.
1-80	Sparks	Samuel, of Henry, and Margaret Lawton, of John; m. by Eld. Francis Bates, Dec. 4, 1736.
2-170	Sparron	Phebe, and Eleazer Sisco, Oct. 24, 1756.
3-298	Spaulding	Erastus G., son of Warren, of Hittsborough, N. H., and Harriet Fisher, of Herman, of Warwick; m. by Ray G. Andrews, Justice, Nov. 11, 1839.
1-88	Spencer	Nathaniel, and Mary Alleton, of John; m. by William Greene, Justice, Oct. 22, 1740.
2-167	"	Capt. John, of East Greenwich, son of William, and Mercy Slocum, of Warwick; m. by James Greene, Justice, Feb. 9, 1752.
2-169	"	Benjamin, of Walter, of East Greenwich, and Sarah Low, of Warwick; m. by Eld. John Gorton, Jan. 20, 1757.
2-175	"	Caleb, and Elizabeth Spencer; m. by Benjamin Arnold, Justice, Mar. 22, 1760.
2-175	"	Elizabeth, and Caleb Spencer, Mar. 22, 1760.

2-173　Spencer Capt. Rufus, of East Greenwich, and Margaret Greene, of Hon. William, dec.; m. by Silas Clapp, Justice, July 12, 1761.
2-213　" Elizabeth, and John Warner, Apr. 28, 1767.
2-182　" Simmons, of John, of East Greenwich, and Amey Briggs, of Joseph; m. by Eld. John Gorton, June 7, 1789.
2-177　" Lawton, of Gideon, of Warwick, and Martha Niles, of Jonathan, of East Greenwich; m. by Eld. John Gorton, Aug. 7, 1791.
2-184　" Thomas, of John, of Warwick, and Mary Vaughn, of East Greenwich, dau. of Christopher; m. by Benjamin Barton, Justice, May 20, 1792.
2-198　" Nancy, and Jeremiah Webb, Dec. 7, 1794.
2-91　" Rufus G., of Charles, dec., and Barbara Wickes, of Stuteley; m. by James Jerauld, Justice, Jan. 24, 1799.
3-293　" Christopher, and Celia Westcott; m. by Eld. Samuel Littlefield, Nov. 18, 1813.
4-401　" William B., of Warwick, and Welthia Carpenter, of Richmond, R. I.; m. by Eld. Thomas Tillinghast, Apr. 20, 1834.
3-295　" Thomas J., of Gideon, and Caroline Remington, of Thomas, (S. B.); m. by Eld. Moses Fifield, Apr. 27, 1834.
3-15　" Mary T., and Joseph W. Arnold, July 29, 1838.
3-299　" Harriet, and Augustus R. Sweet, Nov. 14, 1839.
3-300　" William, of Providence, son of Christopher, and Penelope S. Tiffany, of John; m. by Rev. Moses Fifield, Dec. 23, 1839.
3-303　" David, of East Greenwich, and Sybel Briggs, of Warwick; m. by Rev. Thomas Tew, Jan. 3, 1841.
3-122　" Eliza Ann, and George Mowry, Mar. 6, 1842.
3-127　" Theodesia, and Charles Gorton, May 29, 1843.
3-304　" Raymond G., and Lydia M. Hubbard; m. by Rev. Stephen A. Thomas, May 2, 1847.
3-385　" Hannah, and Benjamin N. Briggs, Aug. 22, 1847.
3-406　" Dexter R., of Ephraim, and Mary H. Tillinghast, of Horace; m. by Rev. Zalman Tobey, Feb. 14, 1848.
4-14　" Eliza, and George W. Whitman, Oct. 8, 1849.
3-401　" William B., of Warwick, and Harriet C. Gorton, of New Bedford, Mass., (also 4-57); m. by Rev. J. Girdwood, Oct. 6, 1852.

4-59   Spencer David A., of East Greenwich, aged 21 years, son of Ezra, and Sally G. Nichols, of East Greenwich, aged 18 years, dau. of Isaac; m. by Rev. B. F. Hedden, Nov. 25, 1852.
1-4   Spicer Peter, of Norridge, Conn., and Mary Busecott, of Warwick, Dec. 15, 1670.
1-102 " Thomas, of East Greenwich, and Mary Chadsey, of William, of North Kingstown; m. by Jabez Greene, Justice, June 1, 1744.
2-221 Spink Deborah, and John Gorton, Aug. 26, 1770.
3-68   " Hannah, and Weeden Clarke, Feb. 11, 1810.
3-50   " Lucy, and Daniel A. Brown, Aug. 3, 1840.
3-166 " Waitey A., and Dudley D. Hall, Apr. 14, 1845.
4-45   " Elcy G., and Nehemiah A. Williams, Sept. 28, 1851.
4-92   " William M., and Dorcas P. Barney; m. by Rev. Stephen A. Thomas, Oct. 24, 1853.
2-168 Sprague Peter, of William, of Cranston, and Mary Carpenter, of Wilbour, of Warwick; m. by Eld. John Gorton, Feb. 19, 1789.
3-289 " Elisha, of North Providence, and Elizabeth Essex, of Warwick; m. by Eld. Samuel Littlefield, Apr. 4, 1805.
3-296 " William H., of Warwick, son of Soloman, of Exeter, dec., and Nancy Rice, of Low, dec., of Warwick; m. by Rev. Moses Fifield, Sept. 19, 1839.
3-321 " Abbie, and David Tefft, Mar. 14, 1842.
3-163 " Susan, and Edwin Hoyt, Nov. 29, 1843.
2-205 Spywood Abigail, and Ishmael West, Mar. 6, 1760.
2-202 " Abigail, and Caleb West, Dec. 28, 1761.
3-289 " James, and Ann Lippitt, (col.); m. by Eld. Samuel Littlefield, Aug, 30, 1804.
3-370 " Betsey Ann, and James M. Cheves, June 27, 1844.
1-2   Stafford Sarah, and Amos Westcott, July 13, 1667.
1-3   " Deborah, and Amos Westcott, Jan. 9, 1670.
1-5   " Thomas, Jr., and Jane Dodge; m. by John Greene, Justice, Dec. 20, 1671.
1-12   " Amos, of Samuel, and Mary Burlingame, of Roger, Sr., Dec. 19, 1689.
1-36   " Thomas, of Samuel, and Anne Greene, of Job, Dec. 25, 1707.
1-66   " Mary, and Samuel Bennett, Jr., July 15, 1716.
1-332 " Samuel, of Amos, and Hannah Bennett, of Capt. Samuel, June 20, 1717.

1-36	Stafford	Thomas, and Audrey Greene, of Richard, July 16, 1719.
1-53	"	John, and Jerusha Westgate, widow of Sylvanus, July 22, 1726.
1-106	"	Phebe, and William Arnold, May 6, 1733.
1-91	"	Susannah, and Alexander McGregor, June 4, 1738-9.
1-23	"	Joseph, of Joseph, and Rebecca Arnold, of Capt. William; m. by William Rice, Justice, May 27, 1739.
1-69	"	Mary, aud Jonathan Greene, July 27, 1740,
1-154	"	Hannah, and Pardon Tillinghast, Nov. 30, 1740.
2-201	"	Mercy, and John Waterman, Jan. 7, 1741.
2-165	"	John, Jr., of John, and Elizabeth Greene, of Major Peter; m. by Eld. Manassah Martin, Oct. 22, 1744.
2-120	"	Barbara, and William Potter, Feb. 2, 1745.
2-166	"	Stuteley, and Sarah Gorton, of Edward; m. by John Walton, Justice, May 26, 1748.
2-68	"	Mercy, and Caleb Hill, Mar. 23, 1755.
2-70	"	Deliverance, and William Havens, Sept. 9, 1764.
2-12	"	Elizabeth, and James Arnold, Jan. 30, 1772.
2-181	"	John, of Stuteley, and Mary Arnold, of Caleb; m. by Eld. Charles Holden, Feb. 11, 1773.
2-82	"	Elizabeth, and Gorton Jerauld, Dec. 18, 1774.
2-67	"	Jane, and William Hathaway, June 4, 1775.
2-139	"	Sarah, and Joseph Arnold, Sept. 6, 1778.
2-162	"	Thomas, Jr., and Polly Rhodes; m. by Eld. Abraham Lippitt, Jan. 1, 1789.
2-129	"	Anna, and Thomas Taylor, Apr. 3, 1796.
2-132	"	Elizabeth, and Samuel Greene, Mar. 19, 1797.
2-166	"	Jonathan, of John, of Coventry, and Hannah Whitford, of George, of Warwick; m. by James Jerauld, Justice, Jan. 6, 1802.
2-199	"	Marbery, and Martin Salisbury Wightman, (also 3-339), July 15, 1804.
3-2	"	Rebecca, and David Arnold, Jr., Nov. 1, 1807.
3-338	"	Pattey, and Thomas Whitford, Apr. 28, 1808.
3-45	"	Alice, and David Blair, Sept. 3, 1809.
3-120	"	Mercy R., and Barton W. Gorton, Dec 3, 1818.
4-76	"	John Raymond, of Thomas R., and Mary Nichols, of Warwick, dau. of Benjamin, dec., of South Kingstown; m. by Eld. Moses Fifield, Nov. 16, 1837.
3-265	"	Sarah, and Willard T. Peirce, Sept. 17, 1838.

WARWICK—MARRIAGES. 113

3-302 Stafford Jeremiah, of Warwick, son of Robey, and Eliza John
son, Cranston, dau. of Benedict; m. by Rev. Junia S.
Mowry, Mar. 25, 1841.
3-268 " Lydia, and Joseph Preston, Sept. 4, 1843.
2-247 Standish Mary, and Clarke Hammett, Sept. 8, 1801.
1-62   Staples Hannah, and Moses Budlong, July 4, 1734.
4-32   Steere Mary, and Jeremiah G. Pearce, Oct. 6, 1850.
4-37   " Seth H., of Glocester, aged 25 years, son of Riley, and
Lucy L. Smith, of same town, aged 20 years, dau. of
Gideon; m. by Rev. Benjamin Phelan, Feb. 23,
1851.
3-375 Stokes Mary Anna, and Abraham R. Carey, Jan. 20, 1847.
1-35   Stone Peter, and Elizabeth Shaw, of John, June 25, 1696.
1-22   " Anne, and William Utter, Sept. 27, 1705.
2-167 " Thomas, Jr., and Elizabeth Carder; m. by John Warner,
Jr., Justice, Mar. 5, 1761.
2-175 " Benjamin, of John, dec., of Cranston, and Mary Straight,
of John, dec., of East Greenwich; m. by Eld. Charles
Holden, May 26, 1763.
2-179 " John, Jr., of John, and Phebe Greene, of Stephen, dec.;
m. by Eld. Charles Holden, Mar. 17, 1774.
2-233 " Mary, and Elisha Baker, May 3, 1778.
2-182 " Olney, of John, dec., and Phebe Arnold, of Simeon; m.
by Eld. John Gorton, Apr. 25, 1782.
2-180 " James, of Cranston, son of Samuel, and Mary Webb, of
William, of Warwick; m. by James Jerauld, Justice,
Feb. 12, 1786.
3-219 " Phebe, and John Miller, Nov. 28, 1806.
3-346 " Eleanor, and Reuben Wickes, Apr. 25, 1808.
3-301 " Jason P., of Coventry, and Eliza Albro, of Warwick; m.
by Rev. Thomas Dowling, Oct. 8, 1839.
3-303 " Elizabeth W., and George Smith, Sept. 1, 1845.
3-392 " Alfred, of Providence, son of William, and Ann M.
Budlong, of Warwick, dau. of George W.; m. by Rev.
Zalman Tobey, Nov. 20, 1848.
4-47   " Harriet K., and Henry C. Sherman, Oct. 30, 1851.
4-51   " Jason P., of Coventry, aged 34 years, son of Nathan K.
and Seldia, and Sarah E. Wickes, of Warwick, aged
21 years, dau, of Reuben and Elizabeth; m. by Rev.
Benjamin Phelan, Mar. 15, 1852.
4-74   " Edwin, and Phebe Randall; m. by Eld. Paul Harrington,
Mar. 25, 1860.

1-44   Straight Henry, Jr., of East Greenwich, and Mary Webb, widow, of Warwick; m. by John Warner, Justice, Aug. 5, 1725.
1-54   "   Mary, and Phillip Westcott, (also 100), Nov. 12, 1732.
1-43   "   Sarah, and Adam Lockwood, Dec. 24, 1734.
2-173 "   Phebe, and Thomas Straight, Dec. 20, 1758.
2-173 "   Thomas, of Coventry, and Phebe Straight, of Warwick; m. by Samuel Gorton, Justice, Dec. 20, 1758.
2-175 "   Mary, and Benjamin Stone, May 26, 1763.
2-178 "   Joseph, Jr., of Joseph, and Mary LeValley, of John; m. by Eld. Charles Holden, Dec. 16, 1773.
2-182 "   Joseph, Jr., of Warwick, now of North Kingstown, and Robe Wightman, of George, dec.; m. by Adam Comstock, Justice, July 18, 1779.
2-173 "   Webb, and Catherine Carder; m. by Eld. Samuel Littlefield, May 31, 1795.
2-99   "   Phebe, and Stephen Bennett, Oct. 12, 1800.
2-105 "   Nabby, and Abel Bennett, May 22, 1803.
4-78   "   Potter P., of Warwick, and Harriet Austin, of Exeter; m. by Rev. Jonathan Brayton, Aug. 2, 1857.
3-408 Sunderland Rhoda A., and Nathan Card, Jan. 27, 1848.
4-31   "   Mary C., and George Bowman, Oct. 7, 1850.
4-62   "   Sarah H., and James S. Tennant, May 1, 1853.
4-50   Sweetzer Seth, Jr., aged 33 years, of Malden, Mass., and Thankful G. Hutchins, aged 22 years, of George; m. by Rev. William H. Richards, Nov. 26, 1851.
1-48   Sweet Nathaniel, of James, and Giffe Kittle, Sept. 7, 1721.
1-43   "   Renewed, and James Hitt, Jr., July 5, 1727.
2-167 "   Phillip, Jr., of Phillip, and Lydia Rice, of Capt. John; m. by William Rice, Justice, Jan. 25, 1740.
1-81   "   Deborah, and Isaac Rice, June 8, 1740.
2-166 "   Eber, and Mary Scranton, of Stephen; m. by Jabez Greene, Justice, Mar. 3, 1747.
2-168 "   Samuel, and Mercy Potter; m. by Eld. John Gorton, Sept. 23, 1754.
2-170 "   Benjamin, of Phillip, and Phebe Wightman, of John; m. by Ebenezer Slocum, Justice, Oct. 8, 1754.
2-23   "   Ann, and Thomas Collins, May 29, 1755.
2-171 "   Mercy, and Peleg Salisbury, Dec. 14, 1758.
2-173 "   Thomas, of Phillip, and Deborah Wightman, of John; m. by Ebenezer Slocum, Justice, Apr. 24, 1760.
2-215 "   Margaret, and Ezekiel Warner, Sept. 25, 1762.

2-75	Sweet Ann, and Jeremiah Hopkins, Sept. 30, 1762.
2-150	" Hannah, and Sawdee Rouse, Apr. 8, 1764.
2-210	" Wait, and William Warner, July 8, 1764.
2-172	" Ceaser, of North Kingstown, son of Ebro, and Tamar Rice (so called), servant of Thomas, Jr., (col.); m. by James Jerauld, Justice, Mar. 21, 1779.
2-220	" Naomi, and Edward Weeden, Oct. 10, 1779.
4-79	" Eliza, and Thomas S. Cheese, May 15, 1808.
3-291	" Stephen, of John, of West Greenwich, and Deborah V. Rice, of Henry, dec., of Warwick; m. by Eld. Thomas Manchester, July 2, 1818.
3-297	" Greene A., and Sarah B. Card; m. by Rev. Thomas Dowling, Sept. 2, 1839.
3-131	" Deborah D., and Job P. Gorton, Oct. 7, 1839.
3-299	" Augustus R., of Warwick, son of William, of Exeter, and Harriet Spencer, of John, Jr., of Warwick; m. by Rev. Moses Fifield, Nov. 14, 1839.
3-158	" Silvia, and David Hall, Dec. 10, 1840.
3-155	" Harriet N., and Charles F. Hopkins, Apr. 4, 1842.
3-25	" Eliza G., and Daniel R. Allen, Oct. 20, 1842.
3-295	" Sion R., of Scituate, son of Joseph, and Hannah Hunt, of Silas; m. by Rev. Jonathan Brayton, Aug. 14, 1843.
4-70	" Lucy Ann, and Lorenzo D. Sherman, Sept. 7, 1846.
3-302	" Pardon, of Cato, and Mary Harry, of John; m. by Rev. Jonathan Brayton, Jan. 11, 1847.
3-291	" Thomas C., of Warwick, son of Daniel, dec., of Richmond, R. I., and Sarah B. Griffin, of Peleg, of Warwick; m. by Eld. Moses Fifield, May 17, 1847.
3-194	" Alice A., and Dyer Kingsley, Jan. 3, 1848.
4-79	" Alonzo B., and Hattie Simmons; m. by Rev. Benjamin Phelan, Nov. 29, 1862.
4-26	Swindells James, of George, and Marie Swindells, of George, all of Providence; m. by Rev. Zalman Tobey, May 13, 1850.
4-26	" Marie, and James Swindells, May 13, 1850.

T

3-395	Taber Mary E., and William C. Burch, Jan. 10, 1847.
4-15	Taft George J., of George, and Abigail R. Odell, of James; m. by Rev. Jonathan Brayton, Aug. 8, 1849.

4-25   Taft Jane W., and Albert H. Knight, Feb. 21, 1850.
2-211 Tallman Bethany, and Smithern Wilcox, Sept. 22, 1760.
1-1   Talman Benjamin, and Elizabeth Gorton, of Samuel, Jan. —, 1735.
1-101 Tanner Lilas, and Samuel Barton, Mar. 23, 1737-8.
3-83   "   Sally, and John G. Dawley, Nov. 30, 1826.
3-311 "   William, of Warwick, son of Palmer, and Eliza S. Tillinghast, of Warwick, dau. of Job, dec., of East Greenwich; m. by Rev. Moses Fifield, Apr. 26, 1835.
3-320 "   Daniel, and Abbie A. Pollard; m. by Rev. Moses Fifield, May 7, 1846.
3-142 "   Susan C., and Stephen A. Greene, Oct, 24, 1847.
4-75   "   Hannah, and Joseph A. Bitgood, Jan. 20, 1860.
2-189 Tarbox Jonathan, of Samuel, of East Greenwich, and Alice Keas, of William, of Warwick; m. by Ebenezer Slocum, Justice, Dec. 19, 1756.
3-326 "   William W., of Whitford, of West Greenwich, and Mary L. Bennett, of Ephraim, of Coventry; m. by Rev. Daniel Slocum, Feb. 11, 1849.
2-129 Taylor Thomas, and Anna Stafford; m. by Eld. Samuel Littlefield, Apr. 3, 1796.
2-121 "   William, of Ambrose, of Warwick, and Mary Reynolds, of Francis, of North Kingstown; m. by Eld. Phillip Jenkins, Dec. 30, 1797.
2-105 "   Betsey, and Edmund Burke, Apr. 5, 1798.
3-359 "   Mrs. Ann, and Christopher R. Whipple, Mar. 31, 1839.
3-312 "   John A., of Warwick, son of John, of Foster, and Emeline S. Thomas, of John, of Warwick m. by Rev. Moses Fifield, June 11, 1839.
3-312 "   Samuel R., resident of Scituate, and Cynthia A. Watson, of Coventry; m. by Rev. Thomas Tillinghast, May 25, 1840.
3-314 "   Thomas T., and Huldah G. Briggs; m. by Rev. M. J. Steere, Apr. 28, 1845.
3-286 "   Lovice C., and Franklin Richardson, Nov. 26, 1846.
4-18   "   Mary E., and Hester McKensie, Nov. 4, 1849.
4-25   "   Josiah, and Zilpha S. Knight, both of Scituate; m. by Rev. Reuben Allen, Mar. 1, 1850.
1-4   Teffe Tabitha, and George Garner, Feb. 13, 1670.
3-317 Tefft Welcome, of Warwick, son of Thomas, dec., of Exeter, and Lucinda Williams, ot Warwick, dau. of Stephen, dec.; m. by Rev. Moses Fifield, Nov. 17, 1840.

3-320	Tefft Samuel H., of Warwick, son of George, dec., of Hopkinton, and Maria F. Johnson, of Warwick, dau. of Levi, dec., of East Greenwich; m. by Rev. Moses Fifield, Nov. 22, 1841.
3-321	" David, of Warwick, son of George, dec., of Hopkinton, and Abbie Sprague, of Warwick, dau. of Christopher, of Cranston; m. by Rev. Moses Fifield, Mar. 14, 1842.
3-312	" Alanson, of Warwick, son of Thomas, of Greene, N. Y., and Robey Himes, of John, of Warwick; m. by Rev. Moses Fifield, Nov. 19, 1843.
3-270	" Esther Ann, and Jason W. Rice, Nov. 16, 1846.
4-19	" Catherine, and Pardon Crandall, Jan. 1, 1850.
3-52	Temple Mary, and William Barbour, Oct. 30, 1840.
3-64	" Janette, and Thomas Begbee, Dec. 29, 1843.
3-305	Tennant Susan, and James M. Scott, May 23, 1842.
3-106	" Ann, and Albert Farnum, Aug. 27, 1843.
3-298	" Ruth, and Isaac Searle, Apr. 7, 1845.
3-316	" John, of Havens, and Ruth Langford, of John; m. by Eld. John Pratt, Sept. 7, 1846.
4-62	" James S. aged 25 years, son of James, and Juda, of Warwick, and Sarah H. Sunderlin, aged 25 years, of Exeter, dau. of William, and Almy S.; m. by Rev. Benjamin Phelan, May 1, 1853.
3-315	Tew John W., of John, and Dorcas Brown, of William; m. by Rev. Thomas Dowling, May 15, 1840.
3-168	" Frances and William Hampson, Oct. 13, 1843.
3-319	" Adam, and Susan A. Walter; m. by Rev. Edward K. Fuller, Jan. 8, 1846.
3-48	Thomas Elizabeth, and Thomas Freeborn, Jan. 30, 1735.
2-189	" George, of Samuel, of North Kingstown, and Phebe Lockwood, of Capt. Amos; m. by Eld. Charles Holden, Sept. 25, 1763.
3-312	" Emeline S., and John A. Taylor, June 11, 1839.
3-310	" Elihu, of Warwick, son of Elihu, of Cranston, and Susan Vickery, of George, of Warwick; m. by Rev. Moses Fifield, Nov. 27, 1842.
3-285	" Mrs. Martha A., and John H. Remington, May 8, 1843.
3-214	Thompson Jane F., and Richard S. Lathrop [also 3-325], Sept. 26, 1848.
4-37	" Mary R., and William M. Halstead, Oct. 16, 1850.
3-348	Thornton Hannah H., and Samuel W. Whitman, Oct. 15, 1812.
3-327	" Ann E., and William H. Wood, Dec. 9, 1844.

2-189 Thurber James, of Dea. Edward, of North Providence, and Mary Rice, of Capt. Randall; m. by Eld. Charles Holden, Dec. 8, 1765.
2-191 " Samuel, of Providence, aud Welthian Turtelot, widow of Abraham, late of Glocester; m. by Eld. Charles Holden, May 27, 1770.
3-318 " Lewis H., of Attleboro, Mass., and Elizabeth G. Arnold, of Warwick; m. by Eld. Thomas Tillinghast, Oct. 8, 1845.
3-57 Thurston Eliza A., and Benjamin R. Briggs, Aug. 23, 1841.
3-322 " Charles F., of Jabez, and Phebe A. Baker, of Pardon, dec.; m. by Rev. Junia S. Mowry, Apr. 4, 1842.
3-323 " Stephen W. of Warwick, son of Whitman, of Exeter, and Abbie R. Johnson, of Warwick; m. by Rev. Moses Fifield, May 2, 1842.
3-159 " Penelope, and James F. Hills, Sept. 19, 1842.
3-315 " Daniel B., of Warwick, son of George A., dec., of Tiverton, and Nancy M. Carder, of Warwick, dau. of James; m. by Rov. Moses Fifield, Sept. 22, 1845.
3-322 " Samuel W., of Warwick, son of John, of Plainfield, Conn., and Esther Martin, of Warwick, dau. of Otis; m. by Rev. Moses Fifield, Nov. 26, 1846.
3-365 " Artemisia, and Joseph P. Brown, May 30, 1848.
1-24 Tibbetts Rebecca, and Fones Greene, Feb. 5, 1712-3.
1-58 " Thomas, and Elizabeth Wood, Nov. 15, 1716.
1-52, 58 " Elizabeth, and Samuel Finney, Mar. 12 or 17, 1726-7.
1-81 " Hannah, and Benjamin Nichols, Feb. 4, 1730-1.
1-16 " William, of Henry, of Warwick, and Judah Perce, of Niles, of Rehoboth, Mass., Apr. 26, 1736.
1-52 " Henry, and Phebe Waterman; m. by Eld. Manassah Martin, Nov. 23, 1738.
1-69 " Dinah, and Francis Matteson, Jr., July 10, 1740.
2-190 " John, of William, dec., and Waite Brown, of Elisha; m. by Richard Pike, Justice, Jan. 7, 1760.
2-13 " Mary, and Elisha Brown, May 21, 1761.
2-191 " Henry, of Henry, and Hannah Remington, of Thomas; m. by Eld. John Gorton, Dec. 15, 1763.
2-217 " Waterman, of Henry, and Mercy Waterman, of John, dec.; m. by Eld. John Gorton, Dec. 13, 1764.
2-110 " Juda, and Pelatiah Mason, Sept, 4, 1766.
2-184 " John, of Thomas, of Warwick, and Robey Dexter, of Coventry; m. by Ebenezer Slocum, Justice, Dec. 13, 1772.

2-78	Tibbetts Phebe, and Nicholas Harris, Feb. 25, 1773.
2-192	" William, Jr., of William, dec., and Sarah Arnold, of Elisha, dec.; m. by James Jerauld, Justice, Feb. 1, 1778.
2-194	" Jonathan, of Thomas, and Rebecca Tillinghast, of Samuel; m. by Eld. John Gorton, July 25, 1784.
2-131	" Jonathan, of Warwick, and Cynthia Weaver, widow of Clement; m. by James Jerauld, Justice, Sept. 2, 1798.
2-90	" George, and Robe Tibbetts, of John; m. by Nathan Arnold, Justice, June 27, 1802.
2-90	" Robe, and George Tibbetts, June 27, 1802.
3-309	" Benjamin, and Henrietta Arnold; m. by Rev. Samuel Littlefield, Jan. 5, 1806.
3-309	" Charles, and Maplet Remington; m. by Eld. Samuel Littlefield, June 1, 1806.
3-218	" Robe, and John Mitchell, Mar. 12, 1809.
3-58	" Julia Ann, and George A. Briggs, June 5, 1836.
3-231	" Ruth B., and Thomas Marble, Aug. 11, 1842.
4-13	" Sophrona A., and Robert Pepperell, Sept. 23, 1849.
2-190	Tiffany Benjamin, of Benjamin, of Warwick, and Mary Olin, of Henry, of West Greenwich; m. by Eld. John Gorton, Nov. 6, 1768.
2-194	" Sylvester, and Frances Hopkins, of Capt. Stephen; m. by James Jerauld, Justice, July 28, 1784.
2-194	" Benjamin, of Thomas, and Eleanor Wickes, of Stuteley; m. by Eld. Phillip Jenkins, Jan. 26, 1794.
2-188	" Lucy, and Seth Burke, Mar. 26, 1795.
3-51	" Susan, and Joseph Baker, July 1, 1819.
3-300	" Penelope S., and William Spencer, Dec. 23, 1839.
3-59	" Roby, and Albert Baker, Oct. 11, 1841.
3-325	" Mahala, and William W. Arnold, June 13, 1842.
3-39	" Elizabeth A., and Dr. Thomas E. Andrew, Nov. 9, 1847.
4-45	" Stephen, aged 29 years, of Griswold, Ct., son of Stephen, and Ann A. W. Clapp, aged 28 years, of Warwick, dau. of Waterman; m. by Rev. Moses Fifield, Oct. 20, 1850.
1-79	Tillinghast Pardon, of Phillip, and Margaret Greene, of Capt. Benjamin; m. by John Wickes, Asst., Jan. 8, 1729.
1-54	" Pardon, of John, of East Greenwich, and Hannah Stafford, of Lieut. James, of Warwick; m. by William Greene, Justice, Nov. 30, 1740.
2-159	" Mary, and John Remington, Dec. 17, 1780.

2-194	Tillinghast	Rebecca, and Jonathan Tibbetts, July 25, 1784.
2-113	"	William, of George, of East Greenwich, and Eleanor Baker, of Joseph; m. by James Jerauld, Justice, Mar. 12, 1797.
3-223	"	Eliza A., and Gulielmus B. Millard, Aug. 23, 1818.
3-226	"	Almy R., and Sylvester K. Merrill, July 4, 1830.
3-263	"	Lydia A., and Otis W. Potter, July 25, 1831.
3-311	"	Eliza S., and William Tanner, Apr. 26, 1835.
3-319	"	Phillip, of Cincinnati, Ohio, son of Joseph R., and Julia A. C. Titus, of Warwick, dau. of Charles W. Cozzens, and adopted dau. of Crompton Titus, dec.; m. by Rev. Thomas Wickes, Oct. 13, 1841.
3-99	"	Rebecca A., and Dexter A. Edwards, Jan. 9, 1842.
3-3	"	Samuel R., of Horace, and Julia A. Searle, of Benjamin G.; m. by Rev. Jonathan Brayton, Feb. 26, 1843.
3-313	"	James B., of Horace, and Lydia W. Budlong, of Samuel; m. by Rev. Moses Fifield, Mar. 25, 1845.
3-288	"	Scynthia, and Thomas M. Remington, Jan. 1, 1846.
3-390	"	Lucy M., and Nicholas C. Briggs, Mar. 29, 1846.
3-101	"	Sally Maria, and Benjamin Essex, Feb. 9, 1847.
3-406	"	Mary H., and Dexter R. Spencer, Feb. 14, 1848.
4-8	"	Samuel, of Warwick, son of Pardon, of Exeter, and Patience T. Dyer, of William T., of Warwick; m. by Rev. Moses Fifield, June 28, 1849.
4-7	"	Ariadna, and Morris Durfee, May 27, 1849.
4-15	"	Benjamin C., of Coventry, son of Pardon, and Ada Blanchard, of Warwick, dau. of Samuel; m. by Rev. Jonathan Brayton, Aug. 26, 1849.
3-319	Titus	Julia A. C., and Phillip Tillinghast, Oct. 13, 1841.
3-321	"	James H., of Providence, and Miranda Pearce, of Warwick; m. by Rev. Stephen A. Thomas, July 19, 1846.
3-102	"	Dorotha, and Calvin Eager, Mar. 18, 1847.
3-318	Torrey	William D., of Attleboro, Mass., son of Samuel, of Wrentham, and Mercy Ann Angell, of Ethan, of Coventry; m. by Rev. Moses Fifield, Aug. 31, 1841.
3-313	Tourjee	James M., of Warwick, son of Thomas, dec., of North Kingstown, and Elizabeth Kingsley, of Warwick, dau. of James, of North Kingstown; m. by Rev. Moses Fifield, June 10, 1839.
3-130	"	Presilla S., and Benjamin Greene, June 10, 1839.
3-324	"	John, son of John and Ellen, and Agnes Blesborough, of Lazarus and Mary; m. by Rev. Charles E. Bennett, Oct. 8, 1848.

4-77	Tourjee Alonzo, and Isabel Harper; m. by Rev. Moses Fifield, Aug. 16, 1855.
4-77	" Isabella, and Elisha O. Sherman, Dec. 7, 1864.
1-77	Townsend Hannah, and John Waterman, June 5, 1729.
3-324	" William, of Exeter, and Mary Knowles, of Coventry; m. by Eld. William Stovyer, May 24, 1842.
1-79	Tripp Phebe, and William Rice, Dec. 10, 1730.
1-66	" Isreal, and Elizabeth Bentley; m. by William Rice, Asst., Sept. 2, 1744.
2-192	" Job, of Isaac, formerly of Pomfret, Conn., and Hannah Rice, of William, dec.; m. by Thomas Aldrich, Justice, May 16, 1757.
2-172	" Ruth, and Jonathan Slocum, Feb. 23, 1759.
3-244	" Susan, and William Nichols, July 1, 1844.
3-310	Trumbull John Kerr, formerly of Ireland, and Betsey Price, of Matthew, of Warwick; m. by Eld. Thomas Manchester, Jan. 27, 1828.
1-57	Tucker Hannah, and James Greene, June 22, 1734.
3-306	Tunguad Mary Ann, and Ebenezer Sidebottom, Apr. 19, 1845.
3-323	Turner Francis S., of Cranston, son of Stephen, and Sarah Jane Maguire, of Daniel, of Warwick; m. by Rev. George A. Willard, June 1, 1848.
2-191	Turtelot Welthian, and Samuel Thurber, May 27, 1770.
3-399	Tyler Hannah M., and William H. Card, June 29, 1846.
4-26	" Anette, and William L. Chase, June 2, 1850.

U

1-22	Utter William, and Anne Stone, of Hugh, Sept. 27, 1705.
1-53	" Sarah, and Amos Lockwood, Dec. 23, 1725.
1-67	" Ruth, and John Dexter, Mar. 3, 1735-6.
1-1	" William, Jr., and Phebe Brown, of Judeth; m. by William Greene, Justice, Jan. 20, 1740.
2-139	" Merebe, and Thomas Barthalake, Sept. 20, 1761.
2-214	" Barbara, and Arnold Wells, Jan. 24, 1762.
2-220	" Sarah, and John Carpenter, Oct. 27, 1765.
2-9	" Ruth, and George Arnold, Dec. 5, 1773.
2-161	" Sarah, and John Rice, Apr. 7, 1785.

V

3-332   Valpey Richard, of Providence, son of Richard, dec., and Susan S. Greene, of Warwick, dau. of Thomas F.; m. by Rev. Moses Fifield, Oct. 31, 1842.

3-331   Van Riper William E., of Warwick, son of Tunis, dec., of New York City, and Betsey A. West, of Warwick, dau. of Amos; m. by Rev. Moses Fifield, Apr. 5, 1847.

2-195   Vaughn David, of East Greenwich, and Sarah Cole, of Nathaniel, of Warwick; m. by Eld. Manassah Martin, Dec. 5, 1745.

2-195   " Christopher, Jr., of East Greenwich, and Elizabeth Freeborn; m. by Joseph Edmunds, Asst., May 10, 1747.

2-26   " Almy, and Elias Dewry, Sept. 25, 1761.

2-195   " David, Jr., of East Greenwich, and Hannah Mathewson; m. by Silas Clapp, Justice, Jan. 24, 1762.

2-184   " Mary, and Thomas Spencer, May 20, 1792.

3-328   " Benjamin, of East Greenwich, and Mellecent Carpenter, of Warwick; m. by Rev. Samuel Littlefield, Oct. 5, 1809.

3-278   " Mary, and William A. Roberts, Jan. 15, 1835.

3-449   " James, of East Greenwich, son of Isaac D., and Maria Congdon; m. by Rev. Jonathan Brayton, Nov. 3, 1845.

4-76   " Lydia, and Reuben Arnold, Feb. 15, 1848.

4-54   " William C., and Elizabeth Remington; m. by Rev. Thomas Tillinghast, Apr. 1, 1849.

4-53   " David C., aged 23 years, of East Greenwich, son of Amos and Ellen, and Elizabeth C. Wilbur, aged 18 years, of Cranston, dau. of Thomas F. and Rebecca; m. by Rev. Philip Crandon, July 5, 1852.

3-329   Vickery Benjamin D., of Warwick, son of Thomas, dec., of Fall River, Mass., and Ann M. Brown, of Jesse, of Warwick; m. by Eld. Moses Fifield, Dec. 28, 1840.

3-310   " Susan, and Elihu Thomas, Nov. 27, 1842.

4-16   " Sally, and Stephen H. Northup, Nov. 15, 1849.

3-124   Vinton Elizabeth, and Lieut. George Sears Greene, U. S. A., July 14, 1828.

3-261   " Cornelia B., and John R. Perry, May 3, 1847.

1-28   Voeghn Jane, and George Hall, M— 11, 1737.

W

3-37 Waite Mrs. Mary, and Charles Allen, Mar. 14, 1847.
3-345 Wakefield Rufus, of Richmond, N. H., and Ruth Atwood, of Warwick; m. by C. Brayton, Justice, Oct. 9, 1811.
1-17 Walch Thomas, and Susannah Wright, both of Providence, Sept. 21, 1703.
3-107 Walker Mary, and William Foster, Oct. 8, 1843.
3-232 " Sally, and Joseph Myrie, Jr., Dec. 12, 1843.
3-405 " Henry, and Susan A. Hutchins, of George; m. by Rev. Jonathan Brayton, Oct. 28, 1845.
3-354 " Edwin S., of Warwick, son of Ebenezer, of Athol, Mass., and Mary A. Nason, widow, dau. of Caleb Carr, of Warwick; m. by Rev. Moses Fifield, Nov. 26, 1846.
4-24 " Angenette, and Henry T. Hall, Nov. 4, 1849.
4-84, 86 " Cynthia A., and Moses W. Collins, Nov. 9, 1855.
4-87 Wallen Andrew, and Sarah Dailey; m. by Rev. M. A. Wallace, Aug. —, 1858.
2-42 Wall Susannah, and Holden Rhodes, Mar. 12, 1769.
3-319 Walter Susan A., and Adam Tew, Jan. 8, 1846.
2-203 Walton John, Jr., and Mary Greene; m. by Benjamin Arnold, Justice, Jan. 6, 1750.
2-240 " Marian, and Caleb Atwood, July 29, 1781.
2-62 Ward Catherine, and Christopher Greene, Dec. 23, 1773.
2-216 " Major Samuel, of Hon. Samuel, dec., of Westerly, and Phebe Greene, of William; m. by Eld. John Gorton, Mar. 8, 1778.
2-62 " Deborah, and Christopher Greene, May 12, 1783.
1-3 Warner Rachel, and Abell Potter, Nov. 16, 1669.
1-4 " John, and Anna Gorton; m. by John Greene, Asst., Aug. 7, 1670.
1-20 " John, Jr., and Elizabeth Coggeshall, Nov. 27, 1694.
1-27 " John, of Warwick, and Susannah Peirce, of Giles, and Elizabeth, of East Greenwich; m. by John Spencer, Justice, Aug. 6, 1713.
1-38 " Ezekiel, of Warwick, and Sarah Bennett, of East Greenwich, May 30, 1717.
1-36 " John, Jr., of Warwick, and Mary Burlingame, of Thomas, of Providence, Oct. 23, 1719.
1-61 " John, Jr., of Warwick, and Abigail Brown, of Judah, of Providence; m by John Wickes, Justice, June 26, 1729.

1-68	Warner Samuel, of Warwick, and Kesiah Browne, of Providence; m. by Stuteley Stafford, Justice, Feb. 19, 1729-0.
1-27	" John, of Warwick, and Elizabeth Cowell, of Boston; m. by Richard Waterman, Asst., Sept. 24, 1730.
1-30	" William, of John, dec., and Susannah Briggs, of Robert, of East Greenwich; m. by William Rice, Justice, Jan. 27, 1739-0.
1-105	" Rachel, and Ephraim Arnold, Jan. or June 18, 1741.
2-201	" Capt. John Jr., of Capt. John and Isabella Risby, of William, late of Newport; m. by Eld. John Hammett, Apr. 16, 1747.
2-204	" Capt. Thomas, and Phebe Greene, of William; m. by Eld. John Hammett, June 22, 1749.
2-142	" Elizabeth, and Holden Rice, June 2, 1751.
2-208	" James, and Rebecca Low; m. by Eld. John Gorton, Jan. 6, 1757.
2-15	" Rachel, and Benjamin Briggs, May 18, 1757.
2-3	" Prescilla, and John Adams, Oct. 2, 1760.
2-215	" Ezekiel, of John, of Warwick, and Margaret Sweet, of East Greenwich, dau. of William; m. by Eld. Charles Holden, Sept. 25, 1762.
2-122	" Lowis, and Azrikam Pearce, Feb. 13, 1763.
2-210	" William, of John, of Warwick, and Wait Sweet, of William, of East Greenwich; m. by Eld. John Gorton, July 8, 1764.
2-144	" Elizabeth, and Jeremiah Richmond, Feb. 23, 1766.
2-213	" John, of Samuel, and Elizabeth Spencer, of Nathaniel, dec.; m. by Eld. Charles Holden, Apr. 28, 1767.
2-231	" Isabel, and David Greene, Jr., Apr. 16, 1772.
2-96	" Anne, and John Lippitt, May 19, 1776.
2-75	" Sarah, and Anthony Holden, Jan. 27, 1780.
2-49	" Phebe, and James Greene, Jan. 6, 1782.
2-224	" Thomas, of Thomas, dec., and Mary Hill, of Nathaniel, dec.; m. by Eld John Gorton, Nov. 24, 1782.
2-255	" Anne, and Nathan Gorton, Dec. 2, 1792.
2-255	" John, of Providence, son of Ezekiel, and Deborah Gorton, of John, of Warwick; m. by James Jerauld, Justice, Dec. 6, 1792.
3-342	" James, and Mary Greene; m. by Rev. Samuel Littlefield, Dec. 15, 1805.
3-155	" Catherine T., and Capt. William Harrison, Jan. 1, 1816.
3-121	" Sarah, and William M. Greene, Dec. 11, 1823.

3-127 Warner Stephen G., and Catherine Celia Greene; m. by Eld. Job Manchester, Feb. 2, 1833.
3-326 " William W., of Warwick, son of Christopher, and Caroline Albro, of Warwick, dau. of Jacob, of Portsmouth [also 3-355]; m. by Rev. Moses Fifield, July 7, 1833.
3-336 " William, of Warwick, and Elizabeth Greene, of East Greenwich; m. by Eld. Job Manchester, Mar. 5, 1835.
" William W., of Christopher, and Susan Barber, of Hazard; m. by Eld. Nathaniel W. Warner, Nov. 7, 1844.
3-351 " Susan A., and Brinton Whitford, Oct. 19, 1846.
4-71 Warren Isabella, and John R. Waterman, Nov. 3, 1805.
4-27 Waterhouse Benjamin, of Richard, of Warwick, and Harriet N. Gardner, of South Kingstown; m. by Rev. Daniel Slocum, June 2, 1850.
1-19 Waterman Wait, and John Roads, Feb. 12, 1684-5.
1-52 " Benoni, of Capt John, and Sarah Wickes, of John, Feb. 11, 1724-5.
1-77 " John, of Capt. John, dec., and Hannah Townsend, of Soloman and Catherine, June 5, 1729.
1-98 " Resolved, of John, dec., and Sarah Carr, of Edward, dec., of Jamestown; m. by Nicholas Carr, Justice, Oct. 12, 1732.
1-52 " Phebe, and Henry Tibbetts, Nov. 23, 1738.
1-52 " Patience, and James Greene, Apr. 10, 1740.
2-201 " John, and Mercy Stafford; m. by Joseph Stafford, Justice, Jan. 7, 1741.
2-207 " John, and Sarah Potter; m. by Eld. Joseph Torrey, June 13, 1754.
2-67 " Hannah, and Nathaniel Hill, Mar. 29, 1761.
2-217 " Mercy, and Waterman Tibbetts, Dec. 13, 1764.
2-176 " Sarah, and William Smith, Nov. 17, 1765.
2-35 " William, of Capt. John, and Phebe Arnold, of Phillip; m. by Thomas Rice, Justice, Mar. 10, 1768.
2-66 " Avis, and Thustian Gardner, Dec. 22, 1768.
2-94 " Phebe, and Benjamin Lockwood, Apr. 5, 1772.
2-232 " Sarah, and Thomas Babcock, Nov. 3, 1774.
2-42 " Anna, and John Clapp, Aug. 31, 1775.
2-218 " John, Jr., and Welthian Greene, Feb. 3, 1782.
2-251 " Sally, and George Greene, Dec. 16, 1787.

2-119 Waterman John, of William, of Warwick, and Phebe Weaver, of Jonathan, of East Greenwich; m. by Eld. John Gorton, July 4, 1790.
2-195 " William, of Coventry, son of Col. John, and Hannah Gorton, widow of Benjamin, dau. of Capt. Oliver Gardner; m. by James Jerauld, Justice, June 9, 1793.
4-71 " John R., son of Dea. John and Welthian, and Isabella Warren, of Thomas and Mary; m. by Eld. Samuel Littlefield, Nov. 3, 1805.
3-117 " Mercy, and James Greene, Oct. 29, 1812.
4-64 " Richard, of John R. and Isabella, and Dianna Maria Chapin, Feb. 15, 1831.
3-342 " Henry, of Millbury, Mass., son of John R., and Sarah L. Greene, of Warwick, dau. of Jeremiah, dec.; m. by Rev. Junia S. Mowry, June 14, 1841.
3 109 " Albert B., of William, and Ann C. Love, of William; m. by Rev. Jonathan Brayton, June 13, 1847.
2-202 Watson Benjamin, of Kingstown, and Mrs. Sarah Westgate; m. by Job Warner, Justice, Sept. 28, 1749.
3-316 " Cynthia A., and Samuel K. Taylor, May 25, 1840.
3-341 " George G., of Warwick, son of James, of Hollowell, Eng., and Sally Russell Carr, of Warwick, dau. of Caleb; m. by Rev. Moses Fifield, Oct. 12, 1840.
4-83, 84 " Harriet N., and Nathaniel S. Carr, Jan. 16, 1857.
1-1 Weaver Clement, of William, and Mary Wickes, of Thomas, prob. ———, 1727.
2-141 " Anne, and Joseph Rhodes, Feb. 4, 1727.
2-211 " Silas, of East Greenwich, son of Benjamin, and Susanna Greene, of Jabez, of Warwick; m. by Ebenezer Slocum, Justice, June 8, 1758.
2-218 " Benjamin, of Benjamin, dec., of East Greenwich, and Susanna Hammett, of Eld. John, dec.; m. by Eld. Charles Holden, Dec. 20, 1772.
2-215 " Caleb, of Abial, and Freelove Cammet, of Isaac; m. by Eld. John Gorton, Apr. 7, 1787.
2-119 " Phebe, and John Waterman, July 4, 1790.
2-197 " Elizabeth, and Liscom Fuller, June 23, 1793.
2-131 " Cynthia, and Jonathan Tibbetts, Sept. 2, 1798.
3-338 " Jonathan R. and Caroline A. Bowen; m. by Rev. Thomas Dowling, Oct. 3, 1839.
3-343 " Lewis, of Rufus, and Phebe Ann Gardner, of Arnold; m. by Rev. Moses Fifield, Dec. 30, 1841.

3-371	Weaver Julia E., and George T. Congdon, Oct. 20, 1842.
3-358	" William G., of East Greenwich, and Sarah B. Lockwood, of Warwick; m. by Eld. Thomas Tillinghast, Dec. 27, 1847.
1-44	Webb Mary, and Henry Straight, Jr., Aug. 5, 1725.
1-88	" Jeremiah, and Freelove Rice, of Thomas; m. by William Rice, Justice, June 19, 1740.
2-17	" Mary, and William Brayton, Aug. 24, 1760.
2-180	" Mary, and James Stone, Feb. 12, 1786.
2-198	" Jeremiah, of William, and Nancy Spencer, of Gideon; m. by James Jerauld, Justice, Dec. 7, 1794.
2-100	" Jeremiah, and Mary Budlong, widow of Moses; m. by James Jerauld, Justice, Dec. 13, 1797.
2-93	" Lydia, and Nathaniel Lockwood, July 7, 1799.
2-186	" Elizabeth, and Abraham Lockwood, Feb. 14, 1802.
3-351	" William, and Hannah Lockwood; m. by Eld. Samuel Littlefield, Sept. 20, 1812.
3-225	" Betsey, and Jacob Matteson, Dec. 4, 1843.
3-224	" Phebe Ann, and Stuteley Matteson, Dec. 4, 1843.
3-352	Webster John, of Providence, son of Isaac, of Kingston, N. H., and Octavia Greene, of Caleb, of Warwick; m. by Rev. Benjamin Phelan, June 9, 1845.
1-3	Weeden Elizabeth, and Moses Mudge, Dec. 17, 1668.
2-263	" John, of Jamestown, and Mercy Chace, of Abraham, of Warwick; m. by Adam Comstock, Justice, Jan. 7, 1776.
2-220	" Edward, of Caleb, and Naomi Sweet, of Anne, both of East Greenwich; m. by Eld. John Gorton, Oct. 10, 1779.
3-31	" Martha A., and William H. Allen, Sept. 7, 1845.
3-340	Weekes William, and Sarah Lippitt; m. by Rev. Samuel Littlefield, Sept. 3, 1809.
3-359	Welch Josiah, of Cranston, and Elizabeth F. Bates, of Warwick; m. by Rev. Edward K. Fuller, July 21, 1845.
3-407	Wellman Susan E., and John L. Smith, Jan. 7, 1849.
1-44	Wells Peter, and Elizabeth Arnold, of Stephen, Feb. 1, 1736-7.
2-200	" John, of East Greenwich, and Barbara Wickes, widow of Richard; m. by Eld. Manassah Martin, Oct. 5, 1740.
1-40	" Peter, and Ruth Slocum, of Ebenezer; m. by William Rice, Justice, Nov. 23, 1740.
2-55	" Penelope, and Oliver Greene, Mar. 20, 1760.
2-214	" Arnold, of Peter, of Cranston, and Barbara Utter, of William, Jr.; m. by Eld. Charles Holden, Jan. 24, 1762.

2-39	Wells	Barbara, and Nathaniel Frothingham, May 13, 1767.
2-218	"	John, and Sarah Holden, of Col. Randall, dec.; m. by Eld. Charles Holden, Dec. 23, 1770.
2-200	"	Barbara, and John Low, Sept. 7, 1775.
2-233	"	Charles, and Rosannah Low; m. by Eld. Samuel Littlefield, Mar. 22, 1795.
3-337	"	Sheffield S., of Warwick, son of James, dec., of North Kingstown, and Susan W. Wood, of William, of Warwick; m. by Rev. Moses Fifield, Apr. 2, 1840.
3-30	"	Harriet A., and Nelson H. Arnold, Nov. 11, ———, Recorded Aug. —, 1845.
3-304	"	Eliza, and Benjamin Wood, Mar. 22, 1846.
3-34	"	Hannah, and Joseph R. Arnold, Mar. 22, 1846.
1-1	Westcott	Jeremy, and Ellen England; m. by John Greene, Asst., July 27, 1665.
1-2	"	Amos, and Sarah Stafford; m. by Benjamin Smith, Asst., July 13, 1667.
1-3	"	Amos, and Deborah Stafford; m. by ——— Carpenter, Justice, June 9, 1670.
1-7	"	Rathvun, and James Hazelton, Aug. 10, 1678.
1-31	"	Stuteley, and Prescilla Bennett, Dec. 21, 1693.
1-100	"	Phillip, of Warwick, and Mary Straight, of East Greenwich; m. by Stuteley Stafford, Justice, Nov. 12, 1732.
1-106	"	Mary, and John Carder, Nov. 30, 1732.
1-99	"	Nathan, and Ann Greene, of Major Peter; m. by Rev. Manassah Martin, Mar. 6, 1735.
2-200	"	Nathan, and Mary Ruttenberge, of Thomas, dec.; m. by Eld. Manassah Martin, June 16, 1745.
2-201	"	Jeremiah, of Nicholas, of Cranston, and Phebe Barton, of Rufus, of Warwick; m. by Eld. Charles Holden, Apr. 26, 1764.
2-151	"	Ann, and William Rhodes, July 21, 1769.
2-228	"	Sarah, and Abraham Baker, May 2, 1773.
2-206	"	Stuteley, of Scituate, and Robey Baker, of Elisha; m. by James Jerauld, Justice, May 24, 1778.
2-209	"	Caleb, of Nathan, and Susanna Greene, of Caleb; m. by Eld. John Gorton, Sept. 10, 1780.
2-211	"	Thomas, of Nathan, and Mercy Arnold, of Caleb; m. by Eld. John Gorton, Feb. 4, 1781.
2-206	"	Nathan, Jr., and Lydia Arnold, of Simon, Oct. 20, 1785.
2-128	"	Penelope, and Benjamin Greene, Nov. 12, 1790.
2-104	"	Susanna, and John Allen, June 2, 1799.

2-135	Westcott Nancy, and John Jerauld, Nov. 23, 1800.
3-293	" Celia, and Christopher Spencer, Nov. 18, 1813.
3-190	" Louisa V., and William Kinnecome, Mar. 1, 1840.
3-339	" Jahleel, of Thomas, dec., and Susan Peirce, widow; m. by Rev. Moses Fifield, May 1, 1840.
3-344	" Peleg W., and Isabella A. Millard; m. by Rev. Thomas Tew, Sept. 7, 1841.
3-156	" Amanda, and Cyrus Holden, June 30, 1842.
4-49	" Caleb, aged 23 years, son of Josiah and Mary H., and Catherine C. Greene, aged 23 years, dau. of Christopher and Julia A.; m. by Rev. S. W. Field, Dec. 15, 1851.
4-65	" Edwin, aged 21 years, son of Jahleel, and Olive C. Shippee, aged 18 years, dau. of Thomas; m. by Rev. Benjamin Phelan, May 22, 1853.
1-53	Westgate Silvanus, of Robert, dec., and Jerusha Davis, of Robert, Dec. 13, 1711.
1-48	" Robert, of Warwick, and Patience Carr, of Edward, of Jamestown, July 9, 1723.
1-93	" Rebeckah, and Benjamin Earl, May 28, 1726.
1-53	" Jerusha, and John Stafford, July 22, 1726.
1-67	" George, of Warwick, and Elizabeth Earl, of Portsmouth; m. by Joseph Brownell, Justice, Oct. 5, 1727.
1-106	" Mary, and John Carder, Jr., Nov. 30, 1732.
1-64	" Sarah, and James Rhodes, Feb. 22, 1732-3.
2-202	" Sarah, and Benjamin Watson, Sept. 28, 1749.
2-205	" Robert, and Mary Hawkins, widow; m. by Jeremiah Lippitt, Justice, Nov. 19, 1753.
2-12	" Hannah, and James Aborn, Nov. 16, 1755.
2-5	" Elizabeth, and Capt. John Adams, Nov. 14, 1757.
2-73	" Mary, and William Hopkins, Dec. 5, 1760.
1-3	Weston Margaret, and John Gorton, Jan. 28, 1668.
2-205	West Ishmael, and Abigail Spywood; m. by Eld. Charles Holden, Mar. 6, 1760.
2-202	" Caleb, and Abigail Spywood; m. by Ebenezer Slocum, Justice, Dec. 28, 1761.
2-212	" Benoni, of Ishmael, and Margaret Dailey, of Timothy; m. by James Jerauld, Justice, Aug. 25, 1782.
2-206	" Sarah, and Ishmael Holden (col.), Apr. 29, 1787.
3-349	" Benoni, and Elizabeth Price (col.); m. by William B. Martin, Justice, Jan. 4, 1822.
3-104	" Martha B., and Charles Fenner, Feb. 8, 1841.

3-355   West Ira, and Amelia Johnson; m. by Rev. Stephen A. Thomas, Nov. 1, 1846.
3-331   "   Betsey A., and William E. Van Riper, Apr. 5, 1847.
1-100   Whaley Ann, and Moses Blanchard, Jan. 1, 1734-5.
3-125   "   Mary Ann, and Stephen C. Griffin, Jan. 1, 1826.
4-53   Wheeler Margaret J., and John B. Howard, May 6, 1852.
4-60   "   Hannah, and Elisha P. Howard, Feb. 4, 1853.
3-353   Wheelock Paul, of Warwick, son of Philetus and Avisee, of Uxbridge, Mass., and Susan G. Allen, of North Kingstown, dau. of Thomas and Alice; m. by Rev. Benjamin Hazelton, Nov. 12, 1826.
1-31   Whipple Mary, and Capt. James Carder, Jan. 6, 1686-7.
1-38   "   Elnathan, and John Rice, Jr., July 25, 1695.
1-29   "   Dorothy, and Malacha Rhodes, May 8, 1699-0.
1-33   "   Anne Phillis, and Moses Lippitt, Nov. 20, 1707.
2-199   "   Eleazer, and Deliverance Rhodes; m. by James Rhodes, Justice, June 24, 1744.
2-73   "   Deliverance, and Joseph Hix, Feb. 8, 1767.
2-28   "   Alice, and Samuel Davis, Nov. 26, 1772.
3-359   "   Christopher R., of Coventry, and Mrs. Ann Taylor, of Warwick; m. by Rev. Thomas Dowling, Mar. 31, 1839.
3-206   "   Lucinda, and Rowland G. Lovell, June 2, 1842.
2-247   Whitaker Thomas, late of Haverhill, N. H., and Rachel Greene, of James; m. by James Jerauld, Justice, Dec. 28, 1786.
3-360   "   John B., of Warwick, son of James, of Seekonk, and Martha Palmer, of John, of Warwick; m. by Rev. Moses Fifield, Mar. 8, 1841.
3-348   White Stowell, of Warwick, and Betsey M. Clarke, of North Providence; m. by Rev. Jonathan E. Forbush, Sept. 18, 1842.
3-357   "   Augustus L., and Patience Phillips; m. by Rev. Stephen A. Thomas, July 30, 1846.
4-14   "   James, of Scituate, and Liza Frazer, of Cranston; m. by Rev. George Uhler, June 21, 1849.
4-22   "   Robert, and Martha Frazer; m. by Rev. George Uhler, Nov. 29, 1849.
4-21   "   Mariah, and George W. Capwell, Dec. 20, 1849.
2-212   Whitford George, of East Greenwich, and Hannah Wickes, of Capt. Thomas; m. by Ebenezer Slocum, Justice, Jan. 15, 1761.
2-212   "   Joseph, and Desire Havens; m. by Eld. John Gorton, Oct. 9, 1761.

2-60	Whitford Mary, and Slade Gorton, Dec. 11, 1777.
2-66	" Thankful, and Benjamin Gorton, Mar. 30, 1780.
2-244	" Sarah, and William Gorton, Nov. 24, 1785.
2-252	" Alice, and David Gorton, Mar. 19, 1789.
2-166	" Hannah, and Jonathan Stafford, June 6, 1802.
3-338	" Thomas, of George, and Pattey Stafford, of John, dec.; m. by C. Brayton, Justice, Apr. 28, 1808.
3-343	" Sarah, and William Wood, Jr., Aug. 27, 1810.
3-351	" Brinton, of Rodman, and Susan A. Warner, of John; m. by Rev. Jonathan Brayton, Oct. 19, 1846.
3-102	" Mary A., and Stephen Essex, Oct. 11, 1847.
4-21	" Margaret, and Joseph O. Brown, Nov. 4, 1849.
4-30	" Thomas W., of Warwick, son of Casey, and Mary L. Cole, of Warwick, dau. of William H.; m. by Rev. Jonathan Brayton, Aug. 4, 1850.
1-40	Whitman Grace, and Jabez Greene, May 23, 1716.
1-75	" John, of George, and Phebe Havens, of Thomas; m. by William Hall, Justice, June 14, 1722.
1-54	" Samuel, and Margaret Gorton, of Samuel; m. by Anthony Low, Justice, Nov. 11, 1724.
1-87	" Deborah, and Malachy Rhodes, Jr., May 27, 1731.
1-52	" George, and Sarah Ladd, of Providence; m. by Eld. Manassah Martin, Aug. 13, 1738.
3-6	" Fannie, and Reuben Alexander, Apr. 22, 1810.
3-344	" Samuel, of Samuel, of East Greenwich, and Experience Arnold, of Caleb, of Exeter, living now in Warwick; m. by Eld. Thomas Manchester, July 11, 1811.
3-348	" Samuel W., and Hannah H. Thornton; m. by Rev. Bela Jacobs, Oct. 15, 1812.
3-356	" Reuben, Jr., of Reuben, and Lydia E. Remington, of Thomas; m. by Rev. Moses Fifield, Apr. 12, 1835.
3-129	" Hannah, and John Grinnell, Nov. 5, 1837.
3-350	" Russell B., of Sterling, Conn., son of Brayton, and Frances F. Albro, of Warwick, dau. of Gardner; m. by Rev. Moses Fifield, Aug. 6, 1846.
3-421	" Henry, of Brunswick, Ohio, son of Peleg, dec., and Susan Allen, widow of John, of Warwick, and dau. of Thomas Westcott; m. by Rev. George A. Williams, Mar. 23. 1848.
4-13	" James A., of Frankfort, N. Y., son of Henry, of Warwick, and Susan Pike, of David, of Warwick; m. by Rev. Moses Fifield, Sept. 18, 1849.

4-14	Whitman George W., of Coventry, son of Caleb, and Eliza Spener, of Edmund, of East Greenwich; m. by Rev. Moses Fifield, Oct. 8, 1849.
4-81	" Ann, and Jeremiah Bailey, Oct. 30, 1863.
3-122	Whitmarsh Elizabeth, and Samuel Gorton, June 3, 1821.
1-5	Wickes Mary, and Francis Gisborne, Jan. 8, 1761.
1-21	" John, of John, dec. and Rose, and Sarah Gorton, of Capt. Benjamin, Dec. 15, 1698.
1-90	" Thomas, and Ann Cole, dau. of Daniel, of Muskoto Cove, L. I.; m. by Edward White, Justice, Feb. 10 or 20, 1701-2.
1-51	" Rose, and Ensign Randall Holden, July 3, 1724.
1-52	" Sarah, and Benoni Waterman, Feb. 11, 1724-5.
1-1	" Mary, and Clement Weaver, ———, 1727.
1-85	" Elizabeth, and Philip Greene, Aug. 12, 1731.
1-11	" Sarah, and James Briggs, Feb. —, 1734-5.
1-20	" Richard, of John, and Barbara Holden, of Charles; m. by Eld. Manassah Martin, Mar. 20, 1735.
2-95	" Sarah, and Nathaniel Peirce, May 22, 1735.
2-200	" Barbara, and John Wells, Oct. 5, 1740.
1-2	" Joseph, of Thomas, and Mary Greene, of Ebenezer, dec.; m. by John Greene, Justice, July 30, 1741.
2-2	" Maplet, and Capt. Josiah Arnold, Dec. 15, 1745.
2-202	" Capt. Thomas, and Mrs. Elizabeth Williams; m. by John Walton, Justice, Oct. 9, 1748.
2-216	" Thomas, of John, and Ruth Brown, of South Kingstown, dau. of William; m. by Rev. James McSparran, Jan. 16, 1752.
2-90	" Sarah, and John Low, Oct. 26, 1755.
2-206	" Renew, and Thomas Wilcox, Oct. 9, 1757.
2-209	" Joseph, and Bridget Price; m. by Eld. John Gorton, June 22, 1758.
2-213	" William, and Hannah Low; m. by John Warner, Justice, Aug. 7, 1760.
2-212	" Hannah, and George Whitford, Jan. 15, 1761.
2-77	" Hannah, and Malachi Hammett, Jan. 10, 1765.
2-214	" Stuteley, of Benjamin, dec., and Elizabeth Greene, of Dea. Thomas; m. by Eld. John Gorton, Dec. 26, 1765.
2-208	" Daniel, of Capt. Thomas, dec., and Freelove Gorton, of Dr. Samuel, dec.; m. by Eld. John Gorton, Nov. 24, 1785.
2-194	" Eleanor, and Benjamin Tiffany, Jan. 26, 1794.

2-257	Wickes Alce, and Isaac Gardner, July 3, 1794.	
2-254	" Powers, of East Greenwich, and Susanna Pearce, of Giles; m. by James Jerauld, Justice, Oct. 1, 1797.	
2-91	" Barbara, and Rufus G. Spencer, Jan. 24, 1799.	
2-57	" Welthian, and John Godfrey, Feb. 24, 1802.	
3-346	" Reuben, of Joseph, and Eleanor Stone, of Josiah; m. by Ephraim Arnold, Justice, Apr. 25, 1808.	
3-346	" Reuben, and Robey Baker; m. by Stephen Budlong, Justice, Apr. 8, 1810.	
4-87	" Mary B., and James Capwell, Apr. 7, 1836.	
3-422	" Alvin, and Lydia Brown; m. by Rev. Henry Tatem, June 9, 1836.	
4-51	" Sarah E., and Jason P. Stone, Mar. 15, 1852.	
2-25	Wightman Sarah, and Benjamin Dexter, Jan. 16, 1745-6.	
2-204	" Elisha, of John, and Sybel Salsbury, of Martin; m. by Eld. John Hammett, Feb. 27, 1752.	
2-170	" Phebe, and Benjamin Sweet, Oct. 8, 1754.	
2-16	" Hannah, and George Briggs, Mar. 8, 1756.	
2-209	" George, Jr., and Rachel Wood, both of East Greenwich; m. by Eld. John Gorton, Feb. 11, 1759.	
2-173	" Deborah, and Thomas Sweet, Apr. 24, 1760.	
2-2	" Mary, and Job Arnold, Mar. 26, 1761.	
2-214	" Phillip, of John, and Mary Gorton, of Othniel; m. by Ebenezer Slocum, Justice, May 27, 1762.	
2-8	" Freelove, and Peleg Andrews, Dec. 12, 1762.	
2-9	" Patience, and William Arnold, of William, July 1, 1764.	
2-223	" Asa, of Samuel, dec., and Mary Cruff, of Thomas; m. by Thomas Rice, Justice, July 30, 1771.	
2-155	" Jemima, and Henry Reynolds, Sept. 27, 1772.	
2-80	" Isabel, and Elijah Johnson, Jr., May 7, 1775.	
2-182	" Robe, and Joseph Straight, Jr., July 18, 1779.	
2-237	" Mary, and Lorey Chase, Apr. 2, 1780.	
2-215	" Daniel, of Elisha, and Lydia Carpenter, of Wilbour; m. by Eld. John Gorton, Oct. 6, 1782.	
2-248	" Hannah, and William Gorton, Oct. 1, 1786.	
2-140	" Sarah, and Joseph Baker, Feb. 28, 1790.	
2-71	" Mercy, and Thomas Holden, June 9, 1793.	
2-110	" Sibbel, and James Reynolds Mitchell, Mar. 9, 1804.	
2-199	" Martin Salisbury, of Daniel, and Marbury Stafford, of John, dec. [also 3-339]; m. by Caleb Jerauld, Justice, July 15, 1804.	
3-23	" Phebe H., and Capt. John W. Arnold, Mar. 7, 1842.	

2-227 Wight Mary, and David Bennett, July 26, 1772.
2-116 " Mary, and Jonathan Nichols, June 27, 1790.
2-116 Wilbour Thomas, of Thomas, of Swansey, Mass., and Mary Gorton, of Dr. Samuel; m. by Eld. John Gorton, Dec. 2, 1764.
3-277 " Elizabeth, and Joseph W. Rice, June 13, 1811.
3-358 " Henry J., of Thomas, and Elizabeth Gorton, of Warwick, dau. of Charles; m. by Rev. Moses Fifield, June 14, 1837.
3-61 " Mehitable, and Beriah S. or L. Brown, June 13, 1839.
3-24 " Mary, and Clark Austin, Mar. 23, 1842.
3-391 " Susan H., and Pardon Burlingame, Apr. 26, 1846.
3-88 " Susan Ann, and Alfred Dawley, Nov. 2, 1846.
4-53 " Elizabeth C., and David C. Vaughn, July 5, 1852.
2-206 Wilcox Thomas, and Renew Wickes; m. by Ebenezer Slocum, Justice, Oct. 9, 1757.
2-211 " Smitern, and Bethany Tallman; m. by Eld. John Gorton, Sept. 22, 1760.
2-10 " Mrs. Alice, and William Arnold, May 2, 1765.
3-49 " Phebe Ann, and Nicholas Brown, Feb. 24, 1840.
3-242 " Mary, and Joseph Nason, Mar. 3, 1842.
3-353 " John, of Stephen, of West Greenwich, and Mrs. Robey W. Bates, of West Greenwich, now of Warwick, dau. of Asel Bennett, dec.; m. by Eld. John Tillinghast, Feb. 2, 1846.
4-18 " George S., of Sylvester, and Mary E. Hunt, of Silas; m. by Rev. John Tillinghast, Jan. 1, 1850.
4-78 " Willard, and Sarah B. Carr; m. by Rev. Jonathan Brayton, Jan. 29, 1860.
4-78 " Susan, and John C. Rice, Sept. 10, 1862.
1-95 Wilkes Sarah, and Nathaniel Peirce, May 22, 1735.
2-202 Williams Elizabeth, and Capt. Thomas Wickes, Oct. 9, 1748.
2-173 " Sarah, and Samuel Baker, Dec. 3, 1795.
2-11 " Sally, and Oliver Arnold, Oct. 11, 1812.
3-160 " Celinda, and William A. Holden, June 8, 1817.
3-317 " Lucinda, and Welcome Tefft, Nov. 17, 1840.
3-360 " Fenner B., of William, and Levinia B. Lake, of Laben, both of Cranston; m. by Rev. Gardiner Dean, Feb. 4, 1844.
3-389 " Mary, and Jeremiah Bennett, Feb. 23, 1846.
4-20 " John M., of Warwick, son of John M. dec., of Wales, Eng., and Mary Blanchard. of Samuel, of Coventry; m. by Rev. Moses Fifield, Dec. 25, 1849.

4-45   Williams Nehemiah A., of Coventry, aged 26 years, son of Olney and Lintha, and Elcy G. Spink, of West Greenwich, aged 23 years, dau. of Thomas, and Mary; m. by Rev. Benjamin Phelan, Sept. 28, 1851.
4-88   " Georgeania A., and William A. Card, Dec. 7, 1870.
3-352 Wilson Austin, of Jonathan, and Sarah Burke, of Christopher, dec.; m. by Rev. Jonathan Wilson, May 4, 1826.
4-43   " William R., aged 19, years, son of Austin, and Olive W. Burguess, aged 19 years, dau. of Zadock; m. by Rev. Zalman Tobey, July 14, 1851.
4-77   " Louis B., and Jannette A. Platt; m. by Rev. Jonathan Brayton, Jan. 25, 1860.
3-350 Wing Freeman, of Judah, of Sandwich, Mass., and Barbara F. Gorton, of Dea. Benjamin; m. by Rev. Thomas Manchester, Feb. 2, 1823.
3-64   Woodmansee Mary, and Isaiah Burrill, Jr., Oct. 20, 1839.
3-340 " Hazard B., of North Kingstown, son of Samuel, and Ann Franklin, of Warwick, dau. of Uriah, dec., of West Greenwich; m. by Eld. Moses Fifield, Oct. 11, 1840.
4-29   " Sarah A., and Alanson F. Hathaway, July 28, 1850.
4-1,3 Woods Marshall, of Providence, son of Alvah, and Anne Brown Francis, of John B., and Anne C., of Warwick; m. by Rev. James N. Granger, July 12, 1848.
1-58   Wood Elizabeth, and Thomas Tibbetts, Nov. 15, 1716.
1-103 " William, and Ann Collins, of Thomas, July 2, 1727.
1-89   " Sarah, and John Blanchard, Oct. 14, 1739.
2-209 " Rachel, and George Wightman, Jr., Feb. 11, 1759.
2-213 " Benjamin, of East Greenwich, and Margaret Preston, of Warwick; m. by Eld. John Gorton, Mar. 13, 1763.
2-215 " Benjamin, of East Greenwich, and Mary Casey, of Warwick; m. by Ebenezer Slocum, Justice, Mar. 17, 1765.
2-263 " William, of William, and Elizabeth Gorton, of William; m. by Eld. Charles Holden, July 2, 1775.
2-162 " Mary, and Thomas Remington, Jr., June 7, 1778.
2-220 " Olney, and Rosanna Remington; m. by James Jerauld, Justice, Mar. 8, 1787.
2-214 " Stuteley, of William, and Freelove Jerauld, of James; m. by Alexander Havens, Justice, Jan. 13, 1803.
3-343 " William, Jr., of Warwick, and Sarah Whitford, of Thomas, of North Kingstown; m. by Alexander Havens, Justice, Aug. 27, 1810.
4-76   " Sarah B. and Oliver C. Budlong, Apr. 27, 1826.

3-56	Wood Mary, and John G. Browning, Nov. 2, 1827.
3-354	" William G., of Warwick, son of Joab, of Coventry, and Fannie T. Burke, of Warwick, dau. of Christopher, dec.; m. by Rev. Moses Fifield, July 4, 1831.
3-357	" Benjamin C., of Casey, and Eliza Eldredge, of Seth; m. by Rev. Benjamin Phelan, Jan. 6, 1836.
3-337	" Susan W. and Sheffield S. Wells, Apr. 2, 1840.
3-204	" Hannah, and Thomas W. Locke, July 18, 1841.
3-345	" John J., and Joanna Potter, of Pardon; m. by Thomas Wilkes, Justice, Oct. 4, 1841.
3-347	" Gardner G., of Providence, son of Caleb, of West Greenwich, and Lucy Ann Reynolds, of Warwick, dau. of Arnold; m. by Rev. Moses Fifield, Dec. 25, 1842.
3-327	" William H., of Stuteley, and Ann E. Thornton, of Stephen; m. by Rev. Jonathan Brayton, Dec. 9, 1844.
3-100	" Emeline, and Joseph P. Essex, Jan. 1, 1846.
3-404	" Benjamin, and Eliza Wells; m. by Rev. Edward K. Fuller, Mar. 22, 1846.
3-241	" Theresa H. A., and Charles T. Northup, Nov. 8, 1847.
1-57	Worden Mary, and Joseph Bucklin, Oct. 23, 1737.
3-193	" Sarah A., and Noah Kingsley, Oct. 6, 1840.
1-2	Worrell John, alias Johnson, and Mary Downe; m. by Benjamin Smith, Asst., Dec. 7, 1668.
1-23	Wright Sarah, and Content Potter, June 1, 1703.
1-17	" Susannah, and Thomas Walch, Sept. 21, 1703.
3-167	" Hannah S., and Ezra Harris, Nov. 27, 1840.
3-420	" Emeline, and James Gardner, Oct. 2, 1848.
4-84	Wye Anna D., and Samuel R. Eddy, Dec. 21, 1859.

X Y Z

2-236	York Elisha, and Job Carpenter, Jr., July 14, 1776.
2-41	Young Sarah, and William Fletcher, Nov. 17, 1796.
3-361	" Willett, of Warwick, son of Elias and Hannah, of Voluntown, Conn., and Mary Sherman, of Warwick, dau. of Asa and Mary, of North Kingstown; m. by Rev. Benjamin Hazelton, Aug. 9, 1826.
3-199	" Amey, and Robinson Lockwood, Sept. 7, 1829.
3-169	" Ann, and Andrew Henderson, Sept. 6, 1841.

WARWICK.

BIRTHS AND DEATHS.

A

2-12   Aborn John, of James and Hannah, Jan. 21, 1756.
        " Edward,   Feb. 11, 1758.
        " Phebe,   May 21, 1761.
        " James,   Apr. 9, 1763.
        " George,   Nov. 30, 1765.
        " Benjamin,   Nov. 19, 1767.
3-6   Alexander Albert Havens, of Reuben and Fannie, Jan. 4, 1811.
        " Mary Frances,   May 11, 1814.
        " Freelove Whitman,   Sept. 24, 1817.
        " Susan Rebecca,   June 16, 1819.
        " Reuben Henry,   Jan. 24, 1821.
        " William Burrell,   Nov. 26, 1822.
2-159 Allen Sarah Bowen, Oct. 14, 1781.
2-240   " Caleb, of Lemuel and Welthian, June 11, 1782.
        " John,   Feb. 11, 1784.
        " John,   d. at sea, Apr. 5, 1800.
        " Robert,   Mar. 4, 1786.
        " Thos. Holden,   Apr. 13, 1788.
        " Charles,   Apr. 14, 1792.
        " Henry,   Feb. 21, 1794.
        " Hannah,   Jan. 2, 1798.
        [NOTE.—1st, born Pomfret; 2d, Providence; 3d,
          East Greenwich; rest in Warwick.]
2-37   " Betsey, of George and Lydia, Jan. 8, 1789.
        " Mason,   Mar. 16, 1793.
3-66   Alverson William, of John, Sept. 18, 1728.
2-102 Andrew Eleanor, of Benoni, June 4, 1771.
2-249   " Rhoda, of Silas and Anna, Sept. 6, 1792.
        " Silas, died Jan. 21, 1801.
2-129   " Stephen, of Peleg, died July 2, 1798.

(10W)

2-129	Anthony Lucy Ann, of Albro and Sarah, Mar. 2, 1800.	
	" Deborah Fry,	Dec. 30, 1801.
3-1	" Alfred,	Sept. 20, 1805.
	" Henry,	Aug. 26, 1806.
4-46	" Catherine C., died, aged 37 y., 11 m., 26 d., Mar. 18, 1851.	
1-34	Arnold Elizabeth, of Israel, Jr. and Elizabeth, Jan. 19, 1699-0.	
	" Isreal,	July 19, 1701.
	" Lydia,	Jan. 8, 1702-3.
	" Benjamin,	Jan. 18, 1707-8.
	" Christopher,	Nov. 7, 1710.
	" Stephen,	Nov. 7, 1710.
	" Sion,	Oct. 31, 1713.
	" Mary,	Feb. 25, 1714.
	" Simon,	Dec. 25, 1717.
	" Elizabeth, wife of Isreal, died Feb. 7, 1718-9.	
1-25	" Stephen, of Stephen and Sarah, May 30, 1709.	
	" Elizabeth,	Mar. 16, 1710-1.
	" Sarah,	Mar. 6, 1712-3.
	" Mary,	July 8, 1719.
	" Peter,	July 27, 1724.
1-25,4	" Sarah, wife of Stephen, died Dec. 5, 1724.	
1-78	" William, of Elisha, and Hannah, Apr. 11, 1710.	
	" Mary,	June 11, 1712.
	" Elisha,	Nov. 25, 1713.
	" Joseph,	Mar. 2, 1716.
	" Nathaniel,	Sept. 15, 1717.
	" James,	Sept. 30, 1719.
	" Isreal,	May 15, 1721.
	" Thomas,	May 25, 1724.
	" Hannah,	Mar. 24, 1727.
	" John,	Apr. 27, 1731.
1-28	" Sarah, of James and Elizabeth, Aug. 31, 1713.	
	" Barbara,	Dec. 31, 1715.
	" Anna,	Mar. 2, 1718.
	" Elizabeth,	June 9, 1721.
	" James,	July 11, 1724.
	" Sion,	June 19, 1729.
	" Roades,	Mar. 19, 1733-4.
1-4	" Sarah, wife of Stephen the Elder, died Apr. 15, 1713.	
1-32	" Susannah, of Phillip and Susannah, July 23, 1716.	
	" Mary,	Feb. 6, 1720.
	" Benjamin,	Nov. 1, 1722.

1-32	Arnold Elizabeth,	Nov. 23, 1724.
	" Phillip,	June 9, 1726.
	" Thomas,	June 22, 1730.
	" Stephen,	Sept. 2, 1732.
1-74	" Prescilla, of Josiah and Elizabeth, Nov. 9, 1717.	
	" Susannah,	Dec. 6, 1719.
	" Dorkis,	Aug. 3, 1721.
	" Josiah,	Apr. 22, 1723.
	" Elisha,	Mar. 8, 1727.
	" "	d. Oct. 27, 1727.
	" Joseph,	June 22, 1725.
	" Christopher,	Sept. 12, 1729.
	" Elisha,	Nov. 23, 1731.
	" Lydia,	Nov. 5, 1734.
1-42	" Rebeckah, of Israel, Jr., and Dorothy, Dec. 5, 1720.	
	" Joseph,	Nov. 14, 1721-2
	" Dorothy, wife of Israel, Jr., died Sept. 10, 1723.	
1-105	" Freelove, of Ephraim and Phebe, Apr. 18, 1730.	
	" Ephraim,	Apr. 19, 1732.
	" Simmon,	July 2, 1736.
	" Uriah,	Sept. 5, 1738.
1-42	" Bathsheba, of Israel, Jr., and Elizabeth, Oct. 2, 1732.	
1-39	" Mary, of Josiah, (of William), Dec. 11, 1732.	
	" Margaret,	Apr. 3, 1735.
	" Benedict,	June 21, 1737.
1-107	" Sarah, of Stephen, Jr., and Hannah, Nov. 18, 1733.	
	" Stephen, died Feb. 12, 1734-5.	
1-106	" Ann, of William and Phebe, Apr. 2, 1734.	
	" Job,	Sept. 26, 1736.
	" William,	Aug. 4, 1738.
	" Thomas,	Oct. 26, 1740.
	" Benedict,	Jan. 5, 1742.
1-54	" Phebe, of John and Desire, May 29, 1734.	
	" Barbara,	Nov. 19, 1735.
	" Stephen, Jr., died from a fall from the mast head coming from Asia, Feb. 12, 1734-5.	
1-63	" Esther, of Simon and Lydia, Oct. 23, 1740.	
	" Benjamin,	July 24, 1742.
	" Phebe,	Mar. 21, 1744.
	" Patience,	Dec. 4, 1747.
	" Isreal,	Feb. 11, 1749.
	" Barlo,	Feb. 11, 1749.

1-54	Arnold	Gideon, of James and Freelove, Sept. 4, 1741.	
2-11	"	Martha,	Apr. 1, 1743.
	"	Hannah,	July 31, 1744.
	"	James,	Dec. 21, 1745.
	"	Elizabeth,	Jan. 17, 1747.
	"	Elizabeth,	d. June 7, 1753.
	"	Eleazer,	Oct. 27, 1748.
	"	Caleb,	June 28, 1750.
	"	Dorcas,	Nov. —, 1751.
	"	Dorcas,	d. Mar. 26, 1757.
	"	David,	July 15, 1753.
	"	George,	Oct. 20, 1754.
	"	Daughter,	Feb. 16, 1756.
	"	Daughter,	d. Sept. 25, 1756.
	"	Peleg,	Apr. 13, 1757.
	"	Peleg,	d. Mar. 20, 1761.
	"	Waite,	Dec. 31, 1758.
	"	Waite,	d. Apr. 27, 1760.
	"	Freelove,	July 12, 1760.
	"	Reuben,	Jan. 25, 1762.
	"	Simon,	Dec. 16, 1763.
	"	Elijah,	Mar. 7, 1769.
1-105	"	Ephraim, of Ephraim and Rachel, May 5, 1742.	
2-1	"	Oliver, of James, Jr., and Elizabeth, Jan. 11, 1745.	
	"	George,	Apr. 9, 1747.
	"	James,	Jan. 9, 1748.
	"	Sarah,	Nov. 7, 1751.
	"	Phillip,	May 15, 1754.
	"	Sarah, of Capt. Josiah and Maplet, May 24, 1748.	
2-2	"	Benedict,	Nov. 20, 1752.
	"	Capt. Josiah, died Sept. 18, 1763.	
	"	Lydia, of Simon and Lydia, Feb. 23, 1752.	
	"	Elizabeth,	Sept. 2, 1758.
2-4	"	Edward, of Stephen and Ann, Mar. 9, 1752.	
	"	Mary,	Oct. 30, 1753.
	"	Benedict,	Mar. 14, 1756.
	"	Anthony, Mar. 16, 1758.	
2-30	"	George, Oct. 12, 1754.	
	"	Mercy (Hopkins), his wife, Aug. 15, 1760.	
	"	Gorton, of George and Mercy, Jan. 25, 1783.	
	"	Benjamin,	Nov. 10, 1784.
	"	Zilpha,	Feb. 25, 1786.

2-30	Arnold Simeon,	Oct. 4, 1787.
	" Joseph Hopkins,	Feb. 17, 1789.
	" Waite,	Sept. 12, 1790.
	" Freelove,	Apr. 16, 1792.
	" Mary,	May 13, 1793.
	" Phebe,	Apr. 2, 1795.
	" George Anson,	Nov. 19, 1796.
	" Son (still born),	Aug. 2, 1798.
	" Aylsey,	Oct. 5, 1799.
	" Elizabeth,	Oct. 5, 1799.
	" Elijah,	Mar. 15, 1801.
2-8	" Susannah, of Thomas, (of Phillip),and Hannah, Dec. 5, 1756.	
	" Elizabeth of Thomas, (of Phillip), and Hannah, Aug. 17, 1758.	
	" Randall, of Thomas, (of Phillip), and Hannah, Dec. 11, 1760.	
	" Bowen, of Thomas, (of Phillip), and Hannah, Aug. 11, 1767.	
	" Frederick, of Thomas, (of Phillip), and Hannah, Apr. 7, 1770.	
2-4	" Lucy, of Oliver and Mary, July 24, 1757.	
	" Mary,	Almy, Nov. 7, 1762.
	" Freelove,	Jan. 23, 1765.
2-6	" Samuel, of Simeon and Hannah, July 9, 1759.	
	" Phebe,	Apr. 16, 1761.
	" Ephraim,	Dec. 17, 1763.
	" Ebenezer,	Nov. 16, 1765.
	" Cyrus,	Aug. 1, 1768.
	" Zeviah,	Apr. 17, 1770.
	" Uriah,	Feb. 10, 1772.
	" Lydia,	Feb. 11, 1774.
	" Freelove,	Nov. 25, 1775.
2-95	" Capt. Joseph, of Joseph and Dianah, Jan. 23, 1762.	
	" Ruth, (Godfrey of Joshua and Mary) his wife, June 17, 1763.	
	" Godfrey, of Capt. Joseph and Ruth, Nov. 7, 1785.	
	" Gorton Whitman,	Oct. 20, 1790.
2-150	" William, of Caleb, July 26, 1762.	
2-116	" Phillip, of Phillip, May 28, 1763	
2-10	" Elizabeth, of David and Waite, Apr. 25, 1766.	
	" Catherine,	May 5, 1768

2-10	Arnold Josiah,	Jan. 30, 1772.
	" Moses,	Aug. 23, 1773.
	" Moses,	d., Feb. 15, 1793.
	" Joseph,	Aug. 24, 1775.
	" Benedict,	Sept. 15, 1777.
	" David,	Mar. 29, 1779.
	" Waite,	Feb. 21, 1781.
	" Lucy Lippitt,	Oct. 19, 1782.
	" Lucy Lippitt,	d. Aug. 26, 1793.
	" John Rhodes,	Sept. 14, 1784.
	" Maria,	June 1, 1787.
2-7	" Daniel of Gideon and Patience,	Mar. 24, 1768.
	" Sarah,	Mar. 12, 1770.
	" Benjamin,	Dec. 24, 1771.
	" Mary,	May 6, 1773.
	" Mary,	d. Oct. 14, 1776.
	" Lucy,	Apr. 20, 1775.
	" George,	Jan. 4, 1777.
	" Patience,	June 9, 1789.
2-9	" Sarah, of George, and Ruth,	Jan. 3, 1774.
	" James Utter,	June 9, 1776.
	" George R.,	Oct. 21, 1783.
2-83	" Rosabella, of Joseph and Anne,	Sept. 10, 1775.
	" Martha,	Sept. 28, 1778.
	" Martha,	d. Feb. 27, 1798.
	" Nathaniel,	Oct. 11, 1780.
	" Abigail,	Feb. 13, 1783.
	" Ruth,	Aug. 9, 1785.
	" Joseph,	Aug. 10, 1789.
2-222	" George Spencer, of Benedict and Lydia (East Greenwich), Aug. 19, 1777.	
	" Stephen, of Benedict and Lydia (East Greenwich), June 4, 1781.	
	" Isabel, of Benedict and Lydia (East Greenwich), July 18, 1786.	
3-1	" Nathaniel, Aug. 10, 1778.	
	" Almy (Greene), his wife, July 8, 1784.	
2-139	" Augustus, of Joseph and Sarah, Dec. 21, 1778.	
	" Samuel,	Aug. 30, 1782.
2-234	" Mercy, of Nathan and Freelove, June 7, 1779.	
	" Elisha,	Oct. 21, 1780.
	" Welcome,	May 8, 1782.

2-234	Arnold Elizabeth,	Jan. 4, 1785.
	" Elizabeth,	d. Oct. 28, 1791.
	" Charles,	Jan. 9, 1794.
2-85	" Russell, of Nicholas and Hannah, Feb. 14, 1780.	
2-238	" Gorton, of Phillip and Robe, Jan. 20, 1781.	
	" Stephen,	Oct. 29, 1784.
	" Stephen,	d. Mar. 24, 1802.
	" Samuel Gorton,	May 8, 1795.
2-1	" Christopher, of Moses and Sally, July 25, 1781.	
	" Elizabeth,	Oct. 22, 1782.
2-9	" Mary Low, of Benedict and Sarah, Dec. 28, 1782.	
	" William,	Nov. 22, 1784.
	" Sarah,	Mar. 19, 1787.
2-245	" Olney Rice, of Phillip, Jr. and Dinah, June 10, 1785.	
2-138	" Jabez Reynolds, of Andrew and Phebe, Mar. 24, 1786.	
	" Phillip,	Oct. 13, 1789.
2-5	" Almy, of William (of Caleb), and Ruth, Sept. 22, 1786.	
	" Caleb,	June 11, 1788.
	" Polly,	Feb. 15, 1791.
	" John B.,	July 28, 1797.
	" William,	June 19, 1799.
	" Augustus,	June 10, 1802.
2-247	" Horatio, of Dutee and Naomi, Apr. 12, 1787.	
	" Mercy,	Oct. 10, 1788.
	" Wanton,	Apr. 8, 1792.
	" Wanton,	d. Feb. 7, 1800.
2-258	" Sally Ann, of Anthony (of Stephen), and Eunice, July 14, 1787.	
	" Whipple, of Anthony (of Stephen), and Eunice, June 2, 1789.	
	" Oliver Cromwell, of Anthony (of Stephen), and Eunice, Jan. 2, 1794.	
	" Russell G., of Anthony (of Stephen), and Eunice, Mar. 16, 1796.	
	" Arteliza, of Anthony (of Stephen), and Eunice, Mar. 19, 1797.	
	" Polly Crawford, of Anthony (of Stephen), and Eunice, Mar. 7, 1800.	
2-116	" Christopher, of Phillip and Freelove, Nov. 20, 1787.	
	" Eben,	May 13, 1790.
	" Anna,	Apr. 13, 1792.
	" Anna,	d. Sept. 25, 1795.

2-116	Arnold James Harvey,	Sept. 23, 1794.
	" Andrew,	Oct. 31, 1798.
3-1	" David Ralph, of Henry, Oct. 17, 1788.	
2-133	" Susanna, of John and Henrietta, Feb. 24, 1789.	
	" Susanna,	d. May 7, 1790.
	" Samuel,	Oct. 13, 1790.
	" Oliver,	Jan. 10, 1793.
	" son,	b. d. Mar. 6, 1795.
	" a daughter,	d. Mar. 6, 1795.
	" daughter,	Mar. 23, 1796.
2-1	" Nathaniel, of Nathaniel and Polly, Jan. 23, 1794.	
3-12	" George Greene, of Isreal and Mary, Oct. 19, 1795.	
2-167	" James Bentley, of Ephraim, Dec. 12, 1796.	
	" William Warner,	Dec. 30, 1798.
	" Simeon,	Mar. 22, 1799.
	" Hannah,	Mar. 22, 1799.
	" Alvin Sanger,	Jan. 12, 1801.
	" Freelove,	Apr. 28, 1802.
2-102	" Holden, of Harris, Jr., and Freelove, May 15, 1797.	
	" Holden,	d. Oct. 10, 1798.
	" Almy,	July 5, 1799.
	" Oliver,	Oct. 18, 1801.
2-7	" Thomas Gorton, of Thomas and Sarah, July 8, 1797.	
	" Thomas Gorton,	d. Feb. 26, 1803.
	" Polly Gorton,	Sept. 21, 1799.
	" Betsey Gorton,	Sept. 24, 1803.
2-32	" James Varnum, of Wanton and Elizabeth, Feb. 14, 1800.	
	" Anna,	Feb. 5, 1802.
2-198	" Warren, of Bowen and Elizabeth, Oct. 6, 1801.	
	" Lucinda,	Jan. 13, 1804.
	" Susan,	Mar. 17, 1809.
2-165	" Sally Fear, of Frederic and Dorcas, Mar. 22, 1802.	
	" Lucy Ann,	Nov. 23, 1803.
	" Almyra,	Nov. 23, 1803.
	" Almyra,	d. Sept. 29, 1806.
	" Alden,	July 17, 1808.
	" Dorcas,	Mar. 19, 1811.
2-180	" Martha, of George and Hannah, Dec. 6, 1802.	
	" Charles Bowen,	Feb. 14, 1805.
	" Albert,	Dec. 26, 1807.
3-2	" Patty, of Nathaniel, Apr. 12, 1806.	
3-32	" John Warner Gorton, Feb. 8, 1808.	

3-1	Arnold Freelove Burlingame, of Elisha and Sarah, Jan. 15, 1807.	
	" Welcome,	Feb. 19, 1809.
	" Elisha,	Feb. 21, 1811.
	" Oliver Cromwell Gorton,	Sept. 13, 1813.
3-2	" Thomas Bradford, of Thomas and Ann, Apr. 6, 1810.	
3-8	" Nathan, of Elisha and Hannah, Jan. 12, 1811.	
	" Mercy Ann,	May 27, 1812.
	" Gorton,	Nov. 12, 1813.
	" Eliza,	June 18, 1818.
3-9	" Lucy Lippitt, of Benedict and Mary, Oct. 2, 1811.	
	" Benjamin Greene,	May 16, 1813.
	" Margaret Wickes,	May 12, 1815.
	" Charles Henry,	Dec. 24, 1816.
3-13	" Charles Greene, of Olney R. and Lydia, Dec. 3, 1812.	
3-11	" Joseph Horatio, of Oliver and Sally, July 15, 1813.	
3-2	" John F., of Thomas and Tavior, May 9, 1827.	
4-56	" William Barkett, of John, died, aged 25 years, Jan. 22, 1849.	
4-56, 61	" Horace, of Stephen, died, aged 28 years, Feb. 19, 1853.	
2-240	Atwood Daniel, of Caleb and Marian, Sept. 13, 1782.	
	" Charles,	Apr. 12, 1786.
	" drownded June 12, 1791.	
	" John Walton, of Caleb and Marian, Apr. 12, 1786.	
	" Ray Ward,	Apr. 16, 1789.
	" Catherine,	May 22, 1792.
	" Charlotte,	Aug. 22, 1796.
2-248	" Ruth, of Nehemiah and Joanna, Dec. 13, 1787.	
	" Stephen,	May 15, 1789.
	" Nathan,	Mar. 10, 1794.
	" Lydia,	Feb. 11, 1801.

B

2-232	Babcock Thomas, of Thomas and Sarah, Mar. 20, 1778.	
2-230	Bailey Mary Ann, of Gideon and Margaret, Apr. 24, 1799.	
2-231	" Gideon,	May 12, 1801.
2-18	Baker John, of William, June 12, 1726.	
	" Hezekiah,	Aug. 2, 1728.
	" Prudence,	Apr. 1, 1731.
	" Jonathan,	Sept. 7, 1733.
	" Benjamin,	Sept. 25, 1737.

2-229	Baker George, Apr. 23, 1750.	
	" Hannah, wife of George, June 6, 1752.	
	" Burton, of George and Hannah, Mar. 25, 1776.	
2-18	" Jeremiah, of Phillip and Hannah, Dec. 27, 1756.	
2-220	" Joseph, of Jeremiah and Rebecca, Mar. 10, 1766.	
	" Hannah,	June 23, 1769.
2-254	" Samuel, of Daniel and Sarah, July 25, 1772, died May 5, 1773.	
	" Samuel, 2d, of Daniel and Sarah, June 30, 1774.	
	" Anna,	Dec. 17, 1775.
	" Mary,	Aug. 3, 1781.
2-7	" Phebe, of Silas and Patience, Jan. 17, 1786.	
	" Moses,	Sept. 7, 1788.
	" Robey,	Dec. 19, 1790.
	" Joseph,	Aug. 20, 1797.
2-114	" Elisha, of William and Truth, Mar. 8, 1791.	
	" Nicholas Parris,	Oct. 28, 1793.
	" Susanna,	Oct. 28, 1793.
	" Henry,	Oct. 31, 1800.
2-120	" Waite, of Charles and Mary, Dec. 10, 1795.	
	" Oliver,	Mar. 10, 1798.
	" Burton,	June 8, 1800.
2-229	" Sally Ann, of Burton and Ruth, Oct. 7, 1799.	
	" Phebe,	July 29, 1802.
3-47	" a daughter,	————
	" George Varnum,	Oct. 19, 1809.
2-229	" Ruth, wife of Burton, born Sept. 18, 1780.	
3-51	" Mary Louisa, of Joseph and Susan, Oct. 19, 1820.	
	" Samuel B.,	————
	" William Tiffany,	Feb. 25, 1824.
4-56	" Burton, died, aged 59y. 7m. 1d., Aug. 4, 1852.	
4-33	Barker Elizabeth, died, aged 83y. 7m., widow of Josiah, born Nantucket, Mass., died in Providence, May —,1850.	
1-73	Barton Phebe, of Benjamin and Mary, Nov. 25, 1728.	
2-13	" Phebe, of Rufus and Catherine, July 21, 1737.	
	" John,	Mar. 6, 1738.
	" Andrew,	Dec. 24, 1740.
	" Rufus,	Feb. 22, 1743.
	" Rebecca,	July 16, 1746.
	" Catherine.	July 16, 1746.
	" Zachariah,	Feb. 11, 1748.
	" Holden Rhodes,	Feb. 23, 1751.

2-13	Barton Waite,	Oct. 20, 1753.
	" Rosamond,	Dec. 31, 1755.
	" Mary,	Feb. 18, 1758.
1-101	" Patience, of Samuel and Lillie, Mar. 26, 1739.	
	" Benjamin,	June 26, 1741.
2-13	" Watey, of Andrew and Sarah, June 9, 1743.	
	" Mary,	Oct. 26, 1745.
	" Joseph,	Apr. 30, 1746.
2-226	" John, of Benjamin and Sarah, Feb. 26, 1777.	
	" Sarah,	Feb. 8, 1781.
	" Benjamin,	May 22, 1785.
1-63	Bates Sarah, of Francis and Mary, Jan. 6, 1729-0.	
	" Benjamin,	Mar. 30, 1732.
	" Esther,	Feb. 15, 1734-5.
1-17	Battey Samson, of John and Margaret, Dec. 18, 1709.	
	" Nicholas,	May 28, 1711.
	" Dinah,	Oct. 12, 1713.
	" Rebeckah,	Sept. 26, 1715.
	" William,	Jan. 20, 1717-8.
	" John,	Mar. 13, 1720.
	" Margaret,	Dec. 13, 1722.
	" Phebe,	Feb. 20, 1725.
	" Caleb,	June 22, 1729.
1-67	" Benjamin, of Nicholas and Hannah, Sept. 7, 1737,	
	" Robert,	Jan. 14, 1740-1.
	" Nicholas,	Oct. 3, 1743.
	" Sylvanus,	Mar. 4, 1745.
1-59	" Anne, of William and Hopestill, Mar. 9, 1741.	
	" Hopestill,	July 26, 1744.
	" Mary,	June 25, 1746.
	" William,	Mar. 3, 1747.
4-11	" William, died, Sept. 23, 1849.	
3-49	Bayley John, of Edmund and Esther, July 20, 1816.	
1-66	Bennett Hannah, of Samuel, Jr. and Mary, July 18, 1718.	
	" Mary,	Jan. 2, 1721.
	" Ann,	Jan. 4, 1725.
	" Freelove,	July 22, 1727.
	" Mary,	July 31, 1729.
1-47	" Mary, of Samuel and Mary, Jan. 2, 1721.	
	" Freelove,	May 9, 1722.
	" Sarah,	Sept. 3, 1726.
	" Hannah,	Nov. 17, 1731.

1-47	Bennett Edward,	Feb. 5, 1738.
2-18	" Caleb, Apr. 30, 1772.	
	" Stephen Wightman, of Caleb, Feb. 19, 1800.	
	" Lydia Ann Wheaton,	Aug. 5, 1802.
	" Thomas Jepherson,	Nov. 26, 1804.
2-231	" Thomas, of Joseph and Mary, May 28, 1775.	
	" Joseph,	Mar. 8, 1777.
	" John,	Feb. 27, 1779.
	" Asa,	Feb. 2, 1781.
	" Tabitha,	Nov. 15, 1783.
	" Mary,	Aug. 19, 1786.
	" Elizabeth,	Feb. 4, 1789.
	" Russell,	Nov. 24, 1793.
	" Almy,	July 3, 1798.
2-190	" John W., of Abel, May 21, 1778.	
	" Elizabeth, (Bennett of David), his wife, Apr. 16, 1783.	
2-227	" Sheldon, of David and Mary, Nov. 29, 1786.	
	" Reynolds,	Apr. 10, 1791.
	" Russell,	Apr. 17, 1792.
3-40	" Penelope, of Joseph, Jr., and Penelope, Feb. 17, 1806.	
	" Mary Ann,	May 11, 1808.
	" Thomas,	Jan. 18, 1810.
	" Amaty A.,	Oct. 19, 1813.
3-41	Benson Martin, Mar. 14, 1781.	
	" Amey (Smith), his wife, May 7, 1785.	
	" Francis, of Martin and Amey, Apr. 1, 1810.	
	" Martin,	Feb. 2, 1812.
	" William Collins,	Feb. 21, 1814.
3-41	Bentley Ellery, of Betsey, Dec. 3, 1804.	
2-17	Blair Mary, of William and Naomi, June 5, 1753.	
	" William,	Sept, 20, 1754.
1-22	Blancher John, of Richard and Mary, Sept. 19, 1697.	
	" Benjamin,	Nov. 17, 1701.
	" Mary,	Apr. 21, 1706.
1-50	" Sarah, of Timothy and Mary, June 25, 1728.	
2-232	Bowen Phillip, of Charles, Jan. 10, 1801.	
	" Peter,	Feb. 21, 1803.
2-228	" James Jabez, of Aaron and Hannah, Mar. 1, 1802.	
	" William,	Mar. 28, 1804.
3-46	" Sarah, of Col. Ephraim, Jan. 30, 1812.	
	" Mary,	July 1, 1815.

WARWICK—BIRTHS AND DEATHS. 149

1-15	Brays Thomas, of Ebenezer and Mary, Dec. 13, 1734.		
		died Aug. 17, 1736.	
2-16	Brayton Joseph, of Thomas, Mar. 3, 1757.		
2-223	" Charles, of Daniel and Elizabeth, Oct. 19, 1772.		
	" Elizabeth,	Sept. 12, 1774.	
	" Sarah,	Sept. 19, 1776.	
	" Ruth Atwood,	Mar. 12, 1779.	
	" Mary,	May 3, 1781.	
	" Susanna,	May 30, 1784.	
	" Sophia Weston,	July 2, 1788.	
2-188	" Ann Marcy, of Charles and Rebecca, Feb. 10, 1799.		
	" Ann Marcy,	d. Feb. 23, 1820.	
	" Charles Atwood,	July 19, 1800.	
	" Charles Atwood,	d. Mar. 27, 1816.	
	" Clarrissa,	Mar. 6, 1802.	
	" Clarrissa,	d. Feb. —, 1803.	
	" George Arnold,	Aug. 4, 1802.	
	" William Daniel,	Nov. 6, 1815.	
3-62	" Charles Ray, of Wm. D. and Anna W., Aug. 16, 1840.		
	" Rebecca Stafford,	Mar. 6, 1842.	
	" Abbie Greene,	Oct. 9, 1843.	
	" Abbie Greene,	d. Feb. 23, 1844.	
	" Anna Clarke,	Dec. 19, 1844.	
	" Francis,	July 9, 1846.	
	" Francis,	d. July 28, 1846.	
	" Francis, 2d,	Feb. 23, 1848.	
	" Francis, 2d,	d. June 26, 1858.	
	" Josephine,	Oct. 11, 1849.	
	" Josephine,	d. Nov. 27, 1849.	
	" Jessie Maxson,	Oct. 11, 1849.	
	" Jessie Maxson,	d. Dec. 14, 1849.	
	" Mary Eliza Waud,	Nov. 12, 1850.	
	" Abbie Greene,	Apr. 17, 1852.	
	" Abbie Greene,	d. June 28, 1852.	
	" Emily Greene,	Apr. 17, 1852.	
	" Emily Greene,	d. Aug. 18, 1852.	
	" George Atwood,	June 16, 1853.	
	" Margaret,	June 13, 1854.	
	" a daughter,	Nov. 27, 1856.	
	" a daughter,	d.————.	
	" William Daniel,	Nov. 16, 1857.	
	" Anna (Waud), wife of William D., died May 12, 1858.		

3-363	Brayton Frances, of Wm. D. and Susan J., Jan. 28, 1868.	
	" Sarah Stafford,	Sept, 22, 1869.
3-80	Briggs Benjamin, Oct. 18, 1736.	
2-16	" Stephen, of George and Hannah, Nov. 5, 1756.	
	" John,	Nov. 4, 1758.
	" Giles,	Feb. 7, 1761.
	" Elizabeth, of George and Sarah, Feb. 13, 1769.	
	" George,	Apr. 29, 1767.
	" Elizabeth,	d. Oct. 11, 1769.
	" Arnold,	Mar. 23, 1770.
	" Isaac,	Sept. 20, 1771.
	" Sarah,	Jan. 20, 1773.
2-252	" Almy, of Joseph and Lydia, Feb. 1, 1770.	
	" James,	Oct. 11, 1771.
	" Samuel,	Jan. 1, 1774.
	" John,	Aug. 11, 1776.
	" Joseph,	Aug. 14, 1778.
	" Miller,	Dec. 16, 1780.
	" Lydia,	Dec. 10, 1782.
	" Nicholas,	Feb. 11, 1785.
	" Amos,	July 10, 1787.
	" Betsey,	May 17, 1789.
	" Catherine,	Apr. 20, 1794.
3-41	" Samuel, of Job, July 21, 1789.	
2-158	" Betsey Ann, of Charles, Jr. and Elizabeth, June 26, 1797.	
2-183	" Sukey Rhodes, of Samuel and Nancy, Aug. 20, 1799.	
	" Wanton Rhodes,	Sept. 5, 1801.
	" Daniel Remington,	Sept. 27, 1803.
	" Betsey,	Dec. 3, 1805.
	" Lydia,	Aug. 21, 1808.
	" Samuel,	Feb. 21, 1811.
	" Warren,	Sept. 4, 1813.
	" Mary Ann,	May 13, 1816.
2-219	" Arnold, of William and Isabel W., Oct. 12, 1800.	
2-144	" George Arnold, of John and Mercy, Mar. 12, 1801.	
	" Mercy Ann,	Jan. 20, 1807.
3-58	" Gilbert Whitman, of Geo. A. and Julia, July 31, 1837.	
	" George Arnold,	July 28, 1844.
4-46	" Joseph P. died, aged 67y. 5 m. 28 d., July 14, 1850.	
3-394	Browning Susannah, widow of John, died in her 88th year, Sept. 1, 1849.	
2-24	Brown Mary, of Elisha and Patience, Mar. 12, 1735.	

2-24	Brown Ruth,	Nov. 27, 1736.
	" Elisha,	Aug. 1, 1739.
	" Waite,	Sept. 23, 1741.
	" Joseph,	Aug. 29, 1743.
	" Frances,	Aug. 7, 1745.
	" Daniel,	Aug. 5, 1747.
	" Patience,	Aug. 5, 1749.
	" George,	July 4, 1751.
	" Hannah,	Apr. 12, 1754.
	" Lucina,	Apr. 12, 1756.
2-250	" Job, of Samuel and Mary,	June 28, 1789.
	" Lydia Greene,	July 24, 1791.
	" Susanna,	Nov. 4, 1793.
	" Sarah,	Feb. 27, 1796.
	" Richard,	Dec. 11, 1798.
	" Richard,	d. Aug. 27, 1799.
2-185	" William, of Elisha and Sally,	Apr. 14, 1797.
	" John,	July 21, 1798.
	" Rice Arnold,	Nov. 16, 1799.
4-33	Elisha, died, aged 77 years, Sept. 3, 1850.	
1-57	Bucklin Mary, of Joseph and Mary, Apr. 13, 1739.	
1-46	Budlong Isabel, of John and Tabitha, Apr. 10, 1731.	
	" John,	Aug. 25, 1733.
	" Sarah,	Jan. 10, 1735.
	" Nathan,	Apr. 12, 1739.
	" William, of John and Renew, Aug. 30, 1748.	
2-140	" Phillip, of Stephen and Huldah, Apr. 15, 1789.	
	" Stephen,	Aug. 1, 1794.
	" Huldah,	Mar. 1, 1798.
	" Susannah,	May 5, 1800.
	" Celia,	Aug. 1, 1804.
3-43	" Moses Lippitt, of Stephen and Isbie, Oct. 26, 1806.	
	" Tabitha Greene,	Mar. 17, 1808.
3-43	" William D.,	Dec. 14, 1809.
	" Lorenzo,	June 27, 1812.
	" Isabella L.,	Mar. 13, 1814.
	" Anne C.,	Mar. 9, 1816.
4-31,33	" Stephen, died, aged 89 y. 1 m. 26 d., Oct. 13, 1850.	
2-188	Burke Rhodes, of Seth and Lucy, May 19, 1797.	
	" Betsey Tiffany,	Mar. 8, 1800.
	" Horatio,	Feb. 15, 1803.
	" William,	July 18, 1805, and d.

2-188	Burke Europy,	Apr. 28, 1808.
	" Seth Chace,	May 6, 1810, and d.
	" Lucy Tiffany,	Jan. 16, 1813.
2-118	Burk Edmund, of William and Lydia, May 13, 1775.	
1-9	Burlingame John, of Roger and Mary, Aug. 1, 1664.	
	" Thomas,	Feb. 1, 1664.
4-40	Burrows Joseph, died, aged 84 y. 4 m. 10 d., Nov. 23, 1850.	
1-9	Burton John, of William and Hannah, May 2, 1667.	

C

3-81	Cady Ezra J., of Joel, Nov. 2, 1813.	
	" Prescilla,	Aug. 22, 1815.
	" Joel E.,	July 9, 1816.
	" Edmund G.,	Sept. 24, 1818.
	" Joseph W.,	Feb. 16, 1821.
	" Alference,	Feb. 3, 1823.
	" Rachel P.,	Nov. 4, 1825.
	" Sally Ann,	Oct. 1, 1827.
	" Alice Elizabeth,	Aug. 19, 1829.
	" John G.,	May 9, 1831.
	" William Sanford,	Feb. 3, 1833.
	" Daniel Webster,	Apr. 8, 1838.
1-13	Cahoone Rebecca, of Nathaniel and Jane, Dec. 11, 1702.	
	" Mary,	Feb. 25, 1703.
	" Sarah,	Mar. 14, 1704.
	" Patience,	Jan. 20, 1706-7.
	" Elizabeth,	May 17, 1708.
	" Anne,	Aug. 28, 1709.
	" Mary,	Dec. 11, 1711.
	" Deliverance,	May 1, 1713.
	" Martha,	May 25, 1715.
1-39	" Joseph, of Joseph and Elizabeth, Feb. 6, 1715.	
	" Nathaniel,	April 5, 1717.
	" John,	July 12, 1719.
	" Abigail,	Dec. 3, 1721.
1-64	" Deliverance, of Samuel and Susannah, Nov. 8, 1723.	
	" John,	Oct. 19, 1726.
	" Mary,	Sept. 4, 1728.
	" Jonathan,	Oct. 13, 1732.
	" Benjamin,	—— 24, 1735.

1-64	Cahoone Daniel,	July 1, 1737.
"	Jonathan,	Sept. 29, 1739.
1-12	Carder John, of John and Mary, Mar. 19, 1673.	
1-31	" James, of Capt. James and Mary, Mar. 26, 1689.	
"	James,	d. May 30, 1689.
"	Son,	Feb. 9, 1693.
"	Son,	d. Feb. 26, 1693.
"	Daughter,	Sept. 28, 1695.
"	Daughter,	d. Oct. —,1695.
"	Mary,	Jan. 2, 1696-7.
"	Mary,	d. June 11, 1712.
"	Daughter,	June 30, 1699.
"	Daughter,	d. July 22, 1699.
"	James,	Sept. 20, 1702.
"	James,	d. May 1, 1704.
1-32	" Sarah,	May 14, 1705.
"	Mary, wife of Capt. James, died age 75 y. Mar 12, 1739-0.	
1-31	" Richard, died at Newport, time of the Indian war.	
"	Mary, wife of Richard, died at Warwick, March 5, 1691-2.	
"	" Capt." James, of Richard and Mary, May 2, 1655.	
"	" Capt."	d. Apr. 25, 1714.
"	Mary Roads,	d. Jan 22, 1692-3.
"	John,	d. Oct. 26, 1700.
"	Joseph, aged 35 years,	d. Mar. 14, 1693-4.
1-14	" Hannah, of Joseph and Bethiah, Apr. 16, 1693.	
"	Mary,	Apr. 17, 1693.
1-30	" Elizabeth, of John and Elizabeth, May 2, 1703.	
"	Mary,	Apr. 16, 1704.
"	Katherine,	Aug. 4, 1705.
"	John,	June 15, 1707.
"	Frances,	Dec. 15, 1708.
"	Susanna,	Apr. 11, 1710.
"	James,	Nov. 11, 1712.
"	Ede,	Feb. 15, 1714-5.
"	William,	Jan. 19, 1716-7.
1-92	" Joseph, of Joseph and Ann, Nov. 15, 1724.	
"	Joseph,	d. Oct. 6, 1732.
"	Mary,	Dec. 7, 1726.
"	Mary,	d. Feb. 24, 1727.
"	Joseph died Feb. 24, 1727.	
1-59	" Elizabeth, of James and Sarah, Feb. 17, 1737-8.	
"	Sarah,	Feb. 2, 1739-0.

1-59	Carder Hannah,	July 13, 1742.
	" James,	Apr. 20, 1744.
	" Frances,	Aug. 19, 1751.
	" Mary,	Apr. 15, 1754.
1-106	" Joseph, of John and Mary,	Aug. 11, 1738.
	" Richard,	Sept. 26, 1739.
	" John,	Feb. 15, 1744.
	" William,	Dec. 26, 1746.
	" Robert,	May 5, 1750.
2-116	" George, of James and Susanna,	June 7, 1766.
4-40	" Sarah (Gorton, of John), died, age 74 y., June 4, 1851.	
1-44	Carpenter William, of Oliver and Sarah, June 9, 1701.	
1-16	" Joseph, of Joseph and Mary, Jan. 7, 1704-5.	
	" Abigail,	Oct. 2, 1705.
	" Anna,	Oct. 2, 1705.
2-19	" Lydia, of Oliver and Martha, Sept. 3, 1744.	
	" Barlo,	Sept. 12, 1747.
2-21	" Lucy, of Wilbour and Sarah, Oct. 7, 1751.	
	" Daniel,	Dec. 17, 1753.
	" Lydia,	Dec. 24, 1755.
	" Sarah,	Oct. 18, 1763.
	" Wilbur,	Dec. 29, 1765.
	" Ann,	Feb. 18, 1771.
	" Job,	Apr. 27, 1773.
	" Sarah, wife of Wilbour, died Aug. 21, 1801.	
3-78	" Elizabeth, of Benjamin and Mary, Aug. 29, 1791.	
	" William,	Nov. 26, 1792.
3-69	" Sally, of Wilbour, Jr., and Patience, Oct. 6, 1813.	
	" Pattey,	Oct. 6, 1813.
2-253	Carr Deborah, of Sails and Mary, Jan. 20, 1790.	
	" Caleb,	Sept. 23, 1791.
2-119	Carvine Anne, of Morgan and Deborah, Mar. 24, 1753.	
2-19	" Sarah,	June 12, 1755.
	" Anstis,	Mar. 22, 1758.
	" David,	Oct. 27, 1760.
	" Dennis,	May 15, 1763.
3-65	Casey Thomas, of Adam and Mary, Nov. 18, 1706.	
	" Silas,	Oct. 20, 1708.
	" Mary,	Sept. 19, 1710.
	" Sarah,	Sept. 22, 1715.
	" Edward,	Feb. 17, 1717.
1-27	" Jesse, of Edward and Hannah, Aug. 23, 1743.	

1-27	Casey Eunice,	July 7, 1745.	
	" Mary,	Sept. 15, 1747.	
	" Edmund,	Sept. 2, 1749.	
2-23	" George A., Feb. 17, 1773.		
3-65	" Susan, of Elisha,	July 24, 1795.	
	" Harriet Lovett, of Elisha, Aug. 24, 1796.		
1-45	Case William, of Edward and Susanna, Feb. 22, 1734-5.		
	" Frances,	Feb. 9, 1735-6.	
	" William,	d. Mar. 4, 1735-6.	
	" Carder,	June 10, 1743.	
	" Israel,	Apr. 1, 1745.	
	" Elizabeth,	Sept. 9, 1749.	
	" Mary,	Jan. 7, 1752.	
4-64	Chapin Dianna Maria, born Uxbridge, Mass., Mar. 29, 1812.		
2-22	Chace Sarah, of Abraham, Mar. 20, 1755.		
	" Joseph,	Sept. 28, 1757.	
	" Lowry,	Nov. 23, 1759.	
	" Gorton,	Oct. 24, 1761.	
	" Charlotte,	Aug. 1, 1763.	
2-236	" Polly Ingraham, of Robai, Feb. 4, 1781.		
2-237	" Sinthia, of Lorey and Mary, Feb. 13, 1781.		
	" Phebe,	July 11, 1783.	
	" Russell,	June 12, 1786.	
	" Gorton,	May 23, 1789.	
	" Wanton,	Apr. 3, 1791.	
	" Maria,	Mar. 1, 1794.	
	" Charlotte,	May 21, 1798.	
1-63	Chase Gideon, of Joseph and Abigail,	Dec. 22, 1712.	
	" Ebenezer,	Jan. 17, 1715.	
	" Paul,	May 22, 1716.	
	" Niome,	July 23, 1718.	
	" Abraham,	July 1, 1720.	
	" Joseph,	Jan. 13, 1723.	
	" Abigail,	Jan. 13, 1723.	
	" Mary,	June 18, 1726.	
	" David,	Jan. 4, 1729.	

[NOTE Joseph, of Gideon and Abigail above, died soon.]

" Abigail, wife of Joseph, died Nov. 25, 1730.

1-66	" Susannah, of Abraham and Susannah, Mar. 23, 1742.		
	" Hannah,	Dec. 21, 1743.	
	" Abraham,	Dec. 26, 1748.	
	" Mercy,	May 7, 1751.	

2-236	Church Arnold, of Lowry and Mary, July 12, 1792.	
2-22	Clapp John, of Silas and Mary, May 14, 1754.	
	" Phebe,	Mar. 14, 1756.
	" Daniel,	May 5, 1757.
2-42	" John, born (N. S.), May 14, 1754.	
	" Anne (Waterman) his wife (O. S.), May 27, 1748.	
	" Silas, of John and Anne, Aug. 29, 1776.	
	" Mary,	Aug. 30, 1778.
	" John Greene,	Aug. 8, 1780.
	" Thomas,	Mar. 26, 1782.
	" Anne,	Sept. 6, 1784.
	" William,	Jan. 24, 1786.
	" Waterman,	Apr. 18, 1788.
	" Mercy,	May 19, 1792.
3-70	" Mary Ann, of John G. and Catherine, Oct. 13, 1810.	
1-50	Clark Mary, of Joseph and Elizabeth, Aug. 16, ——.	
	" Benjamin,	Sept. 3, 1721.
	" Elizabeth,	May 28, 1724.
	" Ann,	June 13, 1727.
	" Ruth,	Aug. 2, 1730.
	" Mercy,	Aug. 24, 1733.
	" Lydia,	July 16, 1735.
	" Hannah,	Sept. 5, 1737.
1-88	" Elizabeth, of William and Elizabeth, Feb. 21, 1732-3.	
	died March 2, 1732-3.	
3-76	" Celia Greene, of Ray and Celia, June 4, 1808.	
	" Ethan Ray,	Jan. 14, 1818.
2-111	Coggeshall George, of John and Sarah, Nov. 21, 1761.	
2-24	" Joseph, of Almy, Mar. 29, 1785.	
3-66	" Mary Ann Sabin, of Joseph and Elizabeth, Apr. 11, 1810.	
1-76	Colegrove Elizabeth, of Francis and Hannah, June 2, 1729.	
	" Mary,	June 2, 1729.
1-56	Cole Sarah, of Nathaniel and Deborah, Nov. 26, 1725.	
	" Nathaniel,	Sept. 3, 1728.
	" Deborah,	Sept. 3, 1728.
2-19	" Mary, alias Vaughn, daughter of Deborah Cole, July 30, 1747.	
2-21	" John, of Nathaniel and Sarah, Mar. 18, 1758.	
	" Lockwood,	Nov. 4, 1759.
3-77	" Charles Gibbs, of Benjamin M. and Mary Ann, Oct. 5, 1823.	
	" Phebe Ann,	Apr. 2, 1825.

1-8	Collins Thomas, of Lieut. Ellyza and Sarah, Oct. 26, 1664.	
	" Ellyza,	June 11, 1666.
	" William,	Mar. 6, 1667.
	" Anna,	Mar. 4, 1669.
	" Elizabeth,	Nov. 1, 1672.
1-25	" Eliza (son), of Thomas and Abigail, Nov. 17, 1693.	
	" William,	Feb. 8, 1694.
	" Thomas,	Jan. 31, 1696.
	" Sarah,	Oct. 31, 1698.
	" Thankful (son),	Aug. 27, 1700.
	" Anna, of Thomas and Anna, 2d wife, July 16, 1707.	
	" Samuel,	May 30, 1709.
	" Abigail,	Nov. 20, 1711.
1-47	" William, of William and Elizabeth, Sept. 6, 1723.	
	" James,	Apr. 6, 1725.
3-73	" Elizabeth, of Thankful and Sarah, Jan. 26, 1728-9.	
3.72	" Sarah,	Apr. 27, 1731.
1-72	" Thomas,	June 5, 1732.
	" Sarah, wife of Thankful, died Nov. 19, 1732.	
	" Lydia, of Thankful and Lydia, Jan. 19, 1735-6.	
2-235	Comstock Ruth, of Adam and Margaret, Dec. 31, 1763.	
	" William,	Mar. 19, 1765.
	" Susannah,	Apr. 11, 1767.
	" Gideon,	Jan. 25, 1769.
	" John,	Jan. 18, 1770.
	" Mary,	Jan. 18, 1770.
	" Daughter,	July 7, 1771.
	" Daughter,	d. July 26, 1771.
	" Daughter,	Aug. 26, 1772.
	" Daughter,	d. Nov. 20, 1772.
	" Freelove,	Oct. 21. 1773.
	" Samuel,	Sept. 20, 1774.
	" Amie,	Feb. 24, 1776.
	" Catherine,	Jan. 28, 1778.
	" Sally,	Apr. 23, 1779.
	" Oliver Cromwell,	Mar. 1, 1781.
	" Samuel,	Jan. 13, 1782.
	" Alpha,	Mar. 21, 1783.
	" Alpha,	d. Aug. 9, 1783.
	" James McGregory,	Feb. 7, 1785.
3-65	Congdon Sarah, of Benjamin, Oct. 23, 1802.	
	" Thomas,	Nov. 15, 1804.

3-65 Congdon Martha, Oct. 9, 1806.
" Eliza, Apr. 27, 1708.
" Mary, of Benjamin and Phebe, June 18, 1811.
" Hannah, June 25, 1814.
2-20 Cooke Lynden Arnold, of Dr. Nicholas and Elizabeth, Oct. 1, 1797.
" Dr. Nicholas died May 20, 1800.
1-50 Cook Samuel, of Samuel and Enfield, July 26, 1720.
" Mary, June 20, 1722.
" Abigail, May 1, 1726.
1-56 Cooper Margaret, of Samuel and Margaret, Dec. 22, 1725.
" Mary, May 13, 1728.
1-52 Corp Thomas, of John, July 21, 1714.
" Susanna, of Abner and Hannah, Mar. 17, 1735.
" Freelove, of Thomas and Rebeckah, Mar. 1, 1741-2.
" Massey, July 18, 1743.
" Elizabeth, Dec. 22, 1744.
" John, Sept. 28, 1746.
2-21 Cory Susanna, of Jonathan, Aug. 18, 1748.
2-20 Cross Susanna, of Samuel and Deborah, Sept. 15, 1729.
" Kezia, Sept. 25, 1733.
" Deborah, Feb. 2, 1735.
" Mary, Nov. 8, 1738.
" Ann, July 30, 1741.
" Abigail, Feb. 7, 1743.
" John, Mar. 13, 1746.
1-17 Culver Hannah, of Samuel and Martha Eland, March 9, 1672.
3-75 Curtis Hiram Augustus, of Rev. David and Rhodia, May 15, 1811.
" James Bolster, Aug. 6, 1813.
" Susan, July 26, 1815.

D

2-25 Dailey Amos, of Susanna (col.), Sept. 15, 1800.
2-28 David Lydia, of Noah and Ann, Jan. 21, 1774.
1-44 Davis Thomas, of Ann, Jan. 10. 1719.
1-12 " John, of John and Rebecca, June 13, 1742.
" John, of Urian and Bersheba, Aug. 11, 1753.
4-64 Dexter Emeline, of Jeremiah, Mar. 4, 1815.
1-89 Dickinson Phillip, dau. of Capt. John and Mary, Oct. 8, 1731.
" Mary, Feb. 18, 1733-4.

1-89	Dickinson Charles,	Mar. 8, 1735-6.
1-12	Doorby Francis, of Francis and Ann, Jan. 20, 1659.	
	" Ellyza,	Mar. 21, 1662.
2-28	Doud Lydia, of Noah and Ann, Jan. 21, 1774.	
3-81	" Oliver, of Ezekiel, Sept. 29, 1798.	
1-83	Dunkens John, Jr., May 10, 1729.	
	" William, of John, Jan. 17, 1731.	

E

1-93	Earl William, [2-45] of Benjamin and Rebecca, Feb. 12, 1726-7.	
	" John,	Jan. 27, 1728-9.
	" Sarah,	Feb. 8, 1730-1.
	" Benjamin,	Nov. 25, 1733.
1-92	Edmunds Caleb, of Thomas and Mary, Jan. 25, 1741-2.	
2-34	" John, of William, Mar. 30, 1751.	
	" Patience,	Sept. 4, 1753.
	" William,	Mar. 23, 1756.
	" Anthony,	Aug. 20, 1759.
2-35	" Benjamin, of Robert and Hannah, Sept. 10, 1775.	
	" Mary,	Sept. 9, 1777.
	" Elizabeth,	Oct. 9, 1783.
	" Hannah,	Apr. 26, 1786.
3-93	Eldredge Richard W., of Thomas and Anne, Aug. 4, 1785.	
	" Thomas, Aug. 4, 1785.	
	" Anna, of Thomas and Barbara, Feb. 1, 1802.	
2-32	Ellis Benjamin, of Jonathan and Sarah, Nov. 22, 1752.	
	" Phillip,	June 11, 1754.
	" Jonathan, of Benjamin and Mary, Nov. 21, 1762.	
	" Mary,	June 26, 1765.
	" Rhobe,	Feb. 25, 1768.
	" Sarah,	May 4, 1771.
	" Lydia,	Mar. 9, 1776.
2-186	" Mary, of Jonathan and Lydia, Oct. 13, 1788.	
	" Benjamin,	Dec. 18, 1795.
2-31	Essex Richard, of Hugh and Rebecca,	Feb. 8, 1748.
	" John,	Aug. 18, 1750.
	" Corpe,	July 23, 1752.
	" David,	Feb. 16, 1755.
	" Elizabeth,	June 1, 1757.
	" Ann,	Oct. 13, 1759.

2-31	Essex Benajah,	Feb. 27, 1762.	
	" James,	May 19, 1764.	
	" Rebecca,	June 26, 1767.	
2-116	" Joseph, of John and Amie, June 6, 1782.		
	" Susanna,	Jan. 30, 1784.	
	" Stephen,	Dec. 10, 1785.	
	" James,	July 4, 1787.	
	" Elizabeth,	May 25, 1789.	
	" Henry,	Oct. 27, 1790.	
	" Mary,	Jan. 19, 1793.	
2-35	" William, of David and Mary, May 23, 1783.		
2-137	" Martha, of Corps and Mary, Oct. 21, 1783.		
	" Thomas,	June 12, 1787.	
	" Richard,	Jan. 30, 1790.	
	" Elizabeth,	Nov. 13, 1792.	
	" Susanna,	July 24, 1795.	
2-136	" Catherine, of Benajah and Penelope, Nov. 23, 1786.		
	" Henrietta,	Dec. 14, 1789.	
	" Ruth,	May 4, 1792.	
	" Lydia,	Dec. 8, 1794.	
	" Anna,	Oct. 25, 1797.	
	" Penelope,	Mar. 20, 1800.	
	" Daniel Fones,	Dec. 13, 1802.	
	" Samuel Fones,	July 29, 1806.	
3-96	" Maria, of James and Susan, Oct. 15, 1813.		
	" Sarah,	Feb. 6, 1819.	
	" Stephen,	Dec. 24, 1822.	
	" John Smith,	Nov. 17, 1824.	
	" James Smith,	Nov. 17, 1824.	
2-32	Estes Mary, of Richard and Mary, Aug. 25, 1747.		
	" Richard,	Feb. 22, 1749.	
	" Thomas,	Sept. 28, 1752.	
	" Frances,	Mar. 5, 1755.	
3-93	Evans John C., of Cranston, Nov. 15, 1805.		

F

1-58	Finney Benjamin, of Samuel and Elizabeth, July 26, 1727.	
	" Benjamin,	d. Aug. 5, 1727.
	" Mercy,	Mar. 25, 1731-2
4-63	Fisher James, Feb. 3, 1798.	

4-63	Fisher Amanda (Potter), his wife, Jan. 28, 1801.	
	" James Potter, of James and Amanda, Oct. 8, 1821.	
	" Alfred,	July 8, 1823.
	" Frances Amanda,	Sept. 20, 1825.
	" Elizabeth Williams,	Jan. 17, 1832.
	" Mariah Louisa,	Jan. 26, 1835.
	" Lewis,	May 8, 1837.
	" Sarah Rhodes,	Jan. 27, 1840.
	" Charles Henry,	Mar. 6, 1842.
	" Emily,	Apr. 3, 1844.
2-38	Fish Mary, of Daniel and Barbara, May 13, 1761.	
2-41	Fletcher William, of Thomas, July 26, 1774.	
	" Sarah (Young, of James), his wife, Feb. 18, 1776.	
	" Abigail Smith, of William and Sarah, Aug. 19, 1797.	
	" Freeborn Olney,	Dec. 28, 1799.
	" Mary Ann,	Dec. 17, 1801.
	" Susannah Dyer,	Feb. 19, 1804.
	" William Henry,	Mar. 18, 1806.
	" Joseph Thompson,	Aug. 1, 1808.
1-76	Foster Ann, of Thomas and Martha, Apr. 18, 1734.	
	" Thomas,	Nov. 3, 1735.
1-99	Frazier Hannah, of Alexander and Mary, May 17, 1728.	
	" Alexander,	Nov. 13, 1729.
	" Massey,	Nov. 19, 1731.
	[NOTE. Another entry reads "and Hannah."]	
4-1	Francis John Brown, of John and Abby, May 31, 1791.	
	" Abby, of John B. and Anne C., Sept. 8, 1823.	
	" Abby,	d. Oct. 19, 1841.
	" John Brown,	Mar. 17, 1825.
	" John Brown,	d. June 22, 1826.
	" Anne,	Apr. 23, 1828.
	" Anne C. (Brown), wife of John B., died May 1, 1828.	
4-2	" Elizabeth, of John B. and Elizabeth, Mar. 12, 1833.	
	" Sally,	Mar. 31, 1834.
	" Sophia Harrison,	May 22, 1836.
	" John Brown, Jr.,	Feb. 11, 1838.
1-49	Freeborn Elizabeth, of Thomas and Elizabeth, Oct. 3, 1736.	
	" Gideon,	June 1, 1738.
	" George,	Nov. 25, 1740.
3-103	Freeman Sally Ann, of Henry, Apr. 26, 1818.	
	" Nonah,	Sept. 1, 1820.
	" Susan Elizabeth,	Nov. 14, 1822.

3-103 Freeman Peter Lafayette,   Jan. 23, 1825.
  " Betsey H.,   Apr. 26, 1827.
  " Mary Jane,   Nov. 12, 1829.
  " Henry F.,   July 9, 1833.
2-37 Fry Thomas, of Thomas and Penelope, Mar. 28, 1747.

G

3-112 Gardiner Mary Wilbour, of John, Apr. 30, 1811.
4-34 " Francis C., of Samuel E., of North Kingstown, dec., and Cynthia (Phillips) died, aged 39 years, Jan. 6, 1851.
2-51 Gardner Lowry, of Silas and Hester, May 15, 1755.
2-64 " Sarah, of Oliver and Mercy, Sept. 5, 1767.
  " Hannah,   June 21, 1769.
  " Mercy,   May 27, 1771.
  " Mary,   Aug. 16, 1773.
  " Mary,   d. Sept. 28, 1773.
  " Oliver,   Feb. 21, 1775.
  " Margaret,   Dec. 23, 1777.
  " Isaac,   Dec. 8, 1779.
  " Elizabeth,   Mar. 9, 1781.
  " Nicholas,   May 19, 1783.
  " William,   June 4, 1787.
  " John,   June 26, 1789.
  " Augusta, of Sarah of Oliver, Apr. 26, 1789.
3-116 " Betsey Wickes, of Wickes and Waitey, Feb. 27, 1804.
  " Thomas,   July 25, 1805.
  ', Malachi Rhodes,   Dec. 21, 1807.
  " Mary,   Feb. 1, 1810.
  " Edward,   Feb. 14, 1812.
1-46 Garardi John, of John and Sarah, Feb. 12, 1721-2.
  " Mary,   Mar. 6, 1723-4.
  " Ephraim,   Mar. 6, 1726-7.
  " Phebe,   Mar. 8, 1729-0.
  " Sarah,   Aug. 9, 1733.
  " Elizabeth,   Aug. 24, 1737.
1-13 Gereoudy John, of John and Deliverance, Dec. 22, 1695.
  " Sweet (dau.),   May 15, 1699.
1-17 Gorton Mary, of Benjamin and Sarah, Oct. 31, 1673, died Jan. 7, 1731-2.
1-12 " Othniel, of John and Margaret, Sept. 22, 1669.

1-12	Gorton Samuel,	July 22, 1672.
	" Samuel,	d. June 5, 1721.
	" Samuel 2d, of John and Elizabeth d. Sept. 9, 1724.	
1-1	" Samuel, of Samuel and Susannah, July 29, 1690.	
1-41	" Hezekiah,	June 11, 1692.
	" Susannah,	June 4, 1694.
1-14	" Ann, of Samuel and Elizabeth, Feb, 19, 1695-6.	
	" Edward,	May 18, 1698.
	" Margaret,	May 12, 1701.
	,' Samuel,	June 2, 1705-6.
1-27	" Alice,	Aug. 5, 1707.
	" Elizabeth,	Sept. 26, 1709.
	" Samuel,	July 14, 1711.
	" Thomas,	Mar. 2, 1713.
	" Benjamin,	Dec. 11, 1715.
	" Ann,	May 22, 1718.
	" Richard,	June 15, 1720.
2-5	" Benjamin, died Dec. 25, 1699.	
	" Sarah, his wife died Aug. 1, 1724.	
1-55	" Patience, of John and Patience, Dec. 12, 1700.	
1-88	" Frances, of Othniel and Mary, Mar. 15, 1707.	
	" Othniel,	Oct. 1, 1718.
2-3	" Elizabeth, wife of Samuel, died Sept. 9, 1724.	
	" John, Sr., died Feb. 3, 1713-4.	
1-45	" Samuel, of Samuel, Jr. and Freelove, Mar. 7, 1717.	
	" Freelove,	Aug. 27, 1718.
	" Ann,	Sept. 7, 1721.
	" Lydia,	Feb. 1, 1722-3.
1-35	" Samuel, of Hezekiah and Avis, May 21, 1720.	
	" Samuel,	d. Nov. 1, 1720.
	" Avis, wife of Hezekiah, died Feb. 17, 1732-3.	
1-47	" Freelove, of Edward and Hannah, May 9, 1722.	
	" Sarah,	July 4, 1724.
	" John,	Sept. 3, 1726.
	" Hannah,	Jan. 16, 1729.
	" Caleb,	Nov. 17, 1731.
	" Edward,	May 24, 1734.
	" Caleb 2d,	Feb. 5, 1738-9.
1-96	" William, of William and Massey, May 30, 1731.	
	" Nathan,	Oct. 11, 1734.
	" Elizabeth,	Jan. 14 or 19, 1737-8.
	" Patience,	Aug. 8, 1740.

1-96	Gorton Mercy,	June 3, 1744.
	" John,	Aug. 13, 1753.
1-84	" Benjamin, of Samuel, Jr., and Mary, July 11, 1732.	
	" Robey,	Jan. 18, 1735-6.
	" Robey,	d. Aug. 31, 1736.
	" Jonathan,	Nov. 25, 1737.
	" Sarah,	Sept. 10, 1739.
	" Elizabeth,	Nov. 28, 1741.
	" Elizabeth,	d. Dec. 27, 1744.
	" Elnathan,	July 4, 1743.
	" John,	June 11, 1745.
1-45	" Zilpha, of Othniel and Theodosia, Feb. 11, 1736-7.	
1-12	" Benjamin, of John, died in his 64y., Apr. 15, 1745.	
2-45	" Phebe, of John (of Samuel), May 13, 1751.	
	" John,	Feb. 25, 1748.
	" Elizabeth,	Feb. 3, 1753.
	" Mary,	Dec. 4, 1754.
	" Bowen,	Dec. 5, 1756.
	" Rhoda,	Nov. 17, 1759.
	" Ann,	Feb. 9, 1762.
	" Benjamin,	Aug. 11, 1764.
2-103	" Benjamin, of Dr. Samuel, Apr. 1, 1754.	
	" Thankful (Whitford, of George), his wife, Aug. 27, 1763.	
	" Mary, of Benjamin and Thankful, Aug. 1, 1780.	
	" Benjamin,	June 17, 1782.
	" Charles Slade,	Jan. 24, 1784.
	" Phebe,	Dec. 6, 1785.
	" Phebe,	d. Oct. 3, 1786.
	" Hannah,	Apr. 15, 1787.
	" Sophia,	Nov. 15, 1788.
	" James Wilbor,	Nov. 3, 1790.
	" George,	Apr. 24, 1792.
	" Barbara Fenner,	Apr. 13, 1794.
	" Silas Casey,	Apr. 7, 1796.
	" Samuel,	Jan. 22, 1798.
	" Barton Whitford,	May 21, 1799.
2-51	" Robey, of Jonathan and Sarah, Jan. 30, 1764.	
	" Robey,	d. Nov. 16, 1797.
	" Samuel,	Jan. 23, 1763.
	" Samuel,	d. May 5, 1793.
	" Sally,	Jan. 17, 1770.
	" Sally,	d. May 22, 1775.

2-51	Gorton Polly,	July 10, 1773.
	" Polly,	d. June 14, 1794.
	" Sally 2d,	Nov. 16, 1776.
2-244	" William of Dr. Samuel, Oct. 15, 1760.	
	" Sarah,	Aug. 29, 1766.
2-63	" Susanna, of Benjamin and Avis, Sept. 21, 1762.	
	" William,	May 10, 1764.
	" John,	Dec. 21, 1765.
	" Joseph,	Sept. 2, 1768.
2-222	" Hezekiah, of Joseph (of Samuel) and Mary, Nov. 21, 1767.	
	" David,	Nov. 24, 1768.
	" Mary,	Mar. 4, 1770.
2-221	" Barbara, of John Jr., and Deborah, July 2, 1771.	
2-227	" Deborah, of John Jr. and Mary Aug. 26, 1774.	
	" William,	June 13, 1776.
	" Mary,	June 1, 1778.
	" Clark,	Sept. 14, 1789.
	" Rhoda,	Mar. 28, 1782.
3-112	" Clarke, of John, Sept. 14, 1779.	
2-1	" Edward, son of Edward, died Oct. 25, 1779.	
3-112	" Almy, of Clarke and Lydia, Dec. 31, 1801.	
	" Eliza,	July 16, 1805.
4-1	" Edward, of Edward, died Oct. 25, 1779.	
2-52	" James W. of Samuel (of Jonathan) and Anne, May 25, 1786.	
	" Lydia W.,	Mar. 29, 1791.
	" Catherine, of William and Sarah, Sept. 16, 1786.	
	" Sarah,	Mar. 27, 1788.
	" Oliver Cromwell,	Apr. 18, 1790.

[NOTE. Latter child born West Greenwich.]

2-64	" Mercy, of Benjamin, (son of Eld. John), Feb. 6, 1790.	
2-66	" George, of Benjamin and Thankful, Apr. 24, 1792.	
3-111	" Gardiner, of Joseph and Cynthia. Apr. 23, 1794.	
2-52	" Samuel, died aged 91ys, 1m, 3d, Jan. 16, 1796.	
3-111	" Warren, of Anthony and Phebe, Nov. 26, 1797.	
	" Catherine,	Oct. 2, 1799.
3-112	" Samuel, of James W. and Hannah, Nov. 30, 1811.	
3-122	" Mercy Ann Arnold, of Samuel and Elizabeth, Feb. 27, 1822.	
	" Elizabeth Sophia,	Jan. 27, 1824.
	" George William,	Jan. 4, 1826.
3-123	" Charles Henry, of Richard and Abbie Ann, Aug. 29, 1826.	
1-1	Greene Deborah, of Capt. John and Ann, Aug. 10, 1649.	

1-1	Greene John,	June 6, 1651.
	" William,	Mar. 5, 1652-3.
	" Peter,	Feb. 4, 1654.
	" Peter,	d. Aug. 12, 1723.
	" Job,	Aug. 24, 1656.
	" Phillis,	Oct. 7, 1658.
	" Richard,	Feb. 8, 1660.
	" Anne,	Mar. 19, 1662-3.
	" Catherine,	Aug. 15, 1665.
1-2	" Audrey,	Dec. 27, 1667.
	" Samuel,	Jan. 30, 1670.
	" Capt. John, died, aged 89 years, Nov. 27, 1708.	
	" Ann, wife of Capt. John, died, aged 82 years, May 6, 1709.	
1-3	" James, of James, June 6, 1659.	
	" Mary,	Sept. 28, 1660.
	" Elisha,	Mar. 17, 1662-3.
	" Sarah,	Aug. 26, 1663-4.
	" Peter, of James and Elizabeth, Aug. 25, 1666.	
	" Elizabeth,	Oct. 17, 1668.
	" John,	Feb. 1, 1670.
	" Jabez,	May 17, 1673.
	" David,	June 24, 1677.
	" Thomas,	in Portsmouth, Nov. 11, 1682.
1-4	" John,	Sept. 30, 1685.
	" James, Sr., died, age 71 years Apr. 27, 1698.	
1-5	" Elizabeth, of Thomas and Elizabeth, July 12, 1660.	
	" Thomas,	Aug. 4, 1662.
	" Benjamin,	Jan. 10, 1665-6.
2-17	" Benjamin,	died, Feb. 22, 1757-8.
1-5	" Richard,	Mar. 5, 1666-7.
	" Welthian,	Jan. 23, 1669-0.
	" Rufus,	Jan. 6, 1672-3.
	" Nathaniel,	Apr. 10, 1779.
1-18	" Mary, of William and Mary, July 8, 1677.	
1-18, 19	" Sarah, of Peter and Elizabeth, Oct. 27, 1685.	
1-19	" John,	Mar. 1, 1686-7.
	" Stephen,	Sept. 19, 1687.
	" William,	July 29, 1690.
1-20	" Elisha,	Newport, Feb. 13, 1693.
	" Barlo,	" Dec. 24, 1695.
1-15	" Anne, of Job and Phebe, Feb. 23, 1685-6.	

1-15	Greene Mary,	Dec. 3, 1687.
	" Deborah,	Feb. 28, 1689-0.
	" Job,	July 5, 1692.
	" Phebe,	Oct. 12, 1694.
	" Christopher,	Mar. 9, 1696-7.
	" Daniel,	Feb. 20, 1698-9.
	" Daniel,	d. Feb. 12, 1700-1.
	" Richard,	Mar. 29, 1701.
	" Rathern,	Mar. 19, 1701-2.
	" Phillip,	Mar. 15, 1704-5.
1-5	" Elizabeth, of Thomas and Ann, May 3, 1687.	
	" Anne,	June 25, 1689.
	" John,	Apr. 14, 1691.
	" Phebe,	May 10, 1693.
	" Phillip,	Mar. 8, 1694-5.
	" Welthian,	Oct. 9, 1696.
	" Deborah,	Oct. 25, 1698.
1-9	" Fones, of " Ensign" James, Jr., and Mary, Mar. 23, 1689-0.	
	" James,	Apr. 2, 1692.
	" Mary,	Mar. 16, 1695.
	" Mary,	d. Oct. 21, 1695.
	" " Ensign" James died Mar. 12, 1712.	
	" Mary, his wife, died Mar. 20, 1721.	
1-62	" Benjamin, of Benjamin and Susannah, June 10, 1691.	
	" Benjamin,	d. Mar. 11, 1714-5.
	" Susannah,	July 16, 1694.
	" Catherine,	Mar. 31, 1698.
1-62	" Thomas, of Benjamin and Susannah, Nov. 30, 1701.	
	" Thomas,	d. Feb. 15, 1702.
	" Elizabeth,	Jan. 26, 1706.
	" Margaret,	Jan. 16, 1706-7.
	" Margaret	d. June 30, 1730.
	" Benjamin,	Feb. 16, 1714-5.
	" Phebe,	Feb. 16, 1714-5.
	" Susannah, wife of Benjamin, died in her 64y., Apr. 11, 1734.	
	" dau. Margaret (Greene) Tillinghast had son born Jan. 22, 1730.	
1-10	" Andery, of Richard and Ellen, Jan. 8, 1693-4.	
	" John,	Nov. 7, 1695.
	" John,	d. Dec. 6, 1695.
	" Amie,	Oct. 4, 1696.

1-10	Greene Isabel,	Sept. 3, 1698.
	" Ellen,	Feb. 19, 1701-2.
	" Mercy,	Apr. 9, 1704.
	" Mercy,	d. May 25, 1711.
	" Mary,	Feb. 16, 1706-7.
	" John, of Richard and Ellenor, Dec. 23, 1709.	
	" Richard died May 24, 1711, in 51 year.	
	" Ellenar, wife of Richard, died Mar. 11, 1719.	
1-11	" William, of Samuel and Mary, Mar. 16, 1695.	
	" Mary,	Aug. 25, 1698.
	" Samuel,	Oct. 22, 1700.
	" Benjamin,	Jan. 5, 1702-3.
	" Anne,	Apr. 5, 1706.
	" Anne,	d. June 30, 1706.
1-9	" Daniel, of Lieut. James and Mary, Apr. 7, 1696.	
	" Elisha,	Aug. 5, 1698.
	" Deliverance,	Feb. 12, 1700-1.
	" Mary,	Sept. 25, 1703.
	" John,	Feb. 26, 1705.
	" Jeremiah,	Dec. 16, 1708.
	" Samuel,	June 8, 1711.
	" Capt. James died Mar. 12, 1712.	
1-14	" Mary, of Peter and Elizabeth, Apr. 6, 1697.	
	" Elizabeth,	June , 1699.
	" Ebenezer,	Feb. 8, 1701-2.
	" Thomas,	Feb. 18, 1704-5.
1-40	" Susannah, of Jabez and Mary, Jan. 30, 1699.	
	" James,	Apr. 24, 1701.
	" Benjamin,	Feb. 16, 1703-4.
	" Jabez,	July 26, 1705.
	" Nathaniel,	Nov. 4, 1707.
	" John,	Feb. 14, 1709-10.
	" Rufus,	June 2, 1712.
	" Mary, wife of Jabez, died Mar. 6. 1712-3.	
1-54	" Mary, of Richard and Mary, Sept. 23, 1700.	
	" Richard,	Apr. 17, 1702.
	" Elizabeth,	Aug. 20, 1710.
	" Thomas,	Apr. 14, 1713.
	" Welthian,	Feb. 19, 1714-5.
	" Thomas father of above Richard died in his 88 year June 5, 1717.	
	" Richard died in his 55 year, Sept. 25, 1724.	

1-24	Greene Rufus, of Nathaniel and Anne, May 30, 1707.	
	" Nathaniel,	May 14, 1709.
	at Boston.	
1-37	" David, of John and Mary, Jan. 4, 1710-1.	
	" James,	Mar. 14, 1712-3.
	" Rachel,	Mar. 16, 1714-5.
	(married Francis Matteson), d. Mar. 8, 1740.	
	" Increase, of John and Mary, Apr. 12, 1717.	
	" Elizabeth,	May 26, 1719.
	" Benjamin,	Sept. 26, 1721.
	" Dina,	Jan. 5, 1723-4.
	" Mary,	Jan. 1, 1724-5.
	" Mary,	d. Oct. 13, 1727.
	" Joseph,	Feb. 19, 1727-8.
	" Peter,	Jan. 8, 1730-1.
1-66-24	" Dinah, wife of Fones, died Mar. 21, 1710-11.	
1-26	" John, of Peter and Kezia, Apr. 23, 1711.	
	" Anne,	Dec. 4, 1712.
	" Richard,	Oct. 3, 1715.
	" Peter,	Mar. 6, 1717-8.
	" Peter,	d. Dec. 4, 1767.
	" Deborah,	Feb. 4, 1720-1.
	" Andrew,	Nov. 17, 1726.
	" Capt. Peter, died in his 69 year, Aug. 12, 1723.	
	[NOTE Deborah and Andrew born at Jamestown.]	
1-29	" James, of William and Sarah, Sept. 8, 1713.	
	" Elizabeth,	Sept. 25, 1715.
	" Sarah,	Sept. 17, 1718.
	" Almy,	Apr. 2, 1721.
	" Stephen,	July 4, 1723.
	" Mercy,	Oct. 31, 1725.
	" Phebe,	Aug. 6, 1728.
	" Freelove,	Feb. 18, 1733-4.
2-24	" James, of Fones and Rebeckah, Dec. 2, 1713.	
	" Dinah,	Dec. 24, 1715.
	" Job,	Aug. 8, 1717.
	" Thomas,	Nov. 22, 1719.
	" Mercy,	Mar. 18, 1723.
	" Fones,	July 29, 1727.
1-32	" Thomas, of John and Deborah, Oct. 29, 1714.	
	" Caleb,	June 11, 1716.
	" Anne,	Feb. 24, 1717-8.

(12W)

1-32	Greene Job,		Mar. 29, 1721.
	"	Benjamin,	May 2, 1720.
	"	Job,	Mar. 29, 1722.
	"	Almy,	Jan. 31, 1723-4.
	"	Richard,	Oct. 4, 1725.
	"	Nathaniel,	Apr, 10, 1727.
	"	Deborah,	May 6, 1729.
1-65	"	Nathaniel, of James and Rebeckah,	June 4, 1718.
	"	James,	Nov. 29, 1720.
	"	Wardel,	Jan. 23, 1723.
	"	Jack,	Nov. 6, 1724.
	"	Patience,	Apr. 7, 1727.
	"	Charles,	July 28, 1729.
1-40	"	Mary, of Jabez and Grace,	Dec. 18, 1718.
1-60	"	Lydia, of Barlo and Lydia,	Mar. 18, 1718-9.
	"	Esther,	Sept, 2, 1720.
	"	Barlo,	Oct. 25, 1724.
	"	Isreal,	Jan. 22, 1726-7.
	"	Martha,	Apr. 30, 1722.
	"	John,	Aug. 5, 1731.
	"	Pellatiah,	Mar. 30, 1735.
	"	Pellatiah,	d. Nov. 25, 1736.
	"	Oliver,	Sept. 10, 1740.
1-43	"	Anne, of John and Mary,	June 30, 1720.
	"	Mary,	Apr. 10, 1723.
	"	Christopher,	Aug. 19, 1725.
	"	Christopher,	d. Mar. 3, 1727-8.
	"	Phebe,	May 3, 1728.
1-18	"	Mary, of Elisha and Mary,	May 23, 1724.
	"	Elisha,	July 7, 1726.
	"	Elizabeth,	June 14, 1731.
1-41	"	Benjamin, of William and Katherine,	Aug. 19, 1724.
	"	Samuel,	Aug. 28, 1727.
	"	William,	Aug. 16, 1731.
	"	Margaret,	Nov. 2, 1733.
	"	Catherine,	Dec. 9, 1735.
	"	Christopher,	Apr. 18, 1741.
	"	Christopher,	d. May 30, 1741.
3-51	"	Mary, of Ebenezer and Marian,	June 8, 1725.
	"	Ebenezer,	Aug. 19, 1727.
1-68	"	Samuel, of Samuel and Sarah,	Dec. 7, 1725.
	"	Mary,	Sept. 8, 1727.

1-68	Greene Joshua,	Feb. 24, 1729-0.
1-57	" James, of James and Elizabeth, Dec. 8, 1727.	
	" Elizabeth, wife of James, died July 14, 1733.	
1-72	" Elizabeth, of Richard and Elizabeth, June 27, 1728.	
	" Thomas,	Oct. 11, 1729.
	" Godfree,	May 31, 1732.
	" William,	Jan. 3, 1733-4.
	" William,	d. Apr. 1, 1736.
	" William 2d,	June 9, 1737.
	" Welthian,	Jan. 1, 1738.
	" Welthian,	d. Mar. 27, 1738.
	" Benjamin,	Jan. 5, 1741.
	" John,	Nov. 10, 1743.
	" Caleb,	Jan. 3, 1746.
1-60	" Usal, of Usal and Susanna, Mar. 22, 1728-9.	
	" Henry,	Feb. 20, 1730-1.
	" Abigail,	Feb. 9, 1732-3.
	" Elizabeth,	Jan. 28, 1735.
2-46	" Mary, of Benjamin and Almy, Jan. 28, 1731-2.	
	" Christopher,	Sept. 7, 1733.
	" Delight,	July 30, 1735.
	" Stephen,	Feb. 19, 1736-7.
1-34	" William, of John and Almy, Mar. 1, 1732-3.	
	" Deborah,	Sept. 27, 1735.
	" Elliner,	June 2, 1737.
1-97	" Temperance, of Daniel and Temperance, Mar. 13, 1732-3.	
	" Temperance, wife of Daniel, died in her 25 year, Mar. 28, 1732-3.	
1-85	" Phebe, of Phillip and Elizabeth, Mar. 25, 1732.	
	" Sarah,	Sept. 10, 1733.
	" Sarah,	d. Jan. 14, 1739-0.
	" Job,	Oct. 24, 1735.
	" Job,	d. Jan. 14, 1739-0.
	" Christopher,	May 12, 1737.
	" Phillip,	Mar. 25, 1739.
	" Phillip,	d. Feb. 6, 1739-0.
	" Elizabeth,	Sept. 2, 1742.
	" William,	Oct. 25, 1746.
	" Sarah,	May 6, 1752.
1-94	" Mary, of Benjamin and Mary, Jan. 28, 1731-2.	
	" Christopher,	Sept. 7, 1733.
	" Delight,	July 30, 1735.

1-94	Greene Stephen,	Feb. 19, 1736-7.
1-58	" Benjamin, of Nathaniel and Phebe,	July 7, 1734.
	" Thomas,	Nov. 11, 1735.
	" Phebe, wife of Nathaniel, died,	May 3, 1737.
1-57	" Elizabeth, wife of James, died July 14, 1733.	
	" Elizabeth, of James and Hannah,	Apr. 11, 1735.
	" Paul,	Feb. 25, 1736.
	" Jabez,	Jan. 12, 1739.
	" Abraham,	Oct. 10, 1740.
	" Hannah,	Oct. 15, 1743.
	" Ruth,	Jan. 7, 1745.
1-62	" Susannah, of Jabez Jr. and Susannah,	Apr. 27, 1736.
	" Mary,	Dec. 1, 1737.
	" Margaret,	Apr. 28, 1740.
	" Catherine,	Mar. 17, 1747.
	" Griffin,	Feb. 16, 1749.
1-93	" Sarah, of Benjamin and Ann,	Sept. 14, 1736.
	" Benjamin,	Apr. 23, 1738.
	" Mary,	Mar. 5, 1739-0.
	" Ann,	Dec. 31, 1742.
1-51	" Comfort, of John and Elizabeth,	July 26, 1738.
	" Stephen,	May 22, 1740.
	" William,	Dec. 24, 1742.
	" Peter,	Apr. 6, 1747.
	" John,	Dec. 12, 1754.
2-50	" William, of James, Jan. 7, 1738, d. Jan. 23, 1738.	
	" Mary,	Jan. 5, 1739.
	" Sarah,	Aug. 17, 1742.
	" Giles,	Mar. 25, 1745.
	" Elizabeth,	July 15, 1748. d. Sept, 2, 1751.
	" Desire,	Jan. 6, 1750.
	" Almy,	May 27, 1752.
1-58	" Jacob, of Nathaniel and Mary,	Mar. 7, 1739.
	" Phebe,	Mar. 20, 1740.
	" Phebe,	d. Oct. —, 1741.
	" Nathaniel,	July 27, 1742.
	" William,	Nov. 1, 1743.
	" Elisha,	Dec. 10, 1746.
	" Christopher,	July 3, 1748.
	" Perry,	Nov. 9, 1749.
	" Mary, wife of Nathaniel, died	Mar. 7, 1753.
1-49	" Richard, of John and Mary,	Apr. 4, 1739.

1-49	Greene Anstress,	July 15, 1740.
	" Almy,	June 15, 1742.
	" Mary,	Jan. 24, 1743-4.
	" Abigail,	May 10, 1745.
	" Ellery,	Dec. 29, 1746.
	" John,	Apr. 26, 1748.
1-64	" Elizabeth, of David (of John), Sept. 21, 1739.	
	" Increase,	Mar. 7, 1743-4.
2-44	" Elizabeth, of David and Alice, Sept. 21, 1739,	
	" Mary,	Dec. 10, 1744.
	" John,	May 12, 1747.
1-69	" Caleb, of Jonathan and Mary, Feb. 24, 1740-1.	
	" Stukeley,	Nov. 14, 1742.
1-4	" Catherine, of Caleb and Ann, Dec. 4, 1740.	
1-39	" Audrey, of Richard and Mary, Oct. 8, 1742.	
	" Mary,	Nov. 25, 1743.
	" Thomas Rice,	June 17, 1748.
	" John Holden,	Mar. 18, 1750.
	" Peter,	Jan. 23, 1754.
	" Keziah,	Feb. 19, 1756.
	" Bethia,	Oct. 26, 1758.
2-52	" Ruth, of Thomas and Sarah, Jan. 5, 1745.	
	" Daniel,	Oct. 10, 1747.
	" Reuben,	Apr. 30, 1752.
2-43	" Deborah, of Daniel and Bethia, May 24, 1745.	
2-44	" John, of Richard and Sarah, Mar. 22, 1746.	
	" Nathaniel,	July 31, 1748.
2-43	" Jonathan, of Increase, May 1, 1746.	
2-62	" Tabitha, of Elisha, Jr., and Isabel, Mar. 8, 1750.	
	" Stephen,	Nov. 5, 1752.
	" Mary,	July 15, 1755.
	" William,	Oct. 8, 1757.
	" Elizabeth,	Nov. 30, 1759.
2-48	" Lewis Sayer, of John and Mary, Aug. 8, 1750.	
	" Job,	Mar. 2, 1752.
	" Eleanor,	May 19, 1754.
	" William,	Mar. 13, 1757.
	" Elizabeth,	Mar. 13, 1757.
	" Ann Mercy,	Mar. 3, 1762.

[NOTE. This family was of Occupassotuxet.]

2-46	" Anne, of Thomas and Phebe, June 15, 1751.	
1-99	" Patience, of James and Patience, Mar. 1, 1753.	

1-99	Greene James,	Oct. 28, 1757.
2-47	" Allen, of John and Patience,	Apr. 9, 1755.
	" Sarah,	May 20, 1757.
	" Thomas,	May 20, 1757.
2-58	" Rhodes, of Stephen and Mary,	Aug. 21, 1755.
	" Phebe,	Feb. 3, 1757.
	" Huldah,	July 5, 1758.
	" Sarah,	Oct. 10, 1759.
	" Mary,	Oct. 12, 1761.
	" Malachi,	Aug. 9, 1764.
	" Almy,	Jan. 5, 1771.
2-50	" Ebenezer, of Ebenezer,	Aug. 3, 1753.
	" Phebe,	Apr. 30, 1756.
	" William,	Nov. 9, 1754.
2-59	" Almy, of Godfrey and Almy,	July 11, 1756.
	" Elizabeth,	Aug. 20, 1761.
	" William,	Sept. 2, 1763.
2-17	" Benjamin died, aged 91y. 1m. 1d.,	Feb. 22, 1757.
2-60	" Welthian, of Christopher and Ann,	Nov. 19, 1757.
	" Job,	Nov. 19, 1759.
	" Phebe,	Jan. 16, 1762.
	" Phebe,	d. Sept. 22, 1786.
	" Ann Frances,	June 2, 1764.
	" Elizabeth,	Dec. 15, 1766.
	" Jeremiah,	Oct. 17, 1769.
	" Daniel Wistrand,	Mar. 22, 1772.
	" Daniel Wistrand,	d. Apr. 6, 1773.
	" Christopher,	Aug. 27, 1774.
	" Mary,	Sept. 20, 1777.
	" Christopher, Sr., slain in action,	May 14, 1781.
2-55	" John, of Potowomut, died	Dec. 8, 1757.
	" Hon. William, (Gov. of R. I.), died	Feb. 23, 1758.
	" Catherine, widow of William, died	Nov. 28, 1777.
2-57	" Thomas, of Nathaniel and Phebe,	Feb. 14, 1760.
2-56	" Phebe, of William Jr. and Catherine,	Mar. 20, 1760.
	" Celia,	June 15, 1762.
	" Ray,	Feb. 2, 1765.
	" Samuel W.,	June 24, 1771.
	" Ann,	June 7, 1774.
2-54	" Sarah, of Thomas and Hannah,	Apr. 8, 1760.
	" Fones,	Mar. 14, 1762.
	" Thomas,	Apr. 3, 1768.

2-225	Greene Timothy, of Paul and Sarah, June 13, 1760.	
	" Hannah,	Mar. 15, 1762.
	" Isabel,	June 18, 1764.
	" Daniel,	June 8, 1766.
	" James,	Feb. 22, 1768.
	" James,	d. Mar. 24, 1772.
	" Patience,	June 12, 1770.
	" Ruth,	June 22, 1772.
	" Sarah, wife of Paul, died Jan. 5, 1773.	
	" James, of Paul and Anna, Sept. 2, 1781.	
2-137	" Mary, of Caleb and Mary, July 24, 1760.	
	" Susannah,	May 12, 1762.
	" Benjamin,	Feb. 18, 1764.
	" George,	Jan. 3, 1767.
	" Dorcas,	Mar. 31, 1769.
	" Caleb,	Feb. 8, 1771.
	" Caleb,	d. Mar. 29, 1771.
	" Caleb 2d,	June 17, 1772.
	" Sarah,	May 31, 1774.
	" Samuel,	Feb. 9, 1776.
	" Henry,	Nov. 23, 1778.
2-55	" Anstress, of Oliver and Penelope, May 9, 1761.	
	" Anne,	Sept. 7, 1762.
	" Hester,	Apr. 12, 1764.
	" John,	Sept. 20, 1765.
	" Mary,	Mar. 3, 1768.
	" Charles Wells,	Jan. 3, 1770.
	" Lydia,	Dec. 21, 1771.
2-57	" George, of Stephen and Mercy, Nov. 8, 1761.	
2-58	" Benjamin, of Nathaniel and Phebe, died Sept. 16, 1762.	
2-64	" Welthian, of Capt. Thomas (of Richard) and Mary, Dec. 12, 1762.	
	" Thomas, of Capt. Thomas (of Richard) and Sarah, Aug. 13, 1769.	
	" Rowland, of Capt. Thomas (of Richard) and Sarah, Nov. 24, 1770.	
	" Benjamin, of Capt. Thomas (of Richard) and Sarah, Mar. 16, 1772.	
	" Rufus, of Capt. Thomas (of Richard) and Sarah, May 10, 1773.	
2-59	" Richard, of Richard and Comfort, ———— ————.	
	" Mary,	Aug. 26, 1765.

2-59	Greene William,	Nov. 5, 1767.
2-63	" Benjamin, of Benjamin and Anne,	Aug. 5, 1765.
	" Thomas,	May 27, 1767.
	" Catherine,	Oct. 20, 1769.
2-246	" Phebe, of John and Mary,	June 22, 1772.
	" Daniel,	Mar. 7, 1774.
	" Eliza,	Jan. 27, 1777.
	" Mary,	Sept. 2, 1778.
	" John,	Dec. 21, 1779.
	" Richard,	Apr. 29, 1781.
	" Ruth,	Apr. 4, 1782.
	" Sarah,	Nov. 7, 1785.
	" Caleb,	June 24, 1787.
	" Phillip,	July 17, 1789.
2-221	" Thomas, of John and Barbara,	July 20, 1772.
	" John Malbone,	May 3, 1774.
2-231	" John of David and Isabel,	June 22, 1773.
2-224	" Anne, of William and Waite,	June 17, 1774.
	" Amos,	Apr. 28, 1778.
	" William,	Mar. 20, 1780.
	" Sarah,	Apr. 9, 1782.
2-230	" Thomas Lippitt, of Wm. and Welthian,	Oct. 16, 1774.
	" Christopher,	May 8, 1776.
	" Harriet,	Apr. 2, 1778.
	" Katherine,	Apr. 8, 1780.
	" Phillip,	July 25, 1782.
	" William Warren,	July 15, 1784.
	" Jeremiah,	Sept. 10, 1787.
2-62	" Anna, of Christopher and Catherine,	Apr. 1, 1776.
	" Catherine,	Oct. 3, 1780.
2-45	" Elizabeth, wife of Phillip, died	Dec. 23, 1776.
	" Phillip, died, aged 86y., 0m., 15 days,	Apr. 10, 1791.
2-61	" Sally, of Elisha and Jane,	Mar. 16, 1779.
	" Franklin,	Sept. 3, 1780.
3-111	" Thomas Rice, Jr. of Thomas R.,	Dec. 21, 1782.
2-242	" William, of James 4th and Rebecca,	Oct. 17, 1783.
	" Mary,	Oct. 31, 1785.
	" Rebecca,	Aug. 25, 1788.
2-62	" Christopher, of Christopher, Jr. and Deborah,	Dec. 8, 1783.
	" Celia,	Jan. 10, 1786.
	" Emily,	Oct. 11, 1787.
	" Nathaniel,	Oct. 9, 1784.

2-62	Greene Richard Ward,		Jan. 21, 1792.
	"	Samuel Ward,	Jan. 28, 1794.
	"	John Ward,	Dec. 8, 1795.
	"	Elisha,	Oct. 11, 1802.
2-242	"	James, of Giles and Rhoda, Apr. 18, 1785.	
	"	Giles Slocum,	Apr. 9, 1791.
	"	Catherine, relict of John, and daughter of William and Catherine Greene, both deceased, died at Boston, Mass., Apr. 30, 1785.	
2-48	"	Warner James, of James and Phebe, July 24, 1785.	
	"	Patience,	May 8, 1788.
	"	Phebe,	May 5, 1792.
	"	Mary,	Apr. 27, 1795.
2-55	"	Christopher Rhodes, of Job and Abigail, Sept. 19, 1786.	
	"	Susanna,	May 5, 1788.
	"	Mary Ann,	May 25, 1794.
	"	Simon Henry,	Mar. 31, 1799.
2-251	"	Richard Wickes, of Thomas Jr., and Barbara, Aug. 4, 1791.	
	"	Raymond,	Jan. 11, 1794.
	"	Charles,	May 25, 1795.
	"	Sally Robinson,	May 25, 1795.
2-128	"	Polly, of Benjamin and Penelope, Feb. 13, 1795.	
	"	Polly,	d. Sept. 8, 1795.
	"	Lucy Ann,	Oct. 25, 1798.
	"	Celia,	Feb. 12, 1801.
2-187	"	George Flagg, of Ray and Mary, Sept. 20, 1795.	
	"	William,	Jan. 1, 1797.
	"	Catherine Ray,	July 18, 1799.
2-105	"	Daniel, died aged 98y, 8m, 19d, Nov. 24, 1797.	
2-133	"	John Stafford, of Samuel and Elizabeth, Apr. 22, 1798.	
	"	John Stafford,	d. Oct. 29, 1798.
	"	Henry,	Apr. 26, 1800.
2-66	"	Benjamin Robinson, of Caleb and Sarah R, May 22, 1798.	
	"	George Sears,	May 6, 1801.
2-101	"	William Wickes, of Nicholas and Hannah, Jan. 8, 1801.	
2-118	"	Daniel, of Christopher and Catharine, Dec. 11, 1801.	
	"	Phebe Eliza,	Feb. 27, 1804.
2-44	"	William, of William, died at Marabee in his 19th year, Aug. 26, 1802.	
	"	Philip, of William, died at River De La Plata, in his 21st year, Mar. 27, 1803.	
2-34	"	Eliza, of Christopher and Anne, Feb. 17, 1804.	

2-34	Greene William Warren,	July 22, 1806.

Children of Thomas Lippitt Greene and Anne (Gibbs) his wife.

3-118,111	"	Thomas Holden, Mar. 17, 1804.	
3-118	"	Sally Holden, June 12, 1805.	
	"	Philip Holden, July 26, 1806.	
	"	Welthian Lippitt, May 19, 1808.	
	"	Anthony Holden, Dec. 25, 1810.	
	"	Louis, Mar. 2, 1813.	
3-115	"	Edgar, of Robert W. and Mary L., Apr. 4, 1807.	
	"	Harriet Franklin,	June 14, 1808.
	"	John Wickes,	Oct. 2, 1809.
	"	Benedict Arnold,	Jan. 17, 1812.
3-113	"	Franklin, of Franklin and Emily, Apr. 22, 1807.	
	"	Christopher,	Dec. 4, 1808.
3-111	"	Welthian, wife of William, died in her 62d year, Sept. 12, 1808.	
	"	William, died Jan. 3, 1809.	
3-114	"	Catherine Frances, of Jeremiah and Phebe, Dec. 10, 1809.	
	"	William,	July 9, 1811.
	"	Mary Ann,	Nov. 7, 1813.
	"	George W.,	June 7, 1815.
	"	George W.,	d. Oct. 21, 1815.
	"	Phebe, wife of Jeremiah, died in her 29 year, Nov. 27, 1815.	
	"	Sarah Littlefield, of Jeremiah and Sarah, Feb. 8, 1818.	
	"	Martha Almira,	May 7, 1819.
	"	Samuel L.,	Feb. 17, 1821.
	"	Jeremiah Albert,	Dec. 30, 1822.
	"	Harriet Manchester,	Mar. 26, 1825.
	"	Harriet Manchester,	d. June 16, 1826.
	"	Eliza Helen,	Jan. 20, 1826.
	"	Phebe H.,	Oct. 21, 1828.
	"	Phebe H.,	d. Nov. 1, 1828.
	"	Sarah, wife of Jeremiah, died Oct. 26, 1828.	
	"	Jeremiah died Apr. 5, 1830.	
4-64	"	Henry W., of Warner J., Mar. 1, 1814.	

Children of Simon Henry Greene and his wife Caroline Cornelia.

4-80	"	Edward Aborn (Providence),	Jan. 24, 1823.
	"	Henry Lekie,	Mar. 31, 1825.
	"	Christopher Rhodes,	Oct. 14, 1827.

4-80	Greene William Rhodes,	Dec. 3, 1829.
	" John Waterman Aborn,	Feb. 19, 1832.
	" Caroline Cornelia,	Aug. 27, 1834.
	" Caroline Cornelia, (Warwick), d.	Sept. 26, 1838.
	" George Frederic, (Providence),	Mar. 9, 1837.
	" George Frederic, d.	Oct. 21, 1837.
	" George Frederic 2d (Warwick),	Aug. 26, 1838.
	" Charles,	Apr. 13, 1841.
	" Charles, d.	Apr. 17, 1841.
	" Francis Clinton,	June 23, 1842.
	" Abbie Susan,	Sept. 29, 1845.
	" Abbie Susan, d.	Oct. 27, 1845.
	" Col. Job. died, Aug. 23, 1808.	
	" Abigail, widow of Job, died, Apr. 18, 1845.	
	" Children of George Sears Greene and Elizabeth, his wife.	
3-124	" Mary Vinton, (Pomfret, Conn.), June 3, 1828.	
	" Mary Vinton, d. (Eastport, Me.), June 6, 1832.	
	" George Sears,	Dec. 17, 1830.
	" George Sears, d. (Warwick, R. I.), Oct. 7, 1832.	
	" Francis Vinton, (Pomfret, Ct.), Aug. 10, 1832.	
	" Francis Vinton, d.	Feb. 22, 1833.
	" Elizabeth, wife of George Sears, died at Eastport, Me,, Dec. 26, 1832.	
3-125	" George Sears, Jr., of George Sears and Martha B., b. (Lexington, Ky.), Nov. 26, 1837.	
4-39	" Mary, died, aged 70y., 4m., 14d. Feb. 28, 1851.	
4-42	" John, died, aged 69y., 6m., July 16, 1851.	
3-125	Griffin Martha Amanda, of Stephen C. and Mary Ann, Aug. 18, 1827.	

H

3-151	Hackstone Anna, of Thomas and Rest, Feb. 27, 1807.	
	" Mary,	Feb. 27, 1807.
	" Susanna,	Sept. 8, 1809.
2-28	Hall Alice, of George and Jane, Sept. 1, 1737.	
	" Abigail,	Jan. 27, 1739-0.
1-59	Hammett Mary, of John and Dorothy, July 29, 1728.	
2-72	" Elizabeth, of Malachi and Maplet, Feb. 8, 1762.	
	" Mary,	July 7, 1764.
	" Mary, d.	Sept. 6, 1764.

2-72	Hammett Maplet, wife of Malachi, died Aug. 8, 1764.	
2-77	" Sarah, of Malachi and Hannah, Oct. 20, 1765.	
	" John,	Sept. 26, 1768.
	" William,	May 7, 1770.
	" Maplet,	May 7, 1770.
	" Mary,	June, 19, 1772.
	" Malachi,	Mar. 23, 1775.
	" Clarke,	
	" Clarke 2d,	July 8, 1780.
	" Hannah,	Aug. 14, 1783.

[NOTE. Clarke 2d, born East Greenwich, Hannah, Warwick]

3-151	" Clarinda, July 26, 1802.	
3-152	Harrison Mary, widow of William, and daughter of Daniel Baker, Aug. 3, 1781, died Oct. 25, 1809.	
	" George, of John and Mary,	May 24, 1807.
	" William,	Apr. 21, 1809.
1-91	Hathaway Elizabeth, of Jeremiah and Ruth, May 7, 1727.	
	" Jeremiah,	May 30, 1730.
	" Caleb,	May 20 or 30, 1732.
2-71	" William, of Caleb and Sarah, Jan. 31, 1757.	
	" Nathan,	Sept. 14, 1758.
3-157	" Caleb, son of Sarah Devout, Jan. 11, 1803.	
2-70	Havens Cynthia, of William and Deliverance, Oct. 5, 1764.	
	" Alexander,	Dec. 22, 1765.
	" Thomas,	Feb. 22, 1768.
	" William,	Jan. 29, 1770.
2-134	" Elizabeth, of Harriet, Jan. 18, 1796.	
2-231	" Alexander, of Thomas and Mary, Sept. 15, 1803.	
1-92	Haynes Edmund, of Josiah and Ann, Sept. 29, 1729.	
	" Ann,	Nov. 28, 1732.
	" Mary,	Dec. 19, 1734.
	" Frances,	Oct. 26, 1736.
2-69	" Sarah, of William and Catherine, Jan. 12, 1735.	
	" John,	Oct. 31, 1737.
	" Josiah,	Feb. 29, 1740.
	" Phebe,	Mar. 28, 1743.
	" Catherine,	Nov. 19, 1745.
	" William,	Apr. 21, 1751.
	" Lucy,	Mar. 24, 1755.
1-19	Hazleton Margaret, of James and Katherine, Mar. 11, 1679.	
1-18	Hill Henry, of Jonathan and Mary, June 24, 1661.	
1-104	" Barnard, of Barnard and Mary, Dec. 23, 1732.	

1-104	Hill Mary,	Mar. 17, 1735-6.
	" Hannah,	July 22, 1737.
	" Gardner,	Jan. 20, 1739-0.
1-55	" Jonathan, of Thomas and Abigail,	Oct. 24, 1737.
	" Elizabeth,	May 28, 1739.
	" Nathaniel,	May 16, 1741.
	" Sarah,	June 25, 1743.
	" Ruth,	Apr. 24, 1745.
	" Hannah,	Feb. 20, 1746.
	" Abigail,	Sept. 20, 1748.
	" Thomas,	July 27, 1750.
	" Naomi,	Dec. 7, 1752.
	" Huldah,	Sept. 18, 1754.
1-13	Holden Frances, of Capt. Randall and Frances,	Sept. 29, 1649.
	" Elizabeth,	Aug. —, 1652.
	" Mary,	Aug. —, 1654.
	" John,	Jan. 1, 1656.
	" Sarah,	Feb. —, 1658.
1-1, 13	" Randall,	Apr. —, 1660.
1-13	" Margaret,	Jan. —, 1663.
1-9	" Charles,	Mar. 22, 1665-6.
1-13	" Barbara,	July 2, 1668.
1-14	" Susan,	Dec. 8, 1670.
	" Anthony,	Oct. 15, 1673.
1-40	" Barbara, of Charles, Jr., and Penelope,	Sept. 13, 1717.
	" Charles,	Apr. 3, 1719.
	" Charles,	d. Sept. 25, 1719.
	" Anthony,	June 10, 1721.
	" Anthony,	d. July 7, 1721.
	" Charles,	Jan. 6, 1722-3.
	" John,	May 18, 1724.
1-31	" Catherine, of Anthony and Phebe,	Oct. 30, 1717.
1 41	" Anthony, of William and Waite,	Sept. 25, 1722.
	" Ann,	Mar. 10, 1723-4.
	" Waite,	Aug. 21, 1726.
	" William,	Oct. 30, 1728.
	" Catherine,	Jan. 12, 1729.
	" Frances,	Jan. 25, 1733.
	" Carder,	Aug. 31, 1736.
	" Mary,	May 2, 1740.
	" Waite,	Dec. 20, 1741,
1-51	" Mary, of Ensign Randall and Rose,	Nov. 17, 1724.

1-51	Holden Randall,	Nov. 25, 1726.
	" Sarah,	Jan. 19, 1729.
	" Sarah,	d. Mar. 11, 1730-1.
	" John,	Jan. —, 1731-2.
1-69	" Welthian, of John and Hannah, Dec. 24, 1733.	
	" Charles,	June 2, 1737.
	" Deliverance,	Sept. 28, 1738.
	" Thomas,	June 7, 1741.
2-114	" Thomas, Jr., Oct. 28, 1757.	
	" Phebe (Burlingame of Elisha), his wife, June 2, 1765.	
	" Caleb, of Thomas, Jr., and Phebe, Feb. 23, 1784.	
	" Celia,	Sept. 6, 1788.
	" Varnum,	July 9, 1796.
	" Catty,	July 9, 1796.
	" Warren,	Feb. 24, 1802.
2-78	" Sarah, of William and Hannah, May 4, 1774.	
	" William Anthony,	Mar. 10, 1777.
2-75	" Ann Gibbs, of Anthony and Sarah, Aug. 14, 1780.	
	" Naomi,	Apr. 1, 1787.
	" Christopher, ol Edward and Sarah, Aug. 30, 1786.	
	" John,	Apr. 9, 1795.
4-42	" Bennett L. died, aged 45y., 2m., 22d. Apr. 26, 1851.	
3-80,157	Holmes James Alonzo, of James and March, Sept. 22, 1815.	
	" Mary P.,	Dec. 6, 1817.
1-86	Howard Mercy, of Benjamin, Aug. 27, 1729, d. Sept. 27, 1729.	
	" Mercy 2d,	Mar. 24, 1730-1.
2-74	" Thomas, of Solomon and Hannah, Dec. 12, 1743.	
2-70	" Benjamin, died Apr. 24, 1758.	
2-262	" Caleb, of Soloman, Oct. 13, 1759.	
2-72	" Mary, widow of Benjamin, died in her 85 year, Feb. 22, 1774.	
3-152	" Clarissa, of William and Mary, Aug. 8, 1810.	
1-27	How Benjamin, died Feb. 3, 1738-9.	
2-77	Hudson Almy, of Capt. Stukeley and Almy, Feb. 20, 1779.	
	" Mary,	Oct. 29, 1782.
3-157	" William Bailey, of Stephen and Lucy, Feb. 5, 1808.	
1-47	Hunt Elizabeth, of Ezekiel Jr., and Eleanor, Apr. 23, 1724.	
	" Ann,	Mar. 17, 1724-5.

I J

4-68 Jencks Hollis King, (b. Cumberland), June 17, 1789.

   Mr. Jenks, in a recorded note, states further that he purchased real estate in Coventry, Nov.—, 1817, which he sold in 1828. Purchased real estate in East Greenwich, March—, 1827, which he sold Feb. 3, 1857. Purchased real estate in Warwick, Feb. 27, 1857, where he now resides. That he removed to East Greenwich, June 19, 1827, and to Warwick, Nov. 20, 1857.

 " Molly (Burr), (b. Rehoboth, Mass.) Nov. 4, 1787.
 " Peter, of Hollis K. and Molly, (Coventry), Feb. 3, 1814.
 " Benj. Burr,   Sept. 9, 1815.
 " Benj. Burr,   (d. Coventry), Jan. 25, 1825.
 " Elizabeth,   Aug. 11, 1817.
 " Catherine Johnson,   Dec. 15, 1819.
 " Marrett,   Nov. 2, 1821.
 " Isaac Burr,   Aug. 29, 1823.

4-89 " Isaac Burr,   (d. Coventry), Nov. 10, 1824.
4-68 " Hollis King Jr.,   June 17, 1825.
 " Annah,   (E. Greenwich), Aug. 8, 1827.
 " George Hiram,   May 23, 1829.
 " Sylvanus Benj. Burr,   Jan. 5, 1832.

2-84 " John, of John and Mary, Mar. 26, 1800.
 " Mary Edmunds,   Jan. 9, 1805.

2-79 Jerauld James, of Dutee and Freelove, Feb. 2, 1746.
 " Sarah,   Apr. 15, 1758.
 " Ann,   June 9, 1760.
 " Susanna,   Nov. 22, 1762.
 " Caleb,   May 11, 1765.

   [NOTE.—James above born East Greenwich.]

2-81 " James, of Dutee, Feb. 2, 1746 d.
 " Mary, widow of James, died Jan. 6, 1798.
 " Henrietta, of James and Mary, Mar. 20, 1769.
 " Elizabeth,   Oct. 2, 1771.
 " Dutee,   Sept. 29, 1773.
 " Dutee,   d. June 27, 1796.
 " Martha,   Aug. 18, 1775.
 " James,   Sept. 21, 1778.
 " Freelove,   Oct. 6, 1780.
 " Henry Rice,   Mar. 24, 1783.
 " Stephen,   June 4, 1785.

2-81	Jerauld Thomas,		Nov. 21, 1787.
	"	Thomas,	d. Sept. 26, 1790.
	"	Mary,	Dec. 1, 1790.
	"	Susanna,	Nov. 24, 1792.
2-80	"	Niles, of Dutee, Jr. and Almy, June 22, 1774.	
2-82	"	Elizabeth, wife of Gorton, died, aged 21y., 8m. Feb. 1, 1775.	
	"	Henry, of Gorton and Phebe, Nov. 18, 1778.	
	"	John Rice,	July 27, 1780.
	"	Edward Gorton,	Mar. 11, 1782.
	"	Sylvester Tiffany,	Nov. 15, 1783.
	"	Elizabeth,	Sept. 21, 1786.
	"	Candace,	Apr. 26, 1790.
	"	William,	July 3, 1793.
	"	Phebe Ann,	Oct. 29, 1797.
	"	Dutee,	Oct. 9, 1799.
	"	Sylvester,	Jan. 29, 1804.
2-84	"	Samuel Arnold, of Caleb and Robe, Mar. 30, 1791.	
	"	Maria,	Mar. 19, 1796.
	"	Daniel Dutee,	Feb. 25, 1798.
	"	Juliann,	Apr. 14, 1800.
2-134	"	Martha, of Elizabeth, Mar. 8, 1795.	
3-170	"	George Warren, of Stephen and Elizabeth, May 8, 1812.	
	"	Albert Augustus,	Mar. 11, 1816.
3-169	"	Joanna, of Edward G. and Sophia, June 6, 1806.	
	"	Anson,	Sept. 18, 1808.
	"	Candace,	May 3, 1810.
	"	George N.,	Dec. 23, 1811.
	"	Christopher,	Oct. 3, 1816.
1-56	Johnson Sindona, of John and Elizabeth, May 9, 1738.		
	"	Submit,	Mar. 27, 1744.
	"	Isaac,	Apr. 22, 1755.
	"	Elizabeth,	June 8, 1760.
2-80	"	Hannah, of Elijah Jr. and Isabel, Sept. 23, 1775.	
	"	Elizabeth,	July 1, 1777.
	"	Elizabeth,	d. Sept. 14, 1778.
	"	Elizabeth 2d,	Sept. 28, 1779.
	"	Gideon Freborn, (at New York.) Dec. 10, 1785.	
3-169	"	Statira, of Elizabeth, Mar. 15, 1803.	
4-99	"	Palmer T., of Palmer T. and Susan J. July 2, 1840.	
	"	Willett A.,	Apr. 10, 1842.
	"	Susan J.,	June 3. 1844.
	"	Emma A.,	July 18, 1846.

4-99 Johnson Sophia L., Oct. 20, 1850.
" Edwin L., Jan. 18, 1854.
" Annie E. July 7, 1857.

K

4-100 King James A. of Sweet and Huldah, Aug. 15, 1841.
Children of Thomas P. R. A. Knox and Lasket his wife.
4-97 Knox Betsey Ann, (b. Foster, R. I.) Apr. 18, 1812, d. June 10, 1813.
" Susan Ann, (b. Jewett City, Ct.) Aug. 12, 1814.
" Susan Ann, d. Sept. 12, 1829.
" Elizabeth Maria, (b. Foster, R. I.) Sept. 28, 1816.
" Elizabeth Maria, d. Jan. 1, 1855.
" Thomas Parker, (b. Foster, R. I.) Sept. 9, 1818.
" Betsey Jones, " Oct. 14, 1820.
" Robert Andrew, (Coventry, R. I.) Dec. 14, 1822.
" Robert Andrew, d. Feb. 16, 1853.
" Jane Gibbs, (Coventry, R. I.) Apr. 16, 1824.
" Hannah Sherman, " Apr. 20, 1826.
" Mary Eliza, " Mar. 18, 1828.
" Alexander Scamels, " Nov. 29, 1830.
" Thomas P. R. A. died, June 12, 1850.

L

2-100 Ladd John Wanton, of Job and Sarah, Aug. 10, 1793.
" Caleb, July 12, 1795.
" Mary Ann, Oct. 11, 1798.
2-99 " Mary, of Caleb and Catherine, Mar. 19, 1799.
" Mary, d. Apr. 13, 1800.
" Joseph Warren, May 24, 1801.
" Alexis, Mar. 10, 1804.
1-28 Lankford Mary, of Jonathan and Ann, Aug. 1, 1733.
4-90 Lawton John Bancroft, of Joseph and Sarah, Nov. 12, 1872.
1-66 Lee Joseph, of John, Jan. 19, 1730-1.
" Benjamin, Aug. 11, 1733.
2-38 Le Valley Margaret, of Peter and Mary, [also 2-144] May 26, 1762.
" Marietta, of William and Phebe, Apr. 10, 1789.

(13-W)

2-38	Le Valley Stephen,	Oct. 4, 1790.
	" William,	May 30, 1795.
	" Maria Sukey,	Mar. 28, 1799.
	" Phebe Ann,	Oct. 24, 1801.
2-36	" Sukey, of Stephen and Anna,	Jan. 15, 1799.
	" Peggy,	Feb. 27, 1801.
1-9	Lippitt John, of John (the younger) and Ann,	Nov. 16, 1665.
1-16	" Moses, of John, "	Feb. 17, 1668.
1-33	" Moses, of Moses and Anne,	Jan. 17, 1708-9.
	" Jeremiah,	Jan. 27, 1710-1.
	" Christopher,	Nov. 29, 1712.
	" Jo,	Sept. 4, 1715.
	" Anne Fillice,	Aug. 29, 1717.
	" Freelove,	Mar. 31, 1720.
	" Mary,	Dec. 2, 1723.
	" John,	Dec. 24, 1731.
1-83	" Catherine, of Moses, Jr., and Waite,	Dec. 19, 1734.
	" Moses,	July 5, 1736.
	" Waite,	Sept. 25, 1738.
	" Waite,	d. Feb. 29, 1739-0.
	" Moses,	Mar. 8, 1739-0.
3-13	" Joseph,	June 28, 1740.
	" Waite,	Apr. 10, 1743.
	" Moses,	May 26, 1745.
	" Abraham,	Oct. 26, 1747.
	" Mary,	June 26, 1749.
	" Rebecca,	Aug. 11, 1751.
	" Joseph,	July 29, 1758.
1-57	" Ann, of Jeremiah and Welthian,	Nov. 15, 1735.
	" Welthian,	Nov. 15, 1737.
	" Welthian,	d. Aug. 25, 1739.
	" Jeremiah,	Dec. 24, 1739.
	" Jeremiah,	d. July 28, 1766.
	" Thomas,	May 19, 1742.
	" Thomas,	d. Feb. 11, 1764.
	" Elizabeth,	Nov. 20, 1744.
	" Welthian,	Mar. 15, 1745.
	" William,	Mar. 7, 1747.
	" John,	Mar. 15, 1750.
	" Moses,	Dec. 16, 1752.
2-89	" Ann Frances. of Joseph and Lucy,	Mar. 30, 1748.
	" Lucy,	Dec. 4, 1749.

2-89	Lippitt Joseph,	Sept. 27, 1751.
	" Sarah,	Aug. 5, 1753.
	" Mary,	Mar. 24, 1756.
	" Thomas,	May. 15, 1758.
	" Bettey,	Sept. 26, 1760.
2-92	" Moses, of Jeremiah, Dec. 16, 1752.	
	" Betsey (Lippitt of Joseph), his wife, Apr. 26, 1760.	
	" Joseph Francis, of Moses and Betsey, Mar. 25, 1788.	
2-91	" Moses died Aug. 8, 1766, aged 57y., 6m., 11d.	
	" Waite, wife of Moses, died Oct. 13, 1768.	
2-93	" Waite, of Moses and Tabitha, Aug. 31, 1769.	
	" Isabel,	July 31, 1773.
2-94	" Joseph, of Abraham and Sarah, Jan. 4, 1771.	
	" Elizabeth,	July 24, 1773.
	" Rebecca,	Mar. 4, 1775.
	" Sal Maplet,	Jan. 1, 1777.
	" Abraham,	Dec. 2, 1778.
	" Ann Phillis,	Jan. 19, 1781.
	" Hannah,	Jan. 14, 1783.
4-55	" Patience (col.), wife of William E., died, aged 84 years, Sept. 13, 1851.	
2-127	Littlefield Mary, of Samuel and Prudence, Sept. 8, 1773.	
	" Edmund,	June 14, 1776.
	" Thomas,	Oct. 24, 1781.
	" Sarah,	July 6, 1792.
1-153	Lockwood Amos, of Amos and Sarah [also 1-53], Apr. 25, 1727.	
1-53	" Sarah,	Jan. 26, 1728-9.
	" Ann,	Dec. 28, 1730.
	" Benoni,	Nov. 26, 1733.
	" Ellis,	Oct. 10, 1735.
	" Mercy,	Nov. 26, 1737.
	" Waite,	Sept. 2, 1742.
	" Phebe,	June 20, 1744.
	" Barbara,	Apr. 24, 1747.
	" Abraham,	Dec. 26, 1748.
	" Millecent,	Apr. 21, 1850.
	" Sarah, widow of Amos, died Jan. 4, 1781.	
1-43	" Ann, of Adam and Sarah, Nov. 17, 1735.	
	" Ann,	d. Apr. 5, 1736.
	" Sarah,	Jan. 27, 1736-7.
	" Abraham,	Aug. 27, 1738.
	" Adam,	Aug. 12, 1742.

1-43	Lockwood Deborah,	Sept. 15, 1745.
	" Almy,	Feb. 17, 1747.
	" Patience,	Mar. 20, 1749.
1-42	" Adam,	June 10, 1752.
	" Abraham,	Oct. 5, 1754.
	" Benajah,	Nov. 20, 1757.
2-91	" Ann, of Sarah, daughter of Adam, Dec. 9, 1753.	
2-92	" Mary, of Amos and Mary, May 21, 1756.	
	" Ann,	May 22, 1760.
	" Amos,	Dec. 9, 1770.
2-95	" Capt. Amos died Mar. 11, 1772.	
	" Abraham died Nov. 11, 1790.	
	" Thomas, of Abraham and Patience, Oct. 5, 1776.	
	" Amos,	Aug. 9, 1780.
2-93	" Oliver, of Nathaniel and Lydia, Nov. 1, 1799.	
	" Charles,	Sept. 17, 1801.
3-198	" Lydia, of Charles and Robey, Mar 23, 1820.	
	" Nathaniel,	July 11, 1825.
	" Charles,	Mar. 30, 1828.
2-98	" Thomas, died in his 57 year, Jan. 24, 1833.	
4-42	" Thomas, died aged 51 y. 1 m. 5 d., Apr. 18, 1851.	
4-46	" Lydia, died aged 82 y. 10 m. 7 d., Dec. 21, 1851.	
1-22	Low John, of Anthony and Mary, Oct. 8, 1702.	
1-21	" Elizabeth, of Stephen and Alice, June 14, 1726.	
	" John,	June 19, 1731.
	" Rebecca,	Oct. 30, 1733.
	" Mary,	Apr. 9, 1735.
	" a daughter,	Aug. 22, 1737.
2-93,123	" John, of John, dec., June 15, 1749.	
2-104	" Sally Holden, of Capt.Samuel and Elizabeth, Nov.14,1797.	
	" Phebe Ann,	May 5, 1801.
3-197	" Anteliza, of Stephen, Jr., and Ruth, Dec. 23, 1805.	
1-55	" Mary Wells, died, aged 75y. 6m., May 2, 1852.	
4-61	" Bennett died, aged 87y. 11m. 27d., Jan. 7, 1853.	

M

1-91	MacGregore James, of Alexander and Susanna, Oct. 1, 1740.	
1-10	Marshall Edward, of Edward and Mary, Apr. 10, 1658.	
	" John,	May 12, 1660.
	" Thomas,	Mar. 1, 1663.

1-10	Marshall Mary,	July 1, 1666.
	" Charles,	Jan. 28, 1667.
	" Martha,	Mar. 16, 1669.

1-34 Martin Sarah, of William (blacksmith) and Hannah, Jan. 28, 1712-3.
  " William, of William (blacksmith) and Hannah, Apr. 27, 1715.

2-107 Mathewson George, of Henry and Comfort, Aug. 9, 1746.
  " Rachel,   June 14, 1748.
2-111 " Chapman, of Daniel and Dorcas, Apr 6, 1771.
1-21 Matteson Sara, of Francis and Sarah, Apr. 13, 1703.
  " John,   Dec. 10, 1704.
  " Hannah,   Oct. 10, 1706.
1-104 " Henry, June 3, 1712.
  " Rachel, wife of Henry, died Mar. 8, 1740-1.
2-107 " John, of Benjamin, Jan. 14, 1748.
2-112 Maxwell John, of Adam and Ann, Apr. 8, 1771.
4-102 McElhaney James, died Feb. 25, 1867.
1-37 Medbury Benjamin, of Nathaniel and Dorothy, Dec. 31, 1718.
  " Mary,   Oct. 16, 1720.
  " Nathaniel,   Sept. 13, 1722.
  " Isaac,   Oct. 13, 1724.
  " Benjamin,   Mar. 31, 1727.
  " Benjamin,   died May 29, 1727.
  " Ann,   Mar. 26, 1729.
  " Sarah,   Jan. 3, 1731-2.
2-109 Millard Lydia, of Nathaniel and Barbara, July 18, 1747.
  " Squire,   Jan. 26, 1749.
  " Samuel,   May 30, 1753.
  " John,   Apr. 30, 1759.
2-112 " Nathaniel, of Esquire and Patience, Feb. 18, 1772.
  " Charles Holden,   Sept. 13, 1773.
  " Pearce,   May 28, 1776.
2-179 " Rice, of Nathan and Ann, Mar. 26, 1775.
  " James,   June 10, 1777.
  " James,   d. Oct. 18, 1778.
  " John,   Mar. 10, 1779.
  " Selah,   Mar. 10, 1781.
  " Robey,   Oct. 12, 1782.
  " Martha,   Aug. 14, 1784.
  " Nathaniel Salisbury,   June 17, 1787.
  " Henry Chace,   Sept. 28, 1789.

2-179	Millard Mary,	Sept. 16, 1793.
2-111	" Martin, of Samuel and Sarah, Jan. 29, 1776.	
	" Hannah,	Oct. 10, 1777.
	" Hannah,	d. Aug. 18, 1797.
	" Elizabeth,	Feb. 14, 1780.
	" Benjamin,	Aug. 26, 1782.
	" James,	Jan. 22, 1785.
	" Samuel,	Sept. 18, 1787.
	" Russell,	Oct. 10, 1791.
	" Sarah Jerauld,	July 12, 1794.
	" Gulielmus B.,	Apr. 28, 1797.
	" Sarah, wife of Samuel, died Sept. 20, 1797.	
2-249	" Joseph Tillinghast, of John Jr. and Eunice, Dec. 30, 1785.	
	" John,	Sept. 14, 1787.
2-197	" Augustus Greene, of Nathaniel and Betsey, Feb. 24, 1794.	
	" Welcome,	June 25, 1796.
	" Juley G.,	May 18, 1801.
	" George Washington,	Feb. 15, 1803.
	" Eliza,	May 17, 1806.
2-135	" Mary, of Rice and Abigail, Apr. 30, 1799.	
	" Sally,	Aug. 11, 1801.
	" Abigail, wife of Rice, born Aug. 11, 1776.	
2-136	" Squire, of Charles and Hannah, Jan. 10, 1800.	
	" John Glasses,	Aug. 18, 1801.
	" Patience,	Nov. 7, 1803.
	" Freelove,	Aug. 19, 1805,
	" Charles,	Apr. 25, 1807.
	" Hannah,	Feb. 14, 1809.
	" Pearce,	Dec. 9, 1810.
	" Nathaniel,	Dec. 17, 1812.
	" Augustus,	Dec. 15, 1814.
3-221	" Susan H., of Samuel and Martha, June 9, 1806.	
	" Edwin,	Nov. 13, 1808.
	" Susan Allen Tillinghast, of Gulielmus B. and Eliza A., July 9, 1821.	
2-111	Miller Polly, of Spicer and Elizabeth, Aug. 3, 1783.	
3-219	" James Williams, of John and Phebe, Sept. 5, 1807.	
	" Susanna Burlingame,	Feb. 22, 1809.
1-16	Mudge Jarvis, of Moses and Elizabeth, Dec. 7, 1669.	

N

3-246　Nicholas William, of Comfort, Apr. 19, 1799.
1-81　Nichols Mercy, of Benjamin and Hannah, Dec. 11, 1733.
1-73　　" 　Enfield, of John, Jr., and Ann, Mar. 4, 1733-4.
2-114　　" 　Margaret, of Thomas and Welthian, Aug. 20, 1758.
　　　　　" 　Thomas, 　　　　　　　　　　　Mar. 29, 1761.
2-115　　" 　Jonathan, of Benjamin and Phebe, Sept. 15, 1769.

O

2-117　Olin David, of Peleg and Phebe, Aug. 3, 1770.
　　　　　" 　Sarah, 　　　　　　May 6, 1772.
　　　　　" 　Polly, 　　　　　　Mar. 5, 1774.
　　　　　" 　Rebecca, 　　　　　Feb. 21, 1777.
　　　　　" 　Peleg, 　　　　　　June 7, 1779.
　　　　　" 　Phebe, 　　　　　　Sept. 19, 1781.
　　　　　" 　John Gorton, 　　　Dec. 31, 1783.
　　　　　" 　Henry, 　　　　　　Apr. 13, 1786.

P

　　　　Parker Isabella, of Thomas and Lusanna (b. Scituate), July 25, 1790.
1-24　Pearce Benjamin, of Benjamin and Mary, June 1, 1732.
　　　　　" 　Benjamin, 　　　　d. June 28, 1736.
　　　　　" 　Pardon, 　　　　　Aug. 1, 1735.
　　　　　" 　Mary, 　　　　　　Oct. 29, 1737.
2-127　　" 　Caleb, of Benjamin and Sarah, Oct. 6, 1781.
3-253　　" 　Samuel Wiley, of Thomas, Sept. 12, 1788.
3-257　　" 　Hannah, of Caleb and Susanna, Oct. 7, 1803.
　　　　　" 　Daniel, 　　　　　　May 23, 1808.
　　　　　" 　Ruth, 　　　　　　　Sept. 22, 1810.
　　　　　" 　Ruth, 　　　　　　　d. Sept. 16, 1813.
　　　　　" 　Mary Russell, 　　　Apr. 8, 1813.
　　　　　" 　Clarrissa Brayton, 　Mar. 11, 1815.
　　　　　" 　Susan, 　　　　　　June 8, 1817.
3-257　Peirce Azrikam, of Samuel and Rebeckah, May 27, 1723.
　　　　　" 　Sarah, 　　　　　　Oct. 12, 1725.
　　　　　" 　Samuel, 　　　　　Mar. 16, 1728.
　　　　　" 　Rebeckah, 　　　　June 17, 1734.

3-257	Peirce Freelove,	Jan. 14, 1735.
1-95	" Ichabod, of Nathaniel and Sarah, Oct. 8, 1735.	
1-11	" Nathan, of David, —— 11, 1739.	
	" Lydia,	Apr. 1, 1741.
2-124	" Sarah, of Samuel, Jr., and Hannah, Aug. 2, 1777.	
1-61	Pigot Richard, of Edward and Ruth, Sept. 2, 1734.	
	" Rebeckah,	Nov. 6, 1735.
1-9	Potter Robert, of John and Ruth [also 1-11], Mar. 5, 1666.	
1-11	" Fisher,	July 12, 1667.
	" John,	Nov. 21, 1669.
	" William,	May 23, 1671.
	" Samuel,	Jan. 10, 1672.
	" Isabell,	Oct. 17, 1674.
	" Ruth,	Nov. 29, 1676.
	" Edward,	Nov. 25, 1678.
	" Content (son),	Oct. 2, 1680.
2-121	" Barbara, of Capt. William and Lydia, June 2. 1756.	
2-126	" John, of William and Mary, May 3, 1778.	
3-260	" Mary, widow of Pardon, died Sept. 11, 1846.	
4-39	" Henry died, aged 69y. 7m. 11d., Mar. 1, 1851,	
2-138	Price James, Nov. 2, 1778.	
	" Asahel Bennett, of James and Nancy, Oct. 19, 1807.	
1-22	Prisse Benoni, of Bridget, Mar. 27, 1685.	
3-264	Prophet Waterman, of Freelove (col.), Apr. 14, 1835.	
1-66,11	Pyner Nathan, of David, —— 11, 1739.	
	" Lydia,	Apr. 1, 1741.

Q R

2-153	Randall Job, of Jeremiah and Bethiah, Apr. 29, 1742.	
	" Elizabeth,	Feb. 14, 1744.
	" Huldah,	Mar. 4, 1747.
	" John,	May 11, 1750.
	" Jeremiah,	Feb. 11, 1752.
	" Joseph,	June 16, 1754.
1-12	Read John, of John and Ann, May 13, 1667.	
4-33	" Anthony, died, aged 65y., 0m., 27d., Aug. 27, 1850.	
2-164	Red John, of Uriel and Tabitha, Sept. 18, 1788.	
1-16	Relfe Alice, of Thomas and Mary, Feb. 13, 1656,	
	" Thomas,	July 12, 1658.
	" Sarah,	Dec. 4, 1661.

1-16	Relfe Deliverance,	Aug. 20, 1666.
1-28	Remington Maplet, of Thomas and Maplet,	July 11, 1712.
	" Mary,	May 17, 1715.
	" Stephen,	June 26, 1720.
	" Thomas,	Aug. 19, 1723.
1-49	" Thomas, of Joseph and Margaret,	Feb. 24, 1718.
	" Joseph,	Jan. 21, 1720-1.
	" Martha,	Mar. 18, 1724-5.
	" Lippitt,	Dec. 17, 1729.
1-69	" Samuel, of Daniel and Ann,	June 1, 1723.
	" Mary,	Aug. 17, 1725.
	" Daniel,	Feb. 11, 1727.
2-142	" Hannah, of Thomas and Abigail,	May 11, 1746.
	" Thomas,	Oct. 24, 1747,
	" Maplet,	June 16, 1749.
	" Sarah,	Jan. 29, 1750-1.
	" Benjamin,	Sept. 2, 1752.
	" Mary,	Mar. 26, 1754.
	" John,	Nov. 2, 1756.
	" Jonathan,	Sept. 9, 1758.
	" James Wolfe,	May 28, 1760.
	" Henry,	July 28, 1764.
	" Abigail, wife of Thomas, died Apr. 14, 1766.	
3-269	" Joseph, of Thomas, Oct. 27, 1785.	
2-149	" Lustrus, of Samuel and Almy, Oct. 27, 1791.	
	" Arnold,	Jan. 27, 1795.
	" Lloyd,	Oct. 24, 1796.
	" Robey,	May 9, 1798.
	" Israel,	Sept. 18, 1794.
	" Fannie,	Apr. 14, 1801.
2-143	" Mary, of Henry and Margaret, Apr. 13, 1792.	
2-145	" Perleg, daughter of Lydia Rhodes, of Peter, May 27, 1794.	
2-99	" John T., of James and Isabella, Mar. 21, 1813.	
	" John T.,	d. Sept. 30, 1815.
4-99	" Henry J.,	Oct. 6, 1817.
	" Sophia L.,	Oct. 10, 1819.
	" Susan J.,	Mar. 10, 1821.
	" Marcella A.,	June 28, 1824.
	" Joseph H.,	Nov. 5, 1826.
	" Thomas P.,	Oct. 2, 1829.
	" James, died May 17, 1829.	
	" John T., died Aug. 8, 1813.	

4-99	Remington John, died July 16, 1852.	
	" Susan J., died Sept. 13, 1858.	
	" Isabella, died Aug. 15, 1864.	
4-55	" Edward Holden, of Daniel and Betsey A., Dec. 29, 1831.	
	" William, of William, died, aged 73 years, June 23, 1852.	
1-18	Renolls James, of James and Mary, (b. Kings Towne) Feb. 20, 1685-6.	
2-162	Reynolds Thomas, of Samuel and Almy, Apr. 6, 1780.	
	" Elizabeth,	Apr. 4, 1782.
2-163	" John Stafford Arnold, of Henry and Millen, Mar. 22, 1782.	
	" Elizabeth Stafford,	Sept. 24, 1787.
	" Mary Arnold,	July 12, 1793.
	" Henry Arnold,	Feb. 10, 1796.
	" Millen Martin,	Apr. 8, 1799.
	" Millen, wife of Henry, died, aged 49 y., 0 m., 19 days, Apr. 25, 1804.	
2-160	" Joseph, of Henry and Anna, Apr. 25, 1785.	
2-87	" Anna, of John, Jr., and Mary, Feb. 5, 1790.	
	" Anna,	d. Mar. 20, 1790.
	" Sarah,	July 4, 1791.
	" Abigail,	May 27, 1794.
	" Mary,	July 28, 1797.
1-19	Rhodes Zachariah, of John and Waite, Nov. 5, 1687.	
	" Mercy,	Nov. 20, 1689.
	" John,	Nov. 20, 1691.
	" Joseph,	Sept. 25, 1693.
	" William,	July 14, 1695.
	" Phebe,	Nov. 30, 1698.
	" Resolved,	May 22, 1702.
	" Waite,	Dec. 16, 1703.
	" John, Sr., died Aug. 14, 1716.	
	" Sarah 2d, wife of John died, Mar. 30, 1730.	
1-29	" Malacha, of Malacha and Dorothy, Apr. 15, 1701.	
	" Malacha,	d. —— 1702-3.
	" Mary,	Sept. 15, 1703.
	" Dorothy,	Nov. 15, 1705.
	" Dorothy,	d. Dec. —, 1705.
	" Malacha,	Apr. 15, 1707.
	" Malacha,	d. Aug. 17, 1714.
	" Dorothy,	Aug. 16, 1709.
	" James,	Dec. 15, 1711.
	" Rebecca,	Apr. 5, 1714.

1-29	Rhodes Rebecca,	d. May 22, 1718.
1-30	" Waite, of John and Catherine,	Dec. 29, 1714.
	" John,	May 5, 1716.
	" Catherine,	Aug. 1, 1717.
	" Charles,	Sept. 29, 1719.
	" Mercy,	Feb. 29, 1720-1.
	" Mercy,	d. Feb. —, 1723-4.
	" Anthony,	May 29, 1722.
	" Joseph,	Aug. 22, 1723.
	" Zachariah,	Sept. 8, 1727.
	" Holden,	May 20, 1731,
	" A son, of John and 2d wife,	Mar. 31, 1734.
	" Catherine, 1st wife of John, died July 25, 1731.	
1-87	" Mary, of Malacha, Jr., and Deborah,	Jan. 29, 1732.
	" Malacha,	June 15, 1734.
	" George,	July 7, 1736.
	" Stephen,	Sept. 27, 1741.
1-64	" James, of James and Sarah,	Nov. 25, 1733.
	" Silvanus,	July 27, 1735.
	" Peleg,	Mar. 9, 1736-7.
	" Silvanus,	July 18, 1739.
	" Robert,	Mar. 21, 1741-2
	" Sylvester,	Nov. 21, 1745.
	" James,	July 9, 1748.
2-141	" Waite, of Charles and Deborah,	Aug. 25, 1740.
	" Peter,	Feb. 24, 1741.
	" Charles,	Oct. 23, 1743.
	" Charles,	d. Apr. 12, 1744.
	" Charles, 2d,	June 29, 1845.
	" Holden, Sept. 22, 1750.	
2-1	" Ishmael (col.), Apr. 1, 1756.	
2-146	" Peleg, of Peter and Hester,	Oct. 22. 1761.
	" Peleg,	d. Dec. 29, 1761.
	" Benjamin,	Mar. 25, 1763.
	" Lydia,	July 27, 1765.
	" Phebe,	Feb. 14, 1768.
	" Anthony,	Nov. 11, 1770.
	" James,	July 11, 1773.
	" Arnold,	Feb. 25, 1776.
	" Rosanna,	Oct. 19, 1778.
	" Charles,	Dec. 19, 1780.
2-149	" James, of Robert and Phebe,	Feb. 10, 1764.

2-149	Rhodes Mary,	Apr. 2, 1768.
	" Sally Fear,	Jan. 7, 1766.
	" Sally Fear,	d. Aug. 10, 1770.
	" Polly,	Apr. 2, 1768.
	" Sarah,	Mar. 9, 1771.
	" Sarah,	d. Oct. 20, 1791.
	" Christopher,	Aug. 16, 1776.
	" Robert,	Sept. 12, 1778.
	" Robert,	d. Oct. 26, 1782.
	" William,	Feb. 11, 1782.
	" Robert, 2d,	Sept. 19, 1787.
	" Robert, 2d,	d. Oct. 9, 1791.
2-42	" Mary, of Holden and Susannah,	Mar. 21, 1769.
	" Holden,	June 10, 1771.
	" Nancy,	Mar. 8, 1774.
	" Isaac T.,	May 22, 1776.
	" Daniel R.,	June 4, 1782.
	" Zachariah,	May 20, 1784.
	" Wanton,	May 22, 1786.
	" Wanton,	d. Sept. 30, 1800.
	" Samuel Remington,	Sept. 28, 1788.
	" Perry,	Mar. 25, 1792.
	" Mary, of Malacha,	Mar. 30, 1769.
	" Peleg,	June 3, 1771.
	" Lydia,	July 30, 1774.
	" Waite,	Feb. 18, 1777.
	" Sarah,	Aug. 27, 1779.
	" Daniel,	June 14, 1781.
	" George,	July 13, 1784.
	" Betsey,	Jan. 24, 1792.
	" Henry,	July 21, 1797.
	" Edward,	July 21, 1797.
2-151	" Mary, of William and Ann,	Apr. 7, 1770.
	" William,	Mar. 21, 1772.
2-156	" Joseph Aborn, of Sylvester and Polly,	June 21, 1772.
	" Betsey,	Sept. 27, 1775.
	" Sally,	Aug. 17, 1777.
2-153	" Sall Ann, of Benjamin and Mercy,	Jan. 31, 1787.
	" Benjamin,	May 17, 1789.
	" Mercy, wife of Benjamin, died, aged 21y., 2m., 16 days, May 24, 1789.	
2-154	" Sion Arnold, of James and Betsey,	Apr. 7, 1791.

2-154	Rhodes John Rice Arnold,	May 2, 1794.
	" Sally Fear,	July 23, 1796.
2-153	" Peleg, of Benjamin and Phebe,	Sept. 8, 1792.
	" James,	Sept. 13, 1794.
	" Amos,	Apr. 17, 1797.
	" Amos,	d. Oct. 31, 1797.
	" Mercy,	Feb. 24, 1800.
	" Phebe, wife of Benjamin, born	Jan. 20, 1777.
2-159	" Ann Mercy, of Peleg and Mary,	Jan, 17, 1798.
	" Ann Mercy,	d. Mar. 15, 1798.
	" James Thomas,	Nov. 20, 1800.
	" Peleg Aborn,	May 4, 1804.
	" Mary, wife of Peleg, died	Nov. 20, 1806.
	" Julia Sophia, of Peleg and Sarah B.,	Dec. 21, 1808.
	" Sarah,	Oct. 21, 1813.
4-55	" Mary, widow of Sylvester, died, aged 97y., 9m., Apr. 12, 1852.	
4-95	" George H., son of Daniel, died, aged 53y., 9m., 2d, Dec. 19, 1877.	
1-38	Rice John, of John, Jr., and Elnathan, Apr. 6, 1696.	
	" Elizabeth,	May 6, 1698.
	" Thomas,	Apr. 26, 1700.
	" Mary,	Sept. 22, 1702.
	" Mary,	d. Apr. —, 1703.
	" Nathan,	June 20, 1704.
	" Barbara,	Apr. 24, 1706.
	" William,	Mar. 25, 1708.
	" Mary,	Jan. 24, 1709.
	" Lydia,	Dec. 30, 1711.
	" Randall,	May 21, 1714.
	" Elnathan,	Aug. 4, 1716.
	" John, Jr., died Jan. 6, 1730-1, aged 86 years.	
2-158	" Freelove, of Thomas and ———	July 22, 1722.
	" Dorothy,	Oct. 30, 1723.
	" Mary,	Sept. 18, 1725.
	" Bethiah,	Nov. 1, 1727.
	" Ellen,	Nov. 26, 1729.
	" Holden,	May 10, 1732.
	" Frances,	Jan. 11, 1734
	" Robe,	Mar. 27, 1736.
	" Anthony,	Apr. 2, 1738.
	" Waite,	Apr. 2, 1738.

2-158	Rice Thomas, of Thomas and ———, 2d wife,		May 11, 1741.
	"	Thomas,	d. Aug. 10, 1742.
	"	Thomas 2d,	Jan. 5, 1744.
	"	William,	Feb. 11, 1745.
	"	Ellen,	June 11, 1748.
	"	John,	Mar. 30, 1750.
	"	John,	d. Apr. 12, 1750.
	"	Josephus,	Dec. 7, 1754.
1-79	"	Abigail, of William and Phebe,	Feb. 20, 1730-1.
	"	Mehitable,	Sept. 25, 1732.
	"	Elizabeth,	Oct. 18, 1734.
	"	James,	Feb. 20, 1736.
	"	James,	d. June 22, 1744.
	"	Hannah,	Apr. 22, 1739.
	"	John,	May 26, 1741.
	"	Mary,	June 18, 1743.
	"	Mary,	d. July 28, 1743.
	"	James,	June 28, 1744.
	"	Mary,	Apr. 24, 1746.
	"	William died Jan. 22, 1746.	
1-38	"	John, of Randall and Dinah,	Mar. 19, 1736.
	"	Job,	Feb. 20, 1736-7.
	"	Olney,	Feb. 12, 1737-8.
	"	Thomas,	Nov. 11, 1739.
	"	Robey,	Feb. 26, 1741.
	"	Fones,	Apr. 3, 1743.
	"	William,	Sept. 28, 1744.
	"	Mary,	Sept. 28, 1744.
	"	Phebe,	Apr. 20, 1746.
	"	Randall,	Oct. 12, 1747.
	"	Nathan,	May 20, 1749.
	"	Elnathan,	Sept. —, 1750.
2-52,144	"	James,	June 6, 1752.
	"	Caleb,	Mar. 20, 1754.
2-144	"	Daniel,	June 5, 1756.
	"	John,	died Jan. 2, 1758.
2-147	"	Barbara, of Major Henry and Martha,	Nov. 4, 1740.
	"	Avis,	Oct. 17, 1742.
	"	Caleb,	Nov. 16, 1744.
	"	Elizabeth,	Feb. 7, 1746.
	"	Mary,	Oct. 19, 1749.
	"	Anne,	July 1, 1752.

2-147	Rice Martha,	Oct. 9, 1754.
	" John, of Major Henry and Phebe,	Jan. 18, 1756.
	" Phebe,	Oct. 14, 1757.
	" Henry,	May 18, 1760.
	" Tibbetts,	Aug. 26, 1777.
	" Major Henry, died Nov. 13, 1800.	
2-144	" Capt. John, died, about 80 years,	Jan. 9, 1755.
2-148	" John, of Job and Anne,	Mar. 22, 1761.
	" Noel,	Apr. 13, 1763.
	" Freelove,	June 19, 1765.
	" Edward,	Sept. 15, 1769.
	" Job,	Feb. 8, 1772.
	" Hannah,	Oct. 31, 1775.
	" Anna,	May 18, 1778.
2-88	" Anthony, of Holden, Sept. 12, 1761.	
	" Martha, his wife, July 7, 1767·	
	" Susannah Cook, of Anthony and Martha,	Aug. 26, 1790.
	" Mary,	Feb. 7, 1792.
	" Sarah Stafford,	July 18, 1795.
	" Elizabeth Holden,	July 26, 1799.
	" Joseph Holden,	Feb. 28, 1803.
2-155	" William, of Olney and Freelove,	Apr. 25, 1763.
	" Dinah,	Mar. 17, 1765.
	" Randall, of Thomas and Freelove,	Oct. 29, 1769.
	" Catherine,	Dec. 13, 1770.
	" Olney,	Feb. 28, 1772.
	" Freelove,	Dec. 15, 1773.
	" Mary,	Sept. 27, 1775.
	" Thomas,	————.
	" Thomas 2d,	Jan. 8, 1780.
	" Phebe,	Mar. 16, 1782.
	" Nancy,	Aug. 19, 1784.
2-152	" Barbara, of Thomas and Rosanna,	Feb. 12, 1776.
	" Anna,	July 17, 1779.
	" Lucy,	May 6, 1785.
	" Lucy,	d. Oct. 19, 1786.
2-164	" Elizabeth, of William and Lucy,	July 28, 1776.
	" Benjamin,	Feb. 3, 1779.
	" Thomas C.,	Aug. 30, 1781.
	" Sally,	Dec. 3, 1784.
	" William,	July 16, 1788.
	" Polly,	Apr. 9, 1792.

2-164	Rice Whipple,	Jan. 31, 1795.
2-141	" Bethiah, of Josephus, Sept. 7, 1778.	
	" Abigail,	Oct. 11, 1780.
	" Hannah,	Oct. 9, 1783.
	" Hannah,	d. Nov. 3, 1801.
	" Phebe,	Jan. 29, 1786.
	" Sally,	May 23, 1788.
	" Thomas,	Jan. 10, 1790.
2-157	" Polly A., of Henry and Susanna, Jan. 15, 1783.	
	" Phebe,	Nov. 15, 1785.
	" Mercy,	May 28, 1791.
	" Deborah,	Apr. 17, 1795.
	" Henry,	died Sept. 28, 1797.
2-161	" Catherine, of Thomas and Sarah, June 14, 1786.	
	" Catherine,	died Mar. 11, 1787.
	" John,	May 8, 1788.
	" Asteliza,	Mar. 21, 1792.
	" William Earle,	July 3, 1796.
	" Immanuel,	May 5, 1799.
2-151	" Oliver Gardner, of Wanton and Mercy, Oct. 9, 1792.	
	" William Warren,	Oct. 27, 1795.
	" Mercy Ann,	Nov. 15, 1798.
	" Benjamin Gorton,	Jan. 2, 1800.
2-255	" George, of William and Sarah, Apr. 24, 1793.	
	" Sarah,	Apr. 2, 1795.
2-276	" Joseph W., of Joseph B. and Sarah, July 23, 1833.	
1-18	Robertson William, of Robert and Sarah, July 25, 1685.	
	Roberts Mark, of Mark and Mary, Apr. 10, 1683.	
	" John,	Dec. 4, 1685.
2-145	" Christy, of John, Sept. 15, 1732.	
	" Phebe,	Oct. 25, 1734.
	" James,	Apr. 18, 1737.
	" Elizabeth,	Mar. 3, 1739.
	" Jonathan,	Mar. 20, 1741.
	" Sarah,	Feb. 26, 1743.
	" Benjamin,	May 17, 1745.
	" Mary,	May 26, 1747.
	" Mercy,	May 25, 1749.
	" Catherine,	Aug. 23, 1751.
3-64	Ruttenberge William, of John and Sarah, Sept. 22, 1720.	
	" Mary,	Aug. 22, 1723.
1-64	" Peter,	June 9, 1725.

3-65	Ruttenberge Mary, of Thomas and Ann, Dec. 10, 1726.
	" Thomas, Feb. 10, 1727-8.
	" Thomas, d. Oct. 10, 1727.
1-38	" John, of John and Mary, Mar. 8, 1793.

S

2-215	Salsbury Martin, of Daniel and Lydia, May 9, 1783.
	" Polly, Nov. 5, 1785.
	" Daniel, Jan. 11, 1791.
	" Lydia, Jan. 1, 1800.
2-245	Sarle Benjamin Greene, of William and Catherine, Oct. 26,1780.
	" William, Feb. 19, 1783.
	" John Fry, Jan. 21, 1786.
	" Lucretia, June 16, 1788.
	" Lucretia, d. Aug. 19, 1788.
3-290	" John W., of Benjamin G., Feb. 13, 1832.
	" George F., Aug. 22, 1834.
1-26	Schreech Teddeman, of William and Sarah, Sept. 4, 1713.
	" John, Feb. 5, 1715-6.
	" William, Feb. 28, 1718.
	" Elizabeth, Sept. 9, 1721.
	" Sarah, wife of William, died Oct. 22, 1739.
4-46	Sheldon Joseph, died, aged 23 y., 11 m., 28 d., Aug. 12, 1851.
2-168	Shearman Tabitha, of Benjamin, Feb. 6, 1754.
2-171	" Gardner, of Benajah, Jan. 30, 1757.
4-70	" Hannah French, of Lorenzo D. and Lucy Ann., Jan. 25, 1847.
	" Alonzo, of Lorenzo D. and Lucy Ann, Nov. 26, 1849.
	" Melissa, Mar. 28, 1851.
	" Abbie Ann, May 13, 1855.
	" Lorenzo Gardner, Jan. 16, 1857.
1-102	Sisson Joseph, of Richard, Apr. 4, 1738.
1-39	Slocum Desire, of Giles and Mary, Jan. 14, 1720-1.
	" Ebenezer, Feb. 17, 1723-4.
1-15	Smith John, of Thomas and Ruth, Aug. 4, 1660.
	" Thomas, Aug. 9, 1663.
	" William, Jan. 10, 1666.
	" Joseph, Feb. 18, 1668.
	" Mrs. Anna, died Nov. 2, 1678.
1-70	" Elizabeth, of Benjamin and Phebe, Jan. 11, 1692-3.

1-70	Smith	Hannah,	Oct. 7, 1694.
	"	Sarah,	May 30, 1695.
	"	Benjamin,	Jan. 21, 1696-7.
	"	Phebe,	Dec. 5, 1699.
	"	Phillip,	Nov. 30, 1700.
	"	Almy,	June 17, 1703.
	"	Lydia,	June 11, 1705.
	"	Alce,	Feb. 3, 1706-7.
	"	Catherine,	Jan. 23, 1708-9.
	"	Giffe,	Apr. 20, 1710.
	"	Stephen,	Feb. 20, 1712-3.
1-18	"	Esther, of Simon and Mary, Oct. 9, 1699.	
	"	Mary,	Apr. 4, 1701.
	"	Christopher,	Oct. 14, 1703.
	"	Phebe,	Dec. 13, 1705.
	"	Simon,	July 1, 1710.
	"	Lydia, wife of Benjamin, died Oct. 1, 1711.	
	"	Simon, of Benjamin and Lydia, died Mar. 4, 1712.	
	"	Benjamin, Jr., died Dec. 20, 1713.	
1-31	"	Joseph, of Daniel and Demis, Apr. 17, 1729.	
	"	Sarah,	Mar. 11, 1730-1.
	"	James,	Mar. 1, 1732-3.
	"	Jonathan,	Aug. —, 1736.
2-165	"	Stephen, of Stephen and Mary, July 15, 1743.	
	"	Benjamin,	Nov. 19, 1744.
	"	Simeon,	Mar. 6, 1745-6.
	"	Mary Abbott,	Jan. 25, 1748.
	"	Sarah,	June 7, 1754.
2-192	"	Benjamin, Nov. 14, 1766.	
	"	Patience Arnold, of Benjn. and Patience, Mar. 20, 1796.	
	"	Sidney Barlow,	June 12, 1798.
	"	Mary Waterman,	Sept. 4, 1800.
4-89	"	Alfred, b. Pawtuxet, Nov. 7, 1802.	
	"	Patience (Phillips), his wife, b. Warren, Mar. 8, 1801.	
	"	Benjamin, of Alfred and Patience, Mar. 28, 1833.	
	"	Caroline Patience,	Nov. 30, 1835.
	"	Mary Cornelia,	Oct. 20, 1837.
		NOTE.—Above two born Providence.	
2-180	Snell	John, of Daniel and Mary, Sept. 10, 1772.	
	"	John,	d. Feb. 26, 1777.
	"	Susanna,	July 3, 1774.
	"	Thomas,	Mar. 9, 1776.

2-180	Snell John,	Aug. 9, 1777.
	" John,	d. Oct. 31, 1778.
	" Lydia,	July 1, 1779.
	" Lydia,	d. Oct. 8, 1780.
	" Kesiah,	Feb. 1, 1781.
	" Mary, wife of Daniel, died Sept. 24, 1804.	
3-290	" William, of Daniel and Rebecca, June 30, 1795.	
2-177	Spencer Thomas, of Pearce, Aug. 30, 1772.	
2-184	" Joseph, of Thomas and Mary, Dec. 23, 1792.	
	" Christopher V.,	Sept. 5, 1795.
	" Waite,	Oct. 10, 1799.
3-293	" William, of Christopher and Celia, Mar. 20, 1817.	
	" Arnold Westcott,	Dec. 5, 1819.
	" Thomas,	Feb. 1, 1821.
	" Edwin,	Oct. 11, 1823.
	" George Washington,	Aug. 15, 1825.
3-40	" Elizabeth, of William B. and Welthian, Nov. 9, 1842.	
1-12	Stafford Mary, of Amos and Mary, Sept. 16, 1690.	
	" Samuel,	Sept. 24, 1692.
	" Mary,	Sept. 21, 1694.
	" Amos,	Sept. 24, 1702.
	" Stukeley,	Nov. 7, 1704.
	" Patience,	Apr. 21, 1707.
	" Patience,	d. Apr. 27, 1711.
	" Freelove,	Oct. 14, 1709.
1-36	" Phebe, of Thomas and Anne, Apr. 11, 1710.	
	" Anne,	Jan. 4, 1711-2.
	" Mercy,	Mar. 12, 1714-5.
	" Job,	Apr. 11, 1716.
	" Samuel,	Jan. 8, 1717.
	" Samuel,	d. ———, 1719.
	" Deborah,	Apr. 9, 1718.
	" Anne, wife of Thomas, died Aug. 24, 1718.	
	" Samuel, died in his 83 year, Mar. 20, 1717-8.	
	" Mary, wife of Samuel, died Mar. 25, 1700.	
1-44	" Mercy, of Joseph (blacksmith) and Susannah, June 2, 1717.	
	" Joseph,	Jan. 16, 1718-9.
	" Susannah,	Aug. 15, 1721.
	" Susannah,	d. Dec. —, 1721.
	" Susannah 2d,	Mar. 10, 1722-3.
	" Susannah, wife of Joseph, died Aug. 29, 1734.	
1-33	" Mary, of Samuel and Hannah, Mar. 27, 1718.	

1-33	Stafford Hannah,	May 2, 1721.	
	" Patience,	Apr. 8, 1724.	
	" Barbara,	June 13, 1728.	
	" Stukeley,	Apr. 25, 1730.	
	" Mercy,	Mar. 26, 1733.	
1-36	" Eleanor, of Thomas and Audrey,	Apr. 25, 1720.	
	" Richard,	Sept. 24, 1721.	
	" Thomas,	Apr. 20, 1723.	
	" Samuel,	Dec. 6, 1724.	
1-35	" Amie,	Apr. 19, 1728.	
	" Samuel,	Feb. 22, 1728-9.	
	" Joab,	Nov. 14, 1729.	
	" John,	May 5, 1735.	
	" Audrey,	Feb. 8, 1731.	
1-53	" Jerusha, of John and Jerusha,	Aug. 24, 1728.	
	" Ann,	May 8, 1731.	
2-172	" Thomas, of Thomas and Rebecca,	July 10, 1767.	
2-183	" Anna, of John and Martha,	Jan. 12, 1775.	
	" Elizabeth,	Mar. 30, 1780.	
	" Thomas Rice,	Mar. 5, 1782.	
	" Marbury,	July 25, 1784.	
	" Pattey,	Feb. 2, 1788.	
	" John Greene,	Apr. 1, 1790.	
2-162	" Rebecca, of Thomas, Jr., and Polly,	Mar. 17, 1790.	
	" Robert Rhodes,	Oct. 3, 1791.	
	" Samuel,	June 13, 1793.	
	" Phebe Smith,	Mar. 7, 1795.	
	" Christopher Rhodes,	Jan. 3, 1797.	
	" Thomas Hill,	July 27, 1799.	
	" Julia Ann,	June, 5, 1802.	
	" Mary Eliza,	Oct. 14, 1804.	
	" Sally Fear Rhodes,	Nov. 23, 1806.	
	" Almira Arnold,	Sept. 21, 1810.	
	" George Washington,	Sept. 2, 1812.	
1-15	Stone Peter, of Hugh and Abigail,	Jan. 28, 1671-2.	
1-17	" Abigail,	Feb. 10, 1677-8.	
1-35	" Elizabeth, of Peter and Elizabeth,	Mar. 25, 1697.	
	" Peter,	Oct. 22, 1698.	
	" Sarah,	Feb. 17, 1699-0.	
	" Abigail,	Sept. 15, 1700.	
	" Prescilla,	Feb. 12, 1702-3.	
	" John,	Sept. 29, 1704.	

2-177	Straight Sarah, of Ruth, July 11, 1767.	
2-178	" Hester, of Joseph and Mary, Oct. 24, 1774.	
2-170	" John Briggs, of Maray, daughter of Joseph, May 5, 1803, died Mar. 16, 1804.	
1-7	Sweet Phillip, of James, July 15, 1655.	
	" James,	May 8, 1657.
	" Mary,	Feb. 2, 1659.
	" Benoni,	Mar. 28, 1663.
	" Valentine, of James and Mary, Feb. 14, 1665.	
	" Samuel,	Nov. 1, 1667.
	" Jeremiah,	Jan. 6, 1668-9.
	" Renewed,	July 16, 1671.
	" Sylvester,	Mar. 1, 1674.
	[NOTE. Five last of above born Providence.	
1-47	" Daniel, of Daniel (miller) and Eleanor, Nov. 2, 1692.	
	" Eleanor,	Mar. 6, 1696.
	" Jeremiah,	May 20, 1700.
	" John,	July 14, 1706.
1-82	" Elizabeth, of Phillip and Elizabeth, Apr. 7, 1712.	
	" Phillip,	Nov. 22, 1713.
	" Pentecost,	Oct. 30, 1715.
	" Welthian,	Jan. 4, 1717.
	" Benjamin,	Nov. 4, 1721.
	" John,	Nov. 3, 1723.
	" Valentine,	Jan. 12, 1725.
	" James,	Aug. 20, 1728.
	" Samuel,	Dec. 7, 1730.
1-49	" Giffe, of Nathaniel and Giffe, June 14, 1722.	
	" Jane,	Mar. 2, 1724.
	" William,	Feb. 18, 1725-6.
1-48	" Neomy, of Daniel, Jr., and Neomy, Dec. 22, 1725.	
	" Eleanor,	Nov. 22, 1727.
	" Daniel,	Dec. 12, 1729:
	" Sarah,	May 5, 1734.
	" Ann,	July 5, 1737.
2-169	" Sarah, of Thomas, July 25, 1752.	
	" Benjamin,	Feb. 2, 1754.
	" Abigail,	Dec. 19, 1755.
3-291	" John R., b. Apponaug, Mar. 27, 1834.	

T

4-39	Taft Robert, died near Stockton, Cal., aged 56y. 1m. 24d., Oct. 29, 1850.	
4-61	" George J., died aged 35y. 10m., Dec. 14, 1852.	
1-1	Tallman Peleg, of Benjamin and Elizabeth, Mar. 25, 1736.	
	" Thomas,	Mar. 28, 1738.
	" Patience,	Dec. 15, 1740.
2-189	" Bethany, of Joseph and Mary, Feb. 1, 1742.	
	" Freelove,	July 18, 1745.
2-129	Taylor Thomas, of Ambrose and Sarah, Sept. 14, 1772.	
2-121	" William, June 4, 1774.	
	" William Francis, of William and Mary, Dec. 19, 1800.	
	" Barbara Elizabeth, of Ambrose, Apr. 24, 1779.	
	" Sarah,	Aug. 27, 1783.
	" Ambrose,	June 12, 1792.
2-129	" Betsey Anna, of Thomas and Ann, Jan. 22, 1799.	
	" John Stafford,	Apr. 3, 1800.
1-15	Tefft Peter, of Joshua and Sarah, Mar. 14, 1671-2.	
4-42	Thompson Festus L., died aged 63y. 5m. 24d., July 28, 1851.	
1-58	Tibbetts, a son of Thomas and Elizabeth, b. and d. Feb.—1717.	
	" Thomas,	Dec. 12, 1719.
	" Thomas, died Aug. 17, 1724.	
1-16	" John, of William and Judah, Sept. 25, 1737.	
	" Almy,	Oct. 21, 1739.
	" Mary,	Jan. 21, 1740-1.
	" Dinah,	Apr. 2, 1742.
	" Judith,	June 16, 1744.
	" Ruth,	Nov. 16, 1745.
	" William,	Oct. 28, 1747.
	" Avice,	June 8, 1749.
	" Caleb,	Apr. 7, 1751.
2-190	" Phebe, of John and Waite, Feb. 10, 1761.	
2-217	" Henry, died Jan. 17, 1765.	
	" Elizabeth, of Henry, died Nov. 15, 1764.	
	" Charles,	died Nov. 14, 1764.
2-217	" Charles, of Waterman aud Mercy, Jan. 25, 1766.	
	" John Waterman,	Jan. 2, 1769.
	" Henry,	Jan. 11, 1771.
2-191	" Hannah, wife of Henry, died, Apr. 28, 1766.	
2-184	" Henry, of John and Robey, Jan. 26, 1775.	
2-110	" Thomas,	May 26, 1783.

2-184	Tibbetts Whitman,	Dec. 10, 1787.
	" Benjamin,	Aug. 13, 1790.
	" Robey,	May 23, 1797.
2-194	" Samuel, of Jonathan and Rebecca, Aug. 16, 1787.	
3-292	" Elizabeth, of George, Feb. 5, 1808.	
	" William,	May 28, 1810.
	" Benjamin,	Nov. 18. 1812.
4-39	" Samuel T., of Jonathan, died, aged 63y., 7m.. 23d., Apr. 8, 1851.	
4-61	Tiffany Jonathan, died, aged 44y., Feb. 6, 1853.	
4-40	Townsend Mary, died, aged 63y., 11m., 19d., Apr. 14, 1851.	
1-66	Tripp Elizabeth, of Isreal and Elizabeth, Mar. 19, 1750.	
	" James,	Apr. 1, 1749.
2-192	" Sarah, of Job and Hannah, Oct. 23, 1758.	
	" Isaac,	Nov. 27, 1760.
	" Lydia,	Sept. 6, 1762.
	" Mary,	Sept. 15, 1764.
2-186	" Stephen, of James and Mercy, Apr. 27, 1775.	
4-101	Twigg Henry, died about June 14, 1866.	

U

1-22	Utter Sarah, of William and Anne, Aug. 1, 1707.	
	" Ailes,	Sept. 27, 1711.
1-1	" Barbara, of William and Phebe, Feb. 16, 1741.	
	" Sarah,	Aug. 26, 1745.

V W

1-46	Wall John, of William and Susanna, Feb. 17, 1723-4.	
	" Ebenezer,	Nov. 13, 1726.
1-35	Walton Mary, of John and Susanna, Oct. 6, 1739.	
2-203	" Welthian, of John and Mary, Aug, 23, 1751.	
	" Marian, born last Friday of May, 1754.	
2-216	Ward William Greene, of Major Samuel and Phebe, Apr. 1, 1779.	
	" Samuel,	Jan. 23, 1781.
	" Henry,	Mar. 17, 1784.
	" Samuel, 2d,	May 1, 1786.
	" Ann Catherine,	Aug. 15, 1788.
	" Phebe,	July 17, 1791.

1-204	Warner John, Jr., June 5, 1673, died Apr. 22, 1712, aged 66 years. [Sic.]	
1-20	" Elizabeth (Coggeshall), his wife, Apr. 23, 1677, died Mar. 13, 1710-1.	
1-20	" John, of John, Jr., and Elizabeth, Aug. 8, 1695.	
	" Elizabeth,	Apr. 19, 1697.
	" Anne,	Apr. 29, 1699.
	" Susanna,	Sept. 4, 1701.
	" Rachel,	Feb. 8, 1703-4.
	" William,	Aug. 31, 1706.
	" William,	d. Mar. 9, 1710-1.
	" Samuel,	Dec. 13, 1708.
1-27	" Mary, of John and Susanna, Sept. 5, 1714.	
	" Prescilla,	Jan. 10, 1715-6.
	" Prescilla,	d. Mar. 17, 1715-6.
	" William,	Mar. 4, 1727.
	" Susannah, wife of John, died Aug. 4, 1727.	
1-36	" John, of John, Jr., and Mary, Aug. 5, 1720.	
	" Thomas,	Mar. 4, 1721-2.
	" Ann,	Aug. 21, 1723.
	" Ann,	d. Nov. 4, 1739.
	" Amos,	Sept. 24, 1725.
	" Mary,	Nov. 25, 1727.
	" Mary, wife of John, Jr., died Jan. 30, 1728.	
1-61	" William, of John, Jr., and Abigail, Apr. 5, 1730.	
	" Elizabeth,	Oct. 23, 1731.
	" Hannah,	Nov. 11, 1733.
	" James,	May 12, 1735.
	" Prescilla,	Jan. 19, 1736-7.
	" Almy,	Feb. 10, 1738-9.
	" Ezekiel,	Oct. 17, 1740.
	" Elisha,	Nov. 8, 1742.
	" Peter,	July 10, 1745.
	" Peter,	d. July 16, 1747.
	" Isabel,	Nov. 24, 1748.
1-68	" Samuel, of Samuel and Keziah, Nov. 25, 1730.	
	" Rachel,	Nov. 4, 1732.
	" Sarah,	May 25, 1735.
	" Phebe,	Apr. 3, 1737.
	" Keziah,	Feb. 27, 1739,
	" Ann,	Oct. 9, 1740.
1-27	" John died Nov. 8, 1732, in 60th year.	

1-30	Warner William, of William and Susannah, Dec. 27, 1740.	
	" Lois,	Nov. 14, 1742.
	" Susanna,	Aug. 25, 1744.
	" Holliman,	Oct. 11, 1746.
	" Mary,	Mar. 23, 1749.
	" Waite,	Aug. 9, 1751.
2-204	" Mary, of Capt. Thomas and Phebe, Sept. 1, 1752.	
	" Sarah,	Nov. 27, 1754.
	" Thomas,	July 26, 1757.
	" Phebe,	May 17, 1760.
	" Anne,	Sept. 5, 1763.
	" William,	Dec. 8, 1766.
2-208	" Elizabeth, of James and Rebecca, Sept. 2, 1757.	
	" John,	July 16, 1759.
	" Amos,	Sept. 4, 1760.
	" Alice,	Jan. 21, 1763.
	" James,	Apr. 12, 1764.
2-215	" Elisha, of Ezekiel and Margaret, Jan. 27, 1764.	
	" Benjamin,	Dec, 27, 1765.
	" Elizabeth,	Aug. 26, 1768.
	" Isabel,	Apr. 14, 1771.
2-210	" Mercy, of William and Waite, Sept. 7, 1764.	
	" Zuriah,	Jan. 30, 1766.
	" Waite,	Sept. 28, 1767.
	" John,	Apr. 16, 1770.
	" William,	June 18, 1772.
	" Elizabeth,	Nov. 24, 1774.
2-213	" Sarah, of John and Elizabeth, Oct. 6, 1768.	
	" Elizabeth,	July 7, 1770.
	" John,	Sept. 18, 1773.
	" Keziah,	Sept. 18, 1773.
2-199	" John, died aged 77y. 7m. 29d., Apr. 7, 1773.	
2-224	" Isabel, of Thomas and Mary, Sept. 13, 1783.	
	" Catherine Townsend,	Dec. 14, 1785.
	" John,	Sept. 16, 1788.
	" John,	d. Sept. —, 1793.
	" Christ'r Townsend,	Oct. 14, 1791.
	" Christ'r Townsend,	d. Sept. —, 1793.
	" John, 2d,	Nov. 6, 1793.
	" Thomas,	Oct. 15, 1796.
	" Mary,	Oct. 15, 1796.
	" Mary,	d. Jan. 23, 1797.

2-224	Warner Thomas, died ———, 1847.	
	" Mary, widow of Thomas, died Mar. 18, 1847. [also 3-356]	
3-342	" Elizabeth Greene, of James and Mary, Sept. 14, 1806.	
	" Stephen,	Aug. 27, 1808.
	" George Greene,	Sept. 15, 1811.
	" James,	Aug. 10, 1813.
3-127	" William Greene, of Stephen G. and Catherine C., Dec. 16, 1832.	
1-199	Warren John, died aged 77y. 8m. lacking 1 day, Apr. 7, 1773.	
1-23	Waterman Elizabeth, of "Ensign" John and Anne, Apr. 18, 1692.	
	" Mercy, of "Ensign" John and Anne, June 27, 1694.	
	" Anne,	May 20, 1696.
	" John,	Feb. 5, 1698.
	" Benoni,	May 25, 1701.
	" Resolved,	Oct. 13, 1703.
1-52	" Mary, of Benoni and Sarah, May 6, 1726.	
	" John,	Aug. 25, 1730.
	" Benjamin,	May 22, 1732.
1-77	" Thomas, of John and Hannah, May 27, 1731.	
	" John,	Jan. 11, 1738-9.
	" Hannah,	Dec. 30, 1740.
	" Hannah, wife of John, died Jan. 12, 1740-1.	
	" Mercy, Dec. 31, 1742.	
	" William, Mar. 6, 1744.	
1-98	" John, of Resolved and Sarah, July 8, 1733.	
	" Edward,	Mar. 30, 1735.
	" Resolved,	Jan. 23, 1736-7.
	" Caleb,	June 20, 1739.
	" Sarah,	Jan. 23, 1741-2.
	" Avis,	Mar. 1, 1744.
	" Phebe,	Apr. 11, 1748.
	" Hannah,	Oct. 12, 1750.
	Note.—Two eldest born Jamestown; rest, Warwick; eldest died soon.	
2-207	" Benjamin, of John and Sarah, July 15, 1755.	
	" Mercy,	Nov. 3, 1756.
	" John,	Sept. 12, 1758.
	" John,	d. Mar. 7, 1759.
	" John, 2d,	Dec. 19, 1759.
	" Mary,	May 22, 1761.
	" William,	May 5, 1763.

WARWICK—BIRTHS AND DEATHS.

2-207	Waterman Sarah,	Sept. 30, 1764.
2-35	" John, of William and Phebe,	Dec. 19, 1768.
	" Mary,	Mar. 10, 1772.
	" Mary,	d. Dec. 10, 1798.
	" William,	Nov. 12, 1774.
	" William,	d. May 25, 1796.
	" Phillip,	Dec. 13, 1776.
	" Phillip,	d. Mar. —, 1777.
	" Benjamin,	Nov. 25, 1778.
	" Benjamin,	d. July 17, 1779.
	" Mercy,	Oct. 14, 1780.
	" Resolved,	Mar. 23, 1791.
	" Resolved,	d. Aug. 11, 1791.
	" Phebe, wife of John, died, Oct. 13, 1801.	
4-71	" John Robinson, of Dea. John and Welthian, Feb. 19, 1783. [also 2-218]	
	" Isabella (Warren, of Thomas and Mary), Sept. 13, 1783. [also 3-33]	
	" Louisa, of John R. and Isabella, [3-33]	Aug. 26, 1806.
	" Maria,	" Mar. 27, 1808.
	" Maria,	" d. Aug. 5, 1808.
	" Richard, [4-64]	Aug. 4, 1809.
	" Maria Almira,	Apr. 25, 1811.
	" John,	Nov. 16, 1812.
	" John,	d, Nov. 26, 1837.
	" Thomas Warner,	Jan. 6, 1815.
	" Thomas Warner,	d. Feb. 1, 1839.
	" Henry,	Mar. 23, 1816.
	" A son,	Sept. 4, 1818.
	" A son,	d. Sept. 10, 1818.
	" Isabella,	Nov, 1, 1819.
	" Catherine,	Nov. 1, 1819.
	" A son,	s. b. Nov. 1, 1819.
	" Maria,	Jan.
	" Maria,	d. Feb. 13, 1823.
	" Sarah Potter,	Sept. 28, 1824.
	" Sarah Potter,	d. Apr. 22, 1832.
	" Isabella, wife of John R., died Jan. 24, 1832.	
2-208	" Cato, servant of Col. John, born Apr. 26, 1785.	
2-119	" Sarah, of John and Phebe, May 15, 1791.	
	" Emma,	Oct. 18, 1793.
4-64	" Abbie Maria, of Richard and Dianna M., Mar. 29, 1835.	

4-64	Waterman Elizabeth Slade,	July 23, 1837.
	" Louisa Chapin,	July 23, 1837.
	" Caroline Chapin,	Dec. 5, 1844.
	" John,	Mar. 7, 1847.
	" Thomas Warner,	June 8, 1849.
	" Frank Arthur,	Oct. 24, 1852.
	" Fannie Alice,	Oct. 24, 1852.
3-424	" Mary, of Col. John, deceased, died in her 86 year, Mar. 4, 1847.	
	" Welthian, widow of Dea. John, died in her 87 year, Mar. 14, 1849.	
1-56	Weaver Daniel, of Clement and Mary, June 9, 1728.	
	" Anne,	Oct. 25, 1729.
	" Robert,	Sept. 24, 1731.
	" Nathan,	July 29, 1735.
1-28	" Phebe, of Benjamin and Mary, July 3, 1741.	
	" Ruth,	July 20, 1743.
2-171	" Phillip, Jr., Sept. 17, 1780.	
2-215	" George, of Caleb and Freelove, Aug. 5, 1788.	
	" Daniel,	Dec. 23, 1789.
	" Nancy,	Aug. 19, 1792.
3-337	Webb Jeremiah, born July 15, 1751.	
2-203	" Thomas, of William and Deliverance, Apr. 10, 1763.	
	" Abigail,	Apr. 13, 1765.
	" William,	Apr. 19, 1767.
	" Mary,	Aug. 11, 1769.
	" Lydia,	Feb. 14, 1772.
	" Jeremiah,	June 7, 1774.
	" Henry,	Dec. 17, 1776.
	" Chace,	Jan. 7, 1779.
	" Freelove,	Oct. 15, 1781.
	" Elizabeth,	Jan. 10, 1785.
	" John,	Oct. 30, 1787.
	" Henry, (grandson)	May 4, 1794.
2-198	" Jeremiah, of Jeremiah and Nancy, May 27, 1776.	
3-351	" Abraham L., of William and Hannah, July 7, 1816; died July 31, 1816.	
2-150	Weiss Charles, Apr. 11, 1781.	
	" John, July 24, 1790.	
1-44	Wells Ann, of Peter and Elizabeth, Sept. 23, 1736-7.	
	" Arnold,	Feb. 11, 1737-8.
	" Elizabeth,	Sept. 18, 1739.

2-44	Wells Elizabeth, wife of Peter, died Sept. 29, 1739.	
2-199	" Penelope, of John and Barbara, June 18, 1741.	
	" Mary,	June 12, 1743.
	" Charles,	Mar. 2, 1744-5.
	" Barbara,	Jan. 28, 1747.
	" Anstress Holden,	Apr. 19, 1752.
	" John Holden, born Sept. 12, 1755.	
2-218	" Charles, of John and Sarah, Jan. 6, 1772.	
	" Rose,	Aug. 10, 1773.
	" Randall,	Apr. 3, 1776
2-233	" Harriet, of Charles and Rosamond, July 31, 1796.	
1-17	Westcott Eleanor, of Jeremiah and Eleanor, Oct. 20, 1659.	
1-9	" Jeremiah,	Oct. 7, 1666.
1-17	" Stukeley,	Oct. 15, 1672.
	" Paris, died in his 3d year, Aug. —, 1673.	
1-8	" Catherine, of Robert and Elizabeth, May 6, 1664.	
1-9	" Zerobabel, of Robert and Catherine, Apr. 15, 1666.	
1-8	" Robert,	Apr. 2, 1668.
	" Dyna,	Feb. 12, 1669.
	" Mary,	July 2, 1672.
1-17	" Samuel,	Sept. 18, 1674.
1-31	" Josiah, of Stukeley and Prescilla, Dec. 2, 1694.	
	" Stukeley,	May 2, 1698.
	" Freelove,	July 5, 1702.
	" Benjamin,	Dec. 31, 1709.
1-54	" Jeremiah, of Thomas and Mary, May 5, 1707.	
1-4, 99	" Hannah, of Nathan and Ann, Dec. 31, 1735.	
	" Keziah,	June 6, 1740.
2-200	" Anne, of Nathan and Mary, Mar. 17, 1746.	
	" Tabitha,	Dec. 17, 1747.
	" Mary,	Oct. 1, 1749.
	" Nathan,	Mar. 4, 1751.
	" Damaries,	Nov. 10, 1752.
	" Caleb,	Aug. 16, 1754.
	" Lucy,	Nov. 3, 1756.
	" Thomas,	July 16, 1758.
	" Almy,	Sept. 15, 1760.
	" Sarah,	Oct. 21, 1762.
	" John,	Feb. 27, 1766.
	" Penelope,	Nov. 4, 1768.
	" Charles,	July 10, 1772.
2-210	" Freelove, of Robert and Sarah, Apr. 15, 1751.	

2-210	Westcott Hannah,	July 29, 1752.
	" Mary,	Dec. 10, 1754.
	" Huldah,	Dec. 20, 1756.
	" Sarah,	Oct. 3, 1757.
2-201	" Waite, of Jeremiah and Phebe,	Mar. 19, 1765.
	" Jeremiah,	Jan. 20, 1768.
	" John,	July 21, 1769.
	" Rebecca,	Apr. 5, 1771.
2-209	" Anne, of Caleb and Susanna,	Dec. 16, 1780.
	" Mary,	June 1, 1782.
	" Josias,	July 28, 1784.
	" Sarah,	Dec. 31, 1786.
	" Catherine Arnold,	Jan. 27, 1789.
	" Almy,	July 5, 1791.
	" Henry,	Aug. 5, 1796.
	" Caleb,	Oct. 24, 1798.
2-206	" Nancy, of Nathan, Jr., and Lydia,	July 25, 1786.
	" Celia,	Feb. 14, 1789.
	" Nathan,	Mar. 4, 1791.
	" Arnold,	Dec. 31, 1793.
2-200	" Amasa, alias Nichols, Mar. 21, 1791.	
3-344	" Henry Augustus, of Peleg W. and Isabella, born Worcester, Mass., Mar. 13, 1843.	
-53	Westgate Silvanus, Feb. 19, 1690.	
	" Jerusha (Davis), his wife, Jan. 17, 1690.	
	" Sarah, of Silvanus and Jerusha, Jan. 10, 1713.	
	" Robert,	Mar. 19, 1716.
	" Silvanus,	July 16, 1719.
	" Silvanus, Sr., lost at sea, Sept. 27, 1719.	
1-48	" Edward, of Robert and Patience, Apr. 23, 1724.	
	" Avis,	Nov. 9, 1725.
	" Patience,	Dec. 16. 1728.
	" Sarah,	Mar. 11, 1731-2.
	" Hannah,	June 1, 1735.
	" Mary,	June 30, 1740.
	" Patience, wife of Robert, died Mar. 27, 1753.	
1-67	" George, of George and Elizabeth, Sept. 16, 1728.	
	" John,	Feb. 1, 1730-1.
	" Prescilla,	Sept. 8, 1732.
	" Mary,	Jan, 7, 1734-5.
	" Earl,	Feb. 26, 1735-6.
2-205	West Benoni, of Ishmael and Abigail, Dec. 24, 1760.	

2-205	West Timothy,		Jan. 14, 1763.
	"	Nancy,	Oct. 26, 1764.
	"	Nehemiah,	Apr. 21, 1766.
	"	Sarah,	Mar. 23, 1768.
	"	Joseph,	Feb. 4, 1770.
	"	Mary,	Mar. 19, 1772.
	"	Abigail,	Mar. 15, 1774.
	"	Robe,	Mar. 6, 1776.
ˍ 80	Whaley Sarah, of Samuel, Aug. 11, 1729.		
1-22	"	Hannah, of Thomas and Ann,	———, 1740.
	"	Hannah,	d. May 9, 1741.
	"	Susannah,	July 13, 1742.
4-73	"	Melissa Vinton, of Phebe Jerusha, June 4, 1846.	
2-199	Whipple Mary, of Eleazer and Deliverance, Jan. 25, 1744.		
	"	James,	July 23, 1747.
	"	Alice,	Oct. 28, 1749.
	"	Mary,	Sept. 27, 1750.
	"	Job,	May 1, 1751.
	"	Joseph,	May 1, 1751.
	"	Almy,	Oct. 8, 1760.
2-262	Whitford Alice, of George, July 16, 1770.		
2-212	"	Silas, of George and Hannah, Jan. 16, 1772.	
	"	Casey,	Jan. 16, 1772.
	"	Barton,	Oct. 14, 1776.
	"	George,	July 9, 1778.
	"	Welcome,	June 29, 1786.
	"	Thomas,	July 14, 1787.
	"	Henry, of Thomas and Patty, Dec. 6, 1808.	
	"	Thomas Wickes,	Mar. 11, 1811.
3-341	"	Silas Casey, of Casey, Nov. 26, 1809.	
1-75	Whitman Mary, of John and Phebe, Feb. 19, 1722-3.		
	"	Sarah,	Dec. 21, 1724.
	"	John,	Dec. 2, 1726.
	"	Elisha,	Dec. 13, 1728.
	"	Phebe,	Sept. 1, 1732.
	"	Mercy,	July 18, 1735.
	"	Phillip,	June 13, 1737.
	"	Waite,	June 12, 1739.
	"	George,	Aug. 12, 1741.
	"	Deborah,	Sept. 5, 1743.
	"	Robey,	June 10, 1745.
	"	Hannah,	Jan. 8, 1747.

1-54	Whitman Samuel, of Samuel and Margaret, Jan. 23, 1724.	
	" Benjamin,	Nov. 2, 1727.
	" Penelope,	April 14, 1729.
	" George,	Nov. 8, 1731.
	" Freelove,	May 22, 1734.
	" Dinah,	Jan. 30, 1735-6.
	" Margaret,	Aug. 22, 1738.
	" Asa,	July 25, 1740.
1-21	Wickes John. son of John, deceased, and Rose, August 8, 1677; died Dec. 27, 1741.	
	" John, of John, Jr., and Sarah, Feb. 26, 1698-9.	
	" Sarah,	Sept. 21, 1700.
	" Rose,	Aug. 12, 1702.
	" Robert,	Dec. 22, 1704.
	" Elizabeth,	Feb. 25, 1706-7.
	" William,	Aug. 26, 1710.
	" Richard,	Oct. 23, 1712.
	" Thomas,	Sept. 8, 1715.
1-91	" Athaliah, of Thomas and Ann, Oct. 10, 1704.	
	" Still born,	Oct. 10, 1704.
	" Mary,	Aug. 15, 1706.
	" Sarah,	Mar. 18, 1708.
	" Thomas,	Jan. 28, 1710.
	" John,	Feb. 6, 1712.
	" Daniel,	May. 10, 1714.
	" Daniel,	d. Sept. 28, 1723.
	" Benjamin,	Aug. 18, 1716.
	" Joseph,	May 31, 1719.
	" James,	Feb. 2, 1722.
	" Samuel,	Feb. 2, 1722.
	" Samuel,	d. Mar. 4, 1722.
	" Robert,	Feb. 2, 1722.
	" Robert,	d. Feb. 16, 1722.
	[NOTE. Mary, above, born East Greenwich].	
1-20	" Sarah, of John and Barbara, Mar. 4, 1735-6.	
	" William, (mariner) of John, died Nov. 21. 1744.	
	" John, died July 4, 1735.	
	" John, Sr., died Dec. 27, 1741.	
	" Sarah, widow of John, died Jan. 31, 1753.	
1-21	" Mary, of John and Sarah, Dec. 11, 1717, died July 18, 1746.	
2-207	" Renewed, of Benjamin and Alice, Aug. 2, 1739.	

2-207	Wickes Stukeley,	Sept. 29, 1743.	
	" Benjamin,	Mar. 27, 1745.	
	" Benjamin, Sr., died Mar. 24, 1757.		
1-2	" Joseph, of Joseph and Mary, May 19, 1742.		
	" Weighty,	Mar. 26, 1744.	
	" Ebenezer,	June 17, 1746.	
	" Daniel,	Nov. 5, 1749.	
	" Marian,	Aug. 2, 1752.	
1-60	" Hannah, of Thomas, Jr., and Thankful, Aug. 3, 1742.		
	" Mary,	Nov. 30, 1744.	
	" Mary,	d. Feb. 4, 1750.	
2-202	" Asa, (dau.) of Thomas, and Elizabeth, June 18, 1750.		
	" Sarah,	Sept. 6, 1751.	
2-216	" Mary, of Thomas and Ruth, Dec. 11, 1752.		
	" Elizabeth,	Nov. 7, 1754.	
2-208	" Mary, of Joseph, July 19, 1754.		
	" William,	July 30, 1756.	
2-201	" Ann, of Thomas, Jr., and Sarah, Jan. 25, 1758.		
	" Benjamin,	July 30, 1760.	
	" Daniel,	Apr. 19, 1762.	
	" Paul Unis,	Feb. 19, 1765.	
3-346	" Reuben, May 24, 1786.		
	" Lois E., of Reuben and Eleanor, Jan. 19, 1809.		
2-208	" Dinah, (colored servants of Thomas), Dec. 25, 1787.		
	" Rhoda, "	June 15, 1790,	
	" Catherine, "	Dec. 14, 1796.	
2-150	Wightman David, of George, July 16, 1750.		
2-204	" John, of Elisha and Sybel, Nov. 4, 1754.		
	" Daniel,	Nov. 19, 1757.	
	" Mary,	Dec. 23, 1759.	
	" Peleg,	Jan. 1, 1762.	
	" Phebe,	Aug. 8, 1764.	
	" Mercy,	Feb. 10, 1767.	
	" Elisha,	June 5, 1769.	
	" Sybel,	Jan. 31, 1772.	
2-215	" Martin Salisbury, of Daniel and Lydia, May 9, 1783.		
	" Polly,	Nov. 15, 1785.	
	" Daniel,	Jan. 11, 1791.	
	" Lydia Ann,	Jan. 1, 1800.	
2-209	" Almy Meriah, of Othniel and Sally, Oct. 30, 1793.		
	" Othniel Gorton,	Dec. 17, 1797.	
	" Phillip, 2d,	Oct. 19, 1799.	

2-209	Wightman Oliver Arnold,	June 13, 1801.
3-339	" Almond Clark, of Martin S. and Marberry S., Jan. 3, 1805.	
	" Daniel, of Martin S. and Marberry S., Dec. 7, 1806.	
3-347	Wilbur Sally Gardiner, of David and Sarah, Oct. 31, 1809.	
	" Harriet Gorton,	Aug. 29, 1811.
	Note.—1st born in Warren; 2d, Warwick.	
3-421	Willard Jane Elizabeth, of George A. and Emerette A., Aug. 3, 1847.	
1-103	Wood William, of William and Ann, May 11, 1728.	
	" Thomas,	June 30, 1730.
	" Humphrey,	May 7, 1732.
	" John,	Oct. 26, 1740.
	" Ann,	Feb. 16, 1741-2.
	" Sarah,	Dec. 28, 1743.
2-220	" William, of Olney and Rosanna, Feb. 17, 1788.	
2-338	" James, alias Godfrey, June 25, 1790.	
2-214	" Burrell, of Stukeley and Freelove, Mar. 11, 1803.	
	" Mercy G.,	Mar. 21, 1806.
	" Eliza,	Apr. 20, 1808.
	" Alanson,	Sept. 5, 1810.
	" Ann,	Dec. 26, 1812.
	" William H.,	Sept. 18, 1815.
	" Charles,	Nov. 11, 1817.
2-205	Worden Esther, of Peter and Mercy, Apr. 19, 1753.	
	" Lucinda,	May 21, 1754.

Y

2-41 Young Sarah, of James, Feb. 18, 1776.

INDEX.

TOWN OF WARWICK.

I.

Names Occurring in their Natural Order.

Marriages commence with page 1, births and deaths with page 137.

A

Aborn, 1 137
Adams, 1
Albro, 1
Aldrich, 2
Alexander, 2 137
Allen, 2 137
Allerton, 3
Almy, 3
Alverson, 137
Amsden, 3
Andrews, 3 137
Angell, 3
Anthony, 4 138
Arnold, 4 138
Ashton, 10
Atwood, 10 145
Austin, 10
Aylesworth, 11

B

Babcock, 11 145
Babson, 11
Backer, 11
Bailey, 11 145
Bagley, 11
Bajnotti, 11
Baker, 12 145
Ballou, 13
Bamford, 13
Barber, 13
Barbour, 13
Barker, 146
Barlow, 14
Barnes, 14
Barney, 14
Barne, 14
Bartlett, 14
Barthalake, 14
Bartholick, 14
Barton, 14 146
Bateman, 14
Bates, 15 147
Battey, 15 147
Baxter, 15
Bebe, 15
Bayley, 147
Beybee, 15
Benjamin, 15
Bennett, 15, 147
Benson, 17 148
Bentley, 17 148
Bicknell, 17
Bigby, 17
Bissell, 17
Bitgood, 17
Blair, 17 148
Blanchard, 17
Blancher, 148
Blesborough, 18
Blount, 18
Bonn, 18
Boss, 18
Bosworth, 18
Bowen, 18 148
Bowman, 19
Bowtwell, 19
Boyd, 19
Bradford, 19
Brayman, 19
Brays, 149
Brayton, 19 149
Brennan, 20.
Briggs, 20 150
Brooks, 21
Brownell, 22
Browning, 22 150
Brown, 22 150
Brussel, 23
Bucklin, 23 151
Budlong, 23 151
Bugbee, 24
Bunn, 24
Burch, 25
Burdick, 25
Burden, 25
Burguess, 25
Burke, 25 151
Burlingame, 25 152
Burrell, 26
Burr, 26
Burrows, 26 152
Burton, 26 152
Burt, 27
Burvee, 27
Busecott, 27
Bushee, 27
Bushnell, 27

Button, 27
Butts, 27
Byles, 27

C

Cady, 27 152
Cahoone, 27 152
Calvert, 27
Cammet, 27
Campbell, 27
Capron, 27
Capwell, 28
Carder, 28 153
Card, 29
Carey, 30
Carpenter, 30 154
Carruthars, 30
Carr, 30 154
Carter, 31
Carvine, 154
Casey, 31 154
Case, 31 155
Caswell, 31
Caucrofte, 31
Ceaser, 31
Chace, 31 155
Chadsey, 32
Champlain, 32
Chapin, 32 155
Chapman, 32
Chappell, 32
Chase, 32 155
Cheese, 32
Cheves, 32
Chipman, 32
Church, 32 156
Chute, 33
Cindrick, 33
Clapp, 33 156
Clark, 33
Clemons, 33
Cleveland, 33
Cobb, 33
Codner, 34
Coggeshall, 34 156
Cogshall, 34
Colburn, 34
Colebee, 34
Colegrove, 156

Cole, 34 156
Collins, 35 157
Collis, 35
Colvin, 35
Comstock, 35 157
Congdon, 35 157
Cooke, 36 158
Cook, 36 158
Cooper, 36 158
Corey, 36 158
Cornell, 36
Corpe, 37 158
Cottrell, 37
Covill, 37
Cowell, 37
Coyle, 37
Crandall, 37
Cranston, 37
Crapo, 38
Cross, 38 158
Cruff, 38
Culverson, 38
Culver, 38 158
Curian, 38
Curtis, 38 158

D

Dailey, 38 158
Daly, 38
Dana, 38
Daniel, 38
Davice, 38
David, 158
Davis, 38 158
Dawley, 39
Deway, 39
Dexter, 39 158
Dickenson, 40 159
Dodge, 40
Deorby, 159
Doud, 40, 159
Douglass, 40
Downe, 40
Draper, 40
Drury, 40
Duffy, 40
Dunkens, 159
Durfee, 40
Dutemple, 40

Dyer, 40

E

Eager, 41
Earl, 41 159
East, 41
Eaton, 41
Eddy, 41
Edmunds, 41 159
Edwards, 41
Eldredge, 41 159
Eldred, 42
Ellis, 42 159
Emerson, 42
England, 42
Essex, 42 159
Estes, 42 160
Evans, 160

F

Fairbanks, 43
Farmer, 43
Farnum, 43
Farris, 43
Faulkner, 43
Fenner, 43
Fifield, 43
Finney, 43 160
Fisher, 43 160
Fish, 43 161
Flagg, 43
Fleming, 43
Fletcher, 43, 161
Fones, 44
Foss, 44
Foster, 44 161
Fox, 44
France, 44
Francis, 44 161
Franklin, 44
Frazer, 44 161
Freeborn, 44 161
Freeman, 45 161
Frothingham, 45
Fry, 45 162
Fullerton, 45
Fuller, 45

G

Gallup, 45
Gammett, 45
Gardiner, 45 162
Gardner, 46 162
Garnardi, 47 162
Garner, 47
Gavitt, 47
Gerreard, 47 162
Gesling, 47
Gifford, 47
Gisborne, 47
Gleason, 47
Godfrey, 47
Gorton, 47, 162
Gould, 50
Groves, 51
Greene, 51 165
Grennell, 60
Griffin, 60 179
Griffis, 60
Grimshaw, 60
Grove, 60
Grummuch, 60

H

Hackstone, 60 179
Hail, 60
Hall, 60 179
Halsted, 61
Hambleton, 61
Hamilton, 61
Hammett, 61 179
Hammond, 62
Hampleton, 62
Hampson, 62
Hanop, 62
Hardin, 62
Hare, 62
Harper, 62
Harrup, 62
Harrington, 62
Harrison, 62 180
Harris, 62
Harrude, 63
Harry, 63
Hart, 63
Harvey, 63

Hatch, 63
Hathaway, 63 180
Havens, 63 180
Hawkins, 64
Haynes, 64 180
Hazard, 64
Hazelton, 64 180
Head, 64
Healey, 64
Heap, 65
Heath, 65
Hebbard, 65
Hedjer, 65
Heenan, 65
Henderson, 65
Henessey, 65
Henry, 65
Herd, 65
Hicks, 65
Hide, 65
Hill, 65 180
Himes, 66
Hiscox, 66
Hitch, 66
Hitt, 66
Hix, 66
Hoksey, 66
Holden, 66 181
Hollis, 67
Holmes, 67 182
Hopkins, 68
House, 68
Houson, 68
Howard, 68 182
How, 69 182
Hoxsie, 69
Hoyt, 69
Hubbard, 69
Hudson, 69 182
Hughes, 69
Hulet, 69
Hull, 70
Hunter, 70
Hunt, 70 182
Hutchins, 70

I

Ingalls, 70
Inman, 70

Irish, 70

J

Jackson, 70
Jacob, 70
Jeffard, 71
Jefferson, 71
Jenckes, 71 183
Jerauld, 71 183
Jessup, 71
Jillson, 72
John, 72
Johnson, 72 184
Jones, 73
Jordan, 73
Joslin, 73
Joyce, 73
Justin, 73

K

Keas, 73
Kee, 73
Keech, 73
Kenyon, 73
Kettell, 74
Kettle, 74
Kimball, 74
Kindrick, 74
Kingsley, 74
King, 74 185
Kinnecome, 74
Kinne, 75
Kippey, 75
Knapp, 75
Knight, 75
Knowles, 75
Knowlton, 75
Knox, 75 185

L

Ladd, 75 185
Lake, 76
Lane, 76
Langford, 76 185
Lanphere, 76
Latham, 76
Lathrop, 76

Lawrence, 76
Lawton, 76 185
Leach, 76
Lee, 76 185
LeValley, 76 185
Lewis, 77
Lippitt, 77 186
Littlefield, 78 187
Little, 78
Locke, 78
Lockwood, 78 187
Lorton, 80
Lovell, 80
Loveland, 80
Love, 80
Low, 80 188
Luther, 81
Lynch, 81

M

MacGregore, 188
Maguire, 81
Mahoney, 81
Malcome, 81
Malone, 81
Manchester, 81
Marble, 81
Mariner, 82
Marks, 82
Marshall, 188
Martindil, 82
Martin, 82 189
Mary Anna, 82
Mason, 82
Masson, 82
Mathewson, 82 189
Matteson, 82 189
Mawney, 83
Maxwell, 83 189
McElhaney, 189
McGregor, 83 189
McKinsie, 83
McMahon, 83
Medberry, 83
Medbury, 83 189
Menden, 83
Merrill, 84
Millard, 84 189
Miller, 84 190

Mitchell, 85
Monaghan, 85
Money, 85
Moon, 85
Moot, 85
Morey, 85
Morrell, 86
Morris, 86
Morse, 86
Mott, 86
Monuel, 86
Mowry, 86
Mudge, 86 190
Mumford, 86
Myrie, 86

N

Nason, 86
Needham, 86
Newell, 87
Newfield, 87
Newman, 87
Ney, 87
Nickerson, 87
Nicholas, 87 191
Nichols, 87 191
Niles, 88
Northup, 88
Noyes, 88

O

Odell, 88
Olin, 88 191
Otis, 89

P

Padelford, 89
Paine, 89
Palmer, 89
Parce, 89
Parish, 89
Parker, 89 191
Pearce, 90 191
Peckham, 90
Peck, 90
Peirce, 90 191
Pepperell, 91

Perce, 91
Perkins, 91
Perry, 91
Phillips, 91
Pigot, 92 192
Pike, 92
Pilgington, 92
Pilkinton, 92
Pirse, 92
Pitman, 92
Place, 92
Platt, 92
Pollard, 92
Pollock, 92
Potter, 92 192
Pratt, 94
Preston, 94
Price, 94 192
Prisse, 192
Prophet, 95 192
Proud, 95
Pulsifer, 95
Putney, 95
Pyner, 192

Q

Quackinbush, 95
Quiman, 95

R

Ralph, 95
Randall, 95 192
Ransom, 95
Rathburn, 95
Ray, 96
Reaves, 96
Red, 192
Reed, 96 192
Relph, 96 192
Remington, 96 193
Renals, 98 194
Reynolds, 98 194
Rhodes, 99 194
Rice, 100 197
Richardson, 103
Richmond, 103
Riley, 103
Risby, 103

Roades, 103
Robertson, 200
Roberts, 104 200
Rodman, 104
Roomes, 104
Ross, 104
Rousemaniere, 104
Rouse, 104
Rowand, 104
Rowan, 104
Ruttenberge, 104 200

S

Salsberry, 105
Salisbury, 105 201
Sailes, 105
Sarle, 105 201
Sayles, 105
Scholfield, 105
Schreech, 105 201
Scott, 105
Scranton, 105
Seabin, 105
Seabury, 105
Seager, 105
Seamans, 105
Searle, 106
Sedgwick, 106
Sephton, 106
Sharples, 106
Shaw, 106
Sheffield, 106
Sheldon, 106 201
Sherman, 106 201
Shippee, 107
Sholes, 107
Shreives, 107
Shute, 107
Sidebottom, 107
Simmons, 107
Singer, 107
Sisco, 107
Sisson, 107 201
Slack, 108
Slocum, 108 201
Smith, 108 201
Smyte, 109
Snell, 109 202
Southwick, 109

Sparks, 109
Sparron, 109
Spaulding, 109
Spencer, 109 203
Spicer, 111
Spink, 111
Sprague, 111
Spywood, 111
Stafford, 111 203
Standish, 113
Staples, 113
Steere, 113
Stokes, 113
Stone, 113 204
Straight, 114 205
Sunderland, 114
Sweetzer, 114
Sweet, 114 205
Swindells, 115

T

Taber, 115
Taft, 115 206
Tallman, 116 206
Talman, 116
Tanner, 116
Tarbox, 116
Taylor, 116 206
Teffe, 116
Tefft, 116 206
Temple, 117
Tennant, 117
Tew, 117
Thomas, 117
Thompson, 117 206
Thornton, 117
Thurber, 118
Thurston, 118
Tibbetts, 118 206
Tiffany, 119 207
Tillinghast, 119
Titus, 120
Torrey, 120
Tourjee, 120
Townsend, 121 207
Tripp, 121 207
Trumbull, 121
Tucker, 121
Tunguad, 121

Turner, 121
Turtelot, 121
Twigg, 207
Tyler, 121

U

Utter, 121 207

V

Valpey, 122
Van Riper, 122
Vaughn, 122
Vickery, 122
Vinton, 122
Voeghn, 122

W

Waite, 123
Wakefield, 123
Walch, 123
Walker, 123
Wallen, 123
Wall, 123 207
Walter, 123
Walton, 123 207
Ward, 123 207
Warner, 123 208
Warren, 125 210
Waterhouse, 125
Waterman, 125 210
Watson, 126
Weaver, 126 212
Webb, 127 212
Webster, 127
Weeden, 127
Weekes, 127
Welch, 127
Wellman, 127
Weiss, 212
Wells, 127 212
Westcott, 128 213
Westgate, 129 214
Weston, 129
West, 129 214
Whaley, 130 215
Wheeler, 130
Wheelock, 130

Whipple, 130 215
Whitaker, 130
White, 130
Whitford, 130 215
Whitman, 131 215
Whitmarsh, 132
Wickes, 132 216
Wightman, 133 217
Wight, 134
Wilbour, 134 218

Wilcox, 134
Wilkes, 134
Williams, 134
Willard, 218
Wilson, 135
Wing, 135
Woodmansee, 135
Woods, 135
Wood, 135 218
Worden, 136 218

Worrell, 136
Wright, 136
Wye, 136

X Y Z

York, 136
Young, 136 218

II.

Names Occurring Promiscuously.

A

Albro, 37
Aldrich, 121
Allen, 18 25 91 116
Almy, 80
Andrews, 107
Anthony, 81 84 108
Arnold, 2 4 7 8 12
  14 18 22 24 25 27
  31 38 39 41 61 64
  67 71 75 83 109
  119 123 133
Arvine, 83

B

Baker, 10 23 109 180
Bannister, 4
Barton, 31 37 100 110
Bates, 18 73 74 109
Baxter, 46
Bellows, 17
Bennett, 34 47 120
  134 148
Bliss, 57
Brayton, 2 9 11 13 16
  17 18 20 21 23 26
  27 28 29 31 32 34
  35 36 39 40 41 44
  46 47 60 61 62 63
  66 67 70 72 74 75
  76 81 85 86 87 88

  92 93 94 95 97 98
  100 103 105 109
  114 115 120 122
  123 126 131 134
  135 136
Brewster, 107
Brownell, 129
Brown, 32 44 58 161
Budlong, 69 133
Burdick, 9
Burleston, 92
Burlingame, 182
Butler, 30
Burr, 183

C

Carder, 93
Carpenter, 128
Carr, 48 125
Casey, 46 88
Champlain, 3 38
Cheney, 20 86
Clapp, 14, 110 122
Clarke, 56
Cleveland, 76
Coggeshall, 34 208
Colburn, 44 103
Colvin, 98
Comstock, 56 68 69
  83 101 114 127
Congdon, 12 42 67
Corey, 71

Corpe, 24 31 84
Couch, 83
Cozzens, 120
Crandon, 122
Crofford, 97
Curtis, 11 33 43 62
  95 104
Cutler, 4

D

Dana, 92
Davis, 214
Dean, 9 134
Dearborne, 44
Devout, 180
Dexter, 62
Dorchester, 92
Dowling, 9 23 63 72
  75 102 113 115
  117 126 130

E

Edmunds, 48 87 122
Ellis, 17
Ervins, 67

F

Fenner, 65
Field, 129
Fifield, 1 2 3 9 11 13
  14 15 16 17 18 19
  21 22 23 25 26 27

29 30 31 32 33 34
35 36 37 38 39 40
41 42 43 44 46 50
59 61 62 63 64 65
67 68 69 72 73 74
75 76 78 80 81 82
83 84 85 86 87 88
89 91 94 97 98
102 103 104 105
106 107 109 110
111 112 115 116
117 118 119 120
121 122 123 125
126 128 129 130
131 132 134 135
136
Fish, 42
Fiske, 10
Forbush, 14 32 35 47
79 86 94 130
Fry, 108
Fuller, 9 10 16 17 19
25 27 29 32 42 46
47 62 68 76 89 95
107 108 117 127
136

G

Gano, 38
Gardiner, 5 47 101
Gerald, 30
Gibbs, 178
Gibson, 37 65
Girdwood, 110
Gladding, 13
Godfrey, 141 218
Goodrich, 21
Gorton, 2 3 5 6 7 10
12 16 17 19 20 22
23 24 25 29 30 31
32 37 42 43 44 46
48 49 56 59 63 64
65 66 69 70 71 73
76 77 78 80 84 85
86 87 88 90 91 93
96 97 98 99 100
101 102 104 105
109 110 111 113
114 118 119 123
124 126 127 128

130 132 133 134
135 154
Granger, 135
Graves, 54 56 78
Greene, 3 4 14 15 23
27 28 31 34 36 37
43 47 48 52 53 54
63 66 67 68 72 76
77 82 87 90 91 92
98 99 100 103 104
106 108 109 111
114 119 121 123
128 132 142
Greenwood, 77

H

Hall, 131
Hammett, 1 5 15 20
33 38 39 51 54 60
82 93 95 100 124
133
Hardman, 10 23 33 75
Harrington, 113
Harris, 12 89
Havens, 16 24 76 97
135
Hazelton, 14 40 70
130 136
Hedden, 20 40 111
Helme, 100
Hill, 7 42
Hitchcock, 38
Holden, 2 6 11 14 15
16 20 24 28 29 30
32 33 34 39 41 43
45 46 48 49 54 55
56 60 61 62 63 65
66 67 68 70 72 73
74 76 77 78 79 80
82 83 84 90 93 96
99 101 103 104
105 108 112 113
114 117 118 124
126 127 128 129
135
Honeyman, 52
Hopkins, 49 140
Hyde, 22

I J

Jacobs, 8 131
Jenkins, 46 116 119
Jerauld, 3 6 7 8 10
11 12 16 17 18 19
20 22 24 25 26 29
30 31 35 40 45 46
47 50 56 58 61 63
64 67 72 75 76 77
79 81 82 84 85 86
89 93 94 97 98 99
102 104 106 109
110 112 113 115
119 120 124 126
127 128 129 130
133 135
Johnson, 14, 72 77

K

Kellogg, 59
Kivan, 94
Knight, 3 42 65

L

Lippitt, 44 45 49 53
54 57 72 78 101
107 112 129
Littlefield, 4 7 8 12
20 29 30 34 35 42
46 50 57 58 61 62
67 71 74 79 89 93
102 110 111 114
116 119 122 124
126 127 128
Lock, 37
Low, 11 45 52 90 131

M

Macreading, 21 86
Macumber, 70
Martin, 5 22 28 30
37 53 65 66 89 99
100 104 108 112
118 122 127 128
129 131 132
Manchester, 8 9 14 19
20 22 25 28 33 41
43 50 59 63 65 68
71 72 73 76 79 83

84 85 86 99 100
115 121 125 131
135
Manning, 6
Matteson, 169
Mawney, 54
McSparran, 132
Mowry, 21 36 59 66
75 81 86 106 113
118 126
Mulchahey, 62

N
Ney, 75
Nichols, 2
Northup, 66

O P
Paine, 20
Palmer, 60
Pearce, 106
Peirce, 47 89
Pendleton, 77
Phelan, 13 17 25 28
29 37 42 46 50 61
67 69 73 81 83 86
92 94 98 107 113
115 117 127 129
135 136
Phillips, 32 91 162
202
Pickering, 85
Pigott, 61
Pike, 118
Place, 32 103
Potter, 41 80 95 161
Pratt, 117
Putnam, 40 41

Q R
Randall, 60
Ray, 52
Remington, 26 70
Rhodes, 1 37 136 193
Richards, 71 73 114
Rice, 5 6 10 12 16
17 18 19 25 30 33
49 53 56 60 67 69
71 72 77 82 83 90
93 94 96 100 101

112 114 121 124
125 127 133
Ripley, 63
Rogers, 70

S
Sands, 55
Searing, 53
Sheldon, 61
Sherwin, 31
Shrieve, 94
Slocum, 3 5 6 10 11
19 36 39 55 60 63
68 70 81 82 87
104 108 114 116
118 125 126 129
130 133 134 135
Smith, 9 34 57 72 77
86 103 128 136
148
Snow, 57
Soule, 49
Spencer, 87 123
Spooner, 97
Stafford, 15 23 53 82
124 125 128
Steere, 21 32 40 47
61 92 97 106 116
Stone, 10
Stovyer, 10 13 43 80
121

T
Tatem, 16 22 35 61
75 133
Tew, 22 110 129
Thomas, 3 10 19 21
25 26 29 31 35 37
40 42 45 60 63 68
72 88 94 95 106
110 111 120 130
Thurston, 57
Tillinghast, 9 21 27
29 50 60 74 83 87
91 93 102 104 110
116 118 122 127
134
Titus, 107 120
Tobey, 1 2 13 14 26
28 32 36 38 44 65

69 74 81 85 88 90
97 105 108 110
113 115 135
Todd, 64 107
Torrey, 125
Townsend, 49 51

U
Uhler, 21 109 130

V
Vaughn, 42 156

W
Waldo, 19
Walker, 13 59
Wallace, 40 123
Walton, 99 112 132
Warner, 1 2 5 9 12
23 27 34 35 44 68
69 70 78 79 87 90
100 105 106 107
113 114 125 126
132
Warren, 211
Waterman, 11 21 83
124 156
Weaver, 19
Werden, 18
Westcott, 2 12 16 67
71 81 109
White, 132
Whitford, 164
Wickes, 22 28 33 80
92 119 120 123
Wightman, 6 33 42
56 96
Wilkes, 46 65 68 136
Willard, 21 88 98 121
Williams, 23 50 131
Wilson, 24 39 50 66
84 85 100 135
Winsor, 6 57 58
Wooding, 3
Worden, 20

X Y Z
Young, 161

III.

Names of Places.

A

Abington, Pa., 37
Aerintos, Eng., 44
Apponaug, R. I., 205
Asia, 139
Athol, Mass., 123
Attleboro, Mass., 118
120

B

Barrington, R. I., 3 83
Boston, Mass., 28 51
54 56 124 169 177
Bristol, R. I., 25 47
82 89 102
Brookfield, N. Y., 33
Brunswick, Ohio, 131
Burrillville, R. I., 13
32

C

Cambridge, Mass., 81
Charlestown, Mass., 57
Charlestown, R. I., 23
74
Chatham, Conn., 35
Chatham, Mass., 1 97
Cincinnati, Ohio, 120
Coventry, R. I., 1 2 3
5 8 9 11 13 14 15
16 17 18 19 20 21
24 25 29 36 37 39
41 42 43 46 56 59
60 61 62 63 65 72
73 74 75 77 78 79
80 82 83 85 86 88
90 91 93 94 95 98
103 104 112 113
114 116 118 120
121 126 130 132
134 135 136 183
185
Cranston, R. I., 2 5 6
8 10 11 12 13 20
21 24 26 27 29 32
36 40 41 43 46 61
62 63 65 67 69 72
73 74 75 76 78 80
81 85 87 88 89 90
93 94 95 99 103
105 106 108 111
113 117 121 122
127 128 130 134
160
Cumberland, Me., 33
Cumberland, R. I., 65
71 80 82 83 183

D

Dartmouth, Mass., 51
53 108
Dedham, Mass., 63
Depere, Wis., 17
Dighton, Mass., 30 43
50
Dorchester, Mass., 33

E

East Greenwich, R. I.,
2 3 4 6 7 11 14
16 17 19 20 21 22
25 27 28 29 30 31
32 33 34 37 39 40
42 44 45 46 47 49
52 53 54 56 57 58
60 64 68 70 71 72
77 79 82 83 84 85
86 87 90 91 93 98
104 105 107 109
110 111 113 114
116 117 119 120
122 123 124 125
126 127 128 131
132 133 135 137
142 180 183 216
Easton, Washington
Co., N. Y., 31
Eastport, Me., 179
Exeter, R. I., 10 21
31 34 35 59 60 74
75 88 111 114 115
116 117 118 120
121 131.

F

Fall River, Mass., 122
Foster, R. I., 18 37 65
97 116 185
France, 45
Frankfort, N. Y., 131

G

Glocester, R. I., 10 64 113 118
Great Britain, 106
Greene, N. Y., 117
Greenfield, N. Y., 58
Griswold, Conn., 76 119
Groton, Conn., 25 26
Groton, Mass., 59

H

Hamstead, L. I., 34
Haverhill, N. H., 130
Heath, Mass., 17
Hittsborough, N. H., 109
Hallowell, Eng., 126
Hopkinton, R. I., 32 38 42 98 117

I

Ipswich, Mass., 22
Ireland, 81 121

J

Jamestown, R. I., 15 48 51 56 72 125 127 129 169
Jewett City, Conn., 105 185
Johnston, R. I., 47 62 74 75 89 90 106
Johnston, Scot. 13

K

Killingly, Conn., 69 100 104
Kingsman, Ohio, 75
Kingston, N. H., 127
Kings Towne, R. I., 4 20 30 44 98 194
Kingstown, R. I. 32 126

L

Lexington, Ky., 179
Little Compton, R. I., 105
London, Eng., 91
Long Island, 34 40
Lowell, Mass., 106
Lynn, Mass., 26

M

Maidfield, Eng., 107
Malden, Mass., 114
Manchester, Eng., 32
Marrabee, W. I., 177
Massachusetts, 80
Mendon, Mass., 69
Meshanticut, R. I., 106
Middleborough, Mass., 61
Middletown, R. I., 34
Millbury, Mass., 126
Marlton, Vt., 63
Muskoto Cove, L. I., 132

N

Nantucket, Mass., 59 146
Naussocut, R. I., 65
Nesocut, R. I., 56
New Bedford, Mass., 110
Newport, R. I., 2 37 38 40 42 45 52 57 66 67 69 82 83 86 104 124 153 166
New Shoreham, R. I., 55 56
New York, N. Y., 122
New York, 68 89 184
Norridge, Conn., 111
North Attleboro, Mass., 107
North Brittain, 22
North Kingstown, R.I., 2 4 6 7 9 10 11 19 22 30 31 34 36 37 38 40 42 46 52 56 59 61 62 64 65 69 70 72 74 85 88 91 96 98 102 104 108 111 114 115 116 117 120 12 130 162
North Providence, R.I., 19 28 111 118 130
Norwich, Conn., 38

O

Occupassotuxet, R. I., 173

P

Pawtucket, Mass., 89 90 106
Pawtucket, R. I., 46
Pawtuxet, R. I., 72 108 202
Perth, Scotland, 36
Pettesquamscutt, R. I., 47
Philadelphia, Pa., 44
Pittsfield, Mass., 75
Plainfield, Conn., 102 118
Plaisfield, Conn., 94
Plympton, Mass., 19 63
Portsmouth, R. I., 36 44 47 51 59 60 84 98 106 108 125 129 166
Pomfret, Conn., 2 121 127 179
Potowomut, R. I., 45 55 64 174
Preston, Eng., 44
Provincetown, Mass., 39
Providence, R. I., 2 3 4 5 13 14 18 21 25 28 30 31 32 37 38 40 41 43 44 45

46 47 48 51 52 57
58 61 64 68 69 71
76 77 80 82 83 84
85 88 89 92 93 94
95 99 103 107 108
109 110 113 115
118 120 122 123
124 127 131 135
136 137 146 178
179 202 205

Q R

Rehoboth, Mass., 14
23 71 77 90 118
183
Rhode Island, 174
Richmond, N. H., 123
Richmond, R. I., 26 63
69 78 89 110 115
River De La Plata, 177
Rye, N. Y., 33

S

Salem, Mass., 108
Salesbury, N. Y., 27
Saint Phillip's Ch., 57
Sandwich, Mass., 135
Saybrook, Conn., 40
Scituate, R. I., 9 10 14
15 16 18 23 39 49
62 63 65 68 75 76
80 81 97 104 105
107 109 115 116
128 130 191

Scotland, 15
Seekonk, Mass., 14, 130
Shaftesbury, Vt., 18
Smithfield, R. I., 20, 22 28 57 86 89 91 92
So. Kingstown, R. I., 1 11 31 40 46 53 64 69 78 87 88 100 112 125 132 135 136
Sterling, Conn, 91 131
Stockport, Eng., 26
Stockton, Cal., 206
Stonington, Conn., 57
Stratford, Conn., 34
Sutton, Mass., 41 61
Swansea, Mass., 34 65 134

T

Taunton, Mass., 27
Thompson, Conn., 102
Tiverton, R. I., 36 86 118
Tolland, Conn., 90

U

Uxbridge, Mass., 109 130 155

V

Valley Falls, R. I., 34
Vermont, 103
Voluntown, Conn., 26 136

W

Waklingford, Conn., 38
Wales, Eng., 134
Waltham, Mass., 43
Warren, R. I., 49 108 218
Warwick, see part first
Waterford, Conn., 23
Waterford, Mass., 44
Westerly, R. I., 11 56 73 76 123
West Greenwich, R. I., 1 2 19 31 35 40 41 49 50 68 74 83 87 88 94 95 98 115 116 119 134 135 136 165
Wickford, R. I., 9
Willimantic, Conn., 72
Wiltshire, Eng., 42
Woodstock, Conn., 14 89
Worcester, Mass., 214
Wrentham, Mass., 120

X Y Z

Yarmouth, Mass., 87.

www.ingramcontent.com/pod-product-compliance
Lightning Source LLC
Chambersburg PA
CBHW051642230426
43669CB00013B/2407